IRISH WATERCOLORS AND DRAWINGS

IRISH WATERCOLORS AND DRAWINGS

WORKS ON PAPER c. 1600-1914

Anne Crookshank and the Knight of Glin

Harry N. Abrams, Inc.,
Publishers

This Book has received the 1994 International Award:

Prix de la Confédération Internationale des Négociants en Oeuvres d'Art

We dedicate this book to
Anne's great grand aunt, Margaret Stokes, and
Desmond's great great grandfather, Edwin, third Earl of Dunraven,
who in the nineteenth century collaborated equally closely
in their work on Early Christian Art in Ireland.

ILLUSTRATIONS

For reasons of space we do not include a list of illustrations. Artists and titles are
listed as captions. It can be assumed that a picture is in a private collection
if no owner is given. Auctioneers and dealers are listed in the photographic credits.

ISBN 0–8109–3466–3

Edited by Alison Wormleighton
Designed by Ted and Ursula O'Brien, Oben Design

First published in Great Britain in 1994 by Barrie & Jenkins Limited,
an imprint of Random House UK Limited, under the title *The Watercolours of Ireland*

Published in 1995 by Harry N. Abrams, Incorporated, New York
A Times Mirror Company

Printed and bound in Singapore

Title page illustration
WILLIAM HENRY BROOKE
Tourists in Ireland, see pages 95–6

Endpapers

Front: FRANCES EDGEWORTH, née BEAUFORT
Vignette from her father, Daniel Augustus Beaufort's Map of Ireland, 1792.

Back: ROBERT AUCHMATY SPROULE
View of Harbour, Montreal, 1830.
(McCord Museum of Canadian History, Montreal, David Ross McCord Collection)

CONTENTS

SPONSORS AND ACKNOWLEDGEMENTS

The authors are greatly indebted to Christie Manson and Woods, who funded our initial photographic and research work and made the book possible. The Department of the History of Art in Trinity College has facilitated the whole process of writing, both clerical and photographic, particularly Eithne Kavanagh, Secretary of the Department, Ruth Sheehy, and Brendan Dempsey, the College's photographer, who has been endlessly patient and efficient over our demands. We are also very grateful for the support and help of Professor Roger Stalley and Dr Edward McParland. The Trinity College Library staff have also been more than useful. The Trinity Trust, particularly Ellen Hanly, have helped enormously by keeping our finances straight.

When the book was virtually written, it became obvious that we would have to seek sponsorship to see it adequately illustrated, and we are extremely grateful to those listed below who have given sums both large and small, and to the others who did not wish their names to appear.

The Esme Mitchell Trust, Belfast and in particular the support of Peter Rankin
The J. Paul Getty Jnr Charitable Trust, London, and the support of Christopher Gibbs
Martin Naughton of Glen Dimplex
The Marc Fitch Fund, Oxford, and the support of John Cornforth
The Alfred Beit Foundation, Russborough
The Irish Georgian Foundation, Dublin
The School of Irish Studies Foundation, Dublin
Rohan Holdings Ltd
George Magan of J. O. Hambro Magan and Co. Ltd.
The Irish Antique Dealers' Association and the support of George Stacpoole
The Dufferin Foundation
The Earl of Belmore
Neil Hobhouse
William Roth
The Dublin dealers, Val Dillon, Cynthia O'Connor and Co., James Gorry, the Wellesley Ashe Gallery, the Jorgensen Gallery, Johnston Antiques and Fleury Antiques
The London dealers, Andrew Wyld of Agnews, Lane Fine Arts, David Posnett of the Leger Gallery, Bill Thomson of the Albany Gallery, Dickinson and Ker and Anthony Mould Ltd.

Innumerable people have generously helped us in our work and we hope that we have listed them all and that they will forgive us if anyone is omitted. First on our list we must thank Olda FitzGerald for, as usual, she had to put up with us both in fair mood and foul, and then Gillen Aitken, our agent, for his patience. We are particularly grateful to Martyn Anglesea of the Ulster Museum, Huon Mallalieu of London, and Christopher Ashe of Dublin for reading the book and for their useful suggestions. Jane Fenlon and her son, Donal, and Shirley Armstrong Duffy helped with research work and the latter with the bibliography; Elizabeth Mayes tidied up our inconsistencies; Helen Litton compiled the index; Mary Read of Christie's Dublin office fielded many a problem; Anne Skelly helped us through the final tasks, Ted and Ursula O'Brien designed the book beautifully and our editor, Alison Wormleighton, proved a marvel.

Elizabeth Kirwan of the National Library of Ireland was generous with her time and help, as were Michael Wynne and Adrian Le Harivel of the National Gallery of Ireland. We must also thank Barbara Dawson of the Hugh Lane Municipal Gallery of Art, Dublin, and Nicola Figgis of the History of Art Department, University College, Dublin who helped us with information about the Irish in Rome.

The Librarians of the Royal Irish Academy were most supportive. No work of this sort would be possible without the Witt Library, London, and it is gratifying that our own photographic collection of Irish painting is being used in the Van Eyck programme of which they are a major partner. The British Museum, and the Victoria and Albert Museum were very helpful as were all the English provincial museums and art galleries we consulted, from Huddersfield, Leeds and Sheffield to Bedford, Bristol and Gloucester, not to mention the Fitzwilliam Museum, Cambridge, and the Ashmolean Museum, Oxford. The Huntingdon Museum and Art Gallery of California and particularly Robert Wark; the Yale Center for British Art; the Royal Ontario Museum, Canada, and Australian and New Zealand libraries and galleries and particularly Joan Kerr of the University of Sydney were all more than kind.

John Turpin of the National College of Art and Design, Dublin, and Peter Murray of the Crawford Art Gallery, Cork, The Abbot Hall Museum and Art Gallery, Kendal, Gervase Jackson Stops of the National Trust, the staff of the Northern Irish National Trust, and members of the British departments of Messrs Sotheby's and Christie's are always generous with their time and expertise.

Among the numerous individuals who have helped are: J H Andrews, Bruce Arnold, Frances Bailey, Toby Barnard, Julian Campbell, Hilary Carey, Harold Clarke, Christina Colvin, Angelique Day, Captain Denham, Honor de Pencier, The Marchioness of Dufferin and Ava, Beatrice Garvan, Nicola Gordon Bowe, Francis Greenacre, Desmond Guinness, Michael Herity, Arnold Horner, Roy Johnston, Brian S Kennedy of the Ulster Museum and Brian Kennedy of the National Gallery, Dublin, Samantha Leslie, Ronald Lightbown, Ciaran MacGonigal, Michael McCarthy, Hector and Randal McDonnell, David M Mitchell, Judge and Mrs Murnaghan, Charles Nelson, Kevin B Nowlan, Oliver Nulty, Eoin O'Brien, Cynthia O'Connor, Richard Ormond, Thomas Pakenham, Laurely Patton, Robert & Mary Raley, Mrs Hugh Roberts, Ann Martha Rowan, Barbara Shapiro, George Stacpoole, Sir Francis Sykes, Glascott Symes, Capt. A. C. Tupper, David White, and Anne Yeats.

Our deepest gratitude must go to all the owners of the works of art we have looked at as well as those we have used.

PHOTOGRAPHIC CREDITS

Agence Photographique de la Réunion des Musées Nationaux (plate 369); Agnew's (plates 92, 135, 136); Amon Carter Museum, Fort Worth (plate 344); Archivio Storico, Accademia Nazionale di S. Luca, Rome (plates 18, 19, 128); Armagh Co. Museum (plates 104, 302); Ashmolean Museum (plate 112); Bank of Ireland (plates 121, 122); Bristol Museums and Art Gallery (plates 158, 183, 203, 208, 209, 307); British Library (plates 4, 6); British Museum (plates 20, 21, 35, 36, 55, 126, 132, 142, 198, 204, 205, 285, 353, 354); J A Brooks (plate 7); Christie's (plates 16, 51, 56, 69, 81, 84, 96, 201, 241, 279, 288, 314, 316, 320, 321, 350, 372, 388); Geoffrey Clements (plates 333, 334); Colnaghi, London (plate 159); Courtauld Institute of Art (plates 15, 17, 78); Crawford Municipal and Art Gallery, Cork (plates 95, 133, 134, 256, 327); Prudence Cumming Associates (plates 25, 26); Davison & Associates (plates 68, 94, 168, 223, 224, 225, 274, 283, 300, 396); K M de Longchamps (plates 150, 151); Brendan Dempsey (plates 1, 2, 3, 9, 31, 32, 33, 34, 37, 38, 39, 42, 44, 46, 47, 57, 88, 89, 90, 99, 106, 110, 115, 119, 149, 162, 163, 167, 169, 173, 178, 180, 181, 184, 185, 186, 189, 193, 212, 213, 216, 220, 230, 232, 233, 234, 236, 259, 263, 269, 272, 277, 278, 280, 282, 284, 286, 287, 291, 292, 293, 294, 297, 301, 305, 308, 318, 319, 324, 330, 331, 365, 366, 383, 390, 392, 394, 397); William Drummond (plate 304); Dyfed Archives Derwydd Collection, Box H13 (page 295); E T Archive (plate 237); Fine Arts Society (plates 210, 363); Fitzwilliam Museum, Cambridge (plates 12, 98, 140); Fogg Art Museum (plates 156, 157); John Freeman (plate 257); Girard College, Philadelphia (plate 59); Gorry Gallery (plates 57, 202, 240, 329, 373, 374, 376); Martyn Gregory Gallery (plate 289); Green Studio (plates 71, 72, 97); J & S Harsh (plates 187, 196, 206, 240, 378); Hazlett Gooden & Fox (plates 82, 130, 131); Hibernian Antiques Ltd (plate 268); Cecil Higgins Art Gallery, Bedford (plate 371); Hocken Library, University of Otago (plate 356); Hugh Lane Municipal Art Gallery (plates 368, 395); Huntingdon Museum and Art Gallery (plates 53, 80, 105, 111, 120, 261); Irish Architectural Archive (plate 312); Irish Georgian Society (plate 139); Jorgensen Gallery (plates 309, 311, 367); David Ker (plates 74, 75, 76, 86, 266); Brendan Landy Photography (plate 298); Leger Galleries (plate 161); Limerick Museum (plate 303); McCord Museum of Canadian History, Montreal (back endpaper); Maggs Bros (plate 8); Manning Galleries (plate 102); Messum Gallery (plate 389); Mitchell Library, State Library of New South Wales (plate 352); Moss Gallery (plate 296); Peter Murray (plates 295, 310, 313, 315, 317, 325, 326); Museum of Fine Arts, Boston (plate 335); National Archive of Canada (plates 340, 341); National Gallery of Ireland (plates 27, 67, 73, 108, 117, 155, 166, 176, 192, 197, 199, 200, 214, 215, 245, 247, 249, 250, 251, 260, 262, 323, 328, 359, 360, 361, 362, 364, 375, 377, 380, 382, 387, 393); National Library of Australia (plate 358); National Library of Ireland (plates 10, 11, 43, 50, 104, 146, 177, 191, 217, 218, 219, 265, 267, and end piece); National Library of New Zealand (plate 357); National Museum of Ireland (plates 30, 221); National Portrait Gallery London (plate 49), National Trust Archive (plate 273); National Trust of Northern Ireland (plate 77); National Trust Photographic Library (plate 182); Natural History Museum, London (plate 152); New-York Historical Society (plate 332); John O'Callaghan (plate 70); Cynthia O'Connor Gallery (plates 114, 179, 211, 258); Oriel Gallery (plate 306); Otago, Early Settlers Museum (plate 355); Pierpont Morgan Library, New York (plate 123); Rhode Island School of Design (plate 13); Rex Roberts (plate 379); Royal Academy, London (plates 124, 239); Royal College of Surgeons, Dublin (plate 398); Royal Ontario Museum (plates 336, 337, 339, 342, 343, 345, 346, 347); Royal Society of Antiquaries of Ireland (plate 188); Royal Society of Arts (plate 127); Scottish National Portrait Gallery (plate 87); Seattle Art Museum (plate 22); Soane Museum (plate 66); Sotheby's (plates 24, 63, 83, 125); George Stacpoole (plates 45, 113); Studio Jane (plate 275); Christopher Thynne (plates 5, 194); Ulster Folk and Transport Museum (plates 175, 386); Ulster Museum (plates 29, 64, 143, 144, 147, 148, 174, 207, 222, 227, 228, 229, 242, 243, 252, 253, 271, 384, 385, 391 and frontispiece); Victoria and Albert Museum (plates 14, 52, 65, 100, 101, 138, 141, 153, 172, 231, 235, 254, 255); Winterthur Museum (plates 60, 61); Andrew Wyld (plate 54); Yale Center for British Art (plates 62, 85, 103, 118, 129, 137, 160, 246, 270).

JAMES HOWARD BURGESS *The O'Cahan Tomb*
(Ulster Museum)

INTRODUCTION

At the outset it must be made quite clear, this book is not a study solely of master-pieces, there is no Irish J.R. Cozens, Girtin or Turner, but there are many visual delights in the works of George Barret, James Barralet, Francis Danby, Frederick William Burton, not to mention the ladies like Rose Barton and Mildred Anne Butler who dominate the late nineteenth century.

As in all our arts, many of the best artists worked abroad, not finding enough patronage at home, and in turn Ireland welcomed, especially in the age of the picturesque, and during the romantic movement, many English artists such as William Pars, the Varleys, and George Fennel Robson, who were attracted to Ireland's sublime scenery in Wicklow, Killarney and Connemara. Indeed there is a possibility that the great Sir Joshua Reynolds came on a visit to Dublin at the invitation of his friend and patron, the Viceroy, the Duke of Rutland. Some sketches of Wicklow scenery, the Scalp, the bridge at Grattan's house, Tinnehinch, and of course Powerscourt waterfall, exist in a sketchbook in the Ashmolean Museum.[1] Rutland was Viceroy between 1784 and '87 and no other mention of the visit has been found so far, though the drawings are considered autograph.

It was not only Ireland's landscape which was noted by travellers but the extraordinary light and effects of climate. For instance, that peripatetic heiress hunter and "parkomane," the German, Prince Puckler-Müskau, described the scenery in 1832 while staying at the dilapidated Bermingham House, Co. Galway, with a hospitable squire. He made an expedition climbing to the top of the famous fairy hill opposite Castle Hacket, not far away. He paints a verbal picture:

> Just at this point the sun set; and Nature, who often rewards my love for her, displayed one of her most wondrous spectacles. Black clouds hung over the mountains, and the whole heavens were overcast. Only just at the point where the sun looked out from beneath the dusky veil, issued a stream of light which filled the whole ravine with a sort of unearthly splendour. The lake glittered beneath it like molten brass; while the mountains had a transparent, steel-blue lustre, like the gleam of diamonds. Single streaks of rose-coloured cloud passed slowly across this illumined picture over the mountains; while on both sides of the opened heavens distant rain fell in torrents, and formed a curtain which shut out every glimpse of the remaining world. Such is the magnificence which Nature has reserved for herself alone, and which even Claude's pencil could never imitate.[2]

There are, however, many pleasures and quixotic excitements in drawings and watercolours other than high art. We have found ourselves overwhelmed by the amount of social, historical material which we have unearthed, ranging from the savage wars of Elizabethan times as depicted by their military map-makers, to the deliciously naïve sketches of gardens and houses by the redoubtable Mrs Delany and her friend Letty Bushe, to the drawings of Irish engineers and officers as far afield as America, Canada, and Australasia. So much of what we treat was done by half-trained amateurs who achieve a near professional standard.

We have been enormously amused by the travellers' tales that we have read in the extensive literature of Irish tourism, which naturally include the horrors of the Irish climate, and the beggary of the Irish peasantry, but it had not occurred to us that Irish hospitality could also have its hazards. For instance, Crofton Croker, a Cork man and a well-known writer on antiquarian subjects, in a particularly amusing passage describes these problems:

> The higher classes in Ireland are ever willing to entertain the traveller and assist in the advancement of his journey, when he has clearly proved it absolutely necessary to proceed, for it is not a matter of question how to get admittance to the first houses in the country, the dilemma is, how to leave them . . . The over-abundant kindness of the host (for an immediate invitation always follows an introduction) seldom permits his guest the free use of his own senses, and to expostulate is vain. If Dr Syntax like, he travels with a sketch-book, and states himself in search of the picturesque, he is hurried from one eminence to another, and assured it affords the best view in the country, as extent and beauty, when applied to the landscape, are generally confounded. A party is arranged to meet him at dinner, each of whom requests a visit; one assures him that a most celebrated castle is on his grounds, while another urges the charms of a glen near his residence in a tone it is impossible to refuse. After a journey of some miles and the loss of an entire morning, this renowned castle may prove but the naked walls of an old tower, dismantled of even its ivy garb, and the "charming glen" perhaps turns out to be neither more nor less than the best fox earth in the country. Thus the circle of acquaintances caused by a single introduction, every one leading to others, goes on increasing like the circles produced by a stone when flung into the water.[3]

Not all visitors took the same views about the landscape. Thackeray, who was amusing on his own weak powers as a landscape draughtsman, had some telling thoughts on Irish beauty spots. He wrote:

> How strange this is, I mean the bad landscape-drawing, in a person [himself] with an exceedingly strong perception of natural beauty. Buildings I can do smartly enough, but there are no buildings here: – only huts built of round stone, and sodded or strawed over – or tumble down modern houses, wʰ are more dismal than any other ruins. I don't think I cared much for Killarney, it is too fine and showy, and looks as if it were there on purpose to be admired, but Westport Bay is a miracle of beauty – and in Connemara I saw 1000 lakes of wʰ 10,000 beautiful pictures might be made.[4]

One of Ireland's greatest contributions to the arts was the remarkable Dublin Society Drawing Schools which, beginning in the 1740s, provided a basic and free training for artists and artisans far earlier than in England, and indeed in most of Europe. Arthur Young, writing in the mid 1770s, said that "Great honour is due to Ireland for having given birth to the Dublin Society, which has the undisputed merit of being the father of all the similar societies now existing in Europe."[5] Ireland looked initially to France rather than England, as the two earliest masters in the Schools were trained in Paris. The emphasis on pastel clearly comes from this training, and the great Hugh

Douglas Hamilton's Roman portrait pastels must be among the masterpieces of their kind in Europe.

As the Schools did not teach oil painting, many of their pupils excelled in watercolour, as did George Barret. He was inspired by his early knowledge of the romantic scenery, with its river, rocks and overhanging woods, of the Dargle valley and by the influence of his friend and contemporary, Edmund Burke, the author of the famous essay on *The Sublime and the Beautiful*. This was written in the mid-1740s when Burke was a student in Trinity College, Dublin, and Barret was a student in the Schools less than five minutes' walk away. Barret's early and excellent use of gouache may, we feel, have been a seminal influence on Paul Sandby.

By the end of the eighteenth and the beginning of the nineteenth century, the English drawing masters and their published aquatinted manuals were available in Dublin, as well as native publications such as William Allen's, *The Student's Treasure a new drawing book, consisting of a variety of etchings, and engravings executed by Irish artists*, first published in 1779. He founded a firm which sold artist's materials, paints, brushes and paper. He also circulated prints. The Revd William Gilpin's works were well known, and John Laporte, who visited and painted in Ireland, published his *Progress of a Watercolour Drawing* in about 1812. Every genteel young lady would have had some drawing book beside her from which to copy. Several oil paintings show amateurs proudly exhibiting their work; for instance, Mrs Jane Reilly of Scarvagh, dated 1775, by Thomas Pope Stevens, fl 1765–80 (on loan at Castletown House), shows her standing in a landscape holding a pencil and displaying a large sketchbook with heads of angels done in red chalk and a landscape on the opposite page. Another example is Benjamin West's portrait of Selina, Viscountess de Vesci, offering a sketch to her husband, who stands beside her. Men are even painted in this way as John Hamilton of Brown Hall and St. Ernan's, Co. Donegal, shows him in a portrait of the 1820s by Martin Cregan standing by the sea with a sketchbook showing a rocky coast and shipping.

The preoccupation with antiquarianism, which goes right through till well into the middle of the nineteenth century, found the art of drawing and watercolour as not only an artistic but a utilitarian method of recording Ireland's extraordinary wealth of dolmens, ruined abbeys, castles and hoary remains. It was a central subject throughout the period from Chearnly to Petrie. Many of Petrie's watercolours of Ireland are obsessed with a feeling for her historic past, and his life's work was important in the emergence of Irish nationalism in the arts in the 1830s and '40s.[6] It was summed up by his *Pilgrims at Clonmacnoise*, which shows not only the archetypal round tower and Celtic cross, but the devout figures at prayer in the graveyard as the sun sets across the Shannon. The tragedy of famine Ireland is little recorded, and strangely the disturbed state of the country in the second half of the century during the land wars, and the land acts, is not reflected in the calm, pastoral art of most of the artists. The age of Mildred Anne Butler, with her sunlit lawns and flower borders, gives no hint of the crumbling Anglo–Irish world. This was recorded occasionally in artistic journalism and caricature.

The origins of modernism are outside the scope of this volume, though we touch on the beautiful blotted technique of Mainie Jellett's studies in the Westminster Art School, which were discontinued quickly under the influence of Cubism. Jack Yeats's superb, airy watercolours on the Norfolk Broads at the beginning of the century slowly give way to a colourful expressionism. Despite the conservative artistic ideas of the new Ireland, the country with its youthful aspirations is surely best expressed by new ideas and new techniques.

Watercolours are often seen as less important and insubstantial things and Judy Egerton comments: "Perhaps the very word 'watercolour' is partly to blame for this, for it may convey, like the phrase 'watering-down,' a sense of dilution and, by implication, of loss of strength . . ."[7] We feel that in their fresh immediacy and quick-sketched liveliness they are often more telling than oils and the beauty of their colour when unfaded does indeed reflect our climate with peculiar vividness. Just as in the *Painters of Ireland*[8] we are unable to discern any particular Irishness about the pictures we are looking at, nothing attempts to remind us of the heights of brilliance and creativity of the great age of the Celtic manuscript. But we hope that the combination of many beautiful images with the sadnesses and amusements of the life and times of our predecessors will illustrate an unfamiliar page of our visual inheritance.

Anne Crookshank
Knight of Glin
Trinity College, Dublin

CHAPTER ONE

IRISH WATERCOLOURS:
THE BEGINNINGS

Watercolour painting in Ireland is of great antiquity. This book, however, will not deal with the fabulous wealth to be found in Irish manuscript painting from the early Christian period, but begins much later, when the old Irish traditions were fading away under the colonial expansion of the Tudors. The well-known woodcuts of John Derricke, published in 1581 in his *Image of Irelande*,[1] are vigorous representations showing the campaigns *(Plate 1)* of the Lord Deputy, Sir Henry Sidney, and the lifestyle of the Gaelic world in its dying stages. We do not know if there were drawings for these woodcuts; certainly they have not survived, but in the *Image of Irelande* Derricke refers to his "Pictures and portractours [portraits] made by painters cunning skill/With gestures of the Irish kern set out by quivering quill."[2] This suggests that he painted in Ireland.

The primitive quality of Irish life held great fascination on the continent, where Lucas de Heere drew[3] a group of Irish about 1575, possibly from life, and Dürer sketched a party of Irish soldiers as early as 1521, showing their distinctive dress.[4] Queen Elizabeth's charter for the City of Dublin, 1582–3, which was drawn in Dublin, includes watercolours[5] probably by herald artists. Other draughtsmen existed as can be seen in the drawing of a giant Irish deer made for Adam Loftus, which we discuss in Chapter 3, and in the watercolour of Trinity College, which was made some years after its foundation in 1592 by Loftus.[6] This drawing, though amateurish, is a bird's eye view of the new, or proposed new, buildings with their Renaissance architectural ornamentation added to the original monastic ruins.

Much of the topography of Ireland is first vividly shown to us by the Elizabethan map-makers, many of whom used the traditional method of working in watercolours on vellum. These map-makers were primarily engaged in surveying the country for the new settlers and depicting the landscape, including the cottages, castles and churches that they found here. Secondly, many show the military engagements, sieges and battles of these Elizabethan conquerors. Of the cartographers, the most pictorial artists were Richard Bartlett, Francis Jobson and, later, Thomas Raven. Bartlett's stunning maps of Ulster[7] use a bird's eye view of the countryside and vividly illuminate the history of the period. For example, his map of Dungannon *(Plate 2)* portrays the shattered stronghold of the O'Neills, now proudly displaying the Cross of St. George of England. It is surrounded by a moat, and the O'Neill ceremonial chair is in its place in the landscape and re-used as a symbol in a scroll in the foreground. Beyond the castle is a *crannog*, where fighting is still going on. The map shows the thatched cottages, one two-storied, in a native Irish *rath*. The composition of this page with its inter-related scrolls and the symbol of the O'Neill throne forms a remarkable artistic work; a picture as well as a map.

Another cartographer, John White (c.1540 –?1606), is an elusive personality and even now is subject to considerable discussion. He seems to have come from the west country like Sir Walter Ralegh, from whom he later leased a property near Lismore, Co. Waterford, but his origins and training are unknown. His remarkable watercolours, done in Virginia where he went first in 1585 and again in 1587, when he was governor of

Ralegh's ill-fated Roanoke Colony, are studies of fish, birds, animals and, most significantly, Indians and Indian life. They include
maps of various localities he visited in the
West Indies and America. Finally, after he
left Roanoke in 1590, he seems to have settled in Ireland for some years. His Irish connections are underlined by the fact that his
American drawings were in an Irish collection, that of the Earls of Charlemont, until
they were bought by the British Museum in
1865. He wrote to Hakluyt in 1593 from
"my house in Newtowne in Kylmore,"
which W.A. Wallace identifies as being Bal-
lynoe,[8] south west of Tallow, Co. Waterford,
part of the Ralegh estate which extended
from Youghal to Lismore. The map of a
nearby area, Mogeely, dated 1598, is now
usually considered to be White's work. J.H.
Andrews points out that it is the earliest Irish
estate map.[9] W.A. Wallace[10] is certain that
White worked in Ireland as surveyor and
draughtsman for Ralegh and noted the close
resemblance of some of the lettering on the
Mogeely map with White's writing on his
American drawings. Regrettably, we know
no marvels of White's draughtsmanship
done in Ireland comparable to his American
masterpieces, but the map with its interesting Celtic interlaced border shows the
wooded terrain now being organized into
named fields with a village shown on the
lefthand side.

A number of other map-makers included
illustrations in their work, such as Francis
Jobson,[11] whose very precise drawing on vellum of the siege of Glin Castle *(Plate 3)* in
1600 was engraved and included in the
record of Sir George Carew's Irish wars in
Pacata Hibernia, published in 1633. Carrickfergus seems to have impressed several
unnamed map-makers[12] with its harbour,
walls, beehive-like huts, cottages and tower
houses along the main street, not to mention
the redoubtable twelfth-century De Courcy
castle and its two churches, all shown with
great pictorial detail and in one instance
including such a detail as the cobblestones in
the castle courtyards *(Plate 4)*.

The Plantation of Ulster was to increase
the cartographical interest in the new buildings and fortifications and the need for map-
making. Thomas Raven was the most gifted
of these men to work in Ireland, starting as
early as 1609. His most elegant creations are
his maps of the Earl of Essex's estates, with a
superb frontispiece of 1635 including figures
of Arithmetic and Geometry standing in an
architectural setting, indicating that he was a
considerable artist in his own right. Through
the frame of the frontispiece *(Plate 5)* we see
Raven taking his bearings with a plane
table.[13] He was also employed in surveying
the new towns which the London Livery
companies were building in Ulster, of which
the best example is the Vintners' estate at
Bellaghy.[14] This shows the manor house and
bawn with its flankers at the end of a street of

1
JOHN DERRICKE
*The Triumphant Return
of the Soldiers (engraving)*

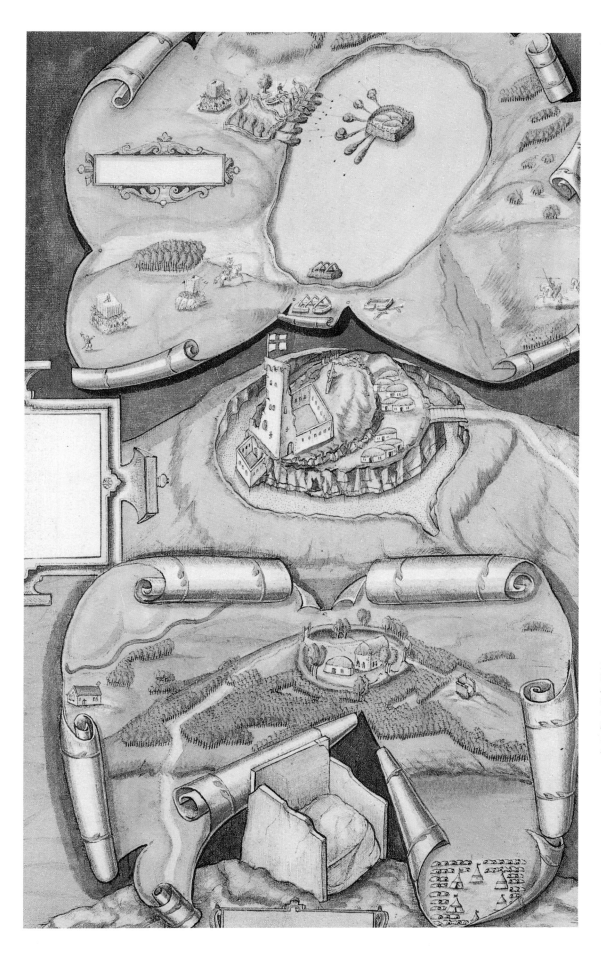

2
RICHARD BARTLETT
*Map of Dungannon,
Co. Tyrone, with the
O'Neill chair in the
foreground, c.1600*
*(National Library of
Ireland)*

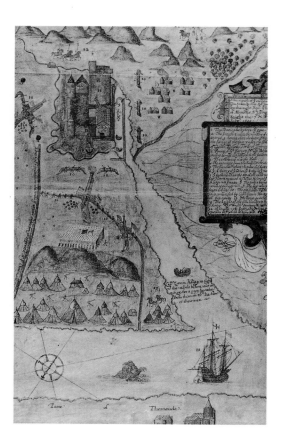

3
FRANCIS JOBSON
Siege of Glin Castle,
Co. Limerick
(Lambeth Palace Library)

4
UNKNOWN ARTIST
Carrickfergus Castle,
Co. Antrim
(British Library)

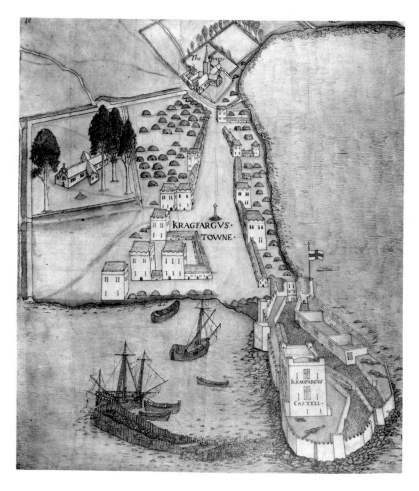

black and white prefabricated frame houses, each with the settler's name, together with the market cross and stocks and the church in a fenced enclosure. These maps are all enormously important from the socio-historical point of view. Equally important is the work of military personnel such as "John Thomas, Solder" [sic], who dated a watercolour of a *Siege of Enniskillen, 1593 (Plate 6),* and depicts everything from helmeted soldiers to tents, artillery, men wheeling supplies, and enemies' heads on stakes surrounded by an encampment. All these drawings have a directness and vivid pictorial quality which so clearly illuminates the harsh colonial settlement of Ireland.

Another aspect of watercolour painting, which we only need to mention in passing, is the work of the heraldic artists. All important charters and documents had initial letters containing a portrait and were often decorated with flowers. In the late sixteenth and early seventeenth century Celtic interlace is still evident, as in the heading of a page in *The Council Book of the Town of Galway, 1632.*[15] A good example of an illustrated book is the *Triumphalia (Plate 7),* a book produced about 1640 in Holycross Abbey, which included a resplendent watercolour of a relic being taken in procession.[16] Both of these examples indicate that the native Irish population still continued the art of watercolour illumination. The heralds who were employed by the Office of the Ulster King of Arms worked out the elaborate ritual of major funerals and they painted watercolour illustrations of processions, coats of arms and other items connected with their profession, though no Irish examples are yet known. They recorded funerary monuments, an example of this being the mid-seventeenth century *Monumenta Eblanae,*[17] as well as designing them. The herald artists worked on manuscript illumination where necessary, as in the giving of charters, peerage creations and the purveying of land titles.

Heraldry was as much employed by native Irish families as by settlers, so many of these craftsmen, most of whom are anonymous, were no doubt of Celtic origin. Their work was frequently of a high order, at times akin to that of miniature painters. An example of this is the initial letter of the Charter of

the Guild of Cutlers, Painter–Steyners and Stationers, founded in 1670.[18] The letter frames a finely painted head of Charles II. Aaron Crossley was warden of this guild in 1685 and in 1688, becoming Master 1689–90. He was the author of the first *Irish Peerage*, published in 1725, and at the end of this he advertises the sort of work undertaken by herald painters at this time which

included, "Esocheons, Hatchments, and all other sorts of Arms, and Pedigrees fairly engrossed and correctly painted . . ."[19] Strickland gives a list of herald painters from the late seventeenth century to the nineteenth which includes a number of painters who also worked in other fields, such as portraiture. Another area where heralds worked was in decorating peerage patents, and Irish examples are larger and far grander than their English counterparts. A splendid example is Viscount Molesworth's letters patent of 16 July 1716 *(Plate 8)*.

Though there is no reason to assume that Wenceslaus Hollar ever visited Ireland, he did make a print entitled *Louving in Ireland*, showing shipping off the coast which is thought to depict Culmore Fort on Inishowen, Co. Donegal. Hollar had engraved a map of Inishowen, presumably worked up from other people's drawings, and the seascape appears to be after Bonaventure Peeters.

Many an amateur artist was at work at this time surveying. An early drawing of Parsonstown House of 1668 is an example and is valuable as it illustrates the elaborate seventeenth-century building. The baronial

5
THOMAS RAVEN
Detail of frontispiece of the Survey of the Essex Estate, 1635

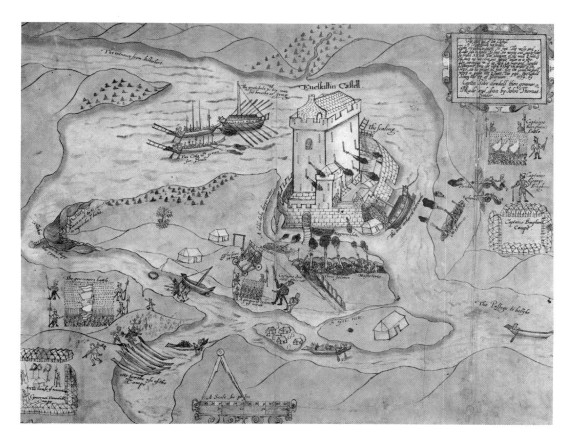

6
JOHN THOMAS
Siege of Enniskillen, Co. Fermanagh, 1593 (British Library)

Birr Castle of today has completely engulfed it. Another example is a ground plan and elevation of "Osbourne's fort," *(Plate 9)* which was done in 1676 by an artist called Trollup, and which depicts a fine, neat promontory fort with elaborate decorated gateways and turrets.

However, the real history of military surveys is continued by Thomas Phillips (c.1635–93), and shows a remarkable change in style from the earlier map-makers and surveyors. He was an engineer brought over to Ireland under the auspices of the Duke of Ormond in 1684/85, when the Viceroy was concerned with the Dutch and French naval threat. In 1685, Phillips's drawings and report were prepared and presented to the Earl of Dartmouth, the Master-General of the English ordnance. Phillips's drawings and watercolours are meticulous in topographical detail and the first of their genre in Ireland. They are also atmospheric in a manner not seen before in this country, and show the influence of the Dutch landscapists at work in England, such as Henry Dankerts, Alexander Kierincx, Jan Wyck, and Jacob Knyff. The clouds above Ben Bulben and the racing water in the Galway view *(Plate 10)* show a proper and new observation of nature.[20]

Slightly earlier than Phillips, Thomas Dineley[21] was one of the first of the many travellers interested in the "curious" to visit

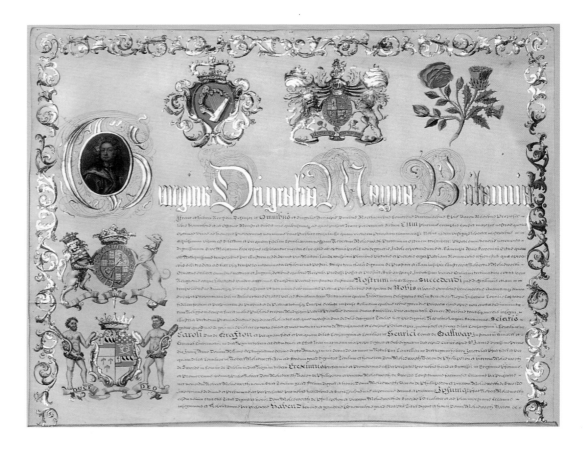

9
TROLLUP
*A View of Osbourne's
Fort, Co. Wicklow, 1676*

Ireland. Dineley, a Worcestershire gentle-man with a legal background, had already travelled in the Low Countries, but unfortu-nately his drawings hark back to the earlier map-makers more than to any contemporary Dutch draughtsman. He worked in pen and ink whereas Phillips's drawings were in coloured wash. Dineley, though naïve, has much charm and an eye for architectural and social detail. He is especially valuable as

10
THOMAS PHILLIPS
Galway, 1685
*(National Library of
Ireland)*

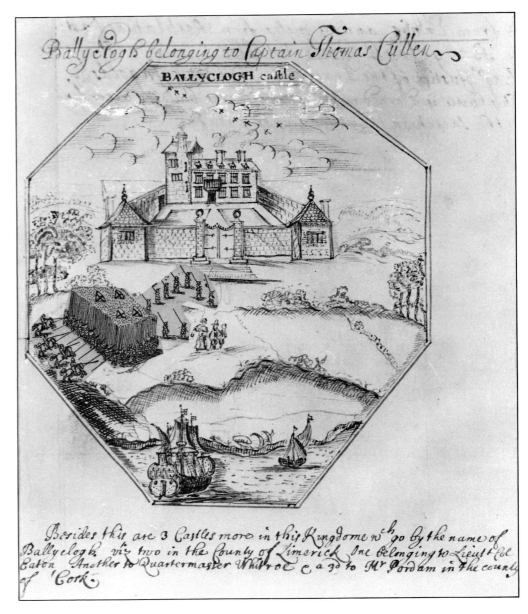

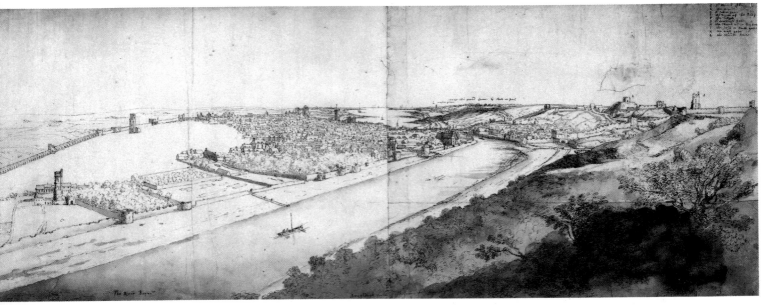

13
FRANCIS PLACE
Detail of a panorama of Dublin, 1698/99
(Museum of Art, Rhode Island School of Design)

many of his illustrations show the old towers evolving into manor houses with dormer-windowed roofs, courtyards and gatepiers *(Plate 11)*.

The century closes on a brilliant note with the visit of the English antiquarian and "virtuoso," Francis Place[22] (1647–1728), who landed in Drogheda in 1698 and travelled via Dublin and Kilkenny, sailing from Waterford in 1699. Most of his work is in pen and ink, though he uses a wash, particularly to establish his foreground. He was a pupil of Hollar and possessed many of his drawings. Place's style was fully matured by the time he reached Ireland so that his finished drawings have the real authority of one of the very first artists to concentrate on landscape painting. The precision and clarity of his views of Kilkenny and Waterford, and the panoramas he painted of Drogheda *(Plate 12)* and Dublin *(Plate 13)* contrast with his more intimate sketchbook work. There his concern with light and shade, the profile of a castle, the homely detail of a country road with the wind blowing *(Plate 14)* give his work an immediacy which carry one along with him on his travels. His virtuosity will be difficult to equal for many a decade.

14
FRANCIS PLACE
The Castle of Granny, Co. Waterford, 1699
(Victoria and Albert Museum)

15
HUGH HOWARD
Carlo Maratta
(Courtauld Institute of Art,
The Witt Collection)

16
HUGH HOWARD
Group of Fashionable
People

CHAPTER TWO

THE EARLY EIGHTEENTH CENTURY

From the late seventeenth and early eighteenth centuries, no drawings or watercolours survive from the oil portrait painters such as Garret Morphey, Pooley or Latham. However, Hugh Howard (1675–1738), trained as he was by Carlo Maratta in Rome, has a beautiful chalk technique well shown in his version of a head said to be a self-portrait by Maratta *(Plate 15)*.[1] This unusual work is unique among early Irish painters. A pen drawing of quality, strongly hatched, of a group of fashionable people *(Plate 16)* has recently been attributed to Howard and shows a more lively side to his work.[2] It came from the collection of the Earls of Wicklow who were descended from Hugh's brother, the Revd Robert Howard, Bishop of Elphin.

There are a few chalk drawings by Henry Trench[4] in the Accademia di San Luca, all student studies of 1705 of very high quality. They are after the antique, including subject pictures from Roman history, *The Death of Tarpea* and *The Schoolmaster of the Falerii*,[5] and some red chalk studies of statues of Bacchus *(Plate 18)*, Apollo and Cleopatra. The latter is signed "Enrico Trench Hibernese," the earliest occasion we know of in which the statement of Irish nationality appears on a signature. A freer drawing of *Hercules Fighting Nessus (Plate 19)* is a study but shows a livelier and stronger drawing style. There was, and still is, an extended Trench family in Ireland, though careful search has not been able to find his immediate branch. Trench studied under Carlo Maratta, and under his pupil Giuseppe Chiari. We also know from a letter written by the Scottish painter William Aikman on 15 July 1725 that Trench was taught, probably during one of his later visits, by the Neapolitan Francesco Solimena.[6] Like Howard and Jervas, he moved in the circle of Lord Burlington, William Kent and Sir John Percival, later first Earl of Egmont. Very interestingly, he was recommended by Dr James Fagan,[7] the Irish priest who was agent for the clergy in England and Ireland, to Lord Shaftesbury who employed him to make drawings for the second edition of his *Characteristics*.[8] Writing to Fagan on 13 February 1712, Lord Shaftesbury advises Trench to practise before going to Naples and says ". . . whilst he studys the antient Originals and sticks to Design and drawing after the noble models of Statuary and Painting here in Italy he will at the same time qualify himself by right Learning for History–Painting, and what is cheif [sic] & principal in his Art."[9] He adds later in the same letter:

Two other artists who studied in Rome in the first decade of the eighteenth century, at the same time as Howard, are the portrait painter Charles Jervas (c.1675–1739) and the virtually unknown decorative painter and illustrator, Henry Trench (fl. 1705–26). Jervas, who became a fashionable portrait painter and Principal Painter to George II, left few drawings, though Vertue states there were a number in the sale after his death. He said that "there is many of his own Studies done at Rome etc. some few heads in Crayons black and white in large frames that were his chief Studies . . ."[3] A portrait of *Matthew Prior* is in the Portland collection and is a humdrum study but his pastel of *Catherine Hyde, Duchess of Queensbury (Plate 17)*, which relates to the portrait in the National Portrait Gallery, is a work of considerable competence and charm.

. . . before he undertakes his Journey I shoud be glad he woud spend a little time in Drawing upon paper only in black and white, or any two Colours . . . taken from . . . fine Statues of the Antients, and particularly from some of the finer sort of Antient *Basso relievo* not only of men and Boys, but animals such as Horses, Lions, and the Poetical Forms of Fawns, Satyrs, Sphinxes and the Like, of which there are at Rome so many fine Remains in Brass and Marble.

17
CHARLES JERVAS
The Duchess of Queensbury
(Courtauld Institute of Art, The Witt Collection)

18
HENRY TRENCH
Bacchus, 1705
(Archivio Storico, Accademia Nazionale S. Luca, Rome)

Trench arrived in Naples on 6 April 1712 and left on 16 September. He had by then completed the task of drawing the headpieces and decorations which Simon Gribelin was to engrave for Lord Shaftesbury. Several of these drawings are of remarkable quality and interest, including that illustrated *(Plate 20)* and his illustration of Shaftesbury's remarks on Tolerance.[10] He also worked as Shaftesbury's agent in buying pictures, receiving substantial payments on occasions, including twenty-two pounds five

shillings as a commission for a transaction worth four hundred pounds with Signor Porcinari.[11] Amusingly, he is paid to take a pair of silk stockings to William Kent when he leaves Naples.[12]

There is a great deal of fascinating correspondence by and about this artist and it is all the sadder that, knowing so much about him, there is relatively little to see. In 1712 he was described as "now the first of all the young Genius's at Rome for painting."[13] He died young and there is a sad reference to his demise as "a very good history painter, but a whore beggar'd him, and he died of the pox."[14] Vertue was more prosaic; he says, "in the middle of Decem[br] 1726 Dyd Mr . . . Trench Painter buried at Padington near Mary Lebon [i.e. Marylebone, not the whore!]."[15]

An Irishman who appears to have been trained in Paris was Nicholas Blakey (fl. 1739–78), whose earliest known oil painting is a portrait of *Field Marshal Keith* dated 1739. Keith worked as a mercenary soldier serving all over Europe, and the portrait is in the French baroque tradition. A few other portraits are known, as many French as English. Blakey may have been in London by 1748, when he is listed in *the Universal Magazine*[16] among a host of well-known artists as one of the "justly esteemed eminent artists."

Blakey worked as an illustrator of a variety of books, including history and travel as well as an edition of Pope, and he collaborated with Francis Hayman. There are two pencil drawings of classical subject matter in the British Museum which are in the French manner, multi-figured allegories *(Plate 21)* and the one in good condition is of remarkable quality. Very little else is known about him except that he died in France.

One of the most important Irish painters who lived in London from the age of twenty-five was Thomas Frye (1710–62). He has become familiar to us today through his series of mezzotints, but began his career by making a number of pastel portraits, including two of young men dated as early as 1734.[17] These are finished works, not drawings for oils, and Frye continued to use pastel as well as oils throughout his life, even

19
HENRY TRENCH
Hercules Fighting
Nessus, 1705
(Archivio Storico,
Accademia Nazionale
S. Luca, Rome)

after he became director of the Bow Porcelain factory in 1744. *The Girl with the Kitten* (British Museum) is one of his finest drawings in black and white chalk done in *chiaroscuro* obviously influenced by Piazzetta's prints.[18] The surviving drawings for the mezzotints are in black and white chalk, such as the slightly sinister *Boy Wearing a Turban (Plate 22)* and his contemplative study of a man which is sometimes said to be a self-portrait. This drawing has a delicacy which enhances the naturalism of the informally posed, half-turned head. It must be among the most sophisticated drawings by an Irish artist of the eighteenth century. Much of the softness of these drawings is lost in the transformation into the mezzotints for which he is so celebrated today. He is one of the few Irish artists who was a considerable influence on his English contemporaries, especially Wright of Derby.[19]

An interesting group of watercolourists and pastellists are the lady amateurs. The earliest of these was Henriette de Beaulieu (c.1674–1729), usually known by her married names, Dering and Johnston. Her birthplace is unknown but was somewhere in France and in the 1991/92 exhibition catalogue of her work she is said to have been

20
HENRY TRENCH
Draft illustration for the frontispiece to Vol. II of the second edition of the Characteristics
(Department of Prints and Drawings, British Museum)

born in 1674.[20] It is probable that she is the Henrietta mentioned in the Huguenot Denizations[21] for 16 December 1687 as arriving in England with her parents, Francis and Suzanna and brother Henry.[22] The will of her daughter, Mary Dering, dated 23 April 1746 and proved on 13 June 1747, identifies the artist as marrying on 23 March 1694 Robert Dering, son of Sir Edward Dering, second Baronet, of Surrenden Dering in Kent.[23] Several members of the Dering family made their careers in Ireland and they were intermarried with the Southwell and Perceval families, who had considerable landed property there.

It is not known where she learned her art but she was practising professionally in Dublin from as early as 1703. It has been suggested that she was taught by Simon Digby, Bishop of Elphin (fl. 1668–d. 1720), who was her second husband's friend and superior. He was one of Ireland's earlier painters but as he is most famous for his miniatures he is really outside the scope of this book. He is recorded as "a great master of painting little watercolours," and inventories taken after his death include many watercolours.[24] One pastel by him survives in a private collection, a portrait of the first Duke of Ormond which links stylistically with English painters like Edmund Ashfield and not with Henrietta Dering. Indeed her second marriage to the Revd Gideon Johnston was not till 1705, when she is most likely to have met Digby, and there is no change in her style between 1703 and her later work.

An artist whom she resembles more closely, however, is Thomas Forster (born c. 1677[25]), by whom work is known from 1690 to 1713 and who is thought to have been in Ireland. His plumbago miniature portraits are of far higher quality than Henrietta Dering's, but they are similar in their Lelyesque poses. She used pastel while Forster used plumbago and Digby usually watercolour. An artist who in the past was said to have been born in Dublin, Edward Lutterell (fl.c. 1673–1724) worked in pastel on roughened copper plates. A drawing by him in the National Gallery of Ireland is not dissimilar to Henrietta's work. It is now generally agreed, however, that Lutterell did not belong to the Irish branch of that family.

Henrietta appears to have had a large practice in the fashionable Dublin world in the years 1703–5. She drew portraits of several of her husband's relatives *(Plate 23)*, including Philip Perceval and the first Earl of Egmont, President of the Trustees of the Colony of Georgia, who sent General Oglethorpe to establish a settlement in Savannah.

Her second husband, Johnston, went as a missionary to Charleston in 1708. Henrietta accompanied him and continued to work there as a portrait painter and is celebrated today as America's first woman painter. Her art was mentioned by her husband in 1709 in a letter: "Were it not for the assistance my wife gives me by drawing Pictures (which can last but a little time in a place so ill-peopled) I should not have been able to live."[26] In a later letter, dated 5 July 1710, her husband notes the problem of obtaining artist's materials and a year later she was exchanging crayons for rice.[27] Her little pastel portraits are delicate and doll-like and derive from miniature and engraved portraits. Her anatomy is poor and her later work appears crude, though this may partly be the result of damage to the drawings due to the American climate. She was still painting in 1725 when she was living in New York, though she died in Charleston in 1729.

The second of these lady amateurs was Letitia (or Letty) Bushe (fl. 1731–d. 1757) who is mentioned frequently in the letters of the third, Mrs Delany (1700–88), from 1731 to 1757. She describes Letty in 1731 as "painting delightfully" and also sadly as losing her fine complexion through "that malicious distemper [smallpox]" which, combined with financial embarrassments caused "a very uncertain fortune,"[28] making her unmarriageable. She was an ideal companion because of her determined good spirits. Mrs Delany mentions Letty drawing from "some prints of Claude Lorraine" and "drawing some beautiful landscapes in the Indian book Mrs Mead gave me."[29] She mentions that Letty painted in oil and also in miniature. Letty helped Mrs Delany to clean watercolours as well as "egging them out."[30]

When Mrs Delany married Dean Delany and came to live near Dublin in 1744/45, Letty Bushe frequently stayed with her for weeks and months on end. It appears from Mrs Delany's letters that Letty stayed regularly with other families as well, though from time to time she lived alone in an apartment in Dublin. Her company was clearly in demand. On 19 January 1744/45, Mrs Delany remarks to her sister "for besides her ingenuity, she has a turn for conversation that is not common, and her good-humour is inexhaustible."[31] Her work was much in demand in the circle of her friends. Lady Knapton of Abbeyleix, writing probably sometime in the mid-1750s, said: "I am afraid Ly. Roden will be very angry wth.me for a request I have to make her, wh. is that

21
NICHOLAS BLAKEY
An Illustration
*(Department of Prints
and Drawings, British
Museum)*

22
THOMAS FRYE
Boy Wearing a Turban
(Seattle Art Museum)

bottom, a pine box for watercolours and brushes.[34] The Dublin Society was also interested in new inventions and gave a silver palette to the makers, George Cowan and Henry Graham, for their range of specimen watercolour paints and the sub-committee on 8 May 1783 considered that they were "rather superior to those invented by Messrs Reeves,"[35] though in fact they were imitations of Reeves's work. A broadsheet, unfortunately undated though it is probably late in the century, issued by "Bushell's Print Shop, Near Crampton Court, Dame-Street," indicates that Dublin was quite well supplied with artist's goods:

Just imported a large Sortment of choice Prints English and French . . . the Etchings of Paul Sanby, Bartolozi, etc. The works of . . . Hogarth, Boydel and Vivares, – Variety of new Drawing Books . . . with Indian Ink, all sorts of Hair-Pencils, and Hog-hair Tools, all sizes of the best primed English Cloths for Painters, large Drawing Paper, French and Dutch; Port-crayons, and chalks, watercolours in shells, Ivories for miniature-Painting, and fine white vellum . . .

It would seem that Letitia Bushe encouraged her friends to paint and she certainly helped Mrs Delany. Letty's few surviving watercolours are charming and naïve but full of incident and detail. They vary from views of Irish landscapes and ruins to a panorama of London. At least two of her paintings emphasize the newly planted surroundings to gentlemen's houses *(Plate 25)* and show them with their gates and encircling trees smaller than the walls, laid out in a formal manner. One is reminded of Swift, who in the 1730s, in *A Dialogue in Hibernian Stile between A and B*, comments, "You have a Country-house, are you Planter. Yes, I have planted a great many Oak trees, and Ash trees, and some Elm trees round a Lo'o'ugh."[36] Indeed, Letty's houses emerge as havens of a new civilization *(Plate 26)* in the wilderness that rural Ireland had been left in, after the wars and depredations of the previous century.

In 1751 Letty made drawings for Richard Barton to be engraved as frontispieces for his *Lectures in Natural Philosophy . . . on Lough Neagh* and his *Some remarks . . . in the County of Kerry*.[37] Of the latter engraving, Mrs Delany

she will let me keep the Drawing Letty is doing for her as it is the only thing of consequence she has attempted. I cannot think of parting with it and it will be no Loss to Ly. R. as she is just going to begin a Landscape in Colors which will be prettier."[32] Lady Knapton clearly painted herself and asks her correspondent to "send for a Box of Colours that Mrs Watson has for me." This reference to a box of watercolours is very early, as Letty Bushe died in 1757, and boxes were not commonplace until the 1770s.[33] It may, however, have only been a "packing" box. Another interesting relic of drawing equipment is the carved mahogany box *(Plate 24)* which was given to the Marquess of Kildare in 1767 by the Guild of Carpenters, Millers, Masons, Helers, Turners and Plummers whose coat of arms is carved on the lid. This velvet-lined box contained a set of drawing instruments including silver compasses and dividers, an ivory parallel rule and, at the

23

HENRIETTA DERING
*A group of nine portraits
of members of the Perceval
and Dering families,
1704-5*

24
*Lord Kildare's
Presentation Box, 1767*

in February 1751 remarked that "the engraver hath not done justice to the delicacy of her pencil."[38] This engraving can lay claim to being the earliest known portrayal of Killarney. The Lough Neagh view is a more conventional landscape showing the shores of the lake.

Letty visited England in 1743 when she painted the very competent panorama of London from Hampstead and views in Bath and Bristol. It is not clear whether her plans for other visits to England ever came to fruition or whether she ever visited London as a girl. This supposition arises because on stylistic grounds it has been suggested by Dudley Snelgrove that she learned her art from Bernard Lens or one of his sons. Bernard died in 1740 before her documented visit, and though Peter Paul Lens visited Dublin about 1737, there is no evidence that he taught there; a *View of Bray* (National Gallery of Ireland) by Letty dated 1736 does not show any marked difference in style from her later work. She must have studied her art in the late 1720s or early 1730s and who taught her remains a matter of speculation.

Mary Granville (1700–88), later Mrs Pendarves and finally Mrs Delany, was a pupil of William Hogarth, Bernard Lens and

25
LETITIA BUSHE
A Country House

correspondence.[41] Mrs Delany copied Letty Bushe's self-portrait, and the hair and part of the costume were worked in hair. She was renowned for her japanning, as were many ladies of that time, like Mrs Conolly of Castletown whose cabinet, with its charming Italianate landscapes and chinoiserie in lacquer, demonstrates how professional lady amateurs could be when imitating textbooks.[42]

The dexterity and artistic skill Mrs Delany showed with her needle, shell and cut paper work, not to mention her brilliant flower collages (discussed in Chapter 7) were unfortunately not paralleled in her watercolours. Though charmingly naïve, these are more important today as rare topographical representations of gardens, buildings and landscapes (Plate 27). Nobody was better taught to so little effect, and as a painter she always remained an amateur. The album of watercolours in the National Gallery of Ireland includes drawings throughout her career in Ireland from 1739 to 1768. These drawings with added washes are stilted and mannered with little feeling for distance or solidity; her trees and rocks often look like sponges. However, she was a very competent copyist, as a chalk drawing dated 1739 shows. It is inscribed by her on the reverse and she states that it is a copy of a pastel (Plate 28) self-portrait of Rosalba Carriera.[43] It is striking how well she draws

the fan painter Louis Goupy. Goupy made her copy the family portraits in oils. She was an admirer of Hogarth's work, writing on 27 May 1731, "I am grown passionately fond of Hogarth's painting, there is more sense in it than any I have seen,"[39] and in the same letter she records that Hogarth gave her some lessons. But this interest is not reflected in her work as a draughtswoman. Her favourite teacher was Louis Goupy, about whom she wrote in 1748 that he was "an incomparable master."[40] Later she was assisted by Letty Bushe, whose miniature of her is reproduced in Lady Llanover's edition of Mrs Delany's

26
LETITIA BUSHE
The Terrace at Leixlip Castle, Co. Kildare

27
MARY DELANY
Castleward, Co. Down, 1762
(National Gallery of Ireland)

31

28 MARY DELANY *Copy after Rosalba, 1739*

29 SUSANNA DRURY *The Giant's Causeway, Co. Antrim, c.1739 (Ulster Museum)*

this, even to her excellent use of chalk, compared with her hesitant landscapes.

In contrast to these amateurs is Susanna Drury (fl. 1733–70), whose background has been described by Martyn Anglesea as "mysteriously obscure."[44] He also notes that her technique of gouache on vellum is similar to work by Joseph Goupy, from whom she might have learned. She may have been in London in 1733 when she painted a now lost panorama of the city from Greenwich Park. However, her masterpiece and her only other known works are the two sets of *Views of the Giant's Causeway*,[45] a pair of which won the Dublin Society Premium for landscape in 1740 *(Plate 29)*. (The Schools and their Premiums are discussed in Chapter 4.) Mrs Delany wrote to her sister on 8 October 1758 that Susanna Drury "who took draughts . . . lived three months near the place, and went almost every day. I can do nothing so exact and finished."[46] These gouaches are, not surprisingly, detailed and portray the basalt columns very accurately. However, this minute portrayal of a natural phenomenon is lightened by the charming rococo figures, and both are subordinated to the overall massing of the landscape. Susanna Drury conveys the Causeway's grandeur by the directness of her manner and highly competent sense of space. Since the work of Francis Place, these are the finest landscapes painted in or of Ireland.

CHAPTER THREE

THE ANTIQUARIANS

The development of antiquarian interests in Ireland was sporadic during the seventeenth century and was linked with the study of natural history. It had, however, an incalculable effect on the development of drawing in Ireland. From as far back as 1586 there is an accurately portrayed sketch,[1] now in the National Museum of Ireland, recording the discovery of the head and antlers of an extinct Irish Giant Deer *(Plate 30)* found in that year and preserved by Adam Loftus, Ireland's Lord Chancellor, who built Rathfarnham Castle in the 1580s. It may, in fact, be the earliest known Irish drawing from Renaissance times. In Loftus's letter of 27 September 1597 to Sir Robert Cecil, Queen Elizabeth's all-powerful Secretary of State, in which he is planning to send the head to Cecil, he describes it as follows: "the rare greatness of it made me . . . set [it] up in the hall of a poor house which I built here."[2] This was, of course, not only extreme modesty but also an attempt to disguise from prying English officialdom the grandeur of his newly built great castle of Rathfarnham.

This drawing seems to have been a unique survival and is not connected with the wave of antiquarian art sparked off a hundred years later in 1683 with the foundation of the Dublin Philosophical Society.[3] William Molyneux[4] was the moving spirit of this organization and it proved to be a milestone in serious research. It was this society that tried to lure to Ireland Edward Lhuyd, the Keeper of Antiquities in the Ashmolean Museum, Oxford, a naturalist, philologist, and student of Celtic Antiquities. Though the Society failed to do this, Lhuyd made two visits to Ireland, and on the second occasion, in 1699, he entered the passage grave at New Grange, the first man to do so since Viking times.[5]

Other members of the Molyneux family, William's brother, Thomas, and his son, Samuel, were also deeply involved in the antiquarian movement. It was Thomas who published in 1726 the drawing of Newgrange[6] made in 1700 by Lhuyd's assistant, William Jones. Thomas Molyneux did not publish Lhuyd's opinions but substituted his own. Newgrange was also the subject of Thomas Wright's work in about 1746. He was an English astronomer, known as "the Wizard of Durham," who came to Ireland and worked as an architect, landscape gardener and antiquarian. It is as a very individual and quirky rococo landscape gardener and designer of follies that he is most famous in England. One hundred and seventy-five of his drawings are in the Avery Library, New York, including some Irish examples such as gates for Tollymore, Co. Down.[7] Seventy-five more are in a private collection in London. His drawings of Newgrange and the sepulchral Mount near Templepatrick were published by Michael Herity.[8] They are examples of the careful delineation of antiquities which fits in with Wright's architectural style.[9] As an antiquarian he published, in 1748, *Louthiana*,[10] a study of castles, earthworks and antiquities in Co. Louth for his patron, Lord Limerick, who was laying out the gardens at Dundalk and Tollymore.

Two other phenomena which exercised the learned attention of the Dublin Philosophical Society in the early years of the eighteenth century were the Giant's Causeway, in Co. Antrim, and Lough Neagh. The Giant's Causeway was first drawn in 1696, very inaccurately, by, according to

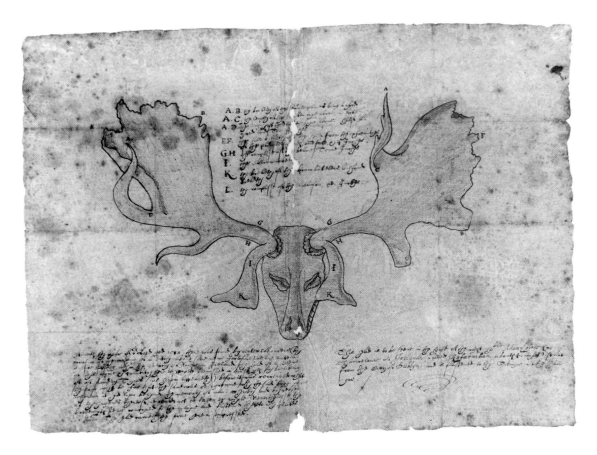

Strickland, "Ireland's earliest engraver of any importance," Edwin Sandys, who died in 1708. It was printed "at the expense of the Dublin [Philosophical] Society."[11] Martyn Anglesea, quoting Thomas Molyneux, records that Sandys was "a good Master in Designing and Drawing of Prospects."[12] He is best known today for the large map of Londonderry during the famous siege of 1689, surveyed by Captain Francis Nevill. It includes buildings, armorials, and even a four-foot long fish found on the quay there, which illustrates the growing interest in natural history inspired by the Society.

New members included George Berkeley, the philosopher, traveller and later Bishop of Cloyne who was described as having "successfully transplanted the polite arts . . . to this northern climate"[13] and who had a collection of pictures in his palace at Cloyne. He, with Thomas Molyneux, was to become one of the founder members of the Dublin Society (now Royal Dublin Society) in 1731. This organization became the focal point of agricultural and artistic education in the eighteenth century and its members included the leading antiquarians.

The influence of these Dublin societies

produced a spirit of enquiry among the nobility and landed gentry in the country and led to the publication of the earliest county histories, such as Walter Harris's *The Ancient and Present State of The County of Down, 1744* and Charles Smith's similarly titled *Waterford*, 1746, *Cork*, 1750 and *Kerry*, 1756. These were published under the aegis of the Physico–Historical Society of Dublin,[14] which was founded to collect materials for a work on the same plan as Camden's *Britannia* to be called *Hibernia or Ireland Ancient and Modern*. Like many other Irish topographical projects, it was stillborn.

Some of Smith's books were illustrated by "prospects" by Anthony Chearnly (fl. 1740–91) of the towns of Lismore, Dungarvan, Youghal, Cork *(Plate 31)* and Kinsale. He signed these "Antho Chearnly gen: Burnt Court delin." He was a country gentleman living in a house next door to the great Jacobean ruin of Burnt Court, Co. Tipperary, a print of which is in Francis Grose's *Antiquities of Ireland* (1791–5). His brother, Samuel Chearnly of Birr (d.1746), was an amateur architect who made a series of entertaining drawings of bizarre garden follies in 1745–6 for Sir Lawrence Parsons of

Birr Castle and a sketch for the Cumberland monument at Parsonstown, the pillar of which, Chearnly says, derived from Perrault.[15] They are rather reminiscent of Thomas Wright and show grottos, fountains and grandiloquent architectural schemes in the Palladian style. Anthony Chearnly's town views were the first engravings of this type and had a wide circulation. Though the views of Kinsale and Youghal were painted in oils, he used watercolours to record ruins and antiquities. Grose included several of these in his book, and in the letterpress he tells us that Chearnly was one of the earliest collectors of antiquarian drawings in the country. Grose also commented that Anthony Chearnly "deserves to be remembered for cultivating the art of design when few practised it in 1740 in Ireland."[16]

It is an insoluble problem to differentiate completely the style of the drawings of the eighteenth-century antiquarians, including Chearnly, as they have all come down to us in collections such as Grose's *Antiquities* and others made, but not published, by fellow antiquarians. These sets are in many cases copies after originals. An example is the set by the Revd James Turner, now in the Royal Irish Academy, with copies after Fisher, Barret, the Revd John Hume, Thomas Roberts, Thomas Ivory, Pope Stevens Reilly, the Revd Mr Seymour, Col. Vallancey and others. Most of Turner's copies are reduced to circular form and treated in a perfunctory manner by a draughtsman with little ability, and they give no concept of what the original drawings were like.

Other collectors, like Austin Cooper, made a better hand of their copies, though he, too, occasionally used Turner, whose work is always weak. Cooper worked in the Treasury Office as a clerk from 1774, becoming chief clerk in the 1790s. He was also Paymaster to the Pensioners on the Civil and Military Establishments and was a land agent to many large estates. The travelling necessitated by these jobs was no doubt the reason he became interested in antiquarianism. From 1796 until 1830, Cooper was Deputy Constable of Dublin Castle. He was also an agent "of the State Lottery, in which it is stated that he drew a purse of £20,000,"[17] which was no doubt why he was able to buy the mansion of Kinsealy and other lands in 1807. He bought William Burton Conyngham's collection of antiquarian drawings. These collections were all interrelated, as these antiquarians formed a small circle of friends of friends and used each other's drawings.

It is less of a problem, however, to isolate Chearnly's hand from the copyists, as Chearnly, unlike later antiquarians, set his ruins within a well-composed landscape viewed from a distance like his town views. There are two views of Ardfinnan, one in Grose *(Plate 32)* and one in Austin Cooper's collection, taken from different viewpoints

31
ANTHONY CHEARNLY
Detail of a view of Cork, 1750 (engraving)

32
ANTHONY CHEARNLY
A view of Ardfinnan,
Co. Tipperary, 1793
(Royal Irish Academy)

33 **JOSEPH TUDOR** *View of College Green and the Parliament House, Dublin*

but both are set ably in landscapes. The Cooper view of Ardfinnan from the south-west is signed and dated "A Cooper pinx[t] 1785" but is also signed "Anthony Chearnly delint 1744," while the watercolour for the engraving in Grose looks more likely to be an original and shows what we think is Chearnly's neat topographical style. The problem also arises of establishing where Chearnly learned his art. His panoramas are undoubtedly influenced by William Van der Hagen's town views,[18] of which Derry and Waterford are the only ones known.

Van der Hagen (fl.1721–45) was a Dutch artist who came to Ireland via England in 1722 and remained till his death in 1745. He can claim to be the father of Irish landscape painting and he also worked as a decorator and scene painter. There is no evidence that he taught, except that the generation of artists of the 1730s and 1740s, like Chearnly, Joseph Tudor (?1695–1759) and William Jones (fl.1746–7), all seem to be influenced by his compositions. We know only one watercolour by Van der Hagen, a study of Derry (though this may be a copy after him rather than by him and has now been lost). We know no watercolours by Jones but four grey wash drawings, for Tudor's engravings of Dublin are in a private collection. In the *View of College Green (Plate 33)*, his handling of architecture, the row of Dutch Billies and the Parliament House itself, is most competently done but the quality of his brushwork suggests that he was more at home in oils. Chearnly's use of watercolour may have been sparked off by its suitability for the peripatetic nature of antiquarian study, though finished work like the Ardfinnan drawing would have been completed at home.

Austin Cooper was also a keen draughtsman, though his style is feeble and his buildings look insubstantial. His best drawing is probably of his family house, Killenure Castle, Co. Tipperary *(Plate 34)*, though it, too, is extremely primitive, like the little thatched building attached to the ruined castle which is where he lived when in the country.

The key figure in the third quarter of the eighteenth century was William Burton Conyngham (1733–96).[19] He was the nephew of the first Earl Conyngham and

34
AUSTIN COOPER
*A South East view
of Killenure Castle,
Co. Tipperary
(Royal Irish Academy)*

had a finger in every antiquarian, architectural and artistic pie as well as holding a number of important public posts, including that of Teller (from 1777) and later Comptroller of the Exchequer in Ireland. He joined the Dublin Society's first Antiquities committee in 1772. This collapsed in a couple of years but he replaced it with his own Antiquarian Society[20] in 1780, with Burton Conyngham as president, and the Revd Mervyn Archdall, Col. Vallancey, Edward Ledwich and William Beauford among the founder members. He made the most extensive collection of drawings of antiquarian subjects and he employed practically every landscape painter in Dublin to make these drawings, though, as we have already mentioned, they have come down to us in the form of copies. A large percentage of the drawings, except those by Francis and Daniel Grose and Thomas Cocking, for Grose's *Antiquities* (1791–5), were from the Conyngham collection. These volumes, though begun by Grose, were finished by Edward Ledwich, who in fact wrote most of the text. Other Conyngham drawings were used by Col. Vallancey in his multi-volume *Collectanea de Rebus Hibernicus* (1770–1804), and by Ledwich in his *Antiquities of Ireland* (1790) which is largely illustrated by William Beauford.

Another collector was Peter Walsh[21] (d.1819), of Belline, Co. Kilkenny, who in about 1769 started collecting drawings of antiquities, including castles, tombs, churches, abbeys and many seventeenth-century buildings which have entirely disappeared. He did not publish them himself,

but a number were copied and used by Sheffield Grace in his various obsessive genealogical studies of the past baronial glories of the Grace family. Over three hundred of these drawings are now in the Victoria and Albert Museum. Walsh was unusual among antiquarian collectors not only because he bought paintings as well, but also because he ran an art school at Belline. Brewer, writing in 1825, mentions Walsh and his collection of paintings, which were housed both in his house and in a gallery nearby which "constituted a sort of academy for students . . ." Brewer says that "several children of the peasantry of this neighbourhood have lately evinced a considerable degree of genius for drawing under Dr Walsh's protection."[22]

This public-spirited behaviour to the local peasant children appears to be unique among antiquarians, and it is interesting to note that the building that housed the art school still stands at Belline.

Charles Tarrant (1730–1818) was a friend of Conyngham and an officer in the Royal Engineers who became Chief Engineer in 1762 and was associated with canal building and with fortifications in Ireland. From 1763 he was a draughtsman to the Board of Ordnance, a department of the Board of Works, and he appears also to have worked as an architect. By 1802 he had been promoted to Major General. He went with Conyngham to the monastery of Batalha in Portugal in 1783. Conyngham went on to Spain and made a close study of the Roman Theatre near Valencia at Saguntum. A drawing by Tarrant in the Cooper collection shows him to have been drawing, as early as 1755, an elevation and plan of a Gothic monument, the Cross in Kilkenny and a ground plan of the stone circles at Lough Gur. His only surviving watercolour dates from a year later, 1756, and is a view of Charles Fort in Kinsale *(Plate 35)*, now in the British Museum. It is surely and freshly handled, and there is a variant of it by Charles Vallancey (Royal Irish Academy, Cooper Collection). Other drawings are mostly connected with his surveying and map-making work.[23] On the Batalha trip, William Burton Conyngham made sketches which are not known but which were described by James

Cavanah Murphy as "elegant."[24] Murphy (1760–1814) had been brought to Conyngham's attention as a gifted draughtsman, and in 1789 Conyngham paid him to make a study of Batalha. The splendid illustrated book,[25] which was such a seminal influence on the Gothic revival, was the result. Murphy, a product of the Dublin Society Schools, contributed only one drawing to Grose, of the Lavabo at Mellifont, but is known for architectural drawings and one landscape of Tynemouth Abbey (Plate 36).

From an antiquarian point of view, Conyngham's patronage and friendship with Gabriel Beranger is of great importance. Beranger (1729–1817), a Huguenot, though born in Rotterdam, came to Ireland at the age of twenty-one and spent his career in this country. He was a print-seller and framer, a teacher of drawing as well as a painter of flower and bird pictures. He eventually obtained a sinecure as Assistant Ledger Keeper in the Treasury in 1780. One of Beranger's bills to the eighth Earl of Meath survives, dated Dublin 1780/1, where he is paid for "Cutting and fixing on blue paper and framing Two Shaddow portraits . . . 3/3" each; eleven more followed soon after. It continues with the framing of flower pieces and repairs and finally "hanging and glueing picture" and supplying "12 Brass headed nails."[26] He was best known as a topographical draughtsman, but one decorative landscape (Plate 37) by him survives and he may have done others in this mode.

Beranger's first sketching trips date from about 1773, though he had painted Dublin topography (Plate 38) before then. It was in 1779 that Conyngham sent him on a tour to the West of Ireland with Angelo Maria Bigari, a Bolognese scene painter. Despite the fact that Beranger was a professional, his work is charmingly naïve; he rules his architectural lines and gets much of his effect from his brilliant clear colour. His figures are fairly cursory, but occasionally they improve, as in the drawing of himself and his friends measuring the Cromlech at Kilternan (Plate 39), where he is copying the work of one of the Vasprés (two brothers who were

37
GABRIEL BERANGER
Imaginary Landscape with Figures

38
GABRIEL BERANGER
*Drimnagh Castle,
Co. Dublin, 1760*
(*National Library of
Ireland*)

39
GABRIEL BERANGER
*The Cromlech at
Kilternan, Co. Dublin*
(*Royal Irish Academy*)

pastellists and visited Dublin in 1777 and 1778). When he signs, it is with a monogram "GB" and the work is usually dated. A convenient summary of his career with forty-seven illustrations from the collection of the Royal Irish Acadamy has recently been published by Peter Harbison.[27] A great many of his watercolours and those of Bigari are included in Grose's *Antiquities*.

These *Antiquities* are puzzling volumes. Grose died within twelve days of his arrival in Dublin on 1 May 1791, on the last of his

visits to Ireland, when John Nixon drew him visiting Howth Head *(Plate 40)*. Dated drawings in his *Antiquities* indicate that he was here in 1770, 1789 and 1790. However, the volumes were edited after his death by Edward Ledwich, many of the illustrations being borrowed from the collection of William Burton Conyngham. The original drawings were by a great variety of artists including Grose's assistant, Thomas Cocking, his nephew Daniel Grose, J.M. Barralet, Jonathan Fisher, the great architect James Gandon, the English and American visitors Francis Wheatley and Henry Pelham, the artist, miniaturist and map-maker who was the half-brother of the famous American painter of Irish parents, John Singleton Copley. Pelham had made a large map of Co. Clare for the grand jury in 1779, and his contribution to the *Antiquities* was, not surprisingly, of Clare subjects.

The volume of drawings in the Royal Irish Academy would not give the impression of many artists at work. As we have already indicated, they are clearly all by a small group of hands trying to achieve a similar style for purposes of engraving. Only occasionally does the style of the artist shine through, particularly in the case of Bigari, with his blocklike buildings and his minute delineation of masonry as well as his very

personal, theatrical figure style. This is very well seen in the *Burial at the Abbey of Banada*, Co. Sligo *(Plate 41)*, with two ladies lamenting by the coffin. Many of Bigari's drawings are in hatched pen and ink with the appearance of engravings. Daniel Grose, Francis's nephew, was also a competent topographer. Though his figures are weak, his handling of perspective is good. In a drawing such as his *Athlumny Castle, Co. Meath*, he shows well his understanding of the architecture of the gabled manor house and its adjoining medieval tower. Francis's convivial servant, Thomas Cocking, uses a very similar style to his master and their work can easily be confused.

After the death of Francis Grose, Cocking went with Daniel Grose (Francis's nephew) to the West of Ireland, and there is a charming view of *Parke's Castle, Co. Sligo (Plate 42)* on the shores of Lough Gill, where three of them are stewing up an alfresco meal in a

40
JOHN NIXON
Francis Grose at Howth Head, Co. Dublin, 1791

41
ANGELO MARIA BIGARI
Burial at the Abbey of Banada, Co. Sligo

42
THOMAS COCKING
*S.E. Aspect of Parke's
Castle, Co. Sligo.*
(Royal Irish Academy)

cauldron. Drawings made on this trip were included in the *Antiquities*. Daniel Grose continued to have an interest in Irish castles and ruins and in the 1820s proposed to publish a third volume of the *Antiquities*. This project was stillborn but the manuscript has recently come to light and been published by the Irish Architectural Archive with an informative introduction which sums up the latest knowledge of the Grose circle.[28] It includes drawings by Daniel Grose, his son, another relative, Lt Arthur Grose, together

43
FRANCIS GROSE
*Tourin Castle,
Co. Waterford*
*(National Library of
Ireland)*

with two by the Revd Charles Moore (whose son was General Sir John Moore of Corunna fame) and four Armagh views by Benjamin Bradford, artists otherwise unknown to us. By the 1820s, Daniel's style was completely out of date, as it had not changed since his youth and must have looked ridiculous compared with George Petrie's brilliant work (see Chapter 9).

To retrace our steps: Francis Grose was an Englishman and a pupil of William Shipley's drawing school in London. Most of his own illustrations in the *Antiquities* are of places near Dublin, and his style is noted for his accuracy in portraying buildings rather than achieving artistic effect. However, in sketches rather than in his finished work he does show a delicacy of style which is well seen in his unfinished study of *Tourin Castle*, on the Blackwater *(Plate 43)*, where the trees and foliage are light and feathery. The same quality comes through in a finished study of *Fishermen in the Stream by Glennan Mill in Co. Tyrone*. Some of the contributors were feeble enough, like the Revd Samuel Wynne, whose pale, feathery watercolours used to turn up frequently in the Dublin art market. A fairly good example is his view of the newly battlemented *Pakenham Hall*, Co. Westmeath *(Plate 44)*.

Another of the antiquarians whom we have already mentioned was William Beauford (1735–1819), whose work is mostly to be found in Vallancey's *Collectanea de Rebus Hibernicus*. In the area of inscriptions, Beauford's work met in 1838 with the disbelief and anger of John O'Donovan,[29] who described Beauford as "a forger of inscriptions and architectural features."[30] He was a notable map-maker in a period when demesne maps by good artists had the prestige of works of art.[31]

There is considerable confusion between

44
Revd SAMUEL WYNNE
Pakenham Hall,
Co. Westmeath

45
Revd WILLIAM LOUIS BEAUFORT
The Falls at Doonas,
Co. Clare

Beauford and a good amateur, the Revd William Louis Beaufort (1771–1849), the son of the map-maker, diarist and Rector of Navan and Collon, the Revd Daniel Augustus Beaufort. William Louis was the pupil in Bristol in 1782 of Nicholas Pocock and a Miss Simmonds and later in Dublin of a James George O'Brien (see Oben, Chapter 5).[32] He painted watercolours on a large scale, such as a view of the *Falls at Doonas at Castleconnell (Plate 45)* and one of a *Distant View of Avondale*. These works have a marked blue tone and concentrate on the landscape, the buildings being far in the distance. Another of his watercolours dated 1789, *A Bridge at Tollymore (Plate 46)*, shows an interest in architecture as the building dominates the scene. The confusion is made worse because the Castleconnell view is signed with a "d," Beauford, but appears to be by the same hand as the Tollymore bridge which is signed with a "t," Beaufort. Strickland combines features of both their biographies and we are not entirely certain of our ground here; if the Castleconnell is by Beaufort, then we do not know of an actual watercolour by Beauford.

In more inaccessible areas of Ireland, local draughtsmen were naturally used,

though it is noticeable that the *Antiquities* did not include Co. Donegal and had only one illustration of Co. Cork. The Revd John Hume (c.1743–1818), who became Dean of Derry from 1783 and lived for many years in Glenalla House near Rathmullen, Co. Donegal, was a competent draughtsman who seems to have covered the North-Western Counties for all the collectors but whose work does not appear in the *Antiquities*. He drew all over Ireland but especially in Counties Cork, Donegal, Tyrone and Fermanagh. In a recently found sketchbook the drawings, dated 1773, vary from *A Mass House at Fannet*, 29 Oct 1773, to views of Strabane *(Plate 47)*, Ramelton and Benburb. As this predates his Derry appointment by ten years, despite the fact that he was born in Oxford he may have had Irish connections. In Austin Cooper's collection there are drawings of various castles in Fermanagh and Tyrone by Hume but unfortunately redrawn by the Revd Mr Turner with his usual heavy hand.

Two figures whom we have hardly dealt with are Col. Vallancey and Lord Portarlington. Vallancey undoubtedly sketched all over Ireland during his tours of duty with the army's military survey of the island.

46
Revd WILLIAM LOUIS
BEAUFORT
*A Bridge at Tollymore,
Co.Down, c.1789*

47
Revd JOHN HUME
The Bridge at Strabane,
Co. Tyrone, c.1773

However, his drawings in Austin Cooper's collection are copies by Cooper, or, worse, by Turner. We have been unable to find any originals by him but his forceful personality made him a figure among antiquarians and he is also an important cartographer. His *Collectanea de Rebus Hibernicus*, which is a gathering of articles on subjects from surveying to archaeology, includes, as we have noted, chapters by authors such as William Beauford and Charles O'Connor.

Lord Portarlington, as the Hon John Dawson and later as Lord Carlow, drew many pictures, found in all the collections. Again few originals can be identified; one signed by him "Lord Carlow pinx" is in the Cooper Collection and is a romantic flickering study of the round tower and ruins at Kildare *(Plate 48)*. It is not typical of the neatness of topographical work and does not show the influence of Paul Sandby. This is perhaps strange as George Harding says that "Lord Portarlington draws in *Sandby's manner* and almost as well – many of the views in *Sandby's* work – (*'The Virtuoso's Museum'*) are taken by the former, who has made a Voyage Pittoresque of *Ireland* worthy of immediate publication, but his modesty will imprison it in the *portfolio*."[33]

Portarlington was an habitué of Sandby's house when in London, and his work is the

48
LORD CARLOW
View of the ruined
Cathedral and Round
Tower of Kildare

source of many of Sandby's Irish drawings and prints despite the Sandby signatures. In fact, it is generally considered today that Sandby did not come to Ireland. In the Hamilton Art Gallery in Australia they have an important collection of Sandby's work, including three major Irish views, all of which are from sketches by John Dawson (Lord Portarlington). They are of *Ross Castle*, *Dromana*, and *The Falls of Polufuca*. Julian Faigan, the author of the Hamilton catalogue, points out that "it seems certain that Sandby did not travel to Ireland himself, for a visit would surely have been alluded to in some way in his correspondence with James Gandon, the architect, whom Sandby had known since the mid 1760s."[34]

A final interesting comment by Harding on Portarlington is that he had a splendid library, including books of drawings, maps and architecture and in this respect was "a phenomenon as in the best House of the Island you can scarce find a common book for amusement – Learning is out of the case."[35] This is surely an exaggeration, but the paucity of books, prints and drawings in Ireland is mentioned by Gandon, who worked for Lord Portarlington designing his house at Emo. He says of Dublin, "I was greatly surprised to find but *one* print-shop. There were two others in which prints were sold, but their trade was that of glaziers."[36]

An Englishman who did come to Ireland was Sir Richard Colt Hoare, the distinguished antiquarian who did so much to improve the idyllic landscape of his seat, Stourhead in Wiltshire. He published his *Tour In Ireland* in 1807, having made the drawings in 1806 while travelling round the country. The book has comparatively few illustrations and his eccentric neighbour, William Beckford, poured scorn on the tome saying witheringly that these were "the meagre notes of this dry, husky traveller whose mind is as dull and vacant as the dignified coal-hole he has selected as a frontispiece."[37] Most of the watercolours for this Irish tour are in the Royal Irish Academy and are distinguished by his competent architectural rendering, though his trees and rocks are weak enough. The two views of Ardfert are undoubtedly his best and the blue wash of the sky gives a translucency which suggests the dusk.

Portarlington was a patron and close personal friend of Jonathan Fisher, who helped

Lady Portarlington with her oil paintings, as she mentions in a letter of the 31 August 1781: "We expect Mr Fisher, a pter, here on Monday, wh will I think incline me to begin the little boys picture, for he will clean my brushes and lay my palette, which is what makes me lazy about beginning a picture."[38] Harding also mentions that she was "a most capital painter in oils . . ."[39] Despite a few drawings in Grose and Cooper, Fisher is not associated with the mainline antiquarian movement, but he was the best artist specializing in straight topographical work in the second half of the eighteenth century. Though he was self-taught, he won a number of Dublin Society prizes, and spent part of his youth in England. A drawing of that early period traditionally attributed to him is of the river at Lymington in Hampshire, and is a typical pen and wash drawing of the mid-eighteenth century. But his style in oil develops into a fully romantic presentation of some of the most sublime scenery in Ireland – Killarney and the Mourne Mountains. If we are right in identifying as a late watercolour by him a *View of the Upper Lake at Killarney* (British Museum), which we now feel was attributed incorrectly to Barker of Bath, it shows the same romantic layers of washes as his paintings, and the pen and ink has disappeared. It is, however, a flat, weak drawing and does not show the directness of his recently discovered sketchbooks (discussed in Chapter 5).

The antiquarians, though of no particular artistic importance, through their peregrinations in search of hoary ruin, dolmen or tumuli but not High Crosses, did an enormous amount to stimulate the appreciation of the picturesque in Ireland. This led many other artists and patrons to search out the beauties of Irish scenery, lake and mountain.

CHAPTER FOUR

THE DUBLIN SOCIETY SCHOOLS

The vital importance of drawing was early appreciated in Dublin. Bishop Berkeley in *The Querist* of 1735 enquired "Whether when a room was once prepared, and models in plaister of Paris, the annual expense of such an academy, need stand the public in above £200 a year?"[1] He clearly had in mind drawing from the antique but he was also a patriotic Irishman and concerned, like his friends Samuel Madden and Thomas Prior, in Ireland's self-sufficient economic development. They were, in their ideas, in the mainstream of the European Enlightenment. In 1740 Madden gave £100 to found a system of Annual Premiums in the Dublin Society which covered agriculture and the arts, painting, drawing and sculpture. Vertue noted this new scheme and wrote that it would ". . . bring forth some eminent Artists – which will eclipse our London proficients of Art . . . [it] may supply and rival the English who want a school or foundation – or some propper encouragement."[2]

In fact, Madden and Prior helped to found the Dublin Society Drawing Schools[3] out of the art school started by Robert West (d. 1770) about 1740. According to Strickland they arranged with West in or before 1744 that he should instruct twelve boys. In 1746 Thomas Prior, in an audience with the Lord Lieutenant, Lord Chesterfield, said that "it is intended to erect a little academy or school of drawing and painting . . ."[4] though it was ten years before they actually did so. The school continued in West's George's Lane premises. The Dublin Society seems to have intended to found a fine art school together with a trade school. This last would have been one of the first in

Europe and the teaching was rather in the manner of the French school the *École Royale Gratuite de Dessin*, founded by Jean Jacques Bachelier much later, in 1767. The Dublin Society Schools were, as we have said, the academy for artists as well as craftsmen, though until the foundation of the Royal Hibernian Academy in 1824 no teaching in oil painting was available in any public art school in Ireland. Berkeley and Madden's views were acceptable in Dublin for, on 24 August 1736, John Esdall in the *Dublin Daily Advertiser* proposed opening a drawing school, stating that "Drawing is the Mistress of all the manuel Arts and Masonary, Carving, Stucco-forming, jewellry, Furniture and Damask Weaving etc . . ."

Robert West, the founding headmaster of the Dublin Society's Schools, is described in an article in *The Citizen* in 1841 as a superb draughtsman. Probably written by Thomas Mulvany, the article states that his drawings from the living model "have never been surpassed and perhaps but rarely equalled."[5] As, regrettably, none of West's drawings have survived, we can only imagine them. His early education in France, where he would have been taught to use chalk and pastel, is mentioned by all the early writers. Pasquin said he "studied under Van Loo and Boucher."[6] O'Keeffe, who was a student in the Schools in 1755, said he was trained in Paris under Boucher and added that "indeed his [R. West's] drawing of what is technically called the Academy Figure was unrivalled."[7] William Carey, the Cork critic, who was extremely well informed, writing in 1826, makes this French education more precise. He says that West "obtained the first prize for drawing in the French Academy under

Carlo Vanloo. West, with all Vanloo's prowess in chalks, drew in a purer style, with more truth and sweetness and without a tincture of that celebrated draughtsman's mannered squareness."[8]

Even a well-known English engraver, William Wynne Ryland, knew of his Paris training. In the interesting *Diary of a Visit to England in 1775* by the Irish clergyman, Dr Thomas Campbell, which was not published till 1854, he remarks that "the best of the English don't think as ill of the Irish as I expected."[9] He continues, "Let me not forget to set down what Ryland told me . . . what indeed I had always heard in Ireland, that old West was the best drawer in red chalks at Paris, of his time, and that for drawing in general he was the best scholar of Venloo[sic]." He then goes on to mention the many Irish mezzotint engravers who were at West's Academy and who dominated "scraping" in England in the eighteenth century.

We have found no reference to West in any French lists of the Académie de St Luc or the Académie Royale, but these are by no means exhaustive. Boucher, who was only *agrée* in the Académie Royale in 1734 was, however, appointed an assistant in 1735, in which year Charles Van Loo was a Professor and his son, J.B. Van Loo, also an assistant. This date, 1735, would fit well as a student period for West, as he set up his drawing school in Dublin in the late 1730s. It is very significant that in the interview Prior had with Chesterfield, the Viceroy said, "The genius of Irishmen is capable of excellence in every art and science, if encouraged. Get masters from the Continent to instruct you. You will soon have painters and sculptors of your own."[10]

The Schools were enormously successful throughout their life and were taken over by the government in 1849. Classes increased in numbers and Sir Vere Hunt mentions seeing "forty boys drawing figures, some of them very clever"[11] on a visit to the Hawkins

49
MATTHEW WILLIAM
PETERS
Self Portrait with Robert West, 1758
(National Portrait Gallery, London)

Street premises in 1813. In 1842, Isaac Weld, who was Secretary to the now Royal Dublin Society, made a speech at the first public Distribution of Premiums in which he estimated that ten thousand artists and craftsmen had passed through the Schools since their foundation nearly a century earlier.[12]

Certainly West's pupils excelled in chalks and pastels. The drawing of West teaching one of his pupils, Matthew William Peters (1741–1814), which is by Peters *(Plate 49)*, is another close hint of West's work and illustrates the point made by Sleator in 1767 that "the Academy has produced many excellent in Chalks, and more than that it could not do, for more it did not teach."[13] From about 1750 West was joined by James Mannin (d. 1779), who was also French-trained and said by Pasquin to have been French, though the name is common in northern Italy. He taught ornament and landscape and was said to be an excellent flower painter. Carey said he taught landscape, flowers and ornament.[14] Undoubtedly the school had a collection of engravings and drawings, of which a very few are now in the National Gallery of Ireland. They include Le Brun, several Natoires – one of a fine rococo fountain – and Roman school works. The manual used was Robert Dodsley's *Preceptor*, published in London in 1749, which included engravings after Le Brun's famous *Passions* and landscape drawings in the rococo taste.

There were a number of private drawing schools in Dublin, several run by French trained artists and some by Frenchmen such as Pierre Mondale Lesat, who advertised his school in 1736, claiming to be "Painter and Medallist, member of the Royal Academy of Paris," and William Bertrand (fl.1765–70), who had been a fellow pupil with West in Paris. Most of his works, exhibited in the Society of Artists between 1765 and 1770, were in crayons or red chalks or were drawings, a word which was interchangeable with watercolour at that time. Other teachers included George Gaven (fl. 1756–75), the portrait painter, who described himself as a Drawing Master in Queen Street, Oxmantown; Thomas Boulger (fl.1761–88), who not only taught in Dublin but set up a school in that Huguenot stronghold, Portarlington, in 1788; and Henry Brooke (1738–1806),

the subject-picture painter, who described himself as a Drawing Master whenever he exhibited in the Society of Arts between 1770 and 1780.

He taught the irrepressible Dorothea Herbert when she was in Dublin staying with relations in 1779 and we learn that he "had always been civil as I was never under any other hand but his own."[15] This hints at the rivalries between drawing masters. The two illustrations to Dorothea's *Retrospections* indicate that Brooke failed, as her work is charmingly primitive. One shows her mother and clergyman-father outside the Rectory of Knockgrafton, receiving tithes in the form of piglets, chickens and other farm produce.

Charles Praval (d.1789) was a Frenchman who arrived in Ireland in 1773, exhibiting two drawings of New Zealand which he said he made as "late draftsman to Mr Banks, during his expedition round the world,"[16] Cook's journey on the *Endeavour*, 1768–71, on which the great botanist, Joseph Banks, sailed. He taught drawing and French, kept a boarding school for young ladies and specifies that he specialized in map-making and geographical drawing. He wrote a couple of books on the French language. The influence of French art and engravings in Ireland for the first three-quarters of the century cannot be stressed too much. In architecture it continues into the nineteenth century, though not in the decorative arts. Recent work is revealing the extent of the circulation of French architectural treatises and pattern books and their influence in Ireland.[17] It pervades all the arts, from stucco ceilings and silver chasing to the painters themselves. Many Irish people had connections with France and saw Paris as a cultural alternative to London. Lord Chesterfield's Francophile remarks, previously quoted, emphasize this.

The mention of map-making brings us to a byway which has no connection with the schools but is most conveniently dealt with here – the so-called French school of Dublin Land Surveyors, John Rocque and Bernard Scalé. They were known for their superb draughtsmanship and, from our point of view, for the magnificent vignettes and cartouches with which their maps are decorated *(Plate 50)*. J.H. Andrews says of them that they were responsible for carrying the estate

50

JOHN ROCQUE
*Detail of a map of
Carton, Co. Kildare, 1760
(National Library of
Ireland)*

map "almost in a single stride, from agent's office to library or drawing room, taking its place among furniture, pictures and other works of art as yet another example of the highest Georgian craftsmanship and taste."[18] He also points out the individuality of each volume and mentions the depiction of farm carts, beehives, spinning wheels and, of course, gardens, houses and different kinds of husbandry. Occasionally other artists contributed to their work, such as Hugh Douglas Hamilton, who made a superb architectural *capriccio* (see pages 66–7), for Rocque's chief private patron, Lord Kildare. Scalé left Ireland in 1779, leaving his pupils Thomas

Sherrard, John Brownrigg and James Vaughan to carry on the tradition.

There were other pupils, including James Williamson (1757– after 1819), who is a very good example of a "Land Surveyor and Draughtsman" largely working in the provinces. Williamson has left us a fascinating autobiography and a book of samples exhibiting his proficiency, together with a series of estate maps from Counties Antrim and Down.[19] His Dutch-inspired figures, which include such motifs as two peasants dragging a ram *(Plate 51)*, are naïve but the maps themselves are well delineated. He was born in London, but came with his parents to Dublin; he worked with his father in Grierson's bookshop and went to the Dublin Society Schools in 1771. He took up miniature painting and hair painting for lockets and rings which he had learned secretly from the Robertson family, whose son Charles had become a famous miniaturist. Williamson's father, however, was working for Scalé and it is clearly in this way that he learned surveying, which he ultimately made his career. Williamson painted topographical landscapes, particularly for Lady Clanbrassil and Lady Glerawly, and continued to paint some miniatures; he also taught painting in Armagh. We have tarried too long on this minor man, but he is a rare example of an artist telling his own story.

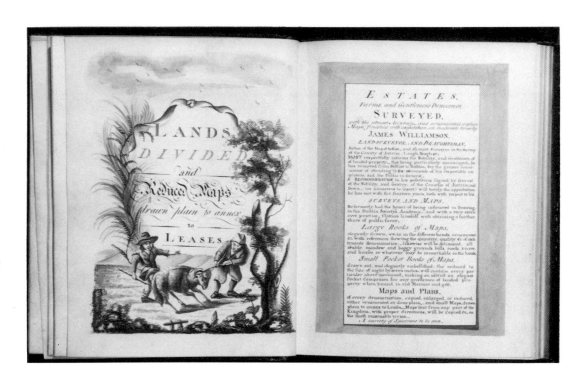

51

JAMES WILLIAMSON
*A page of text and an
illustration of two
peasants dragging a ram
(Ulster Museum)*

After this cartographical digression, we must return to the Dublin Society Schools. Of Robert West's early pupils, George Barret (1732–84) was by far the finest draughtsman in both black and white, in watercolour and in gouache. He does not seem to have used pastel. In the Schools he would only have been taught landscape through the copying of landscape engravings and drawings. Two Watteau landscapes and a Marco Ricci still survive from the original collection. He may have seen Dutch and Italian masters in private collections or in the salerooms in Dublin, where sales were quite frequent. A study of what catalogues remain shows that a high preponderance of the artists were from the Dutch and Flemish schools. The German traveller, Gottfried Küttner, also remarks in 1784 on the same point in Irish collections: "There are very few pieces by Italian great masters, that is true – but the best and most I have seen were Flemish school, or better, Netherlandish. This is now indeed so the case almost everywhere outside Italy, but here more than anywhere else."[20] As far as we can judge, few of Barret's watercolours are directly connected with oils, but a drawing for his *View of Richmond Hill* of 1777 exists in a sketchbook in the Victoria and Albert Museum, and, though close to the oil, there are substantial changes. The foreground tree in the oil is an insertion, and so are the horses and the general romanticized background with strong contrasts of light and shade, unlike the neatly topographical pencil sketch.

The smaller of the V & A sketchbooks may be early, as it contains studies of rocks, water and a little thatched, rustic temple which is identical to one in his etching of the Dargle. This was presumably taken from a plate made for a set of four landscapes of the Dargle and Powerscourt, which were advertised but never published in the early 1760s before he left for England. Many of the trees in the sketchbook are rudimentary in comparison to those in the etching and in his later drawings, where they are beautifully modelled and their species well defined. The marked lighting with which Barret modelled his leaves is described, not unreasonably, by Iolo Williams as "spiky."[21] His capacity to draw an actual tree is also noted by Mallalieu.[22] Another feature of the later drawings

52
GEORGE BARRET
A Bull
(Victoria and Albert Museum)

is the excellent studies of cattle, including a bull *(Plate 52)*, indicating that he was quite capable of drawing animals even though he so often collaborated with Sawrey Gilpin *(Plate 53)* and others. Another amusing aside is a signed drawing by him in the Pierpont Morgan Library of a pair of horses drawing a coach bringing voters to the support of John Wilkes at the famous election contest in Westminster in 1774. It is very rare in showing Barret caricaturing people and it is also unusual to find figure drawings: only one or two are known. We illustrate a pen study which probably includes a self-portrait *(Plate 54)* as it is very close to his pencil self-portrait at his easel in the Soane Museum.[23]

It is interesting that as a student Barret studied landscape, and it is to the credit of the Dublin Society Schools that they must have encouraged it even before the arrival of Mannin, as they exhibited an oil landscape of Barret's in the School show in 1747. It is intriguing that he is included in the following year in a list of "justly esteemed eminent master[s]" published in the *Universal Magazine*.[24] How his work was known in London by this early date is a puzzle.

Edmund Burke is said to have introduced Barret to the Dargle, nearby Powerscourt and its waterfall as well as the owner of these enchanted demesnes, Lord Powerscourt, later to become his earliest patron. Certainly it was Burke who encouraged an interest in wild nature, as the Dargle with its Salvator Rosa-like water, waterfalls, rocks and overhanging trees is only twelve miles away from Dublin. It should be remembered that while

53
GEORGE BARRET
Landscape with horses by Sawrey Gilpin
(Huntingdon Library, San Marino)

54
GEORGE BARRET
Pen sketches of figures including an artist, possibly a self portrait

Barret was at the Dublin Society Schools, a few hundred yards away in Trinity College Burke was a student and writing his *Philosophical Enquiry into the Origin of our Ideas of the Sublime and the Beautiful*. Though this was not published until 1757, the ideas in it must have been part of Burke's conversation and known to friends like Barret. His early oil paintings and his etching of the Dargle *(Plate 55)* adhere to Burke's ideas on the Sublime where he emphasizes the importance of cloudy skies, dark and gloomy mountains, and vast cataracts.[25]

In fact, the Dargle inspired Barret throughout his career and he advised other artists to work in like manner. In an undated letter to another artist who was going to visit the Lake District, Barret wrote advising that "you may in a year or two sufficiently enrich your mind and lay in a stock of materials for your future practice – Care however must be taken that while you are absorbed in the contemplation of nature, the fountain-head of

all that is valuable in art, that you do not forget those examples which the great men of former times have left for your delight and instruction. The study of art and nature must go hand in hand . . ." Later in the letter he adds, "study effects as much or more than mere outlines . . . Do not be engrossed by any one master, so as to become a mimic

but think of all who have been excellent and endeavour to see nature with their eyes. This was the practice of Sir Joshua, Gainsboro, and Wilson – this is all the advice I can give you."[26]

Barret's late gouaches, many inspired by the Lake District, are in contrast to his earlier work, lighter and brilliant in colour, and include many peasant figures. The quality of these gouaches is very high; he has an atmospheric sense of distance and of varied light effects. A typical example shows Ullswater (Plate 56) and the surrounding mountains with, in the distance, a party picnicking by a tent.

These late works are very easily confused with gouaches by John Laporte (1761–1839), also of the Lake District, as well as other rural scenes. Indeed they seem almost impossible to tell apart, though some of Laporte's colouring with his use of yellow is distinctive. The similarity is explained by the fact that Laporte was taught by John

Melchior Barralet (fl.1774–87) who was himself a Dublin Society Schools artist. Laporte travelled to Ireland in 1804, when he signed and dated a view of Dublin Bay seen from the Howth road at Clontarf. A number of other engravings after his picturesque views of the Killarney district and of Leixlip survive.

James Mannin, the second master of the Schools, taught John James Barralet (1747–1815), and quite probably his brother John Melchior. John James's drawing style has a marked affinity with that of George Barret; he too emphasized trees, and his engraving of the Dargle for Milton's Views is very close to Barret's etching, though less dramatic. A study of a tree (British Museum) and his Luttrellstown views have a neat softness in the foliage. They are politely composed on the page and there is no hint of wild nature. He does not appear to have worked in oil at this time though he illustrated several books.

55
GEORGE BARRET
The Dargle, Co. Wicklow
(etching)
(Department of Prints
and Drawings, British
Museum)

56
GEORGE BARRET
Lake View, Ullswater,
Westmoreland, 1781

Facing Page

57 (Top)
JOHN JAMES BARRALET
The Benevolent Lady,
1776

58 (Bottom)
JOHN JAMES BARRALET
The Duchess of Rutland,
in her carriage, 1785

In 1770 Barralet went to England and in 1773 he set up a school in James's Street, Golden Square, later moving in 1777 to St. Albans Street, Pall Mall. While in England, he exhibited a number of drawings of English landscapes, theatrical scenes, classical subjects and English history in the Society of Artists and the Royal Academy. An example of his English period is a drawing, *The Benevolent Lady (Plate 57)*, which is signed and dated 1776. It is a grisaille with a very picturesque treatment of a mounted lady with her groom, distributing largesse to a family of deserving rustics. It is far more finished than most of his Irish works and its sentimentality indicates that it was an illustration; in fact, it was engraved by J. Morris and F. Bartolozzi in 1780. This type of subject hardly exists in Ireland and is closer to French and English examples in subject and style. An engraving entitled *An Italian Fountain* shows his interest, noted by Pasquin, in Vernet. Exotic subjects[27] for his pen were the drawings he made in 1772, working up landscapes from sketches made by others during

Cook's journey round the world on the *Endeavour*.

Barralet returned to Ireland to teach in the Dublin Society Schools in 1779 when Mannin was ill. From this period date a number of topographical drawings as well as portrait groups, such as that of the two Vesey boys and the charming watercolour of the Foster family at Oriel Temple, Co. Louth. A vivacious study of the Duchess of Rutland driving her curricle and whipping up her ponies near Dublin *(Plate 58)* dates from 1785. In a letter dated 2 May 1784 from Lord Carlow to his wife, he describes the Duchess and comments that:

> The principal amusement now in Dublin is parading in a part of the circular road which lies between the [Phoenix] park and the sea. It is the great scene of pleasure and gallantry. The Duchess of Rutland has her six ponies there every morning, Lady Antrim six more, and the other ladies as many as they can get for love or money.[28]

He goes on to say that the Duke rides out

as well but as soon as he met Lady Anne Hatton, with whom he was having a liaison, he dismounted and walked with her. The companion picture shows a distant view of Dublin with a castle in the foreground. These panoramic views with their multiplicity of detail incorporate beautifully drawn trees and attempt considerable action, with the Duchess spanking along with her outriders and nearly coming to grief with a cart full of beer kegs and grain. In both, the backgrounds are delicately handled, with the Hill of Howth on the horizon in one and the smoke of the metropolis drifting in a great plume in the middle distance in the other.

Barralet must have spent some time in Ulster in 1787–9 as there are eight drawings in the Ulster Museum of Glenarm and its neighbourhood, the seat of the Antrim family. He may have been employed teaching the McDonnell children, as some of these drawings are less competent. They were in a folder with a contemporary inscription ". . . Mostly by Mr Barrales [sic] artist and drawing master."[29]

Disappointed by not obtaining a permanent post at the Schools, he finally went to

59 JOHN JAMES BARRALET
The Dunlap House, Philadelphia, 1807 (Girard College, Philadelphia)

60 JOHN JAMES BARRALET
America welcoming Irish immigrants ashore c.1796 (Winterthur Museum)

America in 1795, settling in Philadelphia. An amusing sketch of Barralet's character taken from engravers who had known him was published by William Dunlap in 1834. He is said to have had "all the volatility of France united with Hibernian prodigality and eccentricity. He was a man of talent without discretion or any thing like common prudence; prodigally generous and graspingly poor."[30] His American career included book illustrations, trade cards and stock shares, as well as landscapes and townscapes, including the Dunlap House in Philadelphia *(Plate 59)* where he uses strong colour and gouache.

His landscape *View of Philadelphia from the Great Elm Tree in Kensington*, 1796, a work in watercolour and sepia ink, shows Barralet at his finest. The tree is most sensitively rendered and the lively figures by the boatyard indicate his keen observance of all aspects of people. It was an important work, which impressed his fellow artists into painting the same subject because "Barralet linked a symbol of America's past with the young country's present. The elm where William Penn signed the treaty with the Indians injects a note of history and continuity in this seemingly straightforward rendering of a prosaic scene."[31]

Barralet's best known work is his print of *The Apotheosis of George Washington* and other patriotic American themes, such as *America guided by Wisdom* and *Science Unveiling the Beauties of Nature to the Genius of America*. The watercolour of c.1796 *America welcoming Irish immigrants ashore (Plate 60)*, was significantly decorated with the symbolic Irish harp, the plough and bales of linen. It is fairly close in composition to his engraved certificate for the Hibernian Society of Philadelphia *(Plate 61)*, 1796–8 and might be an alternative design for this.

Barralet, however, had not prospered in

61
JOHN JAMES BARRALET
Hibernian Society Certificate
(engraving)
(Winterthur Museum)

57

62
JOHN MELCHIOR
BARRALET
*A view of the road to
East Grinstead, Kent*

*(Yale Center for British
Art, Paul Mellon
Collection)*

63
ROBERT CRONE
A Tree

the United States, for as late as 1810 he had to pay his rent with a picture, the oil painting *Bridge over the Schuylkill*. It was therefore important for him that in 1812 he was elected Professor of the newly founded Society of Artists of the United States, which he had helped to found.

His brother, John Melchior Barralet, probably went to the Dublin Society Schools before going to London in 1774, where he earned his living teaching. Unlike his brother, John Melchior's interest lay in buildings, and his *View of the Road to East Grinstead (Plate 62)* portrays the rocky defile in an architectural manner. His *View of Maidstone*, dated 1776, is another important work. He seems to have much less interest in trees than John James but the eyes of his figures are smudged in very deeply, a feature also noticeable in his brother's drawings. As a result, a lively genre watercolour like *The Donnybrook Fair* is difficult to attribute to either one or the other.

Other aspects of the Dublin Society Schools' work are found in a number of artists using chalk, crayons or pastel and a group of young men who went on to Italy to further their studies. Robert Crone (c.1718–79) combines both aspects as his drawings are in black chalk, but used with a soft touch and a delicate feeling for tone. In Rome, where he was by 1755, he worked under Richard Wilson who is, of course, noted for his chalk studies. Many of these drawings are for an oil painting of *The Good Samaritan*, an indifferent picture in the Dundee Art Gallery.[32] One was illustrated by Iolo Williams[33] and is signed with initials, "RC"; a second, a finished drawing of the whole picture, was on the art market in the early 1980s.[34] A drawing of a tree *(Plate 63)* probably for this picture was sold in 1987.[35] All these works show that his draughtsmanship was infinitely superior to his painting, and this illustrates the fact already noted that in the Dublin Society Schools students were not taught to use oils. Another drawing of the same subject, in the British Museum, is less Poussinesque and closer to his master, Wilson. If one compares his drawing of a tree with Wilson's *Tall Trees*, one realizes that Crone had not the free style of his master; indeed, he is stiff in comparison. Crone's compositions are made up of marked horizontal receding planes, and his trees are placed formally as frames on either side. Strickland suggests that his chalk drawings were on blue paper, but we have not found this is always so; he uses buff paper as well.

James Forrester (c.1730–76) was also a Dublin Society Schools pupil and a contemporary of Crone's in Rome, having been there by 1755. His one known pre-Roman work is a drawing of *Powerscourt Waterfall (Plate 64)* which is like an inferior Barret. This is particularly so if one compares the cursory, background trees with Barret's Dargle etching, where the foreground trees are spiky and elongated. We think a drawing of O'Sullivan's cascade at Killarney is another early work. Forrester's style develops when he is in Rome, however, and a comparison between the Powerscourt Waterfall and the Waterfall at Terni *(Plate 65)* shows marked differences. The background trees in the latter are feathery and elegant in comparison with the earlier work's inconspicuous and perfunctory draughtsmanship. The water is now heightened with white and falls in a tumult by the much more surely handled trees in the foreground. It is an idealized scene and, however well executed, has none of Barret's realism. Another member of the Irish group in Rome associated with Crone and Forrester was Solomon Delane, but as yet no drawings have been identified as being by him.

64
JAMES FORRESTER
Powerscourt Waterfall,
Co. Wicklow
(Ulster Museum)

65
JAMES FORRESTER
The Waterfall at Terni
(Victoria and Albert
Museum)

66
RICHARD DALTON
*Burton and Charlemont
at the castle of Bodrum,
c.1749*
(*Soane Museum*)

One of the most picturesque Irish figures of the eighteenth century was the Earl of Charlemont, the great Irish connoisseur, patron of Chambers in Ireland and Piranesi in Rome and, more to our point now, a traveller in Greece and the Levant. Charlemont with his group of Irish friends – Francis Pierrepont Burton, later Lord Conyngham, Alexander Scott from Co. Clare, and Richard Dalton (1715–91) as draughtsman – set off from Leghorn to Constantinople in April 1749, following the initiative of the intrepid Bishop of Ossory, the Englishman Dr Richard Pococke, who wrote very interesting accounts of his tours in the eastern Mediterranean and in Ireland. Charlemont had Pococke's travels in his library, but according to Professor Michael McCarthy[36] did not appear to realize the Bishop's trailblazing originality.

Richard Dalton was the son of an impoverished clergyman from Deane in Cumberland and may have been apprenticed at some point to a coachpainter in Clerkenwell. However, according to the architect James Gandon, who must have known him, he "is said to have received his instructions in drawing from the elder West, of Dublin, the preceptor of many early Irish artists, and whose son and grandson for a long period, were Masters of the Figure Schools of the

Royal Dublin Society's establishment."[37] If Dalton was taught by West it was probably before the foundation of the Schools themselves and means that he was either Irish or had close Irish connections. His drawing is not like the products of the Schools, but is sharp and dry. Robert Adam, who disliked Dalton and did not think much of his abilities, thought that *The Antiquities of Greece and Egypt . . .* , Dalton's book of engravings of the trip, when it was published in 1751 was "infamously stupid and ill done that it quite knocked him on the head, and entitled him the name Dulton, which is generally given to him."[38] McCarthy says this did little to dent Dalton's self-confidence and continues to quote Adam by saying that Dalton had "an assurance and that presence of mind that attends his Nation of Ireland"[39] and goes on to say that Adam "must have choked on his haggis when Richard Dalton was appointed Royal Librarian by King George III, four years later."[40] Dalton was a brilliant Librarian and made many important acquisitions for the Royal Library, such as buying the Canaletto drawings and paintings from Consul Smith of Venice.

Accounts of Charlemont's travels have been published and make most amusing reading, as in this description by Charlemont of the state of their clothes when they were entirely broke returning to Paros:

> Our clothes, which had never been splendid, were dirtied and torn by climbing rocks and creeping into caves. My Hussar jacket, which I usually wore, and which was now my only suit, was all in rags. Burton's long plaid banian, at the best the worst of nightgowns, was torn and greasy. But the most wretched figure of all was Dalton our painter, who, having had the misfortune to spill upon his coat a lampful of stinking oil, was now reduced to a waistcoat of green silk, formerly laced with gold, the back of which was pieced with the canvas remnant of an old picture, while the mutilated figures appeared like a sign hung out to testify the poverty of the miserable inhabitant."[41]

Hardy, in his life of Charlemont, states that it has been said to him that Dalton "as an artist . . . was miserable, but exact and faithful: and that his etchings of religious ceremonies, and customs of the Turks, with explanations, though indifferently executed, were remarkably clear and satisfactory."[42] Some of Dalton's drawings have recently been found in the Soane Museum and show that he was no great artist but that he successfully, if feebly, recorded the architecture and sculpture which he saw. A particularly charming watercolour, a variant for plate 30 in his book, shows Charlemont and Burton looking at a sculpted stone at Halicarnassus with Bodrum Castle in the background *(Plate 66)*, and as McCarthy says is "a noteable addition to the iconography of Irish scholar–travellers in the Levant."[43]

The soft style, rather rare in Ireland, which we have seen in Crone's work, is also found in a drawing which belonged to Lord Carlow, the amateur artist. It is the only known drawing by John Butts, an artist who did not attend the Schools. This splendid work *(Plate 67)* has a markedly Claudian effect, and its liquid wash technique, heightened with ink detail and occasional touches of sepia, has a velvety quality. It is very evocative and romantic, with distances which evoke castles, long vistas, water and trees. The foreground trees have the most exquisitely detailed foliage. Pasquin said that "his landscapes were impressive copies from the wild scenes which abound in the County of Cork, and the romantic views on the margin of the Blackwater" and presumably this is a study for one of these.[44] It is very regrettable that there are no more drawings or watercolours known by him but

67
JOHN BUTTS
Landscape Drawing
(National Gallery of Ireland)

it is reminiscent of the little landscapes on delftware which are sometimes attributed to the artist, Peter Shee, who worked for Delamain's Delft factory in Dublin between 1752 and 1757 and is recorded as exhibiting subject pictures in the Society of Artists between 1765 and 1767. Strickland records seeing oil landscapes by him; none are now known. Jeffrey Hamet O'Neal (fl.1763–72), who became a well-known painter of porcelain at the Bow factory, was also a miniaturist and worked as a japanner. A charming drawing by him exists of *Wagonners by a Windmill at Bow* and shows a style like John Nixon, who is discussed in Chapter 5.

The only drawing we know by John O'Keeffe (1747–1833) is of Kilkenny and is by far the best surviving topographical landscape emanating from the Schools of this date. He is recorded as being in Kilkenny in 1767 and making drawings in Indian ink there in that year. The surviving drawing *(Plate 68)* was probably made at this time. It is in pencil and wash and extremely delicately executed. O'Keeffe, who said in his *Recollections*[45] that he went to the Schools aged six, is best known today as a dramatist and in his own day as an actor. Unlike the

work of Butts and Peter Shee but like the Barralets and Barret, the drawing is very precise and detailed, despite the fact that the overall effect is soft and hazy. He described this picture himself in his *Recollections*, saying he made two views of Kilkenny of which he must have been rather proud to discuss them in such detail.[46] Strickland knew of other works and it is regrettable that these have all disappeared as have the views of Belfast which O'Keeffe also mentions. However, the Kilkenny view together with the work of Barret and the Barralets sums up the style of drawing taught in the Schools and probably indicates the techniques of the teachers, Robert West and James Mannin. It is tantalizing, as we have already said, that not a single drawing by either West or Mannin has been handed down to us.

The connection between the art of pastel and the Dublin Society Drawing Schools has been touched on but it is important to stress that they excelled in teaching this medium. All the portrait and figure painters down to Martin Archer Shee could handle it extremely well. Perhaps the most original of the pastellists was Robert Healy (1743–71), who worked entirely in grisaille. He was

68
JOHN O'KEEFFE
View of Kilkenny, 1767
(Rothe House, Kilkenny)

71) when staying at Castletown, Co. Kildare, in 1768/9. John O'Keeffe says in his *Recollections* that Healy excelled in "drawing in chalks, portraits etc. but his chief forte was horses, which he delineated so admirably that he got plenty of employment from those who had favourite hunters, racers or ladies' palfreys."[50] The only horse drawings known today are in the Castletown series. The finest is *Tom Conolly and the Castletown Hunt (Plate 72)* of 1769. Though there is no evidence, it seems plausible that there was a connection between Healy and George Stubbs, who was patronized extensively by Lady Louisa's brother, the third Duke of Richmond; it is possible that Healy may have met Stubbs at Goodwood. In a Stubbs of the Duke's horses at exercise, Lady Louisa is included with other members of the family. The stylistic links are well seen in *Squire Tom Conolly at Full Gallop* and *A Stable Lad Attempting to Catch a Thoroughbred*. These are full of

educated in the Dublin Society Drawing Schools under Robert West about 1765 and, sadly, died young in 1771 "from the effects of a cold brought on while sketching cattle in Lord Mornington's Park" at Dangan, Co. Meath. Pasquin's well-known remark that his pastel grisailles "are proverbial for their exquisite softness: they look like fine proof prints of the most capital mezzotinto engravings"[47] is very true. They are obviously influenced by the mezzotint heads by the Irish artist Thomas Frye, as Michael Wynne[48] has noticed. The most obvious link is between Frye's *Portrait of a Lady with Pearls*[49] and Healy's *Portrait of a Lady* in the National Gallery of Ireland and another of an elegantly beribboned lady *(Plate 69)*, now in a private collection. Apart from the bust portraits in the National Gallery of Ireland, Healy drew many small wholelengths, usually of women. Though some of these are doll-like in the Devis manner, others are better composed. *Miss Cunningham with her Dog*, signed and dated 1770, is gentle and sentimental, while *Mrs Gardiner* carrying her umbrella *(Plate 70)*, with storm clouds massing in the background, is an excellently observed portrait.

Healy's masterpieces are the series of pastels he drew for Lady Louisa Conolly *(Plate*

Nobility, to erect Chinese Turrets, superintend Grottoes, and to ornament Entertainments . . . his Abilities are superlative, as may be seen by his decoration of Lady Moira's Room, which truly bespeaks the Artist's Skill; . . . And his children inherit a Portion of their Father's merit, as witness the lately deceased young Healy, so much esteemed by the Nobility for his great Ability in Drawing, as none could excell him – the eldest of them Youths is falling into his Brother's Business and is a Counterpart of him . . .[52]

The artist with the closest style to Robert Healy is Charles Forrest (fl.1765–80). He was a contemporary of Healy at the Schools

71 (Top)
ROBERT HEALY
Lady Louisa Conolly with a groom, 1768

72 (Below)
ROBERT HEALY
Tom Conolly and the Castletown Hunt, 1768
(Yale Center for British Art, Paul Mellon Collection)

73 (Right)
CHARLES FORREST
An Actor as Major Sturgeon, 1772
(National Gallery of Ireland)

tension and movement and, with their clearly observed landscape backgrounds, they hark back to Stubbs's early work like his *Third Duke of Richmond with the Charlton Hunt* of 1759.[51]

An amusing description of Healy's father and his brother William, who also worked in grisaille, comes from a supposed conversation describing Dublin characters between two imaginary types, Van Trump and Dodderidge, who are walking round St. Stephens' Green:

Vantrump, Pray, who is that dapper alert Man, with them two handsame youths approaching us? Doderidge, . . . that is Healy, of Essex-Qay, and his two Sons, he is the greatest mechanical Genius that now exists, . . . so much admired for exquisite workmanship – he is sent for to the most remote Parts of this Kingdom by the first

and concentrated on small, whole-length pastel portraits in grisaille. The set in the National Gallery of Ireland is of actors *(Plate 73)* and actresses. One family conversation piece with ten figures round a table is known in photograph only,[53] the Fish family from Co. Kildare. His doll-like figures are charming but lack the competence of Healy. He also worked as a miniaturist.

Francis Robert West (1749?–1809), was the son of Robert West. He was taught by his father and succeeded him in the Mastership of the Dublin Society Schools. W.B. Sarsfield Taylor is alone in saying that Francis Robert "received much aid from a cultivation of some years in the French Academy of Arts."[54] He must have been in the Schools with Healy, and his bust portraits in the National Gallery of Ireland are very similar except that he uses coloured chalks. The charming *Seated Man* in the Pierpont Morgan Library is a homely essay and more original. From the catalogues of the exhibitions of the Society of Artists of Ireland, it appears that he mostly exhibited religious pastels, none of which has been identified. They also mention "portraits in conversation" and it is tempting to attribute to West a *Musical Party* recently on the London art market,[55] though it may be too ambitious for him. The cheerful groups of figures in costume (formerly Malahide Castle Collection) are much sketchier but lively enough.

West's most important series of conversation pieces has only recently come to light. It consists of nine ovals, each showing various occupations in the life of the Brooke and Vesey families *(Plates 74, 75, 76)*, done in the late 1770's. They are seen playing billiards, cards and the game of the goose, sewing, taking tea, reading and coming in from picking fruit and flowers in the garden. One even shows three gentlemen in Volunteer uniform studying a map of Ireland, and the ninth shows a group of three in fancy dress assembled to go to a party. With the Castletown Healys, they constitute the only major series of pictures showing Irish upper-class domestic and sporting life.

Another contemporary at the Schools with Healy, and possibly Francis Robert West, was Thomas Hickey (1741–1824), who, though he made a career as an oil painter, is undoubtedly better in his intimate

74-76 FRANCIS ROBERT WEST *Top: Volunteer Officers studying a map*
Centre: Three Ladies with a dog playing cards
Bottom: Two Boys playing a game of goose

77
THOMAS HICKEY
*Mr Eccles of Cronroe,
Co. Wicklow, 1768*
*(National Trust Committee
for Northern Ireland)*

pastel, charcoal and pencil portraits. Most of these show the head and shoulders only and closely resemble Healy's work, as they are grisailles. However, he early came in contact with Gainsborough's painting when he copied, for the Mansion House, Gainsborough's full-length portrait of the Viceroy, the Duke of Bedford, which still hangs in the Provost's House in Trinity College, Dublin. Some of his portraits have the elegant feathery touch one associates with Gainsborough. A good example is the portrait in the Yale Center for British Art of his brother Joseph which is signed and dated 1778. One small whole-length study *(Plate 77)* is known to us, dated 1768, of a member of the Eccles family of Cronroe, Co. Wicklow. It is interesting both for its quiet pose and for its gentle characterization and is important as an example of a full-length study showing the draughtsmanship disseminated by the teaching of the Dublin Society Drawing Schools.

After a chequered career, Hickey spent the latter part of his life mostly in India, where his portrait drawings of British officers in Madras *(Plate 78)* are particularly fine and are studies for a projected but never completed set of seven paintings on the fourth Mysore war, when the legendary

Tipu Sultan was killed at Seringapatam.[56] They are brilliantly sketched in chalk while his earlier work in India in the same medium, like *The Portrait of a Young Lady*, signed and dated 1784, harks back to Hugh Douglas Hamilton[57] and is much more precise.

Hickey accompanied his fellow Irishman, Lord Macartney, on his embassy to China in 1793 as official artist, but his English colleague, William Alexander, did all the work. Farington remarks in his Diary for 28 December 1794, "It seems that Hickey devoted more of his time to writing than to drawing or painting, and Alexander complained that Hickey refused to supply him with paper & pencils when he required them, though a large stock was laid in of which Hickey had the care."[58] However, one not very exciting Chinese study by Hickey, showing a group of what appear to be prisoners, survives in the British Museum.

By far the most famous of the pastellists was Hugh Douglas Hamilton (1740–1808), who attended the Schools from around 1750 to 1756 and probably later. According to O'Keeffe, who was a fellow student, Hamilton "was remarkable for choosing, when drawing the human figure, the most foreshortened view, consequently the most difficult."[59] Not surprisingly, he won several prizes during his school days. He must also have studied in the School of Ornament, which John Turpin says was founded shortly after Mannin's appointment in May 1756, although premiums were offered for damask and linen designs from 1746 (Faulkner's Journal, 3–6 May and 14–18 May 1746). Informal teaching may have occurred earlier even before Mannin's arrival in 1753,[60] three years before his official appointment. Hamilton was not allowed to receive a prize for pattern designing on 9 December 1756 because he was over sixteen. Though he could not receive the prize, he was given £4 in this competition "for the best Design and Inventions of Pattern Drawing and Ornamental foliages . . ."[61]

A remarkable architectural composition of a triumphal arch very much in the French classical manner, signed by Hamilton, appears on the title page of a Survey of Kilkea *(Plate 79)* made by John Rocque in 1760 for the Earl of Kildare, which we have already noted. This shows an entirely new

side to his draughtsmanship and indicates the breadth of teaching in the Ornament School, as the Architectural School had not yet been founded. The foreground shows his deft hand with the foliage of a tree and an elaborate cannon and other military accoutrements which are composed rather like a cartouche. Other ingenious touches are the placing of the index of the various townlands on the side of the arch and the view through a doorway to Kilkea Castle itself. Over all, Pallas Athene floats in the sky with her attendant putti. Hamilton's title page fits in admirably with the Frenchman John Rocque's high rococo cartouches and decorations on later pages. The French basis of the Schools' training is well represented in this little masterpiece. It also illustrates the Earl of Kildare's patronage of pupils of the Schools, of which he was a committee member. Later he was created first Duke of Leinster. His mother, Mary, Dowager Countess of Kildare, then a very old lady, was drawn

78
THOMAS HICKEY
General Baird, 1799

79
HUGH DOUGLAS HAMILTON
Capriccio, title page of Rocques's Survey of Kilkea, Co. Kildare, 1760

80
HUGH DOUGLAS
HAMILTON
*Frances Poole, later Lady
Palmerston*
*(Huntington Library,
San Marino)*

which he is so famous. They usually measure about 9.5 by 7.5 cm (6 by 4 inches) and are drawn on grey paper. Mulvany, writing in 1842, described them as:

> laid in with very few colours, the prevailing tone of which was grey, and then finished with red and black chalk. They were marked with great skill and truth, the features, particularly the eyes, were expressed with great feeling; and as pictures they were not sustained by those depths either of colour or of shadow which alone confer pictorial effect. They had all the appearance of being hurried rather than neglected.[62]

This could not be better expressed. Mulvany also tells the well-known story that, after he got to London,

> he could scarcely execute all the orders that came in upon him, and the writer has heard him declare, that in the evening of each day, a part of his occupation was picking and gathering up the guineas from amongst the bran and broken crayons, in the several crayon boxes into which, in the hurry of the day, he had thrown them.[63]

by Hamilton about this time and he continued to be patronized by the FitzGeralds of Leinster and their relatives, the Conollys of Castletown, till late in his life.

Hamilton worked in Dublin till 1764/5, when he moved to London. In these early years he drew the small oval portraits for

81
HUGH DOUGLAS
HAMILTON
The Rose family, 1775

82 *(Facing Page)*
HUGH DOUGLAS
HAMILTON
*The Fifth Earl of
Guilford*

Few of Hamilton's ovals are dated and this does not help in working out any progression in his style. A portrait of Frances Poole, later Lady Palmerston *(Plate 80)*, dated between 1765 and her death in 1769, is a lively and sympathetic drawing of a pensive lady. An example in very good condition is a portrait of the Hon. Louisa Molesworth, who married William Brabazon, later Lord Ponsonby of Imokilly, in 1769. There appears to be a greater use of colour as his style develops, and before his departure for

Italy backgrounds are often introduced. These are associated with the use of rectangular formats and larger ovals. Among the earliest is the group portrait of *Lord Halifax and his Secretaries*, 1767.

Between 1762 and 1775, Hamilton exhibited as many as forty-six portraits in the London Society of Artists and four in the Free Society of Artists. According to Mulvany, he was charging nine guineas for a likeness when he was in London; presumably that was for a bust-length portrait. This was

83
HUGH DOUGLAS
HAMILTON
A man in red with his horse

not always the case, however, as in 1772 he charged Sir Watkin Williams Wynne six guineas for portrait drawings and two copies of him and his wife.[64] He was doing small whole-length pastels, as he sent two to the Dublin Society of Artists in 1769. Of his London groups, the oval conversation piece, measuring 38 by 48 cm (15 by 19 in) of *The Revd William Rose reading to his parents (Plate 81)*, which is dated 1775, is one of the finest. He captures, with considerable skill, the proud mother and the slightly incredulous father listening attentively to their son, who is dressed in an academic gown.

These London developments are staid in comparison with his style after he goes to Italy in 1778. His portrait of *The Earl Bishop of Derry sitting in the Borghese Gardens* overlooking the roofs of Rome has an informality not yet seen, and is also an excellent townscape (National Trust Ickworth). He continued to use the oval format, and one of his best Roman portraits in this genre is the Earl Bishop's daughter, Lady Erne (National Trust, Ickworth), and another is of Anne, Lady Cowper. Both are highly sympathetic character studies and remind us of Mulvany's comments about his drawing of eyes. While in Rome, he developed the whole-length portrait in pastel to previously unconsidered heights. Several have surfaced over the last few years, including two which form a brilliant psychological contrast. *The fifth Earl of Guilford*[65] is an alert and smart young man *(Plate 82)* basking in his new Roman ruined surroundings portrayed in sunny, pastel colours while the *Young Man in Red*,[66] who has just dismounted from his horse *(Plate 83)*, is gloomily holding his head under the deep shade of trees; the whole conveys an introverted moment. The masterpiece of the Roman years is the portrait of the Irish artist, *Henry Tresham and Canova looking at a study for Canova's Cupid and Psyche (Plate 84)*. The depths of light and shade with which he models the figures in this picture are striking and the contemplative mood of Tresham contrasts so well with the eager, brilliant face of the sculptor.

It is incorrect to say, as is often asserted,

84
HUGH DOUGLAS
HAMILTON
Tresham and Canova looking at Canova's Cupid and Psyche

85
HUGH DOUGLAS
HAMILTON
*Hermes leading
Persephone out of the
underworld*
(*Yale Center for British Art,
Paul Mellon Collection*)

Hamilton's early *jeu d'esprit*. He also continued to draw small ovals, though the neoclassicism which marks his oils does not appear in his pastels. Throughout his career from his London days, Hamilton painted subject pictures, usually in oils. However, a large pastel measuring 70 cm by 50 cm (27 5/8 by 19 5/8 inches), attributed to Hamilton, of the Muse Erato appeared on the London art market recently,[67] and this confirms our view that his pastels retain a rococo character even when the subject is classical. A pen and wash drawing of *Hermes leading Persephone out of the Underworld (Plate 85)* is closer to his classical oils and may be a study for one. It shows a close link with the work of his countryman, Henry Tresham, who was in Italy at this time. (Tresham is discussed in Chapter 6.)

that Hamilton did not use pastels after his return to Ireland in 1792. The splendid pair of small whole-lengths of the second Duke of Leinster and his wife are among these later pastels. The Duke is opening a book of Leinster estate maps, reminding us of

All small pastel portraits found in Ireland used to be attributed to Hugh Douglas Hamilton, but there were a number of minor artists who worked in this lucrative vein. They included George Lawrence (fl.1771–1802), John Cullen (1761–1825/30), who actually worked with Hamilton in London,

86 *Attributed to* WILLIAM HINCKS *View of Portavo, Co. Down*

Bartholomew Stoker (1763–88), and, from the many unidentified works, a large number of others. Nathaniel Bermingham (fl. 1736–74)[68] is one of the most interesting. He started life as a herald painter and is today best known for his exquisite cut paper work, but he also drew pastel profiles which he stuck on black backgrounds and was a very competent draughtsman. In the Dublin Society of Artists catalogues, the following are listed as exhibiting crayon and pastel portraits: John Forster (fl.1773–80), John Warren (fl.1768–77) and William Hincks (fl.1773–97), now known for his highly decorative engravings of the linen industry. Hincks also shows such works between 1773 and 1780. It has been suggested that the pretty view of Portavo, Co. Down *(Plate 86)*, with its lake, well-placed urn and new plantations may be attributable to him. Any pupil of the Schools had abilities in pastel: Sir Martin Archer Shee, for instance, in his early years drew pastel portraits; and an early work of Henry Tresham, dated 1778, of Shag Wilkes in the role of Jessamy in the comic opera *Leon and Clarissa* is very close to the style of Charles Forrest.

Matthew William Peters, whose drawing of Robert West has already been mentioned, is recorded as exhibiting many pastels in London exhibitions. These included oval portraits and fancy pictures. Many of them

have verve but a somewhat cursory line, with only the faces finished and the eyes deep-set and lustrous. A good example is the portrait of *Elizabeth, Marchioness of Lothian (Plate 87)*, 1745–80. Peters's interesting and varied career, his discovery of Rubens and less well-known Italians such as Barocci, which contributed to his use of colour, make his work stand out among his contemporaries. He spent most of his life in England after his visit to Italy at the expense of the Dublin Society.

Pastels were, of course, also painted outside the perimeter of the Schools. The work of William Watson, for instance, who died young, in 1765, is an example. He was the brother of the famous engraver, James Watson, and a friend of Healy. Like Healy, but unlike most Irish pastellists, Watson drew life-size portraits. They were rather in the manner of Francis Cotes and some are even half-length. His *Viscountess Sudeley* in the National Gallery of Ireland, which is signed with a monogram "WW" and dated 1764, is a gentle work in comparison with the

87
MATTHEW WILLIAM PETERS
Elizabeth Chichester Fortescue, later Marchioness of Lothian
(Courtauld Institute of Art, The Witt Collection)

88
WILLIAM WATSON
Lady Capel Molyneux

unsigned *Lady Capel Molyneux (Plate 88)* with its flashy highlights, but they all share penetrating eyes and a very sure technique. A series of five female portraits of the McDonnell family show him as a sparkling and lively artist. Pasquin adds a detail of human interest when he tells us that Watson "was an eminent performer on the German flute." His wife was an embroidress and painter and exhibited in the Society of Artists. She is probably the same Mrs Watson whom we have mentioned earlier as an artists' supplier (Chapter 2).

Several other artists of this period developed outside the aegis of the Schools. Of these, one was the oil portrait painter Charles Exshaw[69] (fl. 1749–71), who was a pupil of Francis Bindon, the painter and architect. He went to France in 1749, where he worked under Charles van Loo and made mezzotint portraits of two of his sons. He was in Rome copying Carlo Maratta, and in 1759 made a fine study of a bearded Old Man now in the National Gallery of Ireland. On his return to Ireland, he became an indifferent portrait painter though, interestingly, he made some etchings showing the influence of Rembrandt.

There is a fascinating book of portrait sketches in the National Gallery of Ireland by Henry Brooke (1738–1806) whom we have mentioned earlier in this chapter as a drawing master. He was the son of Robert Brooke, also a portrait painter, and the brother of Gustavus Brooke, the author of *The Fool of Quality*. The sketchbook is important as it illustrates the method artists used to assist in their compositions. Brooke later worked as a subject picture painter (his *Continence of Scipio* is in the National Gallery of Ireland), but this sketchbook, done early in his career, is largely after engravings and other artists' work and shows the continental and English basis of an Irish painter's repertoire. There is a portrait of an artist with his palette, wearing a fur hat, and another after a painting of Thomas Sheridan *(Plate 89)*, the famous theatrical figure, taken from Lewis's portrait now in the Gallery. An elaborate composition shows a double portrait of a fashionable couple and another is a copy of the well-known half-length portrait by Hoare of the Viceroy, Lord Chesterfield, in 1746. Further sketches, quite loosely drawn, date in the mid-1750s and show Pellegrini-like decorative figures leaning over a balustrade *(Plate 90)* and a female nude bathing. The book has the name of William Brooke, his son, in a childish hand inscribed inside the front cover but the monograms, where they appear on the drawings, are "HB" for Henry Brooke. Though artists' sketchbooks such as this are common enough on the continent, rarer in England, this one is unique to eighteenth-century Ireland.

Alexander Pope (1763–1835), another product of the Schools and a pupil of Hugh Douglas Hamilton, drew many small oval or rectangular portraits from the 1780s which could readily be mistaken for those of his master. His style changes, however, at the turn of the century and he takes up the small watercolour whole-length. He was one of a maddeningly obscure family of portrait and landscape painters, the Popes and the Pope Stevenses, who were very prominent in Dublin artistic circles of the eighteenth century and whose works are now virtually unidentifiable. One member of the family, Thomas Pope Stevens, in a portrait of Mrs Reilly of Scarvagh (on loan, Castletown House), shows her with her pencil, proudly displaying her large sketchbook, open at pages of studies of female heads in red chalk and a landscape. This is a rare example showing the common practice of fashionable ladies at their artistic pursuits.

90
HENRY BROOKE
Two decorative figures
(National Gallery of Ireland)

In 1776 Alexander Pope's name appears in the roll of the Dublin Society Drawing Schools when they were under the Headmastership of Francis Robert West. Later, Pope's father, Stephen Pope of Cabragh, had arranged an introduction to Hugh Douglas Hamilton, who was then in London. He cannot have been with Hamilton long as Hamilton left for Italy in 1778, and indeed Pope exhibited drawings and small portraits in crayon at the Society of Artists in Williams Street, Dublin, in 1777 and 1780, giving a Dublin address. He settled in Cork in 1781. It is not surprising that Pope's early drawings are very close to those of Hamilton, but signed works of 1781 indicate a free rather slapdash manner, whereas the *Portrait of a Lady* (National Gallery of Ireland), which could easily be mistaken for one of his master's works, is signed and dated "Alex. Pope 1783" and represents a far neater and

more accomplished manner very close to Hamilton. When he was in Cork he was charging one Irish guinea for a portrait. He must have been in London by the mid-1780s, as he encouraged the young Martin Archer Shee on his arrival there in 1788. Pope's Regency period will be discussed in Chapter 8.

The Schools were the most significant influence on Irish art, and their foundation makes them the earliest public art school in the British Isles. They were also important because the artistically minded grandees, such as the Earl of Charlemont and the Duke of Leinster, sat on the committees. This was no sinecure as their attendances are recorded regularly. Their influence must have greatly encouraged patronage and undoubtedly the Schools were the cause of the flowering of Irish art from the mid-eighteenth century.

91

JOHN NIXON
*The Cabin on the boat to
Dublin*

92

JOHN NIXON
*The Surroundings of
St. Patrick's Cathedral,
Dublin*

CHAPTER FIVE

GENRE AND LANDSCAPE

Wit, satire and even caricature rollick through our subject at the point when we meet John Nixon. It has been discovered that his father was a merchant in London with property in Scotland.[1] However, he undoubtedly had Irish connections. Strickland, who had access to material now vanished, thought he was from Belfast, while there is a possibility that he or his family had links with Co. Carlow, as there is a watercolour signed and dated by him, "JN 1785," and inscribed by a later hand, *John Nixon's house Co. Carlow*. What is certain is that he worked with his brother Richard, who was an Irish merchant in London, in Basinghall Street. There they lived a life of riotous conviviality as well as being highly respectable men of business. His drawing, *The Feast of the Gods*, signed and dated 1779, is of a debauch, with musicians, women, dogs, drunks and a sleeping man dreaming the whole scene which is set in a cloud over a coastal landscape reminiscent of Dublin and Killiney Bay. Henry Angelo records a number of biographical facts.[2] Nixon was also involved in the theatrical and musical worlds. He clearly visited Ireland regularly, both north and south, from Cork to Derry, and presumably some of these trips were connected with his business.

Everywhere Nixon went he drew, not only landscapes but also everyday subjects – fashionable ladies, travellers, boatmen, beggars, seasick passengers on the packet from Park Gate to Dublin *(Plate 91)*, or even the artist helping the blacksmith to shoe his horse on the way to the Giant's Causeway. His two most ambitious Irish subjects were the *Cove in Cork* (Victoria and Albert Museum), with groups of people about to embark, and a lively street scene in Dublin. This action-packed view takes place outside St. Patrick's Cathedral *(Plate 92)* and shows a cab overturning, drunken figures, beggars, ladies of the town, street vendors, and other characters. There is an even more splendid watercolour of the *Old Pump Room at Bath*, 1792 (Witt Collection, Courtauld Institute of Art), with all its gaieties and inevitable invalids. Nixon was a friend of Grose and was involved in the *Antiquities of Ireland*. There is a memorable sketch of himself with Grose, whose fat figure dominates the view of Ireland's Eye from Howth *(Plate 40)*.

Nixon's style varies enormously. His rough sketches done in pen and watercolour can be very crude, while his finished works are neat, precise, well-coloured drawings. Angelo, commenting on his versatile talents, observed that he "drew characteristics with no mean skill. He could sketch a portrait, with a few scratches of his pencil, of a party whom he had not seen for twenty years, with such marked traits of resemblance as to be known at a glance."[3] This capacity to catch expression, which gives life to all his drawings, leads him easily into the world of caricature. This was probably through his great friendship with Rowlandson, which also accounts for the improvement and softening of his outlines in his later career when his drawings become freer and lighter. Anglesea[4] is of the opinion that Nixon stopped coming to Ireland in 1798 though we cannot be certain of this. He visited and drew in Montreal in 1804.

An artist whose talents also lay in this genre of half caricature was John Boyne (c.1750–1810). He came from Co. Down but left Ireland with his father, a joiner, at

93
NATHANIEL GROGAN
*Study of Peasants after
Egbert Heemskerk*

Interior of the Assembly Rooms in Bath. He is altogether more professional than Nixon, perhaps because he became an art master, and his work has a cutting edge which Nixon's kindlier eye does not depict. Boyne's works have much in common with those of Wheatley and also Rowlandson.

One of the most important Irish artists of the period was Nathaniel Grogan (c.1740–1807), from Cork, who was not trained at the Dublin Society Schools, and although an accomplished draughtsman, is best-known for his oil paintings. His early career was spent abroad in the army and he returned to Ireland at the end of the American War of Independence. As he was advertising on 31 December 1777 in the *Pennsylvania Ledger* for "sign and ornamental painting, with pencil work in general" he must have had some training before he went to America. Pasquin,[5] who was likely to have known, claims that Butts was his teacher.

the age of nine to live in London. He therefore hardly counts in our history but it is irresistible to mention his *Meeting of Connoisseurs*, which is now in the Victoria and Albert Museum, his admirable inn scenes and his

Excellent drawings by him after such Dutch genre masters as Egbert Heemskerk *(Plate 93)* are known. He may have seen engravings after Morland and Walton, as

94 *NATHANIEL GROGAN Castle Hyde, Co. Cork*

hints of their works can be found in Grogan's drawings. He made a number of pure landscape watercolours, topographical views of country seats such as Castle Hyde *(Plate 94)* and the romantic ruins of Kilcrea Castle. Even in these, the figures are very important, and in the view of Kilcrea the foreground group is Dutch in character and also hints at Butts's plump and stubby people. They are very freely painted watercolours, bluish in tone with atmospheric touches such as the crows wheeling round the castle tower. He made a set of twelve oval mezzotints of Cork and scenes on the river Lee which were advertised in the *New Cork Evening Post* in 1796,[6] some of which are really genre scenes with peasants riding and walking to market, boating on the river and labourers digging below Monkstown Castle. His scene of the *Bridge at Blarney Castle* (Wood Collection on loan Limerick University) is really a view of country people dancing and merry-making. His etching of *North Gate Bridge at Cork with Lord Barrymore's Carriage (Plate 95)* is a remarkable piece of work, delicately handled and showing a considerable mastery of the

architectural background as well as the building workers and fashionable ladies in the foreground. The composition of the carriage coming over the bridge is reminiscent of a print of a bridge in Rome by Giovanni Battista Rossi.

Apart from landscapes and genre pieces, Grogan illustrated scenes from books and drew subject pictures. Since our information comes from later Cork exhibition catalogues[7] and little of his work survives, it is unclear in what medium, whether oil or watercolour, they were executed. He was the most interesting artist working in the provinces at this time.

Grogan's two sons, Nathaniel junior and Joseph, followed in their father's footsteps but had nothing like his talent. One of them taught art in Cork. There is an amusing anecdote about Grogan's School in a description of young Lanno Fenwick, who attended classes twice a week in 1812: "Mr Grogan entertains us with praises of Lanno *(Mr Fenwick,* as he calls him), – 'he is so clever, so sensible, so lively, so active, so manly' – (with twenty other so's) 'that

95
NATHANIEL GROGAN
North Gate Bridge,
Cork, c.1770 (etching)
(Crawford Municipal Art
Gallery, Cork)

96
JOHN NATTES
*Carlisle Bridge from the
Old Custom House,
Dublin*

96
JOHN NATTES
*Carlisle Bridge from the
Old Custom House,
Dublin*

everybody must love him.' Mary-Anne [Fenwick, Lanno's sister] hangs her head down to her drawing board, smiles & blushes, while her younger sisters glance at her with an expression that pains me."[8]

John Claude Nattes (1765–1822) may have been born in Ireland, though Hardie thinks he was born in England of Irish parents.[9] This may well be true, as he was trained in London under the Irishman Hugh Primrose Dean, who was one of the group of Irishmen who painted landscapes in Rome. Iolo Williams knew drawings which he thought were by Dean and describes them as "black chalk drawings, rather like a cross between Wilson and the French artist Pillement."[10] Williams thinks this also describes Nattes's drawing style, and an example in the Yale Center for British Art, *Trees in Gosfield Park* of 1811, harks back to this manner. Nattes, from dated drawings, was touring in Ireland in

97
WILLIAM ASHFORD
View of Limerick
(*Limerick Museum*)

1801 and 1807. He clearly intended to publish a book of aquatint views of Ireland, which was to be entitled *Hibernia Depicta* and to be published in 1802. This never appeared but would have been similar, no doubt, to the book he brought out around 1804 entitled *Scotia Depicta*. In Ireland he travelled both north and south, from Co. Down to Co. Kerry.

Nattes's range of subject varies from landscape, including romantic waterfalls and village scenes, to topographical views of houses like Tinnehinch and Castle Bellingham. He drew townscapes, including *Carlisle Bridge from the Old Custom House (Plate 96)* and a lively view of the fruit market on the quays in Dublin with the Four Courts in the background (National Gallery of Ireland). He used pen and wash to produce very precise drawings, though his trees have considerable movement and atmosphere. To us, the influence of Ireland, which must have come to him through Dean, is apparent in these drawings, many of which show a

strong influence from the trees and rocks of Barret – for instance, in the *Waterfall at Mount Kennedy* and *the Bridge on the Road to Lucan*, both dated 1801.

Though most Irish landscape painters were connected with the antiquarian movement, several of them are best treated as a group of their own. William Ashford (1746–1824) is the most obvious of these. Birmingham born, he went to Ireland in 1764 to join the Board of Ordnance, where he worked in the Laboratory section inspecting stocks of arms throughout the country.[11] He did not work in the map-making section with Vallancey but his job meant that he toured Ireland, and his earliest drawings were clearly made on these trips. The six that survive include two views of Limerick from the north-west *(Plate 97)* and the south-west (Limerick Museum), a sketch of Askeaton Castle with rocks on the river Deel, one of the Abbey at Timoleague in West Cork, and lastly two of a mill near Bantry. These are all obviously sketched on

99
THOMAS ROBINSON
*The Glen at Dromore
House, Co. Down, 1787*

They show garden buildings and follies, the stables *(Plate 98)*, the greenhouses, haymaking and guests arriving at the house itself. Big open skies and distant views of Dublin Bay and the Wicklow Mountains give a generous sense of space in contrast to the detailed handling of some of the foreground vegetation. The trees are finely drawn with a feeling for the heaviness of the summer foliage and their distinct varieties rather in the Barret manner. They are executed in a grey monochrome wash and it is unfortunate that we know no other drawings by Ashford, as they are very beautiful. It is likely that much of his work is attributed to others. It is also notable that he was much influenced by the style of the Dublin Society Schools though he cannot have attended them.

Another Englishman who spent his career in Ireland is Thomas Robinson (fl.1785–1810), a pupil of Romney's who was a portrait painter in Dublin before settling in Ulster in the early 1790s, coming under the patronage of Bishop Percy of Dromore. Robinson, who is now best known as an oil painter, worked with the Bishop on his garden designs, including *trompe l'œil* urns and an obelisk painted on wooden boards. He records the latter in a watercolour of a grove *(Plate 99)* which is signed and dated 1799.[13] A number of other sketches for the garden are in the Ulster Museum.

the spot and are boldly executed with strong hatchings either in pen or chalk, some with added wash.[12] One other drawing of Drogheda, which we attribute to him, is a more developed study and also probably dates from his touring years. The treatment of the buildings is similar to that in his sketches of Limerick: they are sharply and surely delineated.

Ashford does not seem to have signed his drawings or his watercolours, so the only other certainly attributed examples are those in the Fitzwilliam Bequest in the Fitzwilliam Museum, Cambridge. They were commissioned, with a number of oil paintings, by the seventh Viscount Fitzwilliam, about 1804/5. With the title page dated 1806 and two views of Fitzwilliam's house in Richmond there are twenty-seven drawings in the album, mostly of the demesne and buildings at Mount Merrion Lodge which give a vivid picture of the life and workings of the estate.

Other English visitors who were painting in Ireland at this time included John Thomas Serres (1759–1825), best known as a marine painter. He was a friend of a number of Irish artists including Ashford, five of whose works he included in a sale he held in London in 1790[14] before going to Italy. He seems, from surviving pictures, to have worked between Dublin and Waterford, where his fine watercolour of *The Exchange at Waterford (Plate 100)* dated 1787, combines a Canaletto-like feel for the architecture and light, with figures very much in the manner of Wheatley. Nicholas Pocock (1740–1821), also a marine painter, visited Ireland on a number of occasions; there are three watercolours known to us, one of the Giant's Causeway and another of the cliff arch at Cushendun, both dated 1793, and a panoramic view of *The Cove of Cork with Spike Island and Two Forts*, which is signed and dated 1811.

By far the most distinguished visitor was William Pars, ARA (1742–82). He was brought to Ireland in August 1771 by Lord Palmerston and visited all the picturesque spots, including Sligo, Lough Key, Adare, Killarney, Lismore, Powerscourt and Leixlip. A watercolour of a particularly charming, formal picnic party on Inisfallen,

100
JOHN THOMAS SERRES
The Exchange at Waterford, 1787

101
WILLIAM PARS
Lough Lene and the Killarney Mountains, Co. Kerry, c.1771

(Victoria and Albert Museum)

102
WILLIAM PARS
The Old Weir Bridge,
Killarney, Co. Kerry,
c.1771
(Victoria and Albert
Museum)

dated 1771, shows a group of elegant ladies and gentlemen, probably the guests of Lord Kenmare, dining at a table, waited on by footmen and a row of redcoats standing behind (Birmingham Museums and Art Galley).[15] He was inspired by the panoramic views of lake and mountains that abound in Killarney, and his watercolour of *Lough Lene and the Killarney Mountains (Plate 101)*, has an atmospheric, breezy feel shown not only in the clouds but in the horseman's coat – tails blowing in the wind as he shelters behind a wall. Andrew Wilton, in summing up Pars's Irish period, says: ". . .his style took another step in the direction of a broader, softer manner; perhaps the gentle hazy atmosphere of Killarney and Roscommon affected his sensitive response as the brighter, clearer air of Greece and Switzerland had done. His wide expanses of mild Irish landscapes are seen in an almost monochrome range of greys, applied in woolly masses without as much careful pen outlining as previously."[16]

Pars's closer views, as in his *Lismore Castle and the Blackwater* (Victoria and Albert Museum) and *The Old Weir Bridge (Plate 102)*, show his able handling of architecture, water, foliage and figures. The old weir bridge was described by George Holmes when he visited Killarney in August 1797: "Quitting the boat we betook ourselves to the Bank, whilst the boatmen prepared to drag the boat through a fall of water . . ."[17] This can be seen both in the Pars drawing and in the Jonathan Fisher which we discuss later in this chapter.

It is interesting to note that when Daniel Augustus Beaufort, the father of William (see Chapter 3), visited Killarney in 1788, he went to view the collection of Mr Herbert at Muckross where "we were well entertained for two hours with some elegant works of Sandby, Rowlandson, Calendar [sic], Tomkins, and Dom. Serres."[18] The

103
CORNELIUS VARLEY
Ardfert Cathedral,
Co. Kerry, c.1808
(Yale Center for British Art,
Paul Mellon Collection)

Herberts seem to have been seriously interested in painting, as another traveller, Alexander Hamilton, a Dublin lawyer, when visiting Killarney in 1804 "sent his compliments [to Mr Herbert] . . . to see his place and had permission with all due civility from his son; he being with two English landscape painters, Gilpin and Barrett, who are taking views of the delightful scenery in this neighbourhood."[19] The next day he saw them taking views "in Lord Kenmare's park." These artists were, of course, William Sawrey Gilpin (1762–1843), the son of Sawrey Gilpin, the collaborator and friend of George Barret, the father of the second watercolourist who was the younger George Barret (1767–1842). Gilpin sketched a good deal in Ireland and was also a landscape gardener. He was the first president of the Old Watercolour Society, and George Barret the younger was one of the original members. He was born in England and spent most of his life there, so we treat him as a visitor. He was a well-known watercolourist, however, and gave up topography for Claudian romance. Killarney must have suited both their styles well.

The brothers John (1778–1842) and Cornelius Varley (1781–1873) were also among the numerous artists who from this time onwards visited Killarney. Cornelius was in Ireland in 1808 and seems to have travelled from Kerry to Armagh. His beautiful

watercolour study of Ardfert Cathedral *(Plate 103)* forms a contrast to the minutely observed outline drawing of a woman spinning *(Plate 104)*, probably done in Markethill. A superb landscape view (Whitworth Art Gallery, Manchester), done in pure watercolour, of an Irish bog with a range of mountains all sodden with the rain is immensely evocative of Ireland's soft and watery atmosphere and gives a brilliant meaning to the word watercolour. His brother John's Irish views were done on a number of visits between 1817 and 1826, and a watercolour of Aghadoe Church, Killarney, signed and dated 1826, is inscribed on the reverse "from a sketch by C. Varley."

We have not found an Irish example comparable to John's luminous Welsh and English landscape panoramas, which remind us of the work of the slightly later George Fennel Robson (1788–1832), who was in the Varley circle. Robson was in Killarney in 1827 and was inspired by the mountain scenery of Scotland and Ireland. Wilton says that "his ability to apply watercolour in deep intense vibrant masses suited him particularly in the large scale landscape of mountainous spaces that Turner made so much

his own . . ."[20] and he goes on to suggest that Robson's best work has "a stillness that brings him close to the Pre-Raphaelite vision of the world . . ."[21] Robson's view of Killarney *(Plate 105)* under sweeping rain clouds and gleams of sunshine epitomizes his highly romantic vision.

Like the Varleys and Robson, John Samuel Hayward (1778–1822) was a member of the enormously influential Old Watercolour Society founded in 1804. He only visited the environs of Dublin in 1805 when he stayed with the Tighe family at Rosanna and painted curiously modern watercolours of Enniskerry, Powerscourt *(Plate 106)*, Luggala and Leixlip. He was influenced by his friend and mentor, Joshua Cristall, in his loose, spontaneous style which appears at its best in his view of *The Village of Enniskerry and the Sugar Loaf.*

Regrettably, no watercolours or drawings survive from the hand of Thomas Roberts, the greatest Irish landscape painter of the eighteenth century, though he, too, was involved with the antiquarians. However, many exist by his brother, Thomas Sautell Roberts (1760–1826), who was a pupil of the Dublin Society Architecture School

106
JOHN S. HAYWARD
View from Powerscourt,
Co. Wicklow, 1805

107
THOMAS SAUTELL
ROBERTS
*View of the Military
Road, Co. Wicklow, 1801*

from 1777 and turned to painting on the death of Thomas in 1778. He exhibited frequently at the Royal Academy from 1789 to 1818, but it is impossible to tell for certain how many of his exhibited works were in watercolour, as only three are so described, although many have subjects similar to known watercolours. As most of them have very high catalogue numbers, this may be an indication, as it would be today, that many were not oils. All but three of the landscapes are of Irish scenes. As his London address changes nearly every year, it would seem he lived in lodgings there and spent more time in Ireland than is sometimes thought.

Roberts was the first Irish artist to hold a one-man show of his watercolours in Dublin. As the result of having obtained the patronage of Lord Hardwicke, the Viceroy, and the Chief Secretary, Charles Abbot, Roberts exhibited forty works in the Parliament House in 1802. In the *Freeman's Journal* for 12 January 1802 this exhibition was advertised: "The subjects principally taken in the County of Wicklow, including the Gold, Copper, and Lead mines; showing the Machinery and manner of working them. The most interesting Views taken from the new Military Roads and close Scenes of the Dargle, Seven Churches, etc. etc; twelve of which are now proposed for publication, to accompany a Tour through that romantic Country . . ." *(Plate 107)*.

An individual who left a manuscript journal for the years 1801–2, now in the Royal Irish Academy, is a unique contemporary critic: we call him the Unknown Diarist. He was a little shocked to have to pay an entrance fee of one shilling to Roberts's exhibition and went on to repeat the advertisement saying that the scenes were "mostly chosen from the more unfrequented parts of the Co. Wicklow, through which the inspection of the new *via militaris* led his Excellency and suite – There are also some fine designs of the Dargle Scenery."[22] Two of these were on the London art market in 1980[23] and show a *View of Powerscourt* with Charles Abbot mounted on a horse and *The Valley of Glencree with Abbot and his suite.* These are finely executed with good horses and figures. They have the blue colour which seems to pervade Roberts's watercolours, though this may be partially due to fading. His *View of Bray (Plate 108)*, signed and dated 1793, has not faded and is not blue in tone but has retained its soft colours with good greens.

The Unknown Diarist remarks on two different styles in Roberts's drawings: one he describes as "an imitation of the effect of oil, dashing careless touches, bright colours, dark shades and frequent & prominent lights" and the other as "just the reverse – softness, nearly fussy, dead colouring, and always autumnal, browns, reds, dusty yellows and sickly olives."[24] None of the known watercolours bear these descriptions out, though the diarist had a keen eye. Naturally, most of Sautell Roberts's watercolours were for engraving, and a large number for his projected *Illustrations of the Chief Cities, Rivers and Picturesque Scenery of the Kingdom of Ireland* were published, though the full work was never completed.

One of the figures already mentioned as connected with the antiquarian set is Jonathan Fisher (d.1809), who is far better known for his oils, prints and aquatints of Irish romantic scenery. The proliferation of picturesque prints at this period is noticeable, and Fisher, who was famous for his series of views of Killarney and Carlingford Lough, also published sixty prints of the *Scenery of Ireland*. Few of his watercolours survive. The *View of the Lymington river with the Isle of Wight in the background* in the Victoria and Albert Museum shows a typical pen and wash eighteenth-century technique, but we are a little dubious, in the light of the sketchbooks recently discovered in the National Library of Ireland, that it is by him at all.

The two sketchbooks which we have newly identified are something of a milestone in watching an eighteenth-century Irish artist at work on site. The condition of the sketchbooks almost seems to summon up the rain pattering on his paper! The drawings, which are in chalk, pencil and watercolour used with great freedom, are often annotated with colour directions and other practical comments. He may have used a camera obscura for some of the panoramas of Killarney. The sketchbooks are preparatory work for the sets of prints. For instance, they include figures pulling up the boats at the old Weir Bridge, Killarney,

108
THOMAS SAUTELL ROBERTS
View of Bray, Co. Wicklow, 1793
(National Gallery of Ireland)

109
JONATHAN FISHER
*View of Carlingford
Harbour from the New
Road to Hillsborough
behind Rosstrevor*
*(National Library of
Ireland)*

which we have mentioned in connection with Pars, and these drawings relate closely to the prints which include this subject. We illustrate a squared-up drawing for a *View of Carlingford Harbour from the New Road to Hillsborough behind Rosstrevor (Plate 109)*, which was engraved by T. Vivares and published by "J. Fisher landscape painter Gt. Ship St. Dublin" in 1772. In the print a tree has been added with some cows and milkmaids on the right of the picture. This version Fisher used as the basis for a small oil painting. These two sketchbooks have, besides picturesque scenery, a number of interesting views of estates, houses and landscape parks. There are several of Curraghmore, one showing a view of the eighteenth century garden front previously unrecorded. Mount Juliet and a number of houses in the Dublin area along the coast are included, many of which have disappeared. The sketchbooks must date from before 1770 when the first set of six Killarney prints was published. He draws upon them for later series, including the Carlingford set of 1772 and his second Killarney series of 1789.

A contemporary, Thomas Walmsley (1763–1806), who popularizes Irish scenery in rather a flashy gouache technique, was obviously much influenced by his training as a scene painter in London. He returned to Ireland in 1788 and worked in the Crow Street Theatre, Dublin. After 1790 he was based in London though he made many visits to Ireland to paint. An interesting work is *Figures and Cattle on a Road*, which is signed with his usual initials *TW*, and has the figures silhouetted against the background. It is a watercolour, though most of his work is in bodycolour. He has chameleon-like changes of technique from one drawing to another, the trees in one looking like crochet while in others they are painted with conventional sweeping strokes, though the end result is similar – dramatic with rich, deep colouring. One of a lighthouse is a romantic Irish version of a Vernet and there are many, like *Lansdowne Abbey, Co. Kerry*, which are amalgams of Irish features, such as High Crosses and ruins with misleading titles. There is no Lansdowne Abbey in Kerry. A lively gouache in his free, scenographic technique is his view of the *Rathfarnham Demesne (Plate 110)*.

John Henry Campbell (1757–1828), another contemporary, though born in Herefordshire was educated at the Dublin Society Schools because his family came to live in Dublin, where his father worked with the King's printer, Graisbery. A drawing dated 1794, of Lodore Falls, Derwent Water (National Gallery of Ireland) has an amateur quality and shows some Dutch seventeenth-century influence. Here he uses pencil,

110
THOMAS WALMSLEY
*Rathfarnham Demesne,
Co. Dublin*
*(Castletown House,
Co. Kildare)*

something rarely seen in his later work. Though he painted a few portrait water-colours, in a rather naïve, coarse style, Campbell is known as a prolific landscape painter, mostly in watercolour, and he exhibited in Dublin from 1800.

111
JOHN HENRY
CAMPBELL
A View of Dublin Bay
*(Huntingdon Library,
San Marino)*

90

His style does not change much over the years. It seems probable that he knew the work of William Payne, who was one of the most successful drawing masters of the day in London, as his technique seems to be based on him. Mallalieu's description of Payne's "exaggeratedly curling branches, and a squiggly manner of foliage drawing"[25] seems to fit Campbell, who is at his best when there is little foliage as in *A View of Shipbuilding near Ringsend*. More typical, and also well painted is his *Ireland's Eye from Howth*, a scene beloved by all artists. He painted mostly round Dublin *(Plate 111)*, frequently very small sketches with a marked blue tone. He clearly turned them out *en masse* and is better on a large scale. A medium-sized watercolour shows him painting a gentleman's demesne in Co. Kildare inscribed *Lake and islands in the lawn of J. Sabine Esq. Branockstown, Co. Kildare*. Another typical work is *Glen of the Downs*, which is signed and dated 1804. A group of pen and ink drawings of Dublin characters and people in Ireland, recently on the Dublin art market, show him as a mild master of caricature. At the beginning of his career, he also made small oval head-and-shoulder watercolour portraits, such as his group of five members of the Caulfield family of Benown, Co. Westmeath, which are signed and dated 1786.[26]

Campbell's daughter Cecilia Margaret (1791–1857) married the horse painter George Nairn in 1826. She was taught by her father and her watercolours resemble his. Again, like her father, she produced an occasional rather sombre oil.

Clergymen were frequently amateur artists, and of this period there is no better example than William Henry Barnard (1767/9–1818), whose grandfather was the Bishop of Derry, and he may therefore have been born in either Co. Derry or Co. Donegal. Though an Oxford graduate who was taught painting by Malchair, he was working in Ireland by 1788, when he painted the Ulster Museum's *Glendalough*. Barnard was in Ireland frequently in the 1790s but settled in a parish in Buckinghamshire. This did not prevent him from travelling on the continent in 1804, 1815 and 1818. He used a soft, spongy tonality and can be amusing, as in his *Carrick-a-Rede Bridge (Plate 112)* showing the

brave, hesitant figure crossing the rope bridge, but in his Dargle view in Yale he deals in an atmospheric manner with the rocks and trees. His *Ponte Rotto* of 1817 is a competent but uninspired Tiber view. Though coloured works are known, he mainly used grey wash.

A near contemporary who visited Ireland about this time, Thomas Sunderland

(1744–1828) used grey-blue and brown washes. Sunderland was a pupil of J.R. Cozens and probably of Joseph Farington. He made his trip to Killarney via Dublin and also visited Cork and Waterford. The trip was probably made about 1806, as one of the views of Ronan's Island appears in Sir John Carr's *A Stranger in Ireland*.

Thomas Leeson Rowbotham (1783–1853)[27] was in Ireland rather later, between 1815 and 1819, when he exhibited in Dublin. His series of drawings of the ornamental grounds of the Marino Casino at Clontarf are the only record of Lord Charlemont's varied garden follies, which included the Gothic Seat, the Root House and the Gothic Room at the head of a lake. Rowbotham spent most of his career in England where he taught in the Royal Naval School, a post in which he was succeeded by his Irish-born son, Thomas Charles Leeson Rowbotham (1823–75), who also painted Irish landscapes, particularly in the Killarney area in the 1860s.

James George O'Brien (fl.1779–1819),

112
WILLIAM HENRY BARNARD
Carrick-a-Rede Bridge, Co. Antrim
(Ashmolean Museum, Oxford)

113

JAMES GEORGE
O'BRIEN (OBEN)
*A View of Adare,
Co. Limerick, 1793*

114

JAMES GEORGE
O'BRIEN (OBEN)
*A View of Fennor Rock
on the Boyne, Co. Meath*

also a product of the Schools, who won their medal for landscape in 1779, had several of his drawings included in Grose's *Antiquities of Ireland*, 1791–5. He exhibited topographi-cal views of ruins in Counties Kilkenny and Dublin in the Dublin Society of Artists in 1780. O'Brien left Ireland in 1798, returning in time to exhibit at the Parliament House in

A Sketch taken from Life by Seignoir Gabrielli. Valued by 12 Connoisseurs at Twenty Thousand pounds!

CRIM.CON.

115
GASPAR GABRIELLI
The Crim Con Case
(engraving)

1801, where he caused much bewilderment by calling himself J. G. Oben. This was recorded by the Unknown Diarist:

This artist though long much esteemed in Dublin was not at the opening of the exhibition recollected by anyone. The pieces of O'Brien had often been admired, but Oben had never been heard of, at length it was discovered that the idea of foreign workmanship being preferred in the London market, had induced him to Germanize his ci-devant appelation.[28]

His earliest known work is a watercolour of the Franciscan Abbey at Adare, Co. Limerick *(Plate 113)*, signed and dated 1793. It is peopled with a stage shepherd holding a crook and talking to his shepherdess. The architectural features of the various ruins, however, are accurate enough and very much in the Sandby manner. His style entirely changes after 1800. The Diarist records that his work in the exhibition was in watercolour, though imitating oils, and Martyn Anglesea, talking of Oben's view of *Fennor Rock* in the Ulster Museum, remarks on the "meticulous detail in the foliage and ferns [which] is created almost entirely by colour-lifting or by the use of stopping out fluid."[29] We illustrate another view of the

Fennor Rock *(Plate 114)*. He adds that there was no body colour but considerable use of gum arabic. No doubt this is why Oben's work at its best, such as in the *Study of a Willow Tree at Beaupark on the Boyne* (Huntingdon Museum and Art Gallery) is limpid in tone and has exquisite clarity which reaches to the far distance. Oben left Ireland again in 1809 for London, where he exhibited at the Royal Academy views of England, Ireland and Wales. Before he left he had held a huge show of seventy landscapes in watercolour at 49 Marlborough Street, Dublin. He died in London.

Gaspar Gabrielli (fl.1805–30) was an Italian brought to Ireland by Lord Cloncurry, by whom he was employed to paint murals at Lyons, Co. Kildare, where Cloncurry's notable collection of antiquities was housed. Gabrielli married Lady Cloncurry's maid and during the famous "Crim Con" case, brought by Lord Cloncurry against his wife for adultery with Sir John Piers, the artist while painting his murals saw the canoodling couple. (This *cause célèbre* was immortalized in Sir John Betjeman's poem on the subject.) A caricature *(Plate 115)* published by McCleary of Nassau Street shows this graphic scene. Gabrielli portrays himself on a scaffold painting the amorous couple

116
GASPAR GABRIELLI
*Tree in the Campagna
near Rome, c.1818*

117
FRANCIS NICHOLSON
*Glanworth Castle, Co.
Cork, c.1805 (NGI)*

the Society of Artists between 1809 and 1813. The catalogues, unfortunately, do not list media, except in the case of pencil sketches, so it is impossible to say how many were watercolour. He painted in Killarney, Wicklow, Tipperary and Wales and also exhibited Italian views. Very few of these have come to light, but one gouache of Poulaphuca, Co. Wicklow, in the Graves Art Gallery, Sheffield, which is dramatic in its *chiaroscuro*, makes a useful lynchpin for further attributions.

Gabrielli's watercolour style is best understood today by his fine series of *Views of Rome*, one of which, *The Arch of Titus from the Roman Forum*, is in pencil and is dated 1818 while the others are in watercolour, including a study of umbrella pines in the Campagna *(Plate 116)*. While in Rome he acted as an agent, sending back pictures, chimney pieces and works of art, particularly for the fashionable architectural practice of Sir Richard and his son, William Vitruvius Morrison.[30]

Henry Kirchhoffer (1781–1860), another Dublin Society Schools product, seems to have almost disappeared as so few works, other than miniatures, by him survive. In the early 1800s, he exhibited at the Society of Artists in Dublin mostly watercolour portraits and miniatures. Later shows in Cork[31] included numerous watercolour landscapes. By 1815 he must have travelled to both Wales and Scotland, and his precise *View of Edinburgh* seems to be his only surviving landscape. A very detailed, charming drawing of the architect Francis Johnston's garden and folly behind his house in No. 60 Eccles Street, Dublin, is closely related to an oil by Kirchhoffer of the same subject which was also in the Johnston collection. This should, in our opinion, be attributed to him, though the architect's collateral descendants believe it to be by Johnston himself.

Though Mallalieu only speculates on a visit to Ireland by Francis Nicholson (1753–1844), we think he did visit Ireland; surviving views of the *Rock of Cashel, Glanworth Castle, Co. Cork (Plate 117)* and a *View of Killarney* do not look as though they had been worked up from other people's drawings. However, Roget says that two watercolours of Ireland exhibited in 1812 and 1813 at the Old Watercolour Society were

and saying, "I think this sketch will astonish his Lordship!/Alas! thy guardian angel sleeps;/Vice claps her hands, and virtu weeps."

Gabrielli's watercolours are usually landscapes, often in gouache, and he exhibited in

done after sketches by Sir Thomas Gage.[32] Nicholson seems to have lived in a circle which included a number of Irish people, such as Lord de Blacquiere and Sir Henry and Lady Tuite,[33] who took him touring to the Lake District. They do not, however, seem to have taken him back to their estates in Westmeath, as the country was in a period of disturbance in the 1790s; nevertheless, it seems extremely unlikely that Nicholson did not get to Ireland with some patron or protégé. Mallalieu illustrates a portrait of the artist by Henry Kirchhoffer, inscribed on the verso "Dublin 1824."[34]

Nicholson's son Alfred, also a painter, was in Ireland for some years from 1813, and his daughter Marianne married the Irish writer and antiquarian, Thomas Crofton Croker (see Chapter 10). Croker, Marianne and her father went on a tour of the picturesque in Counties Cork, Waterford and Limerick in 1821, which made up his *Researches in the South of Ireland* published in 1824. Francis and Marianne drew the views and Croker drew the antiquarian details. These were worked up by the son of Henry Brooke, William Henry Brooke (1772–1860), who was a well-known engraver and illustrator and whose charming sketch of a girl copyist at her easel *(Plate 118)*

118
WILLIAM HENRY
BROOKE
Girl Copyist at her easel
*(Yale Center for British Art,
Paul Mellon Collection)*

119
WILLIAM HENRY
BROOKE *after*
Crofton Croker.
Tourists in Ireland
(lithograph)

we illustrate. Brooke published separately a lithograph after Croker entitled *Tourists in Ireland*, 1828 *(Plate 119)*, showing the trio in a storm with Marianne holding her sketchbook, precariously perched on a wooden cart. Croker had amusingly described this scene in the book, mentioning the excruciating bumps and bruises they had all suffered in their rustic carriage.[35]

Returning to Nicholson *père*, he was not only one of the prime movers in the founding of the Old Watercolour Society in London but also a fine artist. He stressed his foregrounds and frequently used bright colours, though his foliage, to use Mallalieu's adjective,[36] gives a woolly effect. His architecture was, however, well rendered.

Richard Sasse (1774–1849) should be mentioned here, as a contemporary who is known to have visited Ireland, as dated works covering picturesque spots in the Liffey valley, Killarney and the West were exhibited by him in the Royal Academy from 1791 to 1813. His drawings, sometimes in the style of Barker of Bath, are more romantic than Nicholson's detailed, stolid views. His very large *Askeaton Castle* on the river Deel is a typical work and shows the increasing size watercolours were attaining now that their status had been fully accepted since the foundation of the Old Watercolour Society in 1801. Another particularly fine view of *Leixlip Castle on the Liffey* (National Gallery of Ireland) is signed and dated 1812.[37]

Many army officers *en poste* in Ireland left attractive visual records of their stay: a typical example is Lieutenant Carey of the 17th Light Dragoons, who painted a number of views of the Phoenix Park and the Royal Hospital[38] when he was encamped in the Park in the summer of 1792. One of them shows him seated by the Liffey with his hat and horse behind him, sketching away.

A more accomplished visitor who had been in the army is Lieutenant-Colonel Christopher Machell (1747–1827), who between 1784 and 1787 was painting around Dublin but with at least one excursion to Counties Antrim and Down. A patron and friend of Francis Nicholson,[39] he had been Colonel of the 15th regiment of Foot and had lost an arm at the Battle of New York during the American War of Independence. He paints purely landscape scenes in monochrome or grisaille and shows no interest in figures. However, they form a very interesting topographical record of Dublin and its environs (National Gallery of Ireland).

An amateur visitor to Co. Antrim whose style harks back to the eighteenth century was John Baverstock Knight (1785–1859), whose simple, clear and careful views of the Antrim coast should not be forgotten. His *Tievebulliagh from Knocknacarry* (Tate Gallery) is fascinating in showing the changes that have occurred in the landscape, from the barren terrain in Knight's time to the verdant trees which clothe the Glens of Antrim today.

By far the most important and famous recorder of Dublin was James Malton[40] (d.1803), the son of Thomas Malton who had come to Dublin in 1785 and had taught perspective and worked as an engraver. James came with his father from England and worked as a draughtsman for Gandon

121
JAMES MALTON
The Parliament House, Dublin, in its present state, c.1801
(Bank of Ireland)

122
JAMES MALTON
An Imaginary view of the Parliament House, Dublin, in decay, c.1801
(Bank of Ireland)

when he was building the Custom House. His first exhibited works in the Society of Artists in London in 1790 were of Heywood and Castle Durrow (both Victoria and Albert Museum), two seats in the Irish midlands. But most of his watercolours are of Dublin *(Plate 120)* and were either for, or connected with, his engraved series of twenty-five aquatints of the city issued between 1792 and 1799. Apart from their accurate delineation of the architecture of Dublin, they are a masterly and witty record of the everyday street life of the capital during its heyday. They give a particularly good picture of the river Liffey with its rafts of timber and its busy quays, as well as depicting shops of every sort including a butcher's with cattle being driven up for slaughter, fashionable ladies with headdresses taken, as Sacheverell Sitwell suggests, from Heidelhof's *Gallery of Fashion*,[41] ranks of sedan chairmen, beggars, doglife, draycarts, slipes and magnificent carriages. It must be said, however, that these streets are probably emptier and cleaner than they would have been in reality. It is an idealized vision, as is nearly all topography of this period. His two *"capricci"* of the Parliament House, one as it was *(Plate 121)* and the other in an imaginary state of decay *(Plate 122)*, sum up the contemporary view of Ireland's political future after the Act of Union.

CHAPTER SIX

SUBJECT PICTURES

One of the most attractive features of the art of that cantankerous fellow, James Barry (1741–1806), is his drawings. These have been discussed at length by William Pressly in both his book[1] and his Tate Gallery catalogue,[2] and we will therefore not tarry as long on them as their merits might suggest. His earliest known drawing, signed and dated 1762, is in pen and ink and wash of a river landscape *(Plate 123)* and was presumably done in Cork before he went to Dublin in 1763. Its gentle softness is reminiscent of his master, Butts, with overtones of Claude. Unlike his often overblown oil paintings, the drawings and etchings have real strength; but after his visit to Italy and his love-affair with the antique and the Italian Renaissance, his manner changes substantially. In the 1790s, following his years working in the Society of Arts and for the Boydell Shakespeare Gallery, Barry, no doubt influenced by Fuseli, decided to make a series of illustrations to Milton's *Paradise Lost*. These are among his finest studies and include his *Satan and his Legions hurling Defiance toward the Vault of Heaven*, 1792–4 (British Museum) and *Satan at the Abode of Chaos and Old Night*, 1792–5 *(Plate 124)*. These are clearly influenced by his knowledge of the Sistine Chapel ceiling and have heroic stature. The *Chaos and Old Night* is interesting in its foreshortening and its close-up view, entirely different from Fuseli's approach. A Michelangelesque study of the back of a nude horseman *(Plate 125)*, which was recently on the art market, is a very sensual drawing in which he favours pen and strong cross-hatchings, while in other drawings he uses pen and wash.

Barry's subject matter varies from religion to historical allegory. One of his most famous series of studies are the drawings for a proposed allegory of the Act of Union between Ireland and Great Britain *(Plate 126)* of 1801. Despite his equivocal attitude to Ireland in his early career, these drawings show strong nationalist Irish sympathies, as he sees the Union as between equals and the hope for the future in this equality, an attitude which was undoubtedly far from the thought of the English government. He introduces various Irish emblems such as harps and a claddagh ring, and, in the scribes who record the Union, he hints at ancient Irish manuscript illuminators. However, the medallion on the classical altar is an antique medal, which links with a circular drawing of a proposed medal for the Society of Arts showing the twin profiles of Hermes and Perseus, surrounded by roses and shamrocks. The symbolism, which must relate to the Act of Union, is unclear to us.

Towards the end of his life, Barry made a number of self-portraits, of which the one in the Ashmolean is an honest, slightly quizzical study; the profile in the Pierpont Morgan is inspired by antique cameos. His well-known self-portrait *(Plate 127)* in the Royal Society of Arts, in pen, ink and black chalk, shows Barry presenting "himself as the melancholy man, contemplative, self-absorbed and solitary. Disappointed and weary, he unflinchingly confronts the world and finds it wanting. It is a deeply moving study of Romantic pessimism . . ."[3] It is fascinating that Barry, who epitomizes the neo-classic in British art, should also be one of the prototypes of romanticism.

One of the few pupils of the Dublin Society Schools who turned to subject picture

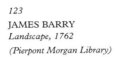

123
JAMES BARRY
Landscape, 1762
(Pierpont Morgan Library)

124
JAMES BARRY
*Satan at the Abode of
Chaos and Old Night*
(Royal Academy)

painting was Jacob Ennis (1728–70), no doubt because he was sent to study in Italy in 1754 by Arthur Nevill, the Surveyor-General. When Ennis returned to Ireland, Nevill became his patron and got him to paint for his Rutland Square house four lunettes after Pietro da Cortona. Apart from these paintings nothing survives except two drawings in the Accademia di San Luca of *Neptune (Plate 128)* and a *Giant,* both competent academic studies though without much flair. Ennis exhibited both portraits and subject pictures at the Society of Artists of Ireland.[4]

Another Irish artist who concentrated on subject pictures was Henry Tresham (c.1751–1814), whose style varies extraordinarily. He begins his career, having been educated in the Dublin Society Schools, using chalk and pastel, exhibiting mostly small whole-length portraits which were probably in the Healy/Forrest manner like the grisaille pastel, signed and dated 1773, showing the actor Shag Wilkes, which we have already mentioned in Chapter 4. Between 1769 and 1775, when he left Ireland, Tresham exhibited in the Society of Artists in Ireland, where he showed, first, a drawing of a Homeric subject.[5] A sensitive and delicate portrait of a man (Ashmolean

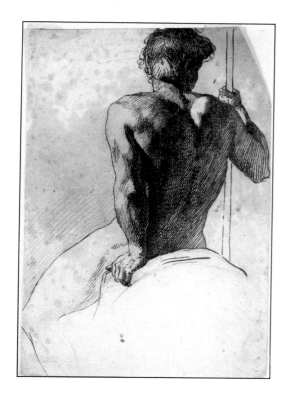

amazed by the number of similar whole-length female statues emerging from the ground *(Plate 130)*. It is in full colour and its apparently amusing subject makes it an arresting watercolour. In fact it shows *The Excavation of Apollo and the Nine Muses* from the Villa di Cassio.

The most fascinating are the drawings done in Malta, one of *Indians from the Coast of Malabar, by a Mediterranean shore (Plate 131)*[6] and another of the Indians manufacturing textiles; both were exhibited in the Royal Academy in 1789. Evidently the French Admiral Suffrien came back from India in 1784 as a result of the Peace of Versailles, and brought a group of Malabar weavers with him. These two drawings, with their simplified backgrounds and carefully posed, sculptural figures, must be among Tresham's finest watercolours.

A charming pen and ink study of *Women Reading*[7] dates from the late 1780s or early

125

JAMES BARRY
Study of a Nude Horseman

126

JAMES BARRY
The Act of Union between Great Britain and Ireland, c.1801

(Department of Prints and Drawings, British Museum)

Museum), dating into the nineteenth century, shows that he did not forsake his early training altogether. He spent some fourteen years in Italy, from 1775 to 1789, in which he developed a full international neoclassic style. He was brought to Italy by the amateur watercolourist, Lord Cawdor, and appears in Hugh Douglas Hamilton's masterpiece of *Canova in his studio with Tresham* of c.1790. *(plate 84)*. He travelled extensively in Italy, in Sicily and in Malta. His three studies of the Earthquake at Messina in 1783 are straightforward, rather blockish views.

The best of Tresham's drawings are genre and landscape, as his subject picture work is always pompous and exaggerated with overtones of Fuseli, Romney, William Hamilton and contemporary Italians. His book *Le Avventure di Saffo*, published in 1784, containing sixteen coloured aquatints, clearly illustrates his neoclassical manner. But his genre subjects and landscapes show another side of his art. *The Ascent of Vesuvius (Plate 129)* has a lively group of figures startled by the sight of the smoking crater, while his excavation scene at an archaeological site shows the grand tourists watching vases and other objects displayed to them. Yet another of the same subject looks like a skit on excavations, as the bewildered onlooker is

127
JAMES BARRY
Self Portrait
(Royal Society of Arts)

128
JACOB ENNIS
Study of a Nude Man as Neptune
(Archivio Storico, Accademia Nazionale San Luca, Rome)

1790s. It is an informal and delicate work, off-the-cuff and less laboured than most of his Roman output. These drawings in turn appear almost lighthearted in comparison

with his British historical subjects such as his illustrations for Bowyer's *Historic Gallery* done after he returned to London. Tresham became Professor of Painting at the Royal Academy briefly between 1807 and 1809, but until his death in 1814 was well-known as an art dealer.

The little known artist James Durno (c.1745–95) was described in the Hayward manuscript as being Irish.[8] There are many Irish links with him that support Hayward's claim: for instance, the Irish sculptor Michael Foye did a bas relief of him;[9] Lord Cawdor, Tresham's patron, owned two paintings by Durno; and the Earl Bishop of Derry also commissioned from him. He was a friend of Tresham in Rome and, finally, his will was witnessed by the Irish sculptor, Christopher Hewetson. There is no evidence of his being educated in Ireland but he did go to the Royal Academy Schools, not an unusual feature for Irish students. He worked with John Mortimer on the ceiling paintings at Brocket Hall and did not go to Italy until 1774, where he stayed till his death. There he earned his living, like so many of his contemporaries, by painting copies of old masters. Only two drawings by him are known, a rough study of *The Murder of Edward, Prince of Wales,* a picture commissioned for the Boydell Gallery and *Agrippina and her children mourning Germanicus (Plate 132).* This, too, despite its finished appearance, is a study for an oil he exhibited in the Society of Artists in 1772. Like much early neoclassicism, it is influenced by French seventeenth-century painting, in this case by a Le Sueur of the same subject in Hampton Court.

Samuel Forde[10] (1805–28) was from Barry's home town, Cork, and, despite his very short life, produced a number of fine drawings. The memoir which appeared anonymously in the *Dublin University Magazine* in March 1845, though overblown and lengthy, does tell us much about the training of a provincial artist in Ireland. There were only two portrait painters in Cork when Forde was eight or ten years old and only one print shop, selling Walmsley's landscapes and Bartolozzi's "red round Angelica Kauffman prints . . . waiting in the window to be framed and glazed, and captivate the eye and sense of the young, warm and

129
HENRY TRESHAM
The Ascent of Vesuvius
(Yale Center for British Art,
Paul Mellon Collection)

130
HENRY TRESHAM
An Archaeological Site

131
HENRY TRESHAM
*Indians from the Coast
of Malabar, c.1789*

greedy beholder."[11] However, he was able to read Reynolds's *Discourses*, Le Brun's *Passions* and Bell's *Anatomy of Expression*.

"Sometimes a roving auctioneer would bring 'a rattling print or two' that astounded him, and at other times the booksellers displayed

132
JAMES DURNO
*Agrippinas and her
children mourning
Germanicus, c.1771*

*(Department of Prints
and Drawings, British
Museum)*

some beautiful wonder to amaze him."[12] Though inevitably partially self-taught, he benefited in his teens from the series of casts from the antique which were given by the Prince Regent and ultimately formed the basis for a new School of Art in Cork in 1818. There Forde worked under the master, J. Chalmers, earning a living teaching and working with his master as a scene and decorative painter.

Forde's drawings are for his subject pictures,[13] including a sketch for the *Fall of the Rebel Angels (Plate 133)*, his last painting, not completed at his death, which is much influenced by Michelangelo's *Last Judgement*.

The critic of the Cork exhibition of 1828 enthused about this picture: "For sublimity and beauty of conception, together with masterly execution, if we mistake not, may vie with at least the best composers of the present day, and bids fair to place the modest artist among the very first of his profession."[14] Other works include groups of classically draped figures in sharp pencil outline, a Norman soldier, studies after antique statues and a beautiful wash drawing of a shrouded figure entitled *The Veiled Prophet of Kohrassan (Plate 134)* which is reminiscent of Fuseli. It seems more likely, though, that he would have known engravings after

133
SAMUEL FORDE
Study for the Fall of the Rebel Angels
(Crawford Municipal Art Gallery, Cork)

Flaxman, or even Blake, which would have inspired him. He was a friend of, and student with, both Daniel Maclise and John Hogan, the sculptor, and knew the art connoisseur William Carey. According to Strickland, his drawings for a Miltonic subject, *The Vision of Tragedy*, were shown to David Wilkie when he visited Ireland, who admired them saying that "he would have thought they were made by some of the old Masters."

The English architect George Richard Pain (1793–1838), who, with his brother James (c.1779–1877), both pupils of Nash, spent their working careers in Ireland, was an accomplished watercolourist. We illustrate as an endpiece to these neoclassical subject picture painters, two remarkable watercolours by George Richard: one in the fantastical Gothick mode, illustrating Horace Walpole's *The Castle of Otranto (Plate 135)*, and the other a classic, Claudian essay of Roman buildings entitled *Caius Marcius at the Ruins of Carthage (Plate 136)*. They are typical of the architectural schizophrenia of the age. In the *Otranto*, where the buildings echo Pain's Mitchelstown Castle, all is collapsing at a thunderclap, and mighty Alphonso appears in the centre of the ruins. Its drama contrasts vividly with the contemplative antiquity of ruined Carthage. They illustrate only too well the theories on the Sublime and the Beautiful with which Barry and Tresham would have agreed. The *Otranto* is signed and dated July 1831 and has all the technical brio of a romantic watercolour, but the pair seem to us to sum up the changing tastes of the turn of the century.

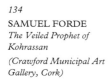

134
SAMUEL FORDE
The Veiled Prophet of Kohrassan
(Crawford Municipal Art Gallery, Cork)

135 GEORGE RICHARD PAIN *The Castle of Otranto, 1831*

136 GEORGE RICHARD PAIN *Caius Marcius at the Ruins of Carthage, c.1831*

137
CHARLES COLLINS
An Egyptian Vulture
*(Yale Center for British Art,
Paul Mellon Collection)*

138
CHARLES COLLINS
A Greater Loon, 1740
*(Victoria and Albert
Museum)*

CHAPTER SEVEN

STILL LIFE AND FLOWER PAINTING

Very few artists worked in this genre until the nineteenth century, when women, especially, became extremely interested in painting flowers from a botanical point of view. However, there are two notable exceptions in the eighteenth century, Charles Collins and Samuel Dixon. Other artists, such as Gabriel Beranger, are known to have painted flowers, though nothing survives.

Our knowledge of Collins and Dixon is very limited. Vertue says of Collins that he was a "bird painter lately dead 1744"[1] and that he died aged between forty and fifty. He must therefore have been born at the end of the seventeenth century.[2] However, no precise evidence has come to light on where or when he was born, or where he was educated. In a report on the sale of the collection belonging to the doctor and property speculator, Gustavus Hume, which took place in Dublin, the *Dublin Evening Post* of 4 May 1786 says that "there are also two pictures most admirably executed; one of live fowl; the other a dead hare, dead birds etc by an Irish master, (Collins) which is allowed by the first judges in point of elegance and performance, to be inferior to none." A work, *A Pheasant*, by him was included in the David La Touche sale in Dublin in Geminiani's rooms in May 1764. These pictures must all have been oils, and his work in that medium is clearly influenced by Dutch painters, as are some of his watercolours. Two different watercolours, one, of 1737, depicting a heron over a pool, and the second of a bittern, dated 1735, are very close in pose to Paul de Vos's *Wading birds in a Landscape*.[3] Other oils in their compositions are often influenced by the work of Jan Weenix.

Some of Collins's watercolours were done as illustrations for ornithological books such as those engraved by H. Fletcher and J. Mynde, published 1736.[4] Iolo Williams considered him far superior to contemporaries working in the same field such as George Edwards, saying that Edwards's "prim hard little lines of white" used to highlight plumage compare unfavourably with Collins in similar passages with his "delicate, sensitive, almost caressing..." brushwork. Williams gives a splendid description of Collins's "masterly drawing of a heron, a wonderfully satisfactory thing for the quality of the plumage, the bold pattern of the pose, and the knowing liveliness with which the bird arches its neck and peers down towards the water . . ."[5] Like Williams, we feel Collins was at his best and grandest drawing large birds, like his *Guinea Hen* of 1743, his superb *Egyptian Vulture (Plate 137)* or his melancholic *Greater Loon (Plate 138)* (now identified as a Great Crested Grebe). John Murdoch,[6] in an entry on this picture, points out that Collins was greatly influenced by the Bolognese naturalist, Ulisi Aldrovandi (1522–1605), whose book on ornithology was reprinted throughout the seventeenth century and to which Collins would therefore have had easy access.

Though we have not seen any watercolours other than of birds, he apparently was involved in illustrating other animals, including exotic beasts from the New World and the East as well as fishes and fungi. Hundreds were listed in the Taylor White Sale, Sotheby's 16 June 1926, and these are discussed by Murdoch. The earliest dated work we know, an oil, is 1729.

Samuel Dixon (fl.1748–69) was the son of a Dublin hosier and brother of John Dixon, the well known mezzotint engraver. According to Strickland, they both studied under Robert West in the Dublin Society Schools. As their attendance is not recorded, it is more likely that they were taught by West before the Schools were officially founded. Samuel Dixon started his career in 1748 as a dealer and watercolourist specializing in gouache drawings of flowers. His work, in both flowers and birds, is influenced by the great French and Dutch painters and in his use of black backgrounds by such contemporaries as G.D. Ehret. But Dixon was mainly a decorative artist and did not study the subjects, birds and flowers, with any scientific discipline. He developed an embossed technique which he called *basso relievo*, and in the designs he introduced birds as well as flowers *(Plate 139)*. The images of birds were frequently pirated from *The Natural History of Uncommon Birds* by George Edwards, which was being published at this time and was much copied. He was extremely careful in his borrowings to include corrections Edwards had inserted in his text correcting his own illustrations.[7] In 1756 Dixon travelled to England, where he stayed till 1758, and from then on he concentrated on setting up a linen-printing industry in Leixlip. Having sold out in 1765, he returned to London where he set up a picture shop.

139
SAMUEL DIXON
Six pictures of his Fruit, Flowers and Birds

He was back again in Dublin in early 1768 when he advertised on 23 April in *Sleator's Public Gazetteer*: "Samuel Dixon Painter . . . hath Just opened Shop . . . where he is making *several New Improvements in his Flowers, Birds* etc etc. And as the Polite Art of Drawing and Painting is daily increasing among the young Ladies and Gentlemen, and many are dispirited for want of Proper Materials, Mr Dixon assures them, that he hath every Article in the Way, accurately prepared, such as Water-Colours, Crayons, fine Vellums, Proper Papers for ditto, a superior kind of Black Lead Pencils etc etc . . ." He goes on to say that he is selling some of the embossed designs uncoloured so that the purchaser might complete them.[8]

Dixon's advertisements in Dublin newspapers give a good insight into his work. In *Faulkner's Dublin Journal* of 21 April 1748 he said he sold "flower-pieces, drawings in indian ink, landscapes in oyl for chimneys and small ditto done on vellum in water-colour fit for ladies closets. . . his set of flower pieces in basso relievo. . . which are a new invention, and are not only ornamental to Ladies Chambers, but useful to paint and draw after or imitate in Shell or Needle-work." He published a second set of *basso relievo* flower pieces in 1750 and another in 1755. By 1750 they were so popular he was already fighting off imitators. At that date the imitators were Irish, Mary Taverner, Zacheriah Deane and McDermott, but later two English artists, Isaac Spackman and William Hayes, followed his example. Dixon dedicated the whole 1750 set to the Earl of Meath; in the 1755 set the individual items are dedicated to the leading aristocratic ladies of Ireland, from the Vicereine, the Duchess of Dorset, to a bevy of Irish countesses and viscountesses. These flower pieces are among the most decorative products of the Dublin art world of the eighteenth century.

Dixon needed to employ a number of assistants to handcolour the reliefs, and they sometimes initialled their work. The best known were James Reilly and Gustavus Hamilton, who later worked as miniaturists. Both were trained in the Dublin Society Schools, as was Daniel O'Keeffe, the brother of the painter and playwright John O'Keeffe (see page 62), who left in his memoirs a

description of Dixon's lively studio. Several examples of the pupil's work *(Plate 140)* are in the Fitzwilliam Museum, Cambridge.

Another botanical painter who was involved in printed textiles was William Kilburn (1745–1818), who Ada Leask[9] thinks was probably taught in the Schools but most of whose career was spent in England. His training under Jonathan Sisson, who owned the linen-printing establishment at Lucan, ended when he went to London about 1766. There he sold his designs to calico printers and shops but later, when he had met the botanist William Curtis, he turned to straight botanical illustration, working for Curtis's *Flora Londinensis*, for which he signed twenty-five plates. Both his work for the textile industry and for the botanists is in watercolour[10] and of a very high order. His plants were drawn life-size; unfortunately, only one watercolour survives (The Library, Royal Botanic Gardens, Kew) for the *Flora Londinensis* plates but it proves the quality of his work in this medium. His textile designs

140
DANIEL O'KEEFFE
Flower Painting with lily of the valley
(Fitzwilliam Museum, Cambridge)

are in gouache and are all based on flowers and natural forms such as seaweeds *(Plate 141)*. They survive in a remarkable album in the Victoria and Albert Museum and are among the most splendid produced in Europe in the eighteenth century.

It is interesting that Dixon felt his work made useful patterns for shellwork and needlework, and one cannot but speculate that Mrs Delany knew them when she lived in Ireland, as she was a notable exponent of both crafts. Later, when she returned to England, her superb mosaic flower paintings *(Plate 142)* bear some generic resemblance to

141
WILLIAM KILBURN
Design for chintz
*(Victoria and Albert
Museum)*

142 *(Facing Page)*
MARY DELANY
Pyracanthus
*(Department of Prints
and Drawings, British
Museum)*

Mespilus
piracantha

Dixon's gouaches, possibly because she uses a black background as he frequently did as well. Both were no doubt influenced by the great Dutch and French flower painters, Louis Tessier, Monnoyer and G.D. Ehret. Though Mrs Delany must have painted flower pieces when she was in Dublin, her masterpieces in this genre all date from after her return to England. Then she spent the summers staying with the Dowager Duchess of Portland at Bulstrode, where they were frequently visited by Ehret.

Her surviving, elaborate cut paper work was created at this time. She had used this art form, as far as can be judged, throughout her career, though only these late works seem to survive. Though undated, her *Broad Crested Cockatoo* and her *Fire-backed Pheasant of Java*, both cut from single pieces of vellum with incredible technical skill, may well date from the Bulstrode period; certainly her "flower mosaicks," her own term, were done at Bulstrode. With these she painted paper to the correct colour, cut out each delicate part and shade of the flower, stem and leaf, and stuck it down on black paper, creating the mosaic effect like a modern collage.[11]

That flower painting and still life were popular in Dublin can be gauged by the fact that so many artists exhibited such paintings in the Society of Artists in Ireland, though again it is not easy to tell how many were in watercolour or chalk. However, two masters in the Schools exhibited such works: James Mannin, between 1765 and 1773, and William Waldron, who had been Mannin's pupil and succeeded him in the Landscape and Ornament School, between 1770 and 1777. Others listed were John O'Keeffe, Mrs Watson, Charles Lewis, Somerville Pope Stevens and William Sadler. In the country the genre was also popular, as *Finn's Leinster Journal* for 25 March 1767 advertises that in Kilkenny in a shop called the "Owl and the Ivy Tree" Irish bird paintings were for sale, "painted with good colours, either glazed and framed, or in bound folio."

A lady of considerable talent was Frances Anne, known as Fanny, Beaufort (1769–1865), who became the fourth wife of Richard Lovell Edgeworth, Maria Edgeworth's father. She was the sister of the Revd William Beaufort, who was mentioned in Chapter 3, and her father was Daniel Augustus Beaufort, the map-maker. In the Huntingdon Library, California, there are a great many highly professional drawings and watercolours of Irish and English plants made by her, mostly between 1790 and 1810.[12] She had drawing lessons from a variety of masters including Nicholas Pocock in Bristol in 1782 and a Miss Simmonds, and, in Dublin in 1785, she was taught by Francis Robert West. She accompanied her parents to London in 1789 and in her father's diary for 22 January and 30 January 1790, it is recorded that she had lessons twice a week from Mr Raymond Deshouillères, on whom we can find no information, who taught her "at ½ guinea per lesson in crayon painting."[13] The family regularly looked at picture collections and knew artists like Paul Sandby, so there was every encouragement for her talents.

Apart from her extremely competent vignette (see front endpaper) done for her father's famous map of Ireland, which was published after much difficulty in 1792, Fanny illustrated a number of Maria's books, and some miniature portraits by her of her family exist. Other members of this highly intelligent and artistic family are mentioned elsewhere in this book.

The nineteenth century saw an increase in the interest in, and need for, painting natural history, as is made clear by the work of John Templeton (1766–1825) and his son Robert (1802–92),[14] whose watercolours and drawings are now in the Ulster Museum. John Templeton, whose house, Cranmore, survives and can claim to be the earliest house in Belfast, was a noted gardener. He was also one of that remarkable generation of Belfast intelligentsia who had supported theoretically, if not actively, the United Irishmen and after the failure of the 1798 rebellion turned their attentions to philanthropic causes. He was a close friend, both before and after the '98 rebellion, of Mary Ann McCracken, the sister of the leading United Irishman in Belfast, Henry Joy McCracken. Templeton was of a merchant family, rich enough to enjoy the leisure pursuit of natural history research. He helped to found the Belfast Academical Institution and supported the Belfast Literary Society and the Belfast Natural History Society,

143
ROBERT TEMPLETON
Shells
(Ulster Museum)

which became the Belfast Natural History and Philosophical Society in 1821.

A keen botanist, John Templeton was in communication with Sir Joseph Banks and other leading figures in London and at Kew. He also created an important manuscript, *Catalogue of Native Plants*, and started a *Flora Hibernica*, assembling text and making watercolour illustrations. A naturalist first and foremost, he always recorded details such as dates and places. He recorded many animals, birds and fish found in and about Belfast, in the market or by fishermen or sportsmen, such as a puffin shot on Belfast Lough. His forty-five drawings of fish show his near miniaturist technique and are

144
ROBERT TEMPLETON
Butterflies
(Ulster Museum)

happily well preserved so that his clear, brilliant colours survive intact. His drawings of shells may in many cases have been copies from other collections, but he and his children went on many collecting expeditions and he credits his daughters, Ellen and Mary, with finding several species of shell in Bangor in 1818.[15]

Robert Templeton, John's son, graduated in medicine in Edinburgh in 1831 and joined the army, travelling widely during his military career and continuing the naturalist hobby instilled in him by his father. His talent as a watercolourist was also put to scientific use, and his superb drawings of shells *(Plate 143)*, butterflies *(Plate 144)*, spiders, monkeys and other specimens were made during his spare time on his postings. These included Ceylon, first in 1835, and then for twelve years from 1839 to 1852, where his stay overlapped with those of Andrew Nicholl and Emmerson Tennent (see Chapter 9). Nicholl is said to have influenced his work but by then Templeton's style appears

fully formed. He had been taught drawing as a boy in the Academical Institution in Belfast by an Italian, Gaetano Fabrini. He had also spent periods in India, Rio de Janeiro and Mauritius (1834), not to mention the Greek Islands and South Africa.

A watercolourist who painted birds, and also drew flowers, butterflies and insects, is Miss Battersby, about whom nothing is known except that she lived for a number of years at No. 16 Mountjoy Square East, which in the *Dublin Directories* is described as belonging to a Mrs Battersby, presumably her mother. She may have been Mary, the unmarried daughter of Robert Battersby of Bobsville, Co. Meath, who in 1763 married Marianne, daughter and co-heiress of Haynes Wade of Lislin, Co. Cavan.[16] Five signed albums of Miss Battersby's work are known, one in the Ulster Museum and the others in the National Library of Ireland, where there is also one small sketchbook which is attributable to her. In the Ulster Museum album she gives her address and

145
MARY BATTERSBY
Blue taild Thrush, 1806
(Ulster Museum)

adds that "all the Birds [are] the size of nature." These drawings are dated between 1804 and 1841. The birds were painted from pets and stuffed specimens; they are magnificent in colour and have an excellent feel for the different quality of feathers, the soft under-feathers contrasting with the strong wing feathers. One drawing of a *Blue taild Thrush (Plate 145)*, dated 1806, is inscribed, "This drawing was taken from a Bird in the collection of Baron Lister, Naturalist remained fifty years in spirits, was taken out dried and stuff'd is now in the Dublin Museum. NB he called it a Starling"; another came from the collection of "Peter Digges La Touche 1810." Most of the drawings are dated and usually give the place of origin of the bird.

The three other volumes of birds in the National Library of Ireland came from the Royal Dublin Society library to which they were given by the artist in 1820 and 1836. The first of these was a volume of drawings from "a collection of stuffed birds in the Dublin Museum" and was given in 1820. On the catalogue page she says, "NB: all the Birds the size of Nature and most of them named by Linn . . . [eaus] except a few lately discovered"; it is signed M. Battersby. This suggests that our identification of her as Mary Battersby is correct. These are the best of all her bird pictures, highly coloured and with many exotic species. Of the other two albums, one is of birds shot in Co. Meath, only one of which is dated, August 1810; the other volume is of birds shot in Pennsylvania in 1834 by Robert Battersby, Esq, MD. Mary Battersby had two doctor nephews called Robert, one in the army, the other the inheritor of Lislin and probably the one referred to in the volume, as no mention is made of army rank. The Pennsylvanian birds include a superb watercolour of a *Blue Jay (Plate 146)*.

The fourth National Library of Ireland volume includes only flower drawings done as botanical specimens. They retain great brilliance of colour and, though she seems less able to handle the texture of flowers than of birds, they are fine. She is at her best when dealing with large-flowered and leafed plants such as a series of different species of passion flower. The sketchbook, which is also obviously by Miss Battersby, includes

insects, butterflies, feathers, flowers and shells as well as her *tour de force*, the word "END" (endpiece) created out of a series of dancing chinoiserie girls, mostly dressed in the costume of the early years of the nineteenth century.

The finest of the Irish bird painters was from Cork. Richard Dunscombe Parker (1805–81) was a gentleman amateur and farmer who lived at Landscape House, Shanakiel, in the Sunday's Well district of Cork. Though nothing is known of his education, Parker was exhibiting in Cork in 1830[17] and again in 1833.[18] In 1842 he is mentioned as showing a Swiss scene[19] in the Art Union Exhibition, so that he must have been known as a landscape watercolourist as well as a bird painter. In 1852, as a gentleman amateur, he exhibited some of his birds at the National Arts Exhibition in Cork.[20] He had exhibited them earlier, in 1843, when the British Association for the Advancement of Science met in Cork. His interest in birds is recorded in 1845, when he is noted as painting "a little eagle" by Dr Harvey in a letter of 30 October.

It is worth mentioning that his brother, Dr Noble Dunscombe Parker, was trained as a doctor in Glasgow and that that

146
MARY BATTERSBY
Blue Jay
(National Library of Ireland)

117

university was one of four in the British Isles that subscribed to Audubon's double Elephant Folio *Birds of America* (1827–38), which Richard might therefore have seen and by which he may have been inspired. From a newspaper cutting stuck into the Dunscombe Parker volume recording the British Association meeting, we see that a Mr Strickland "expressed his gratification at Mr Parker's paintings; in fact, they were only second to Mr Gould's of London, and fully equal to Audubon's. He pointed our particulars in which they far excelled the continental drawings, especially in familiarity with the living habits of the birds and in the plumage." The Belfast naturalist, William Thompson, went even further than Mr Strickland, saying, "in life like appearance they excelled even Mr Gould's, beautiful as the latter were." Parker's work is now known by the 170 pictures, comprising nearly 260 birds, in the collection of the Ulster Museum.[21] The splendid silhouettes of the larger birds, the

settings in which they are placed and the quality of the landscape backgrounds make the link with Audubon very obvious, and they are in the forefront of bird painting. Like Audubon, Parker was a great hunter and he seems to have travelled widely in Ireland. His superb gannets *(Plate 147)* are depicted in front of the Skellig rocks off the coast of Kerry, while his grouse *(Plate 148)* appear to be at Luggala in Co. Wicklow.

Throughout the nineteenth century there was a tradition of women painting botanical studies, of whom Lydia Shackleton[22] (1828–1914) was unquestionably the best. She was a member of the well-known Quaker family from Ballitore and studied art in the Royal Dublin Society Schools in 1850. She was fifty-six when she began her professional career working for Frederick Moore, Keeper of the National Botanic Gardens, Glasnevin, to record numerous species of flowers *(Plate 149)* being cultivated there. Fifteen hundred or so of these survive in

147
RICHARD DUNSCOMBE PARKER
Gannets off the Skellig Rocks, Co. Kerry
(Ulster Museum)

Glasnevin and include a number of master-pieces of botanical illustration. The colour of her watercolours has survived admirably. When her eyes began to fail, she was succeeded by Alice Jacob, also a Quaker, but with much less talent, who taught in both the Dublin and Cork Schools of Art.

Lady Blake (1845–1926), born Edith Osborne at Newtown Anner, Co. Tipperary, was another near professional. Her mother patronized watercolourists and was an early purchaser of the work of the Swiss artist, Alexandre Calame. Mrs Osborne was clearly friendly with Thomas Shotter Boys, whose only known Irish watercolour was painted at Newtown Anner about 1866. She was also a keen sketcher, and a series of her sketch-books done on country house visits in England and Ireland are at Myrtle Grove, Lady Blake's house in Youghal. Mrs Osborne's younger daughter, Grace (d.1926), who married the tenth Duke of St. Albans, was also known as an amateur painter. Edith Osborne, if little educated in the conventional sense, grew up in a lively and educated household where she met many distinguished people; she was herself to become a remarkable linguist, said to be able to speak nine languages including Chinese. As well as

Paeonia officinalis var. 1873.

150 (Above)
LADY BLAKE
The Staircase, Myrtle Grove, Co. Cork

151 (Above Right)
LADY BLAKE
Detail of the Staircase

being a keen natural historian and artist, she took an interest in Irish politics and was a close friend of Anna Parnell, the sister of Charles Stewart Parnell.

Edith married, against her family's wishes, an officer in the Royal Irish Constabulary, Henry Arthur Blake, who came of a good Galway family though too poor for the

152
LADY BLAKE
Homerus Swallowtail Butterfly, 1893
(National History Museum, London)

Osbornes. When in 1881 Blake was appointed a "Special Magistrate," a very dangerous post, the spirited Edith accompanied him everywhere with a cocked revolver at the ready with which she is said to have been a first-class shot. Blake proved his talents by becoming a Governor of a number of British colonies abroad. His duties took him to the Bahamas (1884–7), Newfoundland (1887–8), Jamaica (1889–97), Hong Kong (1897–1903) and finally Ceylon (1903–7).[23]

Wherever she went, Lady Blake painted the flora and fauna as well as interesting places. Two large watercolours, now at Myrtle Grove, were of the Blakes' bathing tent and house at Stanley and the opening of the Placentia Railway in Newfoundland 1888/9 with its triumphal arches and other features. A description of her painting in the Bahamas[24] is unique, as she seems to have carried on her painting with a pet snake entwined round her waist! A great number of her works and lively sketchbooks are still in Myrtle Grove, including three cupboard doors covered with flower decorations of the ginger plant and various lilies, done in 1887 as a present for her husband. The staircase is close-framed with her botanical illustrations *(Plates 150, 151)* and is obviously based, as Dr Ball[25] pointed out, on Marianne North's[26]

120

153
SAMUEL McCLOY
Grapes
*(Victoria and Albert
Museum)*

154
THOMAS COLLIER
Flowers

similarly arranged glazed botanical studies in
the pavilion at Kew Gardens. Dr Ball
arranged for Edith Blake's works to be
exhibited in the Science and Art Museum in
Dublin in 1894, and he considered them
brilliant productions "such as have probably
never before been seen in Dublin." There is
a large collection (195) of her watercolours
of Jamaican lepidoptera *(Plate 152)* in the
Natural History Museum, London, which
show not only her remarkable abilities as a
painter but her scientific knowledge as well.
There is also a large collection of her works
in the Botanic Gardens in Dublin.

Lady Wheeler Cuffe[27] (1867–1967) was,
like Lady Blake, a traveller following her
husband who worked in the Public Works
Department in Burma where she lived for
twenty years. She was a landscapist as well as
a botanical illustrator. About sixty-six watercolours of Burmese and Indian orchids were
given to Glasnevin. One other contributor to
the Glasnevin collection who should be
mentioned is George Victor Dunoyer, who
is discussed in Chapter 9. In Glasnevin there
is a fascinating study in watercolours of
types of apple,[28] which are certainly his best
but least known work. In the Natural
History Museum in Dublin there are studies
of fish by him, and it is clear that he

frequently worked as a painter of natural history as well as of landscapes. A Curator of the Botanic Gardens in Dublin from 1879, the Englishman Frederick William Burbidge (1847–1905) produced very competent work as illustrations for his books and for botanical magazines. Another professional botanist who was an excellent draughtsman was William Henry Harvey (1811–66), who was Professor at Trinity College, Dublin, from 1856. But he drew his delicately detailed illustrations directly on to the lithographic stone and left only very sketchy notes on paper.

Many other artists occasionally painted still life, birds and other natural history subjects. Examples include Robert Hood (Chapter 13), who worked in the Arctic.

Samuel McCloy (Chapter 10) is one whose watercolours of fruit, especially grapes *(Plate 153)*, have that bloom which was felt to give them a living quality, to make them almost edible and succulent, qualities which natural history painters would not have attempted. Thomas Frederick Collier (Chapter 10) is another Irishman who attempted this genre *(Plate 154)* and even Frederick William Burton (Chapter 10) left a superb watercolour of maize cobs *(Plate 155)*.

Other variants of still life painting rarely attract the attention of the watercolourists, but a certain J.E. Newman, giving his address as [32] Philipsborough Avenue, North Strand, [Dublin], painted two particularly delightful compositions. In the *Dublin Directories* he gives his profession in 1846 as

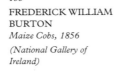

155
FREDERICK WILLIAM
BURTON
Maize Cobs, 1856
*(National Gallery of
Ireland)*

156
J.E. NEWMAN
Perspective rendering of a
desk top
(Fogg Art Museum,
Harvard University)

157
J.E. NEWMAN
Perspective rendering of
an artist's table
(Fogg Art Museum,
Harvard University)

"artist" but by 1851 he calls himself "Professor of Drawing". One wonders if these two watercolours were in the nature of advertisements for his school. One is a composition of a writer's desk-top on which a book lies open at a lengthy and melancholy poem entitled *Richard and Kate (Plate 156)*. The other, more interesting to us, shows an artist's table with paintbox, colour-mixing saucers and brushes, and paintings of romantic baronial ruins *(Plate 157)*. In front of one of these there is a piece of paper used to test out colours, on which Newman has written his name and address. He was clearly also using this paper as a guard to keep the lower of the two watercolours clean. The painting of the graining of the wooden table and the Regency chair with its blue embroidered seat is particularly appealing, and the handling of perspective in both paintings is meticulously worked out, with points of sight and scale noted. The Whatman watermark on the paper dates the works after 1843 though the furniture looks earlier.[29] In a sense, these two compositions are outside the scope of the rest of this chapter but we can imagine, very easily, Mary Battersby settling down at her birds on Mr Newman's table.

CHAPTER EIGHT

THE EARLY NINETEENTH CENTURY

Around 1800 and during the Regency, there was a period both in Ireland and in England when the small whole-length portrait in chalk or watercolour, or a combination of both, became very fashionable. In England Henry Edridge was the principal, but by no means the only, exponent of this popular genre, and Irish painters such as Alexander Pope and John O'Keeffe worked in a very similar manner. Pope, already met with in Chapter 4, changed from pastel to the small whole-length in watercolour in the early years of the century. John O'Keeffe was working in this medium much earlier, as he mentions whole lengths "of William Lewis in the character of Belcour and Capt. Brazer – the first in coloured wash, the latter in bistre, both highly finished."[1] These were done during his acting days in Ireland, from the late 1760s to 1774, and none is known to have survived. They may well have looked like Forrests and, of course, he was also a landscape painter, as we have already mentioned.

Like Pope, O'Keeffe was only a part-time painter. Both had active stage careers, Pope principally in London at Drury Lane and the Haymarket, while O'Keeffe's career was cut short due to blindness and he became a playwright. Pope frequently visited Dublin, and Strickland recounts that he had a long and successful career "owing more to his good looks, his graceful action and melodious voice, than to his powers as an actor." He painted a number of his theatrical contemporaries, such as Mrs Siddons. He was a well-known *bon viveur*, and something of this brushes off on the ample and lively outlines of his particularly fine drawing of J.H. Donaldson *(Plate 158)* standing in a

landscape, signed and dated 1807. The staffage, with its cursive line, makes a splendid frame for Mr Donaldson's plump figure. The *Misses Stoughton*, later Lady Hayes and Lady Ibbetson, playing with a tambourine and a triangle, is a remarkably graceful composition and may be by Pope, in which case it indicates how very like Adam Buck he could be. It is not a signed and dated work.

Pope occasionally uses the conventional classical accessories such as urn and balustrade to set off his sitters, but the serious neoclassic exponent was Adam Buck who was brought up in Cork, where he started his career. Pasquin says in 1796 that Buck was self-taught and "appears to study the antique more rigorously than any of our emerging artists; and by that means he will imbibe a chastity of thinking, which may eventually lead him to the personification of apparent beauty . . ."[2] The earliest drawing we know by him is dated 1795, the year he went to London. It shows a mother seated in strict profile on a Grecian stool holding her child in a precarious pose supported on her foot *(Plate 159)*. It exhibits the curious mixture of neoclassic form and mawkish sentiment which was to be the hallmark of his subject picture style throughout his career. These small works were very popular and were engraved, used as designs on china and used for other decorative purposes. Their titles are self-explanatory and include *Mama, let me not beg in vain; My dear little shock, you must have a dip;* and *Have I not learned my book, Mama.*

Buck's small whole-length portraits, however, are not sentimental; they are usually set against landscape backgrounds yet the figures have a sculptural feel and their outlines

158 ALEXANDER POPE *Portrait of J.H. Donaldson, 1807*
(Bristol Museum and Art Gallery)

159 ADAM BUCK *Mother playing with her child, 1795*

echo his preoccupation with Greek vase painting. Most of the figures are not stationary but gently moving. His feeling for dress is obvious and perhaps is owed to the fact that contemporary clothes were based so much on Greek costume. The scholar, Thomas Hope, had published his influential *Costume of the Ancients* in 1809 and *Designs of Modern Costume* in 1812. These works had considerable impact on Regency dress, and it comes as no surprise that Buck was involved in working for fashion plates later in his career. In 1811 he issued a prospectus for a great work on Greek vase painting which was intended as a continuation of Sir William Hamilton's *Collection of Engravings from Ancient Vases . . .*[3]. Little of this was issued, but a volume of 157 pen and ink drawings, of which 34 were etched in aquatint, survive in the library of Trinity College, Dublin.

Buck's masterpiece is the portrait group of 1813 which was said to be of Thomas Hope,[4] the noted collector and theorist mentioned above, but it is now thought to be a self-portrait of the artist with his wife and two children; a third child, presumably dead, is represented as a bust *(Plate 160)*. Despite its correct portrayal of Greek vases in the background, and its hints of his knowledge of Reynolds and Poussin in the pose of the mother and her youngest child, Buck cannot resist the sentiment of the second son holding a black cat and dipping it into an antique vase. The painter stands four-squarely facing out at us, totally ignoring the domestic scene beside him, and the success of the portrait relies to a great extent on his fascination with the flat pattern-making of the Greek vase painters, whose work he owned and admired so much.

Buck continued to paint portraits till his death, and an excellent and unsentimental late example is *Annie Charlotte Hill* of 1832, in the Ulster Museum. As Anglesea[5] notes, the striking yellow of the grass is due to the fading of a fugitive blue as the rather dark green, hidden by an earlier mount, which appears at the edges, shows Buck's original colour.

A close, but much less competent, follower of Buck was James Dowling Herbert, the author of *Irish Varieties*,[6] well known for its description of the Schools and their master, Francis Robert West. He was in the Schools in 1779 but made his career in the theatre. The Unknown Diarist noted his work in the 1801 exhibition in the Parliament House with a critical eye and mentions twelve drawings in watercolour with figures about twelve inches high "in the manner of Buck of London."[7] In fact, he is a much inferior artist, as his etiolated figure of the second *Lady Cloncurry* proves (National Gallery of Ireland).

A visitor who considered settling in Ireland was George Chinnery (1774–1852). Distantly related to the Irish Chinnerys, he painted Sir Broderick Chinnery's portrait and those of his family when he came to Ireland in 1795. He stayed with the Dublin jeweller, James Vigne, whose daughter he married in 1799. Chinnery painted life-size oil portraits as well as miniatures and drawings. His study of his wife, Marianne, is an appealing, romantic watercolour[8] and has

160
ADAM BUCK
Self Portrait with family
(Yale Center for British Art,
Paul Mellon Collection

the same shadowy hair as appears in his oil portrait of her reading (National Gallery of Ireland). But in the drawing her eyes are compellingly large and black, while the use of pencil in the drapery and background is precise and delicate. An enchanting portrait, signed and dated 1797, of a very young boy clutching his drum *(Plate 161)*, decorated with a crowned harp, is rather less romantic in treatment as it has an outdoor setting with a rudimentary landscape.

Apart from his oils, Chinnery exhibited finished watercolours, now all unknown. Two of these are criticized by the Unknown Diarist. Referring to the exhibition held in 1801, the Diarist says, "To display the versatility of his genius, Mr Chinnery steps out of his natural walk, the study of "the human

161
GEORGE CHINNERY
Boy with Drum, 1797

face divine" to that of nature and the beauties of landscape . . ." He goes on to describe the two drawings: "Sunset Killarney, perhaps natural but parallel stripes of scarlet, black, purple and yellow make but a tawdry appearance on paper. Castle Dermot ruined church. The landscape well, but the building such bright masses of white and green that it appears to have been cut out of something else and pasted into its present situation.[9]

Chinnery was very active in artistic circles, and the artists of Dublin presented him with a silver palette in 1801. However, he left in 1802 for a long sojourn in India and Macao, where he is said to have gone to escape his wife.

Sketches thought to be done in Ireland exist, both portraits and landscapes, including figural doodles in brown pen and ink which show his reliance on Romney. There is a small landscape entitled *County Wicklow* and another, a watercolour of figures on the seashore (Victoria and Albert Museum), which is signed and dated 1801 and is clumsily handled in the Wheatley manner.[10] Chinnery was an artist of great versatility, though too little of his Irish *œuvre* has come to light.

An artist much influenced by him was John Comerford (c.1770–1832); his miniatures are clearly derived from Chinnery, whom he met in 1799. However, Comerford's rather rarely met small, whole-length watercolour portraits are much closer to Buck. An example is his study of *Richard Lovell Edgeworth* in the National Gallery of Ireland, where the face is finely painted but the clothes, boots and landscape are roughly handled.

Topographical painting, whether of ruins or gentlemen's seats, never ceased and had a new impetus in the early nineteenth century when it often shows a considerable social interest and merges with genre painting. Here, as will appear shortly, a new feature occasionally emerges, the intimate interior.

George Holmes (fl.1789–c.1843) was a pupil at the Dublin Society Schools, winning a medal for landscape in 1789. There is very little documentation on his life, though he is known to have gone to London in 1799, where he exhibited at the Royal Academy till 1802. The style of the Schools appears to be changing if Holmes represents it in the

1790s. However, it is very possible that he went to London in the early 1790s, as his signed view of *Rathfarnham Castle (Plate 162)* of 1794, one of a pair, and his undated but certainly early view of *Heywood* is very close in treatment, especially in genre elements such as people and horses, to the paintings of Peter La Cave, a Frenchman working in England and teaching there from at least 1789. The figures in both artists' work ultimately derive, of course, from Dutch masters such as Berchem, whom Holmes could certainly have seen in Ireland as well as in London. His two views of *Fisher Folk by the sea* of 1804 (British Museum) seem to recollect rather feebly Wheatley's similar subjects. Other Irish views such as *Swords Castle* are quite densely painted and show a good sense of colour. His *Kilkenny College from the rear of the Ormond Mill* brings out his ability to deal with water and receding space.

The next date in Holmes's development is *A View of Bristol*, dated 1809 (Bristol Art Gallery); this detailed pencil and chalk drawing contrasts with a far more atmospheric watercolour of Snowdon. The latter, which may be a much later work, shows the influence of John Varley. If this is so, the Holmes we are discussing may be identical with the George Holmes who sent pictures

to the Royal Hibernian Academy from Plymouth in 1841 and 1843. He did many views in Ireland, which were used in various engraved magazines and books varying from Ledwich's *Antiquities of Ireland*, 1790, to Brewer's *Beauties of Ireland*, 1825–6.

Holmes was a drawing master, as is proved by a watercolour sketch (Royal Society of Antiquaries of Ireland) annotated by James George Robertson,[11] who published *The Antiquities and Scenery of the County of Kilkenny* in 1851, with the words "this Sketch was made by George Holmes drawing master from whom William Robertson [the Kilkenny architect and friend of James George Robertson] received some Lessons in his early days." On stylistic grounds one can assume that Holmes also taught watercolour painting to Robert Gibbs, who collaborated with William Robertson on James George Robertson's book. From the watermarks on the paper of the series of drawings Gibbs made of country houses and castles mostly in Kilkenny, Tipperary and Waterford, they date between 1805 and 1809. These have considerable strength and brio, and one drawing of the ruined Clonamichan Castle, Co. Tipperary *(Plate 163)*, shows another, finely detailed side to his draughtsmanship. It is vertically hatched and this

162
GEORGE HOLMES
*Rathfarnham Castle,
Co. Dublin, 1794*

163
ROBERT GIBBS
*Clonamichan Castle,
Co. Tipperary*

163
ROBERT GIBBS
*Clonamichan Castle,
Co. Tipperary*

drawing of hoary antiquity nonetheless is enlivened by the smoke billowing from the cottage in the castle walls. Gibbs was listed as a portrait painter living in Cork in 1810, and a number of his oils survive. Otherwise no dates are known for him at all.

George Holmes was the friend and travelling companion of John Harden (1772–1847), a landed gentleman from Tipperary whose work is still comparatively unknown, as it has remained with his family and only been exhibited[12] and published[13] in the last few years. Harden was, according to family tradition, copying pictures in Dublin in 1794 and travelling round in a gig with friends, sketching from nature. He may have been a law student.

After a trip to England he returned and

164
JOHN HARDEN
*A Family Group, Charles
Lloyd Reading, 1804*
(*Scottish National
Portrait Gallery*)

went on a tour of south-western Ireland in August 1797 with Holmes and another friend, William Sinnett, and Harden's groom, Lyons. Both Holmes and Harden left an account of the trip; Holmes's was published in 1801 as *Sketches of Some of the Southern Counties of Ireland . . . in a series of letters* and some of his watercolours were reproduced in it, while Harden's much more intimate account was finally published in 1953.[14] Holmes praised Harden in 1797 "for his excellent taste . . . for landscape painting, which, as an amateur, I have seldom seen excelled."[15] Harden's Irish diary is full of social comment: he is horrified by the drunken behaviour of the Limerick Bucks and had a great eye for comely girls and a sentimental attitude to worthy peasants dancing, merry-making and flirting to the tune of pipes and fiddle. He had a typically romantic view of nature, extolling crumbling ruins, precipices, waterfalls, distant prospects and hanging woods. Except for some line drawings of antiquities that were done on this tour, no early work seems to have survived.

Nor does any work survive from a trip to England he made in 1799 with the portrait painter, William Cuming, later PRHA, with whom Harden stayed on one of his later visits to Dublin in 1844. In the same year he returned to Tipperary, where he stayed in a number of houses of former neighbours, such as Leap Castle, Sopwell Hall and Cangort Park. He was disturbed by a visit to his old home at Crea and bewailed his neglect of his property through absenteeism.

Our judgement of Harden as an artist depends on work done in England, where he settled after his second marriage in 1803 to the daughter of an Edinburgh banker. In 1804 they went to live in Brathay Hall in the Lake District, close to Wordsworth, whom he knew well. He is at his best as a painter of intimate interior scenes *(Plate 164)*, of his family reading, playing the piano, painting, sewing by candlelight or by the window. Occasionally luminaries appear by chance; for instance the young Constable is shown in a watercolour of 1806 seated in a group round a harpsichord, and there is another of him painting.[16] Harden's figures are extraordinarily well observed and anatomically much better than those of Holmes, whose figures are weak. The composition, the costume, the furniture of the sketches are also carefully thought out and painted with considerable detail and elegance. Most of the interior groups are in pen and ink, or pencil and wash, though some are in watercolour, which he started using out-of-doors in 1803. His landscapes, though very competent, are not so appealing as his figure groups, which reflect his own lively social interests. The two drawings of his family with Tennyson and Hallam *(Plate 165)*, drawn on board ship

165
JOHN HARDEN
On board SS Leeds, 1830, the artist's family with Hallam and Tennyson
(Trinity College, Cambridge)

going from Bordeaux to Dublin in 1830, are charming informal scenes showing them all sitting reading and the future Poet Laureate sprawled on the deck.

The landscapes made on a trip to Ireland in 1812 include one of the upper end of Dawson Street, which shows the demarcation of light and shade in very simplified planes. This quality appears in his best landscape drawings and suggests a close study of classical landscape painters such as Poussin. He is much less interested in atmosphere.

The English painter, Thomas Uwins, writing from Naples in 1830 to Joseph Severn, said, "What a shoal of amateur artists we have got here . . . I am old enough to remember when Mr Swinburne and Sir George Beaumont were the only gentlemen who condescended to take brush in hand, but now gentleman painters rise up at every step and go nigh to push us off our stools. Here my old friend Harden of Brathay, whose good taste and genuine feeling enables him to do beautiful things without parade or pretension."[17] This seems a fitting epitaph for a remarkable amateur.

A professional painter, Thomas Cooley (1795–1873), the deaf and dumb grandson of the well-known Irish architect of the same name, produced some interesting watercolours, though he worked mainly in oils. Two charming pencil and ink studies of a couple playing chess link with an oil of three men by a chess board, but are much superior to this pedestrian painting. Other drawings include portraits of artists such as Sir John Soane and John Flaxman, Turner and Fuseli, and there is a sentimental family group, signed and dated 1848. Most important, however, is *Mr Cooley's Terms (Plate 166)*, an instructive pen and ink drawing showing three portraits of varying size with their prices and sensibly stating, as he was dumb,"half the money to be Paid on the First Sitting."

The only other artist of this period to specialize in painting domestic scenes in watercolour is, like Harden, another amateur, Caroline Hamilton (1777–1861). She was the daughter of William Tighe of Rossana, Co. Wicklow, cousin and sister-in-law of Mary ("Psyche") Tighe and cousin and beneficiary of the last of the "two ladies of Llangollen," Sarah Ponsonby. Caroline Tighe married Charles Hamilton of Hamwood in 1801; all her drawings are still in private ownership.

In 1795 Caroline's mother brought her family back to Rossana after an Italian sojourn and paid John Inigo Spilsbury,[18] who had been art master at Harrow, three hundred pounds a year to teach drawing to her daughters, Caroline and Elizabeth. John Spilsbury was a fine draughtsman, as can be seen in his portrait drawing of Mrs Tighe and the young Caroline.[19] This drawing used to be attributed to Maria Spilsbury, his niece, who later became Mrs John Taylor and came to live in Ireland about 1809. This is too late for her to have done this group, as, from the costume, it dates not much later than 1795. Caroline must later have employed Maria Taylor, who painted several pictures of the Hamiltons and Tighes. She criticized Maria in her diary:

> . . . for when she attempted to paint the passions she failed. . . I chose Mr Hogarth for my model after Mr Spilsbury had left us. Sometimes delighted with the effect of light and shade by candlelight I attempted it, and sometimes observing in company that muscles of the face were set in motion by such and such feelings, I came to express them, by recourse occasionally to Le Bruns *Passions* to convince me that I was right.[20]

It is interesting that amateurs should be so determined to improve that they consulted Charles Le Brun, whose frequently reprinted engravings were a well-known source for the period.

Caroline Hamilton seems to have had two distinct styles: one uses a rather tentative outline, such as her sketch of Betty Phillips, the laundry maid at Hamwood; the other, which is more commonly met, uses *chiaroscuro* washes and simplified outlines. She was a remarkably astute political observer as well as a witty commentator on the ironies of everyday life. In a drawing such as her masterpiece, *Domestic Happiness as acted in this city, a tragi-comic farce (Plate 167)* she shows the results of luxury and vanity beggaring an Irish landlord family. The father and children are being starved, for they are being handed a bone on a plate by a liveried servant while the mother, preening herself at a mirror, has her enormous skirt enveloping pies, chicken and claret which are being sniffed by a cadaverous dog! The father's rent roll is on a chair to the left, the money presumably dwindling due to his wife's excesses.

The Methodist influence of Caroline's mother and her own evangelical leanings distanced her from the usual attitudes of the Irish "Ascendancy." In her memoirs, which came out in a privately printed pamphlet in 1851,[21] she talks of the worldly and corrupting set she lived in as a girl in Dublin up to the 1798 rebellion: "They seemed to have very little or no religion, and very little happiness in domestic life, bad husbands and still more extravagant wives, all wildly in pursuit of pleasure!"[22] Her drawings of the 1798 uprising *(Plate 168)* are telling recollections of the fear which filled the drawing rooms of the time and the claret in which the officers indulged. After the Act of Union she shows the other side of the coin in *Society, 1801,*[23] which portrays the *ennui* that set in after the dissolution of Dublin's Parliament. She could be simply comic as in *The*

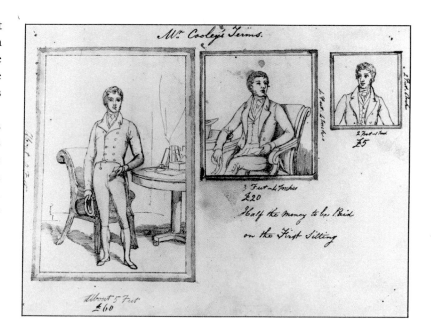

Kingstown to Holyhead Packet,[24] where she depicts an unfortunate horse being winched on to the boat.

Caroline Hamilton's sister, Elizabeth, who later married the Revd Thomas Kelly of Kellyville, Queen's County (Co. Laois), was herself an amateur artist, though not in any

166
THOMAS COOLEY
Mr Cooley's Terms (NGI)

167
CAROLINE HAMILTON
"Domestic Happiness as acted in this city, a tragi-comic farce"

168

CAROLINE HAMILTON
A scene during the 1798 uprising

way as interesting as her sister. One of her sketchbooks recently on the Dublin art market bore a trade card from Allen and Sons[25] of Dame Street, who ran a circulating subscription collection of drawings and prints for "the attention of the artist and Amateur." This was a popular method of learning at this time. Allen offered over a thousand drawings and prints of "Flowers, Fruit, Shells, Landscapes, Figures, and Historical Subjects," and also published little booklets for copying, such as *A new Book of Landskips proper for Youth to draw after (Plate 169)*. They also dealt in artist's materials. Their principal publication was *The Student's Treasure, a new drawing book consisting of a variety of Etchings and Engravings executed by Irish*

Artists after the following great masters (Plate 170), 1804 (first published 1799). The masters included "Cipriani, Bartolozzi, Wheatley, Angelica (Kauffmann) Vivares, West, Bernard, Rowlandson, Stubbs, Zucchi, Mortimer, Howitt, Gilray, Buck, Gainsborough."

Maria Spilsbury was the daughter of Jonathan Spilsbury, the engraver and brother of the John Spilsbury who taught Caroline Hamilton. She had a successful English career, her works even being bought by the Prince Regent. She is described as having "sprightly intelligence, variety of natural expression and line."[26] As we have seen, Caroline Hamilton criticized her attitude to painting. She may have been in Ireland earlier than the date usually given, which is

169

Landscape illustrating Allen's textbook on "Landskip" painting

1809, when she married John Taylor and is known to have been resident in Dublin. Her oils of Caroline's brother's family at Rosanna must, from the age of the children, date from about 1810. Only one drawing certainly by her is known, a view of the interior of the school *(Plate 171)* run by John Synge of Glanmore Castle, whose portrait in his study she also painted. This charity school at nearby Roundwood was where he attempted to teach by the Pestalozzian system indicated by the tables used in the drawing. The forms on the blackboards relate to Synge's book on education, *Relation and Description of Forms.*[27] The drawing is a charming and professional study, and all her oils also show her competence as a draughtswoman.

The two Grattan brothers, George (1787–1819), and William (c.1792–c.1821), were both pupils of the Schools and worked in the genre tradition with considerable skill. Their watercolours are remarkably similar, though George was the more famous in his day because of his oils.

George's watercolours vary from sentimental scenes and an occasional portrait to a topographical view of Christchurch Cathedral *(Plate 172)* which picturesquely shows the shambolic state of Dublin even in those days. Two works in the National Gallery of

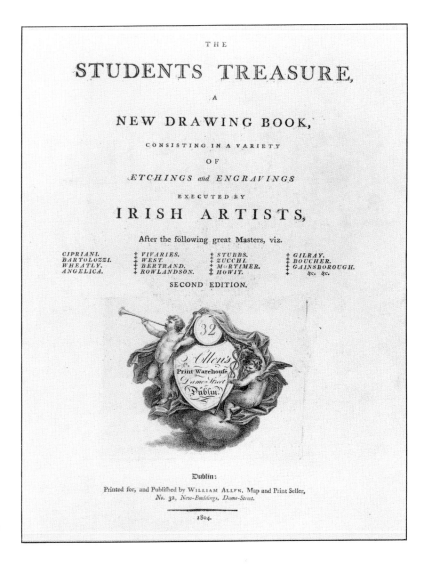

THE

STUDENTS TREASURE,

A

NEW DRAWING BOOK,

CONSISTING IN A VARIETY

OF

ETCHINGS and ENGRAVINGS

EXECUTED BY

IRISH ARTISTS,

After the following great Masters, viz.

CIPRIANI.	‡ *VIVARIES.*	‡ *STUBBS.*	‡ *GILRAY.*
BARTOLOZZI.	‡ *WEST.*	‡ *ZUCCHI.*	‡ *BOUCHER.*
WHEATLY.	‡ *BERTRAND.*	‡ *MORTIMER.*	‡ *GAINSBOROUGH.*
ANGELICA.	‡ *ROWLANDSON.*	‡ *HOWIT.*	&c. &c.

SECOND EDITION.

Dublin:

Printed for, and Published by WILLIAM ALLEN, Map and Print Seller,
No. 32, New-Buildings, Dame-Street.

1804.

170
Title page of Allen's
The Student's Treasure,
1804

170
Title page of Allen's
The Student's Treasure,
1804

171
MARIA TAYLOR
*The Synge School at
Roundwood*

172
GEORGE GRATTAN
Christchurch Cathedral,
Dublin
(Victoria and Albert
Museum

Ireland depict a country dance in the Morland manner, and *A Pilgrim kneeling in front of a crucifix and a pile of bones* in the Salvator Rosa style. Although the pilgrim has a shell badge on his hat, he is in contemporary dress. Grattan appears to be the first artist we have come across who records Catholic, peasant Ireland. Strangely, he uses very hot colouring for these drawings, which are orange in tone.

His brother William's watercolour of a labourer *(Plate 173)* leaning on his fork by a wheelbarrow is a splendidly realistic study of the reach-me-down clothes of an ordinary countryman. William wrote a pamphlet in 1818 bewailing the lack of patronage in Ireland, saying that the "painters of this country. . . are obliged to desert the higher walks of the profession for whatever employment

in the arts the fleeting taste of the moment may offer."[28] This was a familiar enough *cri de cœur.*

A fashionable miniaturist, Sampson Towgood Roch (1759–1847), was the unlikely creator of a number of drawings as evocative of ordinary Irish people as William Grattan's gardener. Roch was the deaf and dumb son of a landed family in Co. Waterford and, though he spent much of his career in London and Bath, he was trained in Ireland and returned there finally in 1822, after the death of his wife living with his family at Woodbine Hill, Co. Waterford. Apart from a work such as his highly finished *Rustics dancing outside an Inn (Plate 174),* which is in a miniaturist technique and utterly idealized, he made quite contrasting pencil sketches, one album of which shows scenes of rural life taken in and about Youghal and Waterford (Ulster Folk Museum).[29] These are rare survivors and are very accurate representations of huxters of every sort of goods from fish, turf *(Plate 175)*, shoelaces and seaweed as well as wool gatherers and other country folk. There are also portrayals of a butterman in his cart who sold milk or buttermilk and of a ferry boat which linked the banks of the Blackwater and the counties of Cork and Waterford. Their expressions are realistically humorous and hard-worn, and their clothing is an important record of rural life at the time.

We find ourselves now in confused territory as we discuss one of the most famous Irish dynasties of artists. We have tentatively tried to disentangle the Brocas family by studying the large collection of sketchbooks and drawings in the National Library of Ireland and the holdings in the National Gallery of Ireland.

The father, Henry Brocas (1762–1837), had two styles. The first was for his caricatures and political sketches which he intended for engraving. The finished watercolour drawing for his only signed caricature drawing, showing the interior of a barber's shop, does not use exaggerations. It was probably done in the 1790s and reminds us of John Boyne (see Chapter 5). It is squared for transfer, though no engraving for it is

173
WILLIAM GRATTAN
A Labourer

174

SAMPSON TOWGOOD
ROCH
*Rustics dancing outside
an Inn*
(Ulster Museum)

known. It is highly amusing, executed with a sharp pen outline and coloured wash. A number of other sketches for caricatures are connected with the Act of Union of 1801, such as a lively sketch which shows a group of carousing diners, bumpers in hand while in a plaque Hibernia hides her face in shame. There are sketches of rustic figures all

175

SAMPSON TOWGOOD
ROCH
*Women carrying Fish
and Turf*
*(Ulster Folk and
Transport Museum)*

showing Brocas's great sense of character and lively drawing.

The second style is for his landscapes, which include rather dull, softly pencilled, rustic views of which a number in the National Library of Ireland are signed and the watercolour examples tend to be in rather dark monochrome. His *Cattle Grazing Beneath Trees* (National Gallery of Ireland) is a more detailed study of foliage with two poorly drawn cattle, while another of *Cattle and Sheep* is a rather feeble effort in the style of Thomas Sydney Cooper. As the National Gallery examples are not signed, it is possible that the identifications are confused. A number of the Gallery's watercolours are of seascapes and coastal scenes. The view of *Carlingford Castle (Plate 176)* is the finest of these and is perhaps early, as it shows the influence of Thomas Sautell Roberts's exhibition of 1801. The later views are more boldly painted with big washes and could well be mistaken for English work. None of these seems to have been engraved, but his small-scale landscape draw-

ings must have had a considerable influence on Petrie.

Henry Brocas's group of watercolours in the National Gallery of Ireland, though not signed, all came associated with his name from the National Museum and ultimately from the Royal Dublin Society. According to Strickland, he was self-taught, and no doubt this explains how un-Irish his watercolours look, having no links with the long-established tradition of the Dublin Society Schools. They are more likely to be based on a study of engravings after English masters. A small sketchbook done early in his career (National Library of Ireland) shows him copying rococo portrait groups in the manner of Henry Brooke (see Chapter 4). A drawing after the English drawing master, William Payne, dated 1796 is in the Library. This English orientation may also explain why it was under Brocas's Mastership of the Landscape and Ornament School, 1800–1837, in the Dublin Society Schools that so many English watercolours by such masters as Peter de Wint, John Varley and

176
HENRY BROCAS, SENIOR
Carlingford Castle, Co. Louth
(National Gallery of Ireland)

139

177
JAMES HENRY BROCAS
*The Moss House on the
Dargle, Co. Wicklow*
*(National Library of
Ireland)*

other artists' work. These range from portraits by Hugh Douglas Hamilton to small topographical views by Lt. R. Smith of the 44th regiment (see Chapter 9).

As well as drawings, the elder Henry Brocas exhibited a number of oil paintings at exhibitions in Dublin from 1800 to 1812, and the problems of his career as Master of the Landscape and Ornament School of the Royal Dublin Society are well documented by John Turpin. Henry Brocas had four painter sons — James Henry, Samuel Frederick, William, and Henry — who unlike their father, fit well into the Irish tradition, though they all studied under him.

James Henry Brocas (c.1790–1846), Henry's eldest son, is a more delicate hand. A drawing signed *JH* in monogram, of Ballynure, Co. Wicklow, 1834, suggests that some sketches, including some of the Dargle, are also by him. Particularly charming examples are of the Moss House overlooking the Dargle *(Plate 177)* and of Tinnehinch, Henry Grattan's house nearby. Strickland describes Brocas as an animal painter who exhibited portraits of cattle and horses in Dublin exhibitions between 1801 and 1816. Presumably, some of the watercolours and drawings of cows and other animals which occur in some of the numerous multi-Brocas sketchbooks and folders in the National Library of Ireland are by him, though others are by his brother William, as proved by a comparison with work in signed sketchbooks by William. Some odd little sketches of individual figures, one of which occurs in a sketchbook signed by James Henry, indicate that he is the author of an awkward though interesting drawing of exhibition visitors to the Dublin Society Rooms in Hawkins Street. In 1834, James Henry settled in Cork, where he lived till his death.

The style of Samuel Frederick Brocas (c.1792–1847) is clear; he is a straightforward topographical artist with a keen interest in urban architecture, as seen in his magnificent *West Front of Trinity College* in the National Gallery of Ireland. This is a signed work, dated 1818, and has almost the quality of a Malton, with its delicately handled figures, perspective and effects of light. He, too, employed engravers, often his brother Henry. He worked in both pencil and watercolour and made a set of views of Dublin in

many others were purchased. This creates a break in the style. As Turpin[30] says, "The Society was anxious to obtain the best examples of up-to-date British watercolour drawing." Brocas occasionally used pen and ink for large sketches using a rather flamboyant cursive line. One of these, in the National Library of Ireland, is signed.

There are a few, somewhat sentimental religious drawings which we also think are by the elder Henry Brocas and some copies, including one after a Nathaniel Grogan, of the church at Glanmire. The religious drawings are done with some care and they would appear to be intended for engraving also, though no record of his engravings of this type survives. We speculate that he may have considered painting altarpieces for the new Roman Catholic churches.

He also drew small portraits, again mostly for engravings for books. A scrapbook in the Library, prepared by his son William, includes many engravings by Henry after

1818. His small-scale drawings are in some ways finer than his large watercolours, as on a big scale he can be stilted. Some drawings of boats in the National Library of Ireland seem to be by him. He exhibited water-colours of North Wales in 1828 in the Royal Hibernian Academy, and he painted the usual picturesque Irish subjects like Killarney and the Dargle Glen. A drawing of Limerick in the National Gallery of Ireland has been wrongly ascribed to James Henry; it is certainly by Samuel Frederick, as it closely relates to a very fine watercolour of the courthouse and St. Mary's Cathedral (Plate 178) executed in pen, grey ink and heightened watercolour, signed and dated 1819, which was recently on the London art market. We illustrate another, smaller and less well-known view of the *Bishop's Palace and Assembly Rooms in Waterford* of about 1812 (Plate 179), as it has a contemporary playbill pasted on the back. A charming

178
SAMUEL FREDERICK
BROCAS
View of Limerick, 1819

179
SAMUEL FREDERICK
BROCAS
Bishop's Palace and Assembly Rooms in Waterford, c.1812

141

180
SAMUEL FREDERICK
BROCAS
*Ballyowen Castle,
Co. Dublin*

181
WILLIAM BROCAS
*A Boy in the Deanery
Garden of St. Patrick's
Cathedral, Dublin,
1836*

watercolour, attributed to Samuel Frederick and almost certainly by him, is of Ballyowen Castle near Lucan *(Plate 180)* and is an excellent example of his rural manner. It shows the family arriving on a sidecar and a horse saddled by the front door. Even though the figures in his many works are naïve and essentially urban, they do show a fascination with people, uniforms, carriages and horses. In another attributed work, *Visitors viewing the Waterfall at Powerscourt*, one sees these Dublin tourists looking out of place in the picturesque surroundings.

William Brocas (c.1794–1868) is the most notable of the brothers. One of his surviving sketchbooks was done when he was staying with his patron, Henry Westenra, MP, later third Lord Rossmore, who lived at the Dell near Windsor; several of the views include Windsor castle. He painted a set of portraits[31] in oils of the Westenra family, now hanging in Florencecourt, Co. Fermanagh. An interesting drawing in this sketchbook shows a study for a whole-length of a Mr and Mrs James, dated 27th August 1838. Mrs James was later the notorious Lola Montez. The sketchbooks, of which there are a number in the National Library of Ireland, also include studies of horses, cavalrymen and dogs, at which he was very good, and genre studies of country people.

Depicting strong farmers with their slipes, donkeys, fishermen, and children begging, these are Morland-like genre scenes. *A Gamekeeper at Desart Court* is dated 1832 and reminds us of Edward Hayes, as does *Mr Galt on Horseback with his Dog* (both National Library of Ireland). Mr Galt was land steward to the Fortescue estate in Co. Louth. There are also several sketches of a fair, probably Donnybrook Fair.

In addition, he exhibited oil paintings of Irish emigrants, though we have not found drawings relating to the subject. William drew small portraits like the one of the Revd Thomas Betagh, a Jesuit priest (National Gallery of Ireland), which was travestied in its engraved form. However, a good engraving after a drawing is of the famous Gothic novelist and playwright, the Revd Charles Robert Maturin. He had a line in fashionable watercolour portraits such as his *Boy in the Deanery Garden of St. Patrick's Cathedral* (Plate 181), which exists in two versions; one signed by him and dated 12th July 1836 gives his address as No.119 Baggot Street. They have the greatest charm and some of the qualities of miniature paintings.

Landscapes showing rustic scenes and fishing boats, both in the National Gallery of Ireland and the National Library of Ireland, are indistinguishable from his father Henry's work, while his view of the Bank of Ireland is virtually identical with Samuel Frederick's engraving of the same subject. This does indicate how inextricably intertwined the family's work is. More interesting are some sketches and watercolours of Antwerp and Rouen indicating that he travelled; one is dated 1840. There are copies after Van Dyck and other old masters.

The youngest son, Henry Brocas (c.1798–1873), would seem to have worked more as an engraver and, in fact, as already mentioned, engraved Samuel Frederick's Dublin views. Strickland says he painted landscapes in watercolour and exhibited a few in the Royal Hibernian Academy between 1828 and 1872, but most of his work was in oils. There is a charming watercolour by him of the celebrations to mark the visit to Crom Castle of the Viceroy, Lord Clarendon, in 1850 *(Plate 182)*; in the National Library of Ireland there are studies for the party and regatta on Lough Erne which took place for this event. Henry Brocas may well have done a somewhat similar work celebrating the coming of age of Catherine Isabella Osborne, the heiress of Newtown Anner, in 1840. The little figures dressed in white, dancing round a pole at Newtown Anner are full of life and movement. This work has been attributed to Catherine Osborne's daughter Grace, Duchess of St. Albans[32] because she inscribed the label, but she cannot possibly have painted it datewise. These multi-figured compositions are handled with great clarity and ease.

182
HENRY BROCAS, JUNIOR
Lord Clarendon's visit to Crom Castle, Co. Fermanagh, 1850

Henry Brocas Junior succeeded his father as Master of the Landscape and Ornament School in the Royal Dublin Society in 1838, retiring in 1854. Strickland, who must have known him, says he was not successful as a teacher because he didn't have his father's energy and ability. As an additional confusion, Henry, like his father, and indeed his brother William, did caricatures which were engraved by McCleary of Nassau Street, who also published a set of Samuel Frederick's Dublin views without his name and with some very slight alterations. A large corpus of Brocas material has recently been found in the National Library and deserves far greater attention than we have been able to give it.

A contemporary painter of town views is Edward Cashin (fl.1823–26), by whom some forty drawings of the main public buildings and streets of Bristol are held in the Bristol Museum and Art Gallery (Plate 183). George Cumberland mentioned him in 1826 as an Irishman "who will come on in

art."[33] He shows both the influence of Malton and, more immediately, Samuel Frederick Brocas, in his architectural handling. We can only assume that he had had some training in the Dublin Society Schools.

Though pure architectural drawings are not touched on in this book, many architects drew and painted outside their professional work, and we have already mentioned the Pain brothers in Chapter 6. For instance, the Englishman Francis Goodwin (1784–1835), the architect of the severely Grecian Lissadell, Co. Sligo, painted a charming watercolour of the old eighteenth-century Gothic gardener's house[34] there in 1834 (Plate 184). His plate of his own design for the grand Gothic gates at Markree,[35] not far away, also shows how ably architects of this period were able to integrate their work into a dramatic, landscape setting.

William Vitruvius Morrison (1794–1838), Goodwin's Irish contemporary, was equally talented in sketching his houses in their surroundings. An excellent example is the finely hatched ink drawing of Shelton Abbey, Co. Wicklow (Plate 185), the seat of Lord Wicklow. Henry Hill (fl.1830–40), the Cork architect, even supplied some illustrations for Hall's Ireland, and his sketchbooks, though obviously centred on architectural subjects, show how able a watercolourist he was. For instance, his view of the main street in Youghal with the Clock Tower is boldly and broadly treated. A single work by William Welland (fl.1843–69), who was one of a family of Dublin architects, survives: a precise drawing of Cahir castle and the bridge over the Suir. It is dated 1843 and is a typical example of the carefully competent architect's studies of the Victorian period.

Sandham Symes (d.1894) is naïve in comparison but his little watercolours of Irish buildings, both vernacular and otherwise, have considerable charm, as witnessed by his Ballybrittain Castle, Co. Offaly, 1837 (Plate 186), which shows the archetypal cluster of ruined tower, farmhouse and offices. He also records such events as a balloon ascent in 1848, in the Rotunda Gardens.

Probably the finest watercolourist/architect working in this tradition is the Englishman, William Joseph Booth (c.1795/6–1871) who was surveyor and architect for the Drapers' Company between 1822 and

1854 and designed many of the buildings on their estates in Ulster. He had been at the Royal Academy Schools and travelled in Italy and Greece. Many of his designs in Moneymore and Draperstown were executed, and his superb series of watercolours of these towns, their buildings and the surrounding landscapes, often taken before his own work had been constructed, are among the most memorable social documents of rural Ireland[36]. The drawings are in the Draper's Company.

Thomas Manly Deane (1851–1933), a member of the famous Cork family of architects, was another practitioner later in the century. A number of drawings and

184
FRANCIS GOODWIN
*Gothic Gardener's House,
Lissadell, Co. Sligo, 1834*

185
WILLIAM VITRUVIUS
MORRISON
*Shelton Abbey,
Co. Wicklow*

sketchbooks by him are in the National Gallery of Ireland and show enormously varied subjects, from architectural detailing to a lady playing tennis or studies of sculpture and flowers in Italy. There is a particularly charming sketch of a man driving a cart as well as straightforward landscape views.

A fascinating sideline on architectural practice is a watercolour by the landscape artist, George Miller (fl.1815–19), probably an Englishman, mentioned by Strickland as living in Kilkenny in 1815–19, who was a pupil of Barker of Bath. This is a staffage surround with the centre left empty, clearly for an architect's ideal view, and such a one exists in a watercolour inscribed obviously much later by the architect James George Robertson (1816–99), of *Shankhill Castle, Co. Kilkenny (Plate 187)*, which has a nearly identical staffage surround clearly by Miller.

This type of short cut must have been a convenient aid but it is rare to find such a good example. One of Miller's watercolours, in an entirely different vein, is his *Interior of St. Patrick's Cathedral* (National Gallery of Ireland), which shows him handling

186
SANDHAM SYMES
*Ballybrittain Castle,
Co. Offaly, 1837*

187
GEORGE MILLER *and*
J.G. ROBERTSON
Shankhill Castle,
Co. Kilkenny

architecture very competently. His water-colour of the Cottage Orné at Kilfane, Co. Kilkenny *(Plate 188)*, was invaluable for the recent reconstruction of this building in its picturesque site.

An artist whose work connects with the Brocases is the itinerant artist William Turner de Lond (fl.1767–1826), presumably so named in order to avoid confusion with William Turner of Oxford and, perhaps presumptuously, with the great Turner himself. Very little is known of him except his visits to Ireland and later to Scotland, where he settled in Edinburgh for some years. He

exhibited twenty-four paintings in Limerick in 1821, including the large oil of *The Entry of George IV into Dublin* (National Gallery of Ireland), 1821, and various paintings done in Limerick and Killarney.[37] The catalogue does not mention mediums so that we cannot be certain whether watercolours were shown, but it seems likely, as amateur work was included.

This exhibition attempted to wake up the commercial burghers of Limerick to the importance of the fine arts and to the fact that there was no school of art in the city. The introduction regarded the exhibition as a "touchstone for public feeling"[38] and therefore an encouragement for Limerick civic pride. The exhibition also included works by one of the Brocases, J.S. Alpenny, St. John Long, Sadler and a number of English painters including Sandby and Wilson.

From this catalogue we gather that Turner de Lond travelled extensively in Italy, as he includes views of Calabrian scenery, Tivioli and Rome, and in Tuscany near Florence. Some of these may well have been watercolours. He was also in Paris where he painted a portrait of Bonaparte against a background of the Tuileries gardens and Les Invalides; the entry states "the scenery sketched on the spot, by Mr Turner." There was a pair to this of the Duke of

188
GEORGE MILLER
The Cottage Orné at
Kilfane, Co. Kilkenny
(Royal Society of
Antiquaries of Ireland)

Wellington in St. Paul's Cathedral. Gouaches are beginning to surface; one, of Cahirconlish House in Co. Limerick, the seat of the Wilson family, was signed and dated 1821, and on stylistic grounds a pair of Limerick city views can also be attributed to Turner. One, showing St. Mary's Cathedral, the Courthouse and Quays on the Shannon, is now in the Limerick Museum, though in a faded state. Its pair, however, showing a carriage in Bank Place with St. Mary's Cathedral and the courthouse in the background *(Plate 189)*, survives in an excellent condition. Sometime ago we attributed it incorrectly[39] to Samuel Frederick Brocas, who was painting in Limerick at much the same time. In fact, it is less dry than Brocas and the gouache technique is very freely handled. Other paintings exhibited in Limerick by Turner were religious subjects.

James Hore (fl. 1829–37), is best known for his topographical oils of Dublin. He was an amateur who came from a Wexford gentry family, the Hores of Harperstown and Seafield.[40] No reference book gives his dates but he is first heard of in 1829 on a Grand Tour of Italy, where he was painting a watercolour of the Piazza del Popolo in Rome in a highly theatrical manner. A drawing inscribed "View of the Protestant Burying ground at Rome drawn by James Hore Esq" is done with a thick, soft pencil and surely executed. The inscription continues, "The tomb most marked in the drawing is that of Ly Charlotte Stopford who died at Rome 29th Feb[y] 1828 – to be given to James Earl of Courtown or his son." Lady Stopford was a daughter of the fourth Duke of Buccleuch and the wife of James, Viscount Stopford, later fourth Earl of Courtown and a cousin of the artist. Another drawing of the Arch of Constantine and the Coliseum is in very much the same manner. As these show, Hore was particularly interested in architecture, but one landscape has been recorded, a view of the Gondo tunnel on the Simplon

189
WILLIAM TURNER
DE LOND
Courthouse and Quays,
Limerick

190
JAMES HORE
The Gondo Tunnel

191
WILLIAM ROE
Clondalkin Tower,
Co. Dublin

(National Library of
Ireland)

Pass *(Plate 190)*, which shows echoes of Francis Towne's magnificent alpine watercolours of 1781. Hore's work must date from his journey to or from Rome in 1829 and the rocky, glacial appearance of the scenery is idealized, as contemporary lithographs record stunted trees.[41]

As we can see, genre and landscape watercolours were commonplace at this time, partly because of the proliferation of the Irish bourgeoisie. Dublin was, since the Act of Union, mainly a city full of doctors, lawyers and civil servants. The walls of their town houses and country villas were profusely decorated with miniatures, drawings and watercolours of family interest and landscapes by both professional artists and family amateurs. Comparatively few members of the aristocracy or Members of Parliament now had a Dublin house. The taste of the early Victorian interior was for elaborate clutter, and even the country houses of the nobility and more important gentry, where there were often collections of great works of art, were engulfed with decorative minutiae. The surround of every chimneypiece was profusely hung with silhouettes, drawings and miniatures producing a rich effect.

A man whose work would have ideally adorned the drawing rooms of the period was William Roe (fl.1822–c.52), who was a very delicate draughtsman trained at the Dublin Society Schools, where he obtained several prizes between 1822 and 1827. His work looks as though intended for engraving, though no engravings of it have been recorded. He also spent a short time in London. His earliest exhibited works at the Royal Hibernian Academy in 1826 were watercolour portraits, though later he concentrated on landscapes. His view of the road near Clondalkin Round Tower *(Plate 191)* shows his very finished style, and his freer studies are well represented by a delightful drawing showing the Wooden Swannery on a little tree-begirt island in the Lake at Marino, Lord Charlemont's landscape park near Dublin. The great first Earl had taken much trouble in obtaining the swans from William Brownlow of Lurgan in the 1780s.[42]

Roe exhibited at the Royal Hibernian Academy between 1826 and 1847 but he moved to Cork about 1835 and exhibited at the first Cork Art Union exhibition, in 1841, watercolour genre scenes of Irish peasantry. His series of pencil drawings of Cork and its environs dated from 1837–9.[43] In the 1842 Art Union exhibition, Roe was represented by two watercolours, *Kerry Peasantry, Killarney* and *Irish Peasant Emigrants Bound for America*, both described by the (Cork) *Examiner's* correspondent as "so Irish, so true, so natural even if perhaps a little inclined towards caricature."[44] About the emigrants the correspondent goes to town, but this criticism is important both as a social document predating the Famine and as a description of a type of watercolour by Roe of which we have no knowledge. It continues:

> While we admire the humour and power of the other, the *Emigrants*, we cannot but regret that it is too true, too frequently seen. The locale of the picture is in the New-street, . . . and the group consists of a number of comfortable, well-clad peasants – men, women and children – the *Banithee* and her decent partner, – the *Colleen Dhas* and the *Bouchall Oge* – and the little, sturdy, plump, cake-munching *gossoon*. Their worldly goods are heaped on two cars, which are tilted on their shafts – the horses standing free. Two majestic, long-snouted,

huge-eared Porkers would suggest the idea that the emigrants were about bearing to another land the *Lares* of their abandoned home, the most prominent figure in the group is that of a well-limbed, clean-ankled, brown-necked *Bouchal, dressed to the life, standing to the life, and holding his kippeen* to the life. He is the very *beau ideal* of Irish ease and Irish bashfulness – a junction most paradoxical, but true – the one natural – the other accidental, and easily accounted for by the presence of a rosy, roguish, bright-eyed damsel, whose eloquent smile speaks volumes for her admiration of Paddy's proportions and elegance . . .[45]

Watercolours of Blarney and the Old Mill, Blackpool, dating 1844, show William Roe's watercolour technique to have been considerably inferior to his delicate pencilling. Though he was included in the Cork exhibition of 1852, this may have been posthumously.

192
JOSEPH ALPENNY
Portrait of Edward Hayes, 1812
(National Gallery of Ireland)

193
EDWARD HAYES
The Greenhouse at
Newtown Anner,
Co. Tipperary, 1818

Edward Hayes (1797–1864), a Tipperary man, was one of the best practitioners of the decorative small picture. He was taught at the Dublin Society Schools and by Joseph Alpenny or Halfpenny (1787–1858), whom

194 *EDWARD HAYES Self Portrait*

we include here. Alpenny is said by Strickland to have been Irish and seems to have gone to England as a young man. He was in the Royal Academy schools from 1805 to 1808, but he was in Ireland by 1810 and exhibiting prolifically in Dublin, from 1812 to the early 1820s,[46] drawings and watercolours, portraits, landscapes, religious, literary, Irish historical and military subjects. The latter are still unusual at this date. He returned to London about 1825 where he published *A New Drawing Book of Rustic Figures* in that year. One of his only surviving watercolours is his particularly charming study of the young Edward Hayes, dated 1812 *(Plate 192)*. A number of pencil studies survive, done by Hayes after Alpenny and dating from 1814, one of which is inscribed by Hayes "pupil to J.S. Alpenny."[47] Neat and of merely decorative interest, they show castles and landscapes probably in the Tipperary area where Alpenny was also working. In 1813, he exhibited in Clonmel. An 1818 drawing by Hayes of the greenhouse at Newtown Anner, also in Co. Tipperary *(Plate 193)* is very finely delineated and shows considerable improvement.

These early works do not herald his romantic later style or his brilliant fashionable figure groups. These are often of children, like the young Talbots,[48] or fashionable ladies, but a volume of portraits of young officers or members of a club in the library at Longleat show some telling character studies, such as one of Lord Mount Charles and a self-portrait of the artist painting *(Plate 194)*.

Another, less known aspect of Hayes's work is his landscapes; many of these are merely good examples of contemporary topography, but some have an obsessive vortex-like composition, such as his cobwebby study of a woodland stream *(Plate 195)* and his similar background to *The Babes in the Wood*.[49] This particular treatment is almost Pre-Raphaelite and probably represents his late style. He was a teacher and a miniature painter and also painted the occasional oil.

Edward Hayes was the father and teacher of Michael Angelo Hayes (1820–77), who achieved great success as a watercolourist and oil painter of military and sporting subjects, horses and animals. These included parades such as the fine *St. Patrick's Day at*

Dublin Castle of 1864 (Cavalry and Guards Club, London). He painted a few landscapes but no portrait groups. His watercolours were sometimes on the grand scale, such as his well-known *16th Lancers breaking the Square at Aliwal (Plate 196)* dated 1846, which was exhibited at the London New Watercolour Society in 1852 and for which he charged the enormous sum of three hundred pounds. A detailed account of the battle and the personalites shown was given in the catalogue. In an earlier exhibition, 1849, he had shown his *Third Light Dragoons at the Battle of Moodkee* and, in 1855, *Heavy Cavalry Charge at Balaclava*, which are also fully described in the catalogues.

These military triumphs where the horses are so superbly orchestrated depend on his theoretical studies of the horse in motion. In 1876 he delivered his paper on *The Delineation of Animals in Rapid Motion*,[50] in which he appears to reach the same conclusions as Muybridge, Marley and other photographers did a little later in rejecting the flying gallop. He had used this in his earlier work, but avoids it in the major watercolours. His set of aquatints of *Car Driving in the South of Ireland*, which do include the flying gallop, are dated as early as 1836. They were extremely popular, were often reprinted and clearly made his name. A fine view of Sackville Street *(Plate 197)* is dated 1858 and shows "the Palatial Mart of the Messrs McSwiney and Co," the shop of his brother-in-law. From exhibition catalogues it is clear that he painted quite a number of ordinary landscapes and townscapes.

To Michael Angelo Hayes may be attributed an enormous watercolour, at least 2.5 metres (eight feet) high, of the interior of St. Patrick's Cathedral, in the Deanery at the cathedral. It shows a christening

195
EDWARD HAYES
A Woodland Stream

196
MICHAEL ANGELO
HAYES
*Lancers breaking the
Square at Aliwal, 1846*

party[51] and is an impressive work, dating, from the costume, to the 1840s, and is possibly a preliminary effort at painting watercolours on the scale needed for his military pieces.

Michael Angelo Hayes was in the thick of the bitter controversy which tore asunder the Royal Hibernian Academy during the 1850s, and he made a number of comments on the state of art in Ireland to the Select

197 *MICHAEL ANGELO HAYES A view down Sackville Street, Dublin, 1858 (National Gallery of Ireland)*

Committee on Art Union Laws in 1866. His principal theme was the well-known truism that Irish artists only achieved fame if they went abroad – no doubt he had Maclise and Foley in mind – and that the upper classes in the main bought old masters, backing this up with the information that in the Dublin Exhibition of 1853 out of the 1023 paintings only a mere handful were by Irishmen.[52]

Many oil portrait painters were good watercolourists and used the medium occasionally. Even Martin Archer Shee, whose skill as a pastellist has already been mentioned, painted in watercolour, for instance a small, three-quarter-length portrait, exhibited in the Royal Academy in 1792 of John Williams who wrote under the pseudonym, Anthony Pasquin *(Plate 198)*. His invaluable but quirky *Memoirs of the Royal Academicians and Authentic History of the Artists of Ireland*, published in 1796, from which we quote so often, is the seminal source for the history of Irish art in the eighteenth century. In the biography of his father written by the younger Shee, he mentions this picture, though he does not make it clear if the work exhibited in the Royal Academy was an oil or a watercolour, and he describes the work as a "somewhat sombre but vigorously-painted picture, [which] came in for a fair share of praise on the part of the newspaper critics."[53]

Stephen Catterson Smith the Elder (1806–72), when he first came to Ireland, to Londonderry in 1839 and later to Dublin in

1845, drew portraits in crayon and pencil. He was much influenced by Alfred Chalon, whose "haute tonnish" watercolour portraits and drawings of the British and Irish aristocracy were so readily popularized by Lady Blessington's annual *Book of Beauty*. His portrait of Lady de Tabley (National Gallery of Ireland) is a typical example; she was the wife of a distinguished patron of the arts, the first Lord de Tabley, who was of Irish descent. Smith's self-portrait *(Plate 199)* is in coloured chalks and is a much more penetrating study. His son, Stephen Catterson Smith the younger (1849–1912), was an accomplished draughtsman of both figure and landscape, and a number of studies by him are in the NGI.

A contemporary of the elder Catterson Smith is Thomas Bridgford (1812–78), who was a friend of Maclise and admired by Thackeray when he visited the Royal Hibernian Academy in Dublin in 1841.[54] But he also drew portraits in both oil and pencil heightened with white, many of them rather

198
MARTIN ARCHER SHEE
A portrait of John Williams (Anthony Pasquin), c.1792
(Department of Prints and Drawings, British Museum)

199
STEPHEN CATTERSON SMITH THE ELDER
Self Portrait
(National Gallery of Ireland)

London address, and in 1853 he became Headmaster of the Cork School of Design for three years. Though fashionable ladies and their children, some with elaborate furnishings, predominate, there is an interesting watercolour dated 1855 of fisherfolk and boat builders on the shore posing by a boat (National Museum of Ireland). He also painted comic pictures of monkeys riding hounds and pigs; dog fights and horse dealers' yards, some done for *Barney Bryan's Sketchbooks*.[55] In one of these yards the conspiratorial faces of the horse dealers, and even the horse being exhibited, make it quite clear that the "swell" is about to be fleeced *(Plate 201)* The prints in *Barney Bryan's* sketchbook are initialed "RRS" but some watercolours for them are signed with a monogram "BB", presumably for Barney Bryan. His ordinary work is signed "RR Scanlan". He is a highly competent and very lively artist and even in his portrait work achieves a high standard. This is well illustrated by his posthumous portrait signed and dated 1855, of Henry, Earl of Mount Charles, who died young in 1824, and is shown riding with his groom with Windsor Castle in the background, commemorating his notorious mother, Lady Conyngham and her liaison with the Prince Regent. A more

200
THOMAS
BRIDGFORD
Portrait of Martin Archer Shee, c.1846
(National Gallery of Ireland)

stiff, including his competent likeness of Shee wearing his academy medal *(Plate 200)*.

Robert Richard Scanlan (fl.1826–76) was an Irishman who spent many years in England. Though he did paint in oils, most of his work is in watercolour, group portraits, genre and animal scenes. He no doubt came back to Ireland quite frequently, as he painted Irish subjects even while giving a

201
ROBERT RICHARD
SCANLAN
A Horse Dealer

typical subject is his spirited *Donnybrook to Dublin (Plate 202)*, a car driving scene which was lithographed with another, *Dublin to Drogheda* in 1841.

An Italian, Felice Piccioni (fl.1830–42), was brought to Belfast by the printmaker and publisher, Marcus Ward, who was also a patron of Andrew Nicholl (see Chapter 9). Nicholl's humble parents and other members of his family circle were portrayed by Piccioni in five drawings in the Ulster Museum. The portrait of the father, a cobbler, is a moving study. Piccioni worked in a similar vein to Scanlon, using chalk, charcoal and wash. His earliest known interior scene shows three daughters, Gertrude, Christina and Adelaide, of the Domville family *(Plate 203)* whose crest appears in quatrefoil medallions on the carpet. An interesting detail is the Regency villa, similar in style to those designed by Sir Richard Morrison, portrayed as an overdoor. He moved about the country as he was in Cork in 1842 drawing members of the Briscoe family of Fermoy. A characteristic study is his *Sportsman with his gun and dog*, signed and dated 1840. The last work we know is a family group done in Belfast which, from the costume, dates sometime in the 1850s. This would extend the *floruit* dates given by

Strickland. It shows his characteristic interest in furniture, carpeting and decoration. Strickland says that while he was in Cork he drew caricatures. Scanlan and Piccioni are two of many artists, mostly unidentified or amateurs, who worked in this vein in Ireland.

Samuel Lover (1797–1868) was another watercolourist who also worked in miniature. He had a very versatile career as a novelist, book illustrator, poet, song writer and performer, so that his painting reflects these interests and is also curtailed by them. His work varies from the small whole-length in chalk and watercolour, and similar half-lengths, to subject pictures like his *Flow on thou Shining river* from Moore's *Melodies*. This is a watercolour executed in something of a miniaturist technique and "brings together Lover's interest in literary and musical subject matter, in landscape and 'the antique' in costume and theme."[56] There are a number of his watercolours in the National Gallery of Ireland, including a romantic sketch of *Lucy Lover*, dated 1840, which is unfinished and contrasts with the more staid *Meta Lover*, his aunt, which is a sympathetic study in brown and pink. These portraits link with the work of the elder Catterson Smith and Thomas Bridgford whom

202
ROBERT RICHARD
SCANLAN
"Donnybrook to Dublin"

we have already discussed. He too drew Martin Archer Shee but as a younger man than Bridgford and shows him seated at his easel in a very relaxed pose, pausing between brushstrokes. It is a remarkably fine pencil drawing, which recalls the direct clarity of Ingres. His pencil drawing of an Irish piper is freer in handling and shows the melancholy, frustrated nationalism of Ireland at the time.

Lover's career moves from the neat Regency portrait to the literary, romantic subject matter loved by the Victorians. Much of his life was spent in England and he once said to Burton, remarking sadly on the state of the arts in Ireland and the paucity of patrons in Ireland, "A man here [in Ireland] has no purchase – nothing to work from, if he have any talent he must depend there on himself alone and consequently spins himself out like a spider."[57] Perhaps this explains not only his travels but also the variety of his work. He visited America from 1846 to 1848, touring with a theatrical company, and a lively drawing of a street scene, with a procession moving in front of the Cathedral in New Orleans, survives (Plate 204).

The period from the end of the Napoleonic wars, 1815, to the Famine, 1845–7, and its grim aftermath, is one of declining patronage, and artists are constantly bewailing the impossibility of making a living. Emigration was the only solution for the great artists, while the lesser talents scratched out a meagre living with book illustration and various jobs which involved artistic training, such as the Ordnance and Geological Surveys discussed in the next chapter.

203 FELICE PICCIONI *The Domville Children*

204
SAMUEL LOVER
The Cabildo, New Orleans
(Department of Prints and Drawings, British Museum)

CHAPTER NINE

THE ROMANTIC PERIOD: LANDSCAPE AND TOPOGRAPHY

Three landscape painters who started their careers together were James Arthur O'Connor (1792–1841), Francis Danby (1793–1861) and George Petrie (1790–1866). O'Connor was the impoverished son of a Dublin printseller and engraver and may have attended the Dublin Society Schools,[1] where he early became a friend of Danby and Petrie, who are known to have been at the Schools. It used to be thought that they all worked on an oil picture of a *Lakescene* about 1813,[2] though this is now doubted;[3] but they certainly all visited London together to see the Royal Academy in the same year.

Two watercolour, monochrome sketches in the Royal Academy, both done on the London visit, *The Vision*, after Rembrandt's *The Angel appearing to the Shepherds*, and *A Landscape with Horseman*[4] emphasize O'Connor's early interest in light and shade. He soon went home, only returning to live in England in 1822. Few of his drawings survive; they include some done in Mayo *(Plate 205)* in 1818, one of *Irishtown and Sandymount* and some sketchbooks of 1822 of an English tour (National Gallery of Ireland). All these show him to have been a neat outline draughtsman, as does all his topographical work even up to the German sketches of 1833. They are all old-fashioned and do not change in style. Most of his drawings were intended as studies for his oils, many of which are of fine quality and by which he should be judged. An unusual drawing is a little, free pen sketch of himself holding his mahlstick *(Plate 206)*, which is signed and dated 1824.

O'Connor's friend Francis Danby is in a totally different class. Though his early

Irish topographical views, such as his conventional *Castle Archdale* (National Gallery of Ireland), hark back to the eighteenth century, one of them, *Ringsend from Beggar's Bush (Plate 207)*, has a clarity of light and distance which give it a limpid atmosphere. He developed quickly when he settled in Bristol in 1813, where he immediately succeeded in selling drawings to John Minthorn, a fancy stationer. These were of Co. Wicklow, and his early drawings of the Bristol Channel and the Downs have the spatial and tonal qualities of the watercolours by Thomas Sautell Roberts of the Wicklow mountains and the area round Dublin. These were exhibited in Dublin throughout the first decades of the century and Danby must have known them. Many of his Bristol oils do derive from the later work of William Ashford but, as far as we can tell, not his watercolours. These are among his finest work; his *Avon at Clifton (Plate 208)* of 1821 has been called by Francis Greenacre[5] a "masterpiece of British watercolour drawing," and he comments on the careful observation of the sunset's dying moments. Danby's ability to handle hills and mountains, cliffs and rocks can be seen at different times in his career, from the early views of *St. Vincent's Rocks on the Avon Gorge (Plate 209)*, with their splendid clarity of form, to the mountainous scenery in Norway, which he visited in 1827, and the Alps when he was in Geneva in the later 1830s. A different aspect of his work is the Claudian *View of Killarney*[6] (Mellon Bank Corporation, Pittsburgh), which is a romantic recollection of the famous beauty spot rather than a topographical essay.

Danby was always interested in genre, peopling the foregrounds of his more

intimate landscapes with figures not only walking, boating and fishing, but also working, carrying loads, breaking stones, and boats at work on the river. These details contrast with the nereids and tritons which cavort in his watercolour *Amphitrite,* or the fairies who float and dance in his imaginary illustrations, such as *Oberon and Titania* (Yale Center for British Art).[7] His imaginary landscapes are very atmospheric and sometimes Turneresque, and his few pencil studies show a very sure free drawing style. Danby's watercolour *Le Pont de la Concorde (Plate 210),* done in Paris about 1831, is full of these genre details but at the same time suggests the glow of a still evening, with the buildings bathed in the gentle golden light of the setting sun. He had fled to Paris to escape creditors and because of the scandal of his private life.[8] The black chalk drawings of two of his children done about 1828 are unusual and particularly sympathetic. Despite his comment that "Ireland to me is a desert without an interest"[9] he kept drawings of Ireland, certainly of Killarney, as he still had some with him in Paris in 1837,[10] and the surviving drawings show that he worked them up at that time, as they have no stylistic link with his early Irish work. He never returned to Ireland but ended his days living by the sea at Exmouth.

George Petrie (1790–1866), the third of the trio, was not only a painter, antiquarian, archaeologist, musician and writer, but also

an avid collector of folklore and the leading light in the new scientific approach to ancient Irish history and artifacts. He must have had a compelling personality, as he was the centre of a wide circle of learned and artistic people, who included his biographer, William Stokes, the doctor; John O'Donovan, the linguist on the Ordnance Survey; Sir Samuel Ferguson, the antiquarian; Frederick William Burton, the painter; Sir William Wilde, the doctor; and the third Earl of Dunraven, the archaeologist.

Petrie came of an artistic family: his father was a miniature painter and portraitist who

207
FRANCIS DANBY
*Ringsend from Beggar's
Bush, Dublin*
(Ulster Museum)

dealt in coins, jewellery and antiquities. He was educated in the Dublin Society Schools where he won a Silver Medal. In 1808, when he was 18, he made his first painting tour in Wicklow. He went on several trips to Wales and in 1813 , as we have mentioned, he was in London with his fellow students, Francis Danby and James Arthur O'Connor. Unlike them, he had some means and an introduction to Benjamin West, the President of the Royal Academy. Though impressed by London, he returned home and made his career in Ireland.

This got under way with his ninety-seven illustrations *(Plate 211)* to Cromwell's *Excursions through Ireland*, published in 1821, though the first prints date from 1819. These books of engravings, the equivalent of our modern coffee-table volumes, were very popular, the taste having been set in England by such works as William Gilpin's *Observations on the River Wye, 1782.*

208
FRANCIS DANBY
The Avon at Clifton, 1821
*(Bristol Museum and
Art Gallery)*

209
FRANCIS DANBY
*St. Vincent's Rocks on
the Avon Gorge*

*(Bristol Museum and
Art Gallery)*

Books concentrating on British landscape were illustrated by the most famous artists, like Turner. Petrie went on to work for Brewer and Wright though he found the publishers and engravers extremely slow to pay, and this may account for the fact that he virtually stopped making illustrated books early in his career. Brewer's *Beauties*

210
FRANCIS DANBY
Le Pont de la Concorde
with l'Assemblée
Nationale, *Paris 1831*

of Ireland came out in 1825, and in Brewer's correspondence he makes it plain that a large number of "Seats" must be included. He described the Duke of Leinster's Seat as follows: "Carton *(Plate 212)* is ugly enough, but the Duke's name is 'a tower of strength'."[11] Petrie writes from Parsonstown Castle, Birr, in 1820:

> Today I have been till now (four o'clock), sketching a nobleman's seat here (Lord Rosse's) which, though very fine, cost me a great deal too much time; but in fact, it has been the same with all the subjects of that character which I have hitherto done; less than four or five hours will not suffice for one sketch. The weather continues broken and windy. I should not have been able to sketch today but for the leeward side of a haycock, which I had the good fortune to meet with.[12]

The concern for illustrating "Seats" was justified, as Brewer was flattered when Christopher Bellew, of Mount Bellew in Co. Galway, offered to accommodate Brewer and Petrie and collect them from the mail coach stop in his carriage, if they would include his house.[13] Wright's *Guides to Wicklow and Killarney* came out in 1821 so Petrie must have been very busy during the early 1820s. As so much of his work was for engraving, most of these early watercolours are monochromatic, done in sepia and grey ink.

It is clear that "Seats" were not his main interest and William Stokes writes an evocative passage which shows where Petrie's taste really lay:

> It has been already shown how closely related in his mind were the studies of nature, and of those old surviving monuments of the land, with which they are witnesses of its history, become themselves objects of a peculiar beauty, and give to the reflecting mind a larger enjoyment of the landscape. Hence many of his pictures show the effects of that combination so strangely frequent in Ireland, where the ruin and its surroundings unite in giving a

211
GEORGE PETRIE
Dalkey Castle, Co. Dublin

212
GEORGE PETRIE
Carton, Co. Kildare

213
GEORGE PETRIE
Trim Castle, Co. Meath
(Royal Irish Academy)

beautiful handling of foliage, particularly in an example such as the *Trim Castle (Plate 213)* where the ivy which covers the gates like a head of hair sweeps across the watercolour and continues down the broken walls. When treating distant hillsides, the texture has a marbled effect. However, he is not particularly good at figures and much prefers stillness, though he often achieves interest by great curved lines that create almost abstract shapes within his landscapes.

Stokes mentions Petrie's early interest in George Barret,[15] but we can see no influence from Barret's watercolours; the foliage painting may, however, owe something to Jonathan Fisher, whose work was so well known through the many engravings after him, some in sepia. Henry Brocas the Elder, who was a master at the Dublin Society Schools when Petrie was a pupil, also seems to have influenced him. Stokes correctly sees a link between Petrie and the poetry of Wordsworth. "The poetry of Wordsworth had made a deep impression upon him . . . in both we find the same perception of the beautiful, the same dwelling on scenes of simple nature . . ."[16]

national character to the scene, and so in a large proportion of his works, we have the feeling and skill of the painter in union with the knowledge of the antiquarian.[14]

Petrie was fascinated by the Aran islands and visited them in 1821 and 1822 as well as later in his life. He was the first artist to visit them and in 1821 he planned to write a book on them, though this was never finished.

The style of the early drawings is simple, clearly necessary for the engravers. He uses layers of wash which are accented by his

Petrie's career as an artist was interrupted by his appointment to be Head of the Topographical Department of the Ordnance

214
GEORGE PETRIE
The Twelve Pins,
Co. Galway
(National Gallery of
Ireland)

215
GEORGE PETRIE
*Gougane Barra, Co. Cork,
c.1831*
*(National Gallery of
Ireland)*

Survey of Ireland in 1835 till its disbandment in 1846. During this period he was too busy at his researches to do much painting, and he did not exhibit between 1836 and 1839. This was particularly unfortunate, as his work in the early 1830s had reached a remarkable level of excellence and he was now using full colour as he was to later when he returned to fulltime painting in 1846. *The Twelve Pins (Plate 214)* of 1831 is an example of a sublimely barren landscape, empty except for a shepherdess, and surprisingly, in full, but cold, sunlight. The reproduction of it in coloured lithograph in 1835 gives no hint of its splendour. The late 1830s was also the period when he was most concerned with collecting Irish music and with his work collecting and cataloguing for the Royal Irish Academy. He also published his *Ecclesiastical Architecture of Ireland* in 1845. After 1846 he earned his living by painting.

Gougane Barra (Plate 215), of which there are many versions, one exhibited as early as 1831, is Petrie's masterpiece, with amazing light effects and shafts of sunlight achieving beautiful tonal values. Another famous work is *Pilgrims at Clonmacnoise*, which is found in near monochrome examples as well as in colour. From the drawings in the sketchbooks

in the Royal Irish Academy, Petrie stands out as a master in pencil; his architectural detailing is extremely delicate and deft in both outline and shadow. He became PRHA briefly in 1857 but resigned in order to assist the government enquiry. He had been an RHA since 1828, the only member at that time who worked exclusively in watercolour.

It is interesting that he is singled out by Thackeray in his *Irish Sketchbook* in 1842 when he visited the Royal Hibernian Academy in Dublin, then so neglected that only two other people visited while he was there. After admiring Burton and Bridgford and mentioning the Art Union making a stir, Thackeray says of Petrie's drawings that they are "exceedingly beautiful, and, above all, trustworthy: no common quality in a descriptive artist at present."[17]

Petrie's assistant and pupil, George Victor Dunoyer[18] (1817–69), was Dublin-born. He worked in the Ordnance Survey with Petrie and after its collapse taught drawing in St. Columba's College before joining the Geological Survey of Ireland, where he was employed for the rest of his life. His faint pencil sketches are extremely precise but he is at his best when he uses wash, as in his

216
GEORGE VICTOR
DUNOYER
*Drimnagh Castle,
Co. Dublin*

217
HENRY MacMANUS
An Irish Hedge School
(National Library of
Ireland)

218
HENRY MacMANUS
A Horse and Cart
(National Library of
Ireland)

(Plate 216) show his ability to mass trees and architecture. His thirteen small notebooks now in the Royal Society of Antiquaries of Ireland show his interest in people and are full of vignettes of everyday life. Another of Petrie's assistants was William Frederick Wakeman (1822–1900), who at his best can be mistaken for Petrie, from whom he derives his style, but does not inherit his spirit. A typical study is of *Ballygrennan Castle*, Co. Limerick. Many of these drawings by Dunoyer and Wakeman are in the Royal Irish Academy.

An interesting teacher who started his work in the old watercolour style with an emphasis on architecture and standard foreground figures was Henry MacManus (1810–78), whose watercolour of the *Courthouse at Armagh* (Armagh Museum) is an early work of 1830, competently handled. Later he worked as a portrait painter and an illustrator, and also exhibited many watercolour landscapes in the Royal Hibernian Academy. His work for Hall's *Ireland*,[19] probably done about 1840, comprises quick and sure drawings of genre subjects treated without sentimentality. The best of these is probably his *Irish Hedge School (Plate 217)*, where a rather menacing schoolteacher listens to a varied age group reciting while the rest of the class pummel each other in the background, and a lively drawing of a country cart *(Plate 218)* with its solid wheels drawing a well-dressed peasant family presumably to church. He later developed a free and sketchy manner, seen in his drawing of *Donegal Castle* (National Library of Ireland) of 1873.

In his *Irish Times* obituary (25 March 1878) they stress his importance as Headmaster of what were formally the RDS Schools, which were taken over by the government in 1849. He became Professor of Painting in the Royal Hibernian Academy in 1873. He was also head of the Glasgow School of Design, 1845–9. The obituary adds, "It was he who trained up to art, all we may say of its present members."

Another contributor to Hall's *Ireland* was William Willes (d.1851), a pupil of Grogan who went to the Royal Academy Schools and lived in both London and Cork. His drawings in brown and blue washes are well composed as vignettes, and are lively

watercolours of Moorestown Castle and Shelton Abbey. His antiquarian watercolours give the wrong impression as they are very coarse and rough. In this field his chalk drawings are better. A pair of sketchy chalk and pencil drawings heightened with white of *Carrickfergus* and *Drimnagh Castle*

characterizations of children in action as can be seen in his *Goalers – Hurley – Hurling (Plate 219)*. He also painted landscapes and seascapes with a very delicate touch. He ultimately became the first Master of the School of Art in Cork, the year before he died, and in the Crawford Art Gallery there are a number of academic nude studies and other charcoal drawings by him which date from the 1830s.

The National Gallery of Ireland owns a large number of drawings by William Howis (1804–82) and his son William Howis, Jr. (1827–57). Howis was a product of the Dublin Society Schools under Robert Lucius West and went on to become an oil painter exhibiting in the Royal Hibernian Academy, at the beginning of his career mostly portraits, turning to landscapes and watercolours later on. He also worked as a restorer and adviser on art and is said to have copied a number of James Arthur O'Connors which were later attributed to O'Connor.[20] The drawings are mostly sketchbook landscapes, figure studies both academic and genre of workmanlike quality. His son, William Howis, Jr., follows in his father's footsteps.

An antiquarian watercolourist *(Plate 220)*, Henry O'Neill (1798–1880), who sometimes worked with Petrie but usually disagreed with him, is now known by very few watercolours and mostly through aquatints

219
WILLIAM WILLES
*Goalers – playing
Hurley*
*(National Library of
Ireland)*

and lithographs. His lithographic portraits of the Young Irelanders, including Smith O'Brien, are well known; a set of twenty large watercolours shows the apartments in the Richmond Bridewell used in 1844 by Daniel O'Connell, Charles Gavan Duffy *(Plate 221)* and others, including T.M. Ray who commissioned the series. They are a magnificent record of their surroundings and include bedrooms, the dining room and the Governor's gardens complete with model castle on a mound and a tent. They are the best record that we know, of middleclass

220
HENRY O'NEILL
Castle Roche, Co. Louth

165

interior decoration and furnishings of the period in Ireland.

O'Neill published in The Kilkenny Archaeological Society's *Journal* on the Cross of Cong,[21] and in his *Fine Arts of Ancient Ireland* and in his *Round Towers*[22] he sought to refute Petrie's views on the origin of round towers with his own theory that they were pagan.

His self portrait (National Gallery of Ireland) shows a delicate touch and a feeling for three-dimensional form. His landscapes include quiet, pastoral scenes, and a watercolour of 1839 shows the tenantry feasting outside Crom Castle. It has strong links with the work of the younger Henry Brocas. Despite their later controversies, early in his career he sometimes collaborated with Petrie, and this brought him into contact with the Belfast topographical artist, Andrew Nicholl (1804–86). The National Gallery of Ireland's *A Seated Man in a Wood* shows the influence of Nicholl with its deep tones, though unlike Nicholl, O'Neill dapples in his leaves.

Andrew Nicholl was the son of a boot and shoe maker and appears to have been totally self-taught though encouraged by his elder brother, William, who was in business in Belfast and an amateur artist. Both the brothers were founder members of the Belfast Association of Artists in 1836. Belfast was at this time not only a thriving industrial city but also an intellectual and artistic centre. It saw the foundation of the Belfast Natural Historical and Philosophical Society as well as the Linen Hall Library. Though its liberalism had been dampened after the 1798 rebellion, men like James Emerson, later Sir James Emerson Tennent, who was to be Nicholl's most important patron, adhered to forward-looking ideals.

In our opinion Nicholl must have been aware of the aquatints of William Daniel, whose book, *A Voyage round Great Britain*, was published in London between 1814 and 1825 and shows many features which can be seen in Nicholl's early views of the Antrim coast, some of which are dated 1828. These, despite their charm, are quite naïve with their

221
HENRY O'NEILL
Charles Gavan Duffy's Bedroom in the Richmond Bridewell, 1884
(National Museum of Ireland)

hard-edged outlines. But Nicholl used Daniel's series of flat washes and also his curiously stylized compositions with cattle by smooth water and heaving waves with rocking boats. Martyn Anglesea has remarked that the figures in *West view of the Giant's Causeway from the Stookans (Plate 222)*,[23] a man flanked by two bonneted ladies seen from behind and placed dead-centre, are very close to the work of Caspar David Friedrich, but though this is true it must be pure coincidence.

Nicholl's style developed during a visit to London made under the patronage of Emerson Tennent between 1830 and 1832. Anglesea says that Nicholl copied from paintings in the Dulwich Gallery,[24] his favourite artists being Cuyp, De Wint and Copley Fielding, whose rustic manner with brownish tones Nicholl clearly turned to but without the elegant genre additions of Copley Fielding. Anglesea adds that Nicholl must at this time have seen his first Turners. Turner was a major influence throughout his career; even some of his much later

Ceylonese seapieces and sunsets are clearly Turneresque. This visit to London, and another in the 1840s, was important for the development of his style, which ultimately loosened up and became more atmospheric. This can be seen in his *Richmond Hill, London*, of 1842, which clearly shows the influence of Peter de Wint. His drawing of figures and cattle, though never brilliant, also improved. He discovered various techniques such as scraping-out and, for foliage, split-brush, used by painters like John Glover. A series of brownish-toned pictures in the National Gallery of Ireland show this phase, and much of the finest of them is *A Pointer in a pond with waterlilies*. This work combines the flat areas of colour in the background and stylized haycocks of his early work with the mixed techniques of his later years. The reeds are scraped out and he uses split-brush for the trees.

The first mention of his flower paintings is in a sonnet written in 1830 by Emerson's sister, Eliza, on receiving "a beautiful

222
ANDREW NICHOLL
West view of the Giant's Causeway from the Stookans, 1828
(Ulster Museum)

223
ANDREW NICHOLL
*Flower Piece with
Mussenden Temple in the
background*

224
ANDREW NICHOLL
*Native Trees and a
Coconut Palm*

coloured drawing of flowers" from Nicholl.[25] These flower paintings are usually composed with wild flowers, mostly poppies, cornflowers, and daisies, in the foreground and a landscape seen behind or through them. The flowers are often imaginatively coloured, the poppies blue as well as red, and the topographical landscape microscopically observed, with a recognizable building such as Dunluce Castle, the Mussenden Temple *(Plate 223)* or Kingstown Harbour very faintly discernible in the distance. These would appear to be totally original compositions, and because the scale of the flowers and buildings is so irrational they have a surrealist quality.

The next fifteen years saw Nicholl living in Dublin and later in London working for the book trade and teaching. It was at this time that he probably got to know Petrie and Henry O'Neill, with whom he collaborated on several publications including *Picturesque Sketches of some of the finest landscape and coast scenery of Ireland.*[26] His patron, now Sir James Emerson Tennent, went to Ceylon (now Sri Lanka) as Colonial Secretary in 1845 and seems to have arranged that Nicholl should have the post of Teacher of Landscape Painting, Scientific Drawing and Design in the Colombo Academy. Nicholl was taught mapping and engineering drawing in London before he sailed, and the

Ulster Museum has an example of the design work he carried out in Colombo.

He toured with Tennent in Ceylon, going as far as the ancient capital of Kandy, as his patron wanted him to illustrate the book he published in 1860 on Ceylon.[27] His recent training can be seen in some rather dry architectural drawings in the British Museum of Hindu temples which form a contrast with the freer studies of native trees

225
ANDREW NICHOLL
Convolvulus

and a coconut palm *(Plate 224)*, bungalows and lakes, not to mention botanical drawings of fruit and flowers. He uses a frieze of white convolvulus as the base of his watercolour of the shrine at Jassna *(Plate 225)*, though the building is not intermingled with the flowers. This continues the frieze effect of his Dublin flower paintings of the 1830s. His dramatic seascapes of the Indian Ocean with squalls and waterspouts *(Plate 226)* show how well he had digested Turner's art. In these sketches he uses wash almost exclusively, in direct contrast to the careful drawing of the architectural works.

He returned to London about 1849/50 and seems to have lived between Dublin, Belfast and London for the rest of his long life, dying in his house in London aged eighty-three. It is impossible to make a chronology of his work as he rarely dates his drawings and confuses the issue by signing sometimes well after the date he painted. Several of his Cingalese drawings, for example, have RHA after his name, which honour he only achieved ten years after his return in 1860. Throughout his career he repeated subjects like the Giant's Causeway and Staffa and the banks of flowers. Some of these are of an extremely indifferent quality, and there is a theory that these were turned out by his daughter Mary Anne, who was also an artist. They were clearly done as potboilers. However, the finest of Nicholl's flower pieces do remain among the most memorable and beautiful watercolours that Ireland has produced.

Nicholl taught throughout his career and it is almost certain that his most distinguished pupil was an amateur, a Belfast doctor, James Moore (1819–83). The only documentary evidence that Moore was a pupil is a note pencilled on one of his own drawings: "Mr Cranfield, Westmoreland Street, Dublin. Tinted paper stone colour same quality as that purchased by Mr Nicholl."[28] Most of his works are in the Ulster Museum. However, if one looks at his view of Glenarm dated 1844,[29] it is obvious that he has learned much from Nicholl. A few years later he had developed a lively, personal style with

226
ANDREW NICHOLL
Waterspout

227 (Top)
JAMES MOORE
Maze Race Course, 1852
(Ulster Museum)

228 (Above)
JAMES MOORE
*Glenarm, Co. Antrim,
1856*
(Ulster Museum)

and the birth date which is usually given, 1817, seems too late as it would make him an infant prodigy of thirteen. There is no indication of his education and, though he exhibited only portraits for the first three years in the RHA and then did not exhibit for nine years, when he did he had changed to being a landscape painter. He contributed twenty-five illustrations to Hall's *Ireland*,[31] published in 1841, and working for this could explain why he did not exhibit. Though he seems always to have lived in Ireland, he travelled to Scotland before 1842 when he exhibited *Loch Lomond* and several other Scottish subjects in the RHA. He also visited England and Wales and stopped exhibiting in the RHA in 1880. His style in pencil drawing is clearly intended for lithography, for which he was given a prize by the Royal Irish Art Union in 1846. His watercolours vary from architectural subjects like the fine *O'Cahan tomb in Dungiven Church* (frontispiece), which is monochromatic, heightened with white, to the fully romantic *View of Errigal, 1870* (Ulster Museum), or *The Grey Man's Path, Fairhead (Plate 230)*. These are carefully delineated with rather strong yet somewhat muddy colours and he tends to be weak on his distant perspective.

Burgess set up an art school in Belfast in 1850 while his contemporary Jeremiah Hodges Mulcahy (1804–89) did the same in Limerick in 1842. Mulcahy's early training is not known and he may have learned from prints, but he certainly knew and worked with the marine painter Captain (later Admiral) Richard Brydges Beechey, when Beechey was surveying the River Shannon in the 1840s. A number of Beechey drawings were in Mulcahy's collection, which was partially sold in 1980[32] and, like Mulcahy, his work in pencil and watercolour is intended as studies for his oils. A watercolour study of a man-o'-war is inscribed "painted for me by Capt[n] Beechey R.N. Limerick 1844 . . . ."[33] Mulcahy drew some very similar studies of naval vessels and yachts in the Shannon. When in Limerick, Beechey also painted extremely competent watercolours, including two of Askeaton Castle and Castle Connell.

There are numerous sketch drawings by Mulcahy[34] but not many finished works. One Claudian landscape with a bridge,

spontaneous, broken brushwork which is notable in his *Gardens at Versailles* of 1845, *Coleraine Regatta* of 1847 and *Maze Race Course (Plate 227)* of 1852. In their freedom they prefigure the twentieth century and were probably only possible because he was an amateur. He also painted a more finished type of watercolour, like *Glenarm (Plate 228)*, 1856, and the large exhibition piece, *Slieve Bernagh from the Trassey Bog, Mourne Mountains,* 1870, of which Martyn Anglesea comments, "The vigorous style of brushwork on heavy, rough wove paper, bears much similarity with the English watercolourist, Thomas Collier who carried on the David Cox tradition."[30] A very charming example of a late work is his *Antonia at Annadale (Plate 229)*.

Another Belfast artist is James Howard Burgess (c.1817–90), about whom very little is known. He exhibited first at the Royal Hibernian Academy watercolour portraits,

dated 1833, is a study for a picture for the Cork Exhibition of the following year. Finished works include a classical landscape (inscribed "this was my first composition") and a study of Roman ruins after Panini, dated 1823, which seem to confirm that he learned from prints. There are a number of *capricci* dated in the 1830s but most of his drawings are pastoral subjects or straight landscapes.

The nineteenth century had its share of military topographers, of whom a few seem worth mentioning: Lieutenant Colonel Charles Hamilton Smith (1776–1859), Charles Vallancey Pratt (1789–1869), and Captain Robert Smith (1792–1882). Charles Smith was Flemish by birth and a visitor in Ireland; several of his sketches, including *Glanmore Castle*, appear as illustrations in John Carr's *The Stranger in Ireland*, published in London in 1806, though they are, surprisingly, credited to Carr. His visit

229
JAMES MOORE
*Antonia at Annadale,
Belfast*
(Ulster Museum)

171

230
JAMES HOWARD
BURGESS
*The Grey Man's Path,
Fairhead, Co. Antrim*

231
ROBERT SMITH
*Baggot's Town Castle,
Co. Limerick*
*(Victoria and Albert
Museum)*

must have been in the earliest years of the century, and two sketchbooks of his drawings of Ireland and Scotland are in the Huntingdon Collection in San Marino, California. They indicate that he travelled very widely and to a number of unusual places like Buncrana on Lough Swilly, as well as Killarney and round Dublin. They are lightly washed pencil sketches.

Charles Vallancey Pratt (1789–1869) is a more interesting figure, presumably christened after Charles Vallancey. After a career in the army, he settled at Stoneville, Delgany.

In a list he made of drawings and watercolours he had painted in England and Scotland, under the date 1805, Pratt recorded, "These Sketches were made from Nature during my Cadetship at the R. Military College G^t Marlow, when under the instruction of the late eminent Artist W. Alexander Professor of Landscape drawing at said College."[35] He also recorded when he painted the "colour on spot," differentiating this with "Tinted" or just "Colour." This is a useful confirmation of the importance of military college instruction and that the quality of the teachers remained high, as Alexander, who has already been met with as Lord Macartney's fellow artist with Hickey on the famous embassy to China, was an excellent watercolourist.

Pratt was extremely antiquarian-minded, recording and commenting carefully on the places, ruins and villages which he painted in Ireland, often in full watercolour with a rather soft green tonality. One drawing of the ash tree at Rathmichael was sketched in company with Samuel Lover. The earliest Irish view is dated 1807, and then there is a gap till 1813, from when there is a continuous series till the year of his death, 1869. He wandered all over Ireland. A large collection of these watercolours was on the Dublin market in 1982. He was an officer in the 69th regiment and sketched abroad, presumably wherever he was posted in the

232
THOMAS DE RIENZI
*The Barracks at Fermoy,
Co. Cork, 1822*

British Isles and in Jersey (1813), Spain (1814), etc.

Captain Robert Smith was Irish and an officer in the 44th regiment. His work is in minute pencil or ink, most carefully and meticulously drawn. The drawings include ruins *(Plate 231)* and country houses and he was obviously extremely interested in architecture. A collection of drawings is in the Victoria and Albert Museum. In 1832 he went to India and criticized the repair work on the Qutb Minar in Delhi carried out by his namesake, the engineer Colonel Robert Smith (1787–1873), with whom he can be easily confused. Captain Smith returned to Ireland and finally became a Herald in the Office of Arms in Dublin Castle.

An enormous number of officers drew extremely well as a result of their military education and having time to practise. A typical album of landscapes, house views and other subjects is by Captain Thomas de Rienzi of Clobemon, Co. Carlow, which includes a drawing of his new house dated 20 August 1826, and a splendid view through the window of the barracks at Fermoy *(Plate 232)* looking over the parade ground, 1822. By far the most charming drawing, however, shows himself and Betsy Nelson on a wheelbarrow *(Plate 233)*, done in Jersey where he was *en poste* in 1824.

Philip Bedingfield (d.1897), also an army officer, made a tour of Ireland about 1863,

going to quite out of the way places such as the Loop Head peninsula and Scattery Island, Co. Clare, with its round tower and churches. Nearby, on the southern bank of the Shannon, he painted an attractive watercolour of the estuary with Carrigafoyle Castle *(Plate 234)* and Lislaughton Abbey. Bedingfield was a very proficient artist, as his view of Reginald's Tower and the quays at Waterford shows. He handled architecture particularly well.

These artists were considerably facilitated by the improvements in public transport, such as the canal systems which flourished in many parts of the country from the third quarter of the eighteenth century and the

233
THOMAS DE RIENZI
*Self Portrait with Betsy
Nelson on a
wheelbarrow, 1824*

234
PHILIP BEDINGFIELD
Carrigafoyle Castle,
Co. Kerry, 1863

stage coach "cars" run so efficiently by Bianconi from 1815 to the 1860s, when the age of steam fully took over. It was also the period when the technical development of watercolours was improving. In the 1830s William Winsor and H.C. Newton produced their easily carried sketching boxes with their colours in little pans, and in 1846 metal tubes containing moist watercolours were introduced by the same firm. Hard cake colours were not abandoned, however, as they were suitable for out-of-door sketching, and the new tubes made of lead were heavy and cumbersome.[36]

CHAPTER TEN

THE VICTORIANS

The great names in the mid-nineteenth century in Irish painting were Daniel Maclise, William Mulready, Frederick William Burton and the Doyles. Of these, Mulready (1786–1863),[1] though born in Ennis, Co. Clare, left the country at the age of five and we feel that, despite the brilliance of his drawings and watercolours and his great influence on English art through his teaching, he has no place in our survey. It is worth noting, however, that he was mentioned in the Limerick exhibition catalogue of 1821 which we discuss on page 146. He was regarded as Irish and incorrectly as a Limerick man who contributed to the honours of his native city. This contemporary effort to emphasize his Irish nationality would not have caused any pleasure to the artist who, according to Marcia Pointon,[2] did his best to conceal his Irishness because of Ireland's unsavoury and troublesome reputation in England, whereas Wilkie could take pride in his Scottishness. It is ironic that it is Wilkie and not Mulready who paints the Irish whiskey still.

Daniel Maclise (1806–70) was also born in Ireland, though he spent most of his career in England. On the other hand, he had his first artistic education in Cork, and he kept close Irish contacts and frequently illustrated Irish themes. Maclise was the son of a Scottish Presbyterian shoemaker who settled in Cork, and after a short and unsuccessful period as a bank clerk, 1819–20, he studied in the Cork Institute, which housed the casts after the antique presented to Cork by George IV. The School of Art in Cork was founded the following year, 1822. Cork had a small but flourishing artistic and intellectual community at this time, including such

figures as Dr Woodruffe, who lectured on anatomy; Richard Sainthill, the antiquarian and bibliophile; and the writer and critic, Thomas Crofton Croker, who had many English connections and went to live in London in 1818. Croker, who was an admirer of Grogan, made a few neat pen and ink drawings for Hall's *Ireland*. They include the birthplace of James Barry and a sketch of a decayed medieval house in the main street of *Kilmallock*.[3] Croker has already been noticed in Chapter 5 when he married into the Nicholson family of artists.

Fellow students of Maclise were Samuel Forde (see Chapter 7) and the sculptor, John Hogan. According to Strickland, Maclise opened a studio in Patrick Street, Cork, and specialized in small pencil portraits minutely done with great attention to detail. But Maclise had an eye for the main chance, for, in 1825, he drew a profile head of Sir Walter Scott[4] when he visited Cork, and through lithographing it, Maclise made his name locally. He was also introduced to the sitter, who autographed the original drawing. In 1826, with a number of friends, he made a trip to Dublin, where he drew many army officers and probably his portrait of Colonel John Townshend of Castle Townshend, which is dated the same year. Later he went on a walking tour with three school friends in Co. Wicklow and travelled slowly back to Cork, sketching all the way, sometimes now using a less precise and more fluid manner which is shown in a drawing of himself under a tree *(Plate 235)* sketching the Rock of Cashel.[5]

Not only did Maclise make the usual topographical sketches of ruins, but there are fairy drawings. These were influenced by

235 DANIEL MACLISE *Self Portrait Sketching, c.1826 (Victoria and Albert Museum)*

236 DANIEL MACLISE *Disraeli, c.1833 (engraving)*

237 DANIEL MACLISE *Thackeray seated, 1832 (The Garrick Club)*

his friend Crofton Croker's *Fairy Legends and Traditions of the South of Ireland*, which had been published in 1825. He, in fact, made some illustrations for the second edition of 1826 and this was the beginning of a considerable output of Irish and, later, English book illustration. In 1827 he went to London and studied at the Royal Academy Schools, obtaining a silver and a gold medal in 1829 and 1831 for his history painting. Meanwhile, in 1828, the Mechanics Institute in Cork held an exhibition of his portrait drawings. He kept up his connections with Ireland and was never forgotten by his native town. His younger brother, Joseph Maclise (c.1815–c.1880) was a surgeon and lived with Daniel in London for many years. He was a great anatomical draughtsman and must have learned much from Daniel, as his illustrations to his *Surgical Anatomy*, 1851, are magnificent *(Plate 398)*.

Maclise continued to earn his living with portrait drawings, many made for *Frazer's Magazine*, which was edited by an Irishman, William Maginn, also a native of Cork. These portraits, which include Disraeli *(Plate 236)*, Carlisle, Coleridge, O'Connell and other notabilities, have a sharpness that makes a comparison with Ingres obvious and are among the most lively portrait drawings of their time. His most famous drawing is of Paganini (Victoria and Albert Museum),[6] who is shown playing against a fainter background of the orchestra listening. We also illustrate *Thackeray (Plate 237)*, 1832, to whom he was introduced by Maginn. This is not a drawing for the magazine, so is much more informal and shows Thackeray sprawling on a chair. Naturally, once Maclise's fame increased he turned to oils, but watercolour drawings, portraits, landscapes and illustrations always poured from his hands.

The watercolour of around 1831, of an unknown man seated in his study[7] (Scottish National Portrait Gallery) is an early example of a figure in an elaborately furnished interior which was to become a feature of his greatest oil portraits, such as his famous *Charles Dickens seated in his study*. His group of Sir Francis Sykes and his family *(Plate 238)*, about 1837, dressed in medieval costume and armour associated with the neo-Gothicism of the Eglinton tournament, is a large and sumptuous watercolour cleverly utilizing the S-shape of the spiral staircase to enliven the composition of the group walking down it.

Apart from his illustrative work, his drawings in later years were mostly preparatory for his large oils and frescoes. Of these, by far the finest is the huge cartoon for *The Meeting of Wellington and Blucher (Plate 239)*,[8] 1858/9, for the fresco in the Royal Gallery in the Houses of Parliament, Westminster. This frieze-like composition of contemporary history shows the artist's intense interest in the accurate portrayal of military costume. This is apparent in other circumstances in his *Eva and Strongbow* (National Gallery of Ireland), for which he made a close study of Irish antiquities. In both pictures the tragedy of war dominates, and in the Waterloo scene the attitude of Wellington to the horrors of battle is expressed in his melancholy countenance. In *Eva and Strongbow* Maclise, as has been said, "depicts the Marriage as a sacrificial event, illustrating, . . . the subjugation of a free people and the destruction of an ancient culture."[9] This clearly reflects his own views.

An important survival of what was probably an extensive genre is the depiction of the Irish peasant, as can be seen in *The Irish Peasant's Grave*, 1843 *(Plate 240)* by John Tracey (1813–73). These peasant subjects had been touched on by Maclise in a happy vein in his *Snap-apple Night* of 1833, but Tracey's attempt at reality is a new feature, even if by our standards the characters look remarkably well fed. It must be remembered that 1843 was only two years before the Great Famine. The picture was bought by the Irish Art Union and was engraved. Most of Tracey's pictures are on classical themes but the occasional Irish subject includes *Larry O'Toole and his wife praying for a Son And Heir to the Half Acre*, a subject taken from Carleton's *Phelim O'Toole*. Carleton's novels painting the life of the Irish peasantry

238
DANIEL MACLISE
The Sykes family, c.1837

were of enormous importance, though not apparently to Irish painters, who usually avoided this unpalatable subject till the second half of the century.

It was Maria Edgeworth, not Carleton, who interested David Wilkie (1785–1841) in Irish subjects, though she was also his sternest critic, pointing out that in *The Peep-o-Day Boys Cabin*, 1835–6, he needed "more negligence, more slovenliness, more recklessness in the costume." Wilkie was in Ireland in 1835 in the West and South-west but not in the North, so that the title of this picture is incorrect, as Peep-O-Day Boys were Northerners; his original title *The Sleeping Whiteboy* is accurate. The drawing for the sleeping youth is rather weak in comparison to the vibrancy of most of his Irish sketches, such as the sidecar pelting along *(Plate 241)*, done in Dublin on 15 August 1835.

Another English visitor with an interest in Irish genre was Francis William Topham (1818–77), who came to Ireland three times, in 1844, 1862 and 1868. He painted many peasant scenes, from the highly finished *Pilgrims at a Well* (British Museum) to the more vigorous and spontaneous *Cabin Interior with Mother and Child* inscribed "Claddagh Galway 1844" *(Plate 242)*.

Probably the best-known visitor was Erskine Nicol (1825–1904), who spent four years with the Department of Science and Art in Dublin between 1846 and 1850; afterwards, though he returned to his native Edinburgh, he paid annual visits to Ireland. He is famed for his often comic peasant Irish subjects, and there is no doubt that he was influenced by Wilkie. Though *Paddy at Versailles* (Ulster Museum) is typical of the satirical vein in which he sometimes depicts Irishmen with simian features, he also drew straightforward, even moving, subjects of peasant life, including *The 'Merican Difficulty (Plate 243)* of 1862 which gives a brilliant effect of concentration on the old lady's face as she struggles through a newspaper account of the American Civil War hoping that her children were not casualties. His scene of the *Seafront at Bray* (National Gallery of Ireland), with the bourgeoisie at play, a brougham trotting by and a servant delivering the vegetables to the basement of one of the newly built seaside terrace houses, is perhaps one of his most attractive works.

239 (Facing Page)
DANIEL MACLISE
Detail of Meeting of
Wellington and Blucher,
1858/9
(Royal Academy)

240
JOHN TRACEY
The Irish Peasant's
Grave, 1843

241
SIR DAVID WILKIE
A Dublin Sidecar, 1835

An unexpected painter of the Irish peasantry was a visitor, Elizabeth Thompson (1846–1933), the English wife of an Irish general, Sir William Butler, and today known for her famous military paintings. On her honeymoon she went to Kerry, and in her diary[10] she describes her shock at the poverty of the inhabitants living amid the grandeur and colour of the Killarney mountains and the exquisite effects of light. She was a Roman Catholic and therefore attended mass at the tiny chapels with the peasants. Her watercolours, mainly landscapes, include a moving study of those peasants praying at the door of a *Chapel of Ease* in Co. Kerry and a striking picture of wild horses in the mountains of Glenaragh. Later, in 1905, she spent some time painting and drawing in Co. Mayo. Her social conscience about Irish conditions led her to paint her famous oil, *Evicted* (University College, Dublin) in Ireland in 1889.

To Maclise, drawing and watercolour were an adjunct to his main work, but Frederick William Burton (1816–1900) was an artist who worked totally in this medium. Born in Corofin, Co. Clare, the son of a country gentleman, Burton came with his family to Dublin at the age of ten for his education. He went to the Dublin Society Schools and studied under Robert Lucius West and Henry Brocas senior, whose genre paintings he found particularly influential. Burton was a precocious genius and exhibited his first work, a religious subject, in the Royal Hibernian Academy when he was aged sixteen. For the first years of his career

he worked as a miniature painter, much influenced by Samuel Lover, who gave him lessons in the art.

As well as portraits, he exhibited subject picture watercolours in the RHA, taking his themes from literary sources as well as Irish peasant scenes, of which he was one of the earliest exponents and which link his work with the new interest that we have noted earlier in this chapter among English visitors. Of these his most famous are *The Blind Girl at the Holy Well* of 1839 and *The Aran Fisherman's Drowned Child* (National Gallery of Ireland) of 1841. This had been in his thoughts since his visit to Aran with Petrie in 1839, and Margaret Stokes said that there were "at least fifty preparatory drawings in pen and pencil for the picture . . . , which show how the subject grew on the painter's brain till he found the true arrangement and grouping by which to concentrate all feeling on the parent's sorrow . . . "[11] It is not surprising that when it was first engraved by the Royal Irish Art Union in 1840 it became the most popular print the Union had published.

In a sense this picture reflected the new, widely disseminated, archaeologically minded spirit of the times, and the various societies and organizations such as the Archaeological Society of Ireland which were being founded. Burton was intimately involved with its leaders, with the circle of Petrie, O'Curry, O'Donovan and Larcom with their Ordnance Survey researches, and also with the doctors, Sir William Wilde and William Stokes, both notable antiquarians; all were actively investigating Ireland's past with a new, more academic and scientific approach. In the next generation, Whitley and Margaret Stokes, children of William Stokes, continued their association with Burton, helping him with their linguistic and archaeological researches.

Burton was also a close friend of Thomas Davis, the leader of the Young Ireland movement, a political group of the 1840s which attempted to create a cultural identity for Ireland and which hoped that Burton might realize their dreams on paper. He drew a cover for their magazine, *The Spirit of the Nation*, but he was not prepared to be involved in their active nationalism. He encouraged Davis to turn his attention to poetry and song rather than attempting to create a nationalist art.

Burton's portraits in the later 1830s and 1840s were no longer minatures, but in chalk or watercolours. The finest example is his portrait group of *Lady Gore Booth and her two daughters (Plate 244)*, exhibited at the Royal Hibernian Academy in 1845. The Renaissance-style, pyramidal composition of this watercolour, with its Venetian overtones, is supported by his exquisite handling of Lady Gore Booth's voluminous, shot-silk skirt. It is interesting that Burton made detailed studies of hands, arms, drapery and other details in the true Raphaelesque manner and, despite the fact that he lived in Germany for many years, it was to Italy that he looked for inspiration in his youth.

He paid two short visits to Germany in 1842 and 1844 but went to live there in 1851 at the invitation of Maximilian II of Bavaria, as a curator of the royal collection. He stayed for seven years, sending pictures back to London for exhibition, mostly peasant German subjects including the very large *Tyrolese Boys trapping birds*, which he sent to the Old Watercolour Society in 1859. These watercolours tend not to be his best work, though the study in the Ashmolean, for the architecture in the *Franconian Peasants Waiting for Confession,* 1855 (National Gallery of Ireland), is a fine watercolour, better than the finished work. Burton

243
ERSKINE NICOL
The 'Merican Difficulty,
1862
(Ulster Museum)

244
FREDERICK WILLIAM
BURTON
Lady Gore Booth and
her two daughters, 1845

245
FREDERICK WILLIAM
BURTON
Helellil and Hildebrand,
The Meeting on the
Turret Stairs, 1864
(National Gallery of
Ireland)

returned to London in 1858, where he lived for the rest of his life, becoming part of the Rossetti circle, though he made numerous visits to Ireland to see his old friends.

These influences must have inspired Burton's masterpiece *Helellil and Hildebrand, The Meeting on the Turret Stairs (Plate 245),* 1864 – perhaps the most famous of all Irish

watercolours. This was based on the translation of a Danish ballad by Whitley Stokes, and with its brilliant colour and romantic medievalism it is very Pre-Raphaelite. The artist's friend George Eliot, of whom he painted a famous portrait (National Portrait Gallery), said of it, "The subject might have been made the most vulgar thing in the world – the artist has raised it to the highest pitch of refined emotion . . . "[12] *The Times* critic goes even further and states that the picture is "a personification of that lofty woman worship which was at the very heart of chivalry."[13] Despite these raptures it must stand in the forefront of Victorian watercolour painting. Another picture which rises above its sentimental subject is *The Dream (Plate 246)*. He produced a number of medieval subjects, such as a young page with a helmet entitled *Recuyer – the Knight's Esquire*, 1864 (Victoria and Albert Museum). But after his appointment to the Directorship of the London National Gallery in 1874, he gave up painting.

One aspect of Burton's work has yet to be mentioned, his Irish landscapes. These he painted throughout his career, and in a letter of 1840 to Robert Callwell, Burton

rhapsodizes about the Connemara mountains *(Plate 247)*:

> This is a paradise – at the end you see the Tusk mountains and no others with an outline of surpassing beauty, and if such an evening as I had a light over them that bears you to the seventh heaven – I shall never forget the amethystine glow – that filled the whole atmosphere and tinged the silvery rocks of Maam Turk with ineffable loveliness – but every prismatic colour was visible on the mountains all softened by this violet sort of smile.[14]

His great love of nature, coupled with his learning, is parallel to the spirit of John Ruskin. On his visit to Scotland in 1848 Burton made a detailed analysis of the colours at every time of day and he did much the same in Ireland.[15] His understanding of light, and scientific study of colour means the half lights in his landscapes are particularly fine. His Irish studies are among the finest ever produced and remind one of the young Turner.

A very different character and an artist who frequently worked on a very large scale

246
FREDERICK WILLIAM
BURTON
The Dream
*(Yale Center for British Art,
Paul Mellon Collection)*

247
FREDERICK WILLIAM
BURTON
Landscape
*(National Gallery of
Ireland)*

248
JOHN FAULKNER
*A farrier's forge in
Co. Wicklow*

and also in oils was John Faulkner (fl. 1848–90). His birth date is unknown but he was accepted into the Royal Dublin Society Schools[16] in 1848 and from 1853 exhibited at the Royal Hibernian Academy, at first subjects near Dublin and in Co. Wicklow. He became an RHA in 1861. His style does not seem to vary much, and only a small number of his works are dated but from exhibition catalogues one can work out his travels. He must have gone to Scotland about 1861 when he exhibited *The Pass at Glencoe*, and he sent other Scottish works in the next few years. The first Cork view is shown in

1863 and scenes from Donegal and Sligo in 1864. A watercolour of the Shenandoah Valley, dated 1869, indicates that he went to America before resigning from the RHA in 1870, due, according to Strickland, to some mysterious scandal. However, he was back in Ireland, though not exhibiting, by the mid-1870s, as there is a dated work, *Derryneen Bridge, Connemara* of 1875. He didn't attempt to exhibit till 1880 and then seems to have settled in London. The only continental work was shown in 1887 and is of *Coblenz from the Moselle*. He was alive in 1890 when he showed a view of *Lough Gill* in the New Watercolour Society in London, and must have died shortly afterwards.

Faulkner's landscapes vary from quite precise studies of English villages like Rickmansworth,[17] a *Farrier's forge in Co. Wicklow (Plate 248)*, pastoral scenes and peasants walking along the banks of a river, to sweeping mountain panoramas, stormy seascapes and views of great lonely empty spaces. His colours, like those of Burton, often have a pre-Raphaelite brilliance. He did not work for the engravers as his life span saw the beginning of the age of photography. His pictures have an atmospheric quality which highlights the vaporous Irish climate. His marine paintings are particularly accomplished, with waves dashing on the rocks and speeding storm clouds flowing overhead, as in his *Off Cape Clear, Co. Cork* (The Whitworth Art Gallery, Manchester).

It seems likely that Faulkner was influenced by Edwin Hayes (1820–1904), who was in Dublin exhibiting during Faulkner's youth. Hayes, though born in Bristol, came to Ireland when young, was educated at the RDS Schools and lived in Ireland till 1852. From exhibited works, he seems to have returned to Ireland regularly, showing an Irish subject in the Royal Hibernian Academy as late as 1893. Though he painted mostly in oils, his marine watercolours have great verve and unite in one the movement and power of the sea, sky and sailing boats.

An artist who is, sadly, rarely found is Henry Newton (fl.1844–56). From comments made by Isaac Weld on 18 December 1844,[18] when he lists Newton among a group of English and Scottish artists resident in Ireland, we can be certain that he was English, but what works are known are all of Ireland, ranging from Co. Antrim to Dublin. There is a group of his work in the National Gallery of Ireland, which includes three very fine views of the Glens of Antrim, including the waterfall at Esna Larach. The detail and feeling for light in them is beautiful and in *Below Esna Larach Waterfall (Plate 249)* the effect of the beam of sunlight is dramatic. One of his best works is a quietly contemplative view of pleasure grounds round the ruins of Monkstown Castle, Co. Dublin, which is a valuable record of a Victorian water garden. He makes a very subtle use of greens bathed in the evening sunlight.[19]

The small watercolour portrait which was so popular in the first half of the nineteenth century continues to appear occasionally in the work of portrait painters, especially Thomas Alfred Jones (c.1823–93). This artist, whose origins remain mysterious, was brought up by the philanthropic Archdale family and educated at both the RDS Schools and Trinity College. After spending three years abroad, from 1846, he settled in Dublin where he became a prominent portrait painter and finally succeeded Stephen Catterson Smith as PRHA in 1880 and was the first President to be knighted. Jones's watercolours have a strongly Pre-Raphaelite feel, using their small strokes of brilliant colour. His subject matter, though mainly Irish, includes Faust, Tennyson, Shakespeare and Dante. His unfinished literary pictures in the National Gallery of Ireland are in carefully correct costume. His Irish pieces have sentimental titles, though his *Molly Macree* (National Gallery of Ireland) is a straightforward portrait study of a young colleen. More sombre is *A Prayer for the Absent (Plate 250)* depicting a mother with a newspaper on her lap and her daughter, clearly a Crimean subject.

An amazing watercolour panorama of Dublin, dated 1856, seen from the steeple of St. George's Church, Dublin, which fascinates visitors to the National Gallery of Ireland, is by James Mahoney (1810–79) who was born in Cork. He travelled widely in his youth and from time to time throughout his career, studying in Rome and travelling elsewhere on the continent including Spain. He seems to have lived in Cork, exhibiting there till 1856 and in Dublin at the Royal Hibernian Academy from 1842 to 1859. He moved

249
HENRY NEWTON
*Below Esna Larach
Waterfall, Co. Antrim*
*(National Gallery of
Ireland)*

on to London where he exhibited at the
Royal Academy between 1866 and 1877 and
became an associate in 1867 of the New
Watercolour Society. Fired with cosmopolitan enthusiasm in 1841 in Cork, Mahoney,
with an artist friend, Samuel Skillen (1819–
47), founded the Cork Art Union and was
very active in the arts in his home town.[20]
Most of his own contributions in 1841 to the
Art Union exhibition were Italian subjects;
later French and Spanish themes predominate. A large number of his exhibited works

appear to have been watercolours. Apart
from the panorama, Mahoney is famous
today for his fresh and fluent watercolours
of the Great Exhibition held in Dublin
in 1853, opened by Queen Victoria and
Prince Albert *(Plate 251)*. Their colours
remain so sharp and the scenes so lively that
he can be counted as one of the most interesting Irish Victorian watercolourists.

There is, however, confusion over his
work as an illustrator of magazines and
books. Though Strickland gives a long list of

these in his annotated copy of his Dictionary in the National Library of Ireland, he admits to having made a mistake and that there were two artists of this name, one purely an illustrator. Forrest Reid[21] gives an account of an Irish youth employed as an errand boy who attracted the attention of the engraver Edward Whymper by his scribblings, and developed into an illustrator. His name was James Mahoney, he apparently also came from Cork and his death date is the same as the watercolourist's, 1879, though he was younger, being born in 1847. The water-colourist Mahoney used different methods of signing, but great confusion naturally arises as they both apparently use a very sim-ilar monogram and were contemporaries in London. The watercolourist worked as an illustrator before the year in which the other was born, as he did sketches of the famine in west Cork for the *Illustrated London News* in 1847. However, they both appear to have illustrated magazines and books in London

250
THOMAS ALFRED
JONES
A Prayer for the Absent
(National Gallery of
Ireland)

251 JAMES MAHONEY *Queen Victoria and Prince Albert in the Paintings and Sculpture Hall of the Dublin Great Exhibition, 1853 (National Gallery of Ireland)*

in the 1870s. Perhaps the most serious confusion is which of them drew the illustrations for the Household Edition of Charles Dickens's works, *Little Dorrit, Our Mutual Friend* and *Oliver Twist*. We leave this problem unresolved.

A watercolourist, until recently little known, was Samuel McCloy[22] (1831–1904), from Lisburn, near Belfast. He started his career at the Belfast Government School of Design, 1850–51, and went on to the Training School of Masters in South Kensington. From there he got a post as Master of the School of Art in Waterford, where he married and was still working in 1874. In that year he returned to Belfast where he worked freelance, designing cards for Marcus Ward and damasks for the linen trade. He was also an illustrator and ended his days living near London at Sydenham. As a watercolourist McCloy was a typical Victorian sentimentalist, as is shown in *The Bather*,[23] which shows a nude girl felicitously using a convenient branch as a sensible protection against prurient eyes. Apart from genre subjects like *The Bridal Dress (Plate 252)* he painted straight interiors and landscapes like *Strickland's Glen, near Bangor*. The Pre-Raphaelite detail of this picture with the sun dappling the leaves over the stream produces a most

sensitive result. He was obviously devoted to nature. His fruit and flower paintings are mentioned on page 122, but his masterpiece is *Espaliered Apple Blossom (Plate 253)*, where the detail of the blossoms and leaves creates a subtle overall design. His wife, E.L. Harris, painted children's heads in her husband's manner.

Thomas Frederick Collier (fl.1848–88) had a broken career and must not be confused with the Englishman Thomas Collier (1840–91). Trained at the RDS Schools from 1848, he was exhibiting extensively at the Royal Hibernian Academy from 1850, when he showed one of his fruit pieces, which are close in style to William Henry Hunt, Samuel McCloy and other Victorian watercolourists discussed in Chapter 7. But he mainly painted landscapes, of which not many are known today. The *Women Seated under a Tree (Plate 254)*, dated 8 August 1855, has a beautiful, lilting composition with a flowing rhythm which makes one wish that in 1860, when at the peak of his career as Headmaster of the College of Art in Cork, he had not had a drunken fit, breaking many of the plaster casts and having to leave the School and his family under a cloud. This disaster clearly did not affect his ability to paint. He exhibited only once again in the

253
SAMUEL McCLOY
Espaliered Apple Blossom
(Ulster Museum)

Royal Hibernian Academy, in 1888, but he showed till 1874 in England at the Royal Academy and elsewhere, and a watercolour of *Appleblossom*, dated 1879, was in the sale-room recently. His death date is not known.

A pupil of the Cork Art School in 1852/3 was John Kemp[24] (1833–1923), who settled, after training at the Royal Academy, in Gloucester. There he made his career as the founder–principal in 1859 of the Gloucester School of Art, where he taught for thirty-two years. Few watercolours by him survive; one, *A Street Scene in St. Malo (Plate 255)*, signed and dated 1861, shows him to have been a highly proficient practitioner in the Samuel Prout manner. He painted Irish scenes such as the watercolour of the *Mourne Mountains from Greenore* and the oil of *Killaha Castle near Killarney*, showing that he must have visited his native land quite frequently. He exhibited in England but is best known as a teacher, his most famous pupils being Philip Wilson Steer, who painted his portrait, and the *Punch* caricaturist George Belcher. Kemp did not emigrate to Australia as has been suggested. After his death in 1923 the local Gloucester Society of Artists arranged a memorial exhibition in his honour. About a hundred paintings were on view, including one finished only five years before his death. The City Museum and Art Gallery in Gloucester holds a number of his works, including some late pure watercolours of Venice which are not as good as his more precise early style, seen in his *Rouen Cathedral*, which is dated 1860.

A family of artists from Cork called Stopford produced two generations of artists. Robert Lowe Stopford[25] (1813–98) was Dublin-born but settled in Cork, where he worked as a teacher and became an art

254
THOMAS FREDERICK COLLIER
Women Seated under a Tree
(Victoria and Albert Museum)

correspondent of the *Illustrated London News.* Robert Lowe Stopford had a long career painting mostly local Cork views, including a splendid view of *Queenstown (Cobh), Co. Cork (Plate 256),* and another of Cork harbour from St. Aubyns. Three detailed drawings of the building of viaducts on the Great Southern and Western Railway in Co. Cork are in the possession of the Crawford Art Gallery. Stopford travelled in England

255
JOHN KEMP
A Street Scene in
St. Malo, France, 1861
(Victoria and Albert
Museum)

Facing Page:

256 (Top)
ROBERT LOWE
STOPFORD
View of Queenstown
[Cobh], Co. Cork
(Crawford Municipal Art
Gallery, Cork)

257 (Bottom)
WILLIAM HENRY
STOPFORD
Flamborough Head,
C.1871

painting, but his work can usually be described as competently dull.

His son, William Henry Stopford (1842–90), is much more exciting. He was born in Cork, studied under his father and in the School of Art in Cork before going to South Kensington. Later he taught in St. Martin's Place School of Art and became Headmaster in Halifax School of Art.[26] He specialized in cliff views using a pre-Raphaelite technique and to some extent colour. His *Flamborough Head (Plate 257)* of c.1871 has a dizzy viewpoint, looking down sharply on a rocky stack from the top of the cliffs and on to the gulls wheeling round it. Another, slightly less spectacular, view of a cliff face with caves is a brilliant study of rock structure and very evocative of the sound of the sea and the gulls. In 1890 it was recorded that the lithograph of his *Blarney Castle* sold 140,000 copies in America alone.[27] This must make it the most popular view painted by any Irish artist, satisfying the Irish emigrants with a sentimental vision of the source of their "gift of the gab."

Henry Albert Hartland (1840–93) was from Mallow. He studied at the Cork School of Art and began his career working in a picture dealer's and doing scene painting in Cork and Dublin. He left Ireland in 1870 and lived mostly from then on in Wales, Liverpool and London, though he paid many visits to Ireland. His work was particularly popular in Liverpool and a number of watercolours are in the Walker Art Gallery. One of his finest paintings is his brooding *Last Ray of Evening, Shannon Bridge* of 1876 in the Victoria and Albert Museum. This is a set piece and has all the technical skill so admired in his day as well as an ability to paint atmosphere. His *Bog of Allen (Plate 258)* is a superlative representation of windswept

258
HENRY ALBERT
HARTLAND
The Bog of Allen

259
JOHN DOYLE
*Susannah and the Elders
(lithograph), 1837*

trees and the lonely distances of the bog. Some of his lighter pastoral scenes are reminiscent of Faulkner.

An entirely different artist stylistically was William Davis (1821–72), but Davis and Hartland have in common the link with Liverpool. Davis spent most of his life there, though he paid visits back to his home near Leixlip. There are very few watercolours known by him and he appears to have used the medium only in connection with his oils. The fine example *Ploughing* (Walker Art Gallery) is a detailed finished watercolour, but it is so close to an oil of the same subject also in the Walker Art Gallery that they must be connected, though it could not be called a study. Davis was influenced by the

Pre-Raphaelites, and the minute precision of the brushwork in this watercolour is clearly derived from them.

We finish this chapter with the Doyle dynasty, who, as far as this book is concerned, combine the problems we have met with when discussing Mulready and Maclise – i.e. that though both were born in Ireland, Mulready left as a young child while Maclise remained until his mid-twenties, but most of his career was spent in England. John Doyle (1797–1868) was, like Maclise, born and educated in Ireland. He was from a Wexford family but born in Dublin and trained in the Schools and under Gaspar Gabrielli and the miniaturist John Comerford. In Ireland he worked as a horse painter and produced rather stiff oils, exhibiting frequently in Dublin. According to Strickland he emigrated to London in late 1821. The family kept up links with Ireland, as the third son, Henry Edward, was born in Dublin in 1826 or 1827 and received his art education in Dublin. In 1869 he became Director of the National Gallery of Ireland, where he was famous for his brilliant buying. He was, however, not a watercolourist, though a number of portraits and studies in the NGI show him as a competent, academic draughtsman.

John Doyle is best known today as the caricaturist "HB" though his caricatures are not in the usual exaggerated mode of Gilray

and Rowlandson but achieve their effect through their detailed realism. A good example is his charming lithographic drawing of the young Queen Victoria in 1837 out riding with Lord Melbourne and Lord Palmerston, which he entitled *Susannah and the Elders (Plate 259)*. This is a perfect example of Thackeray's comment that "they did not appeal to 'grinning good-natured mechanics', . . . but caused one to smile in a quiet gentleman-like kind of way."[28]

The most famous of his children was Richard (Dicky) Doyle (1824–83), who was born and lived in London and does not seem to have had much contact with Ireland, though he was taught by his father and would therefore have inherited the traditions of the Schools. As Isaac Weld, secretary of the Dublin Society, remarked on 18 December 1844, "Master Richard Doyle [was] . . . a grandson of this Society."[29]

Doyle was a very fine watercolourist and best known for his illustrations, his fairy pictures and the old cover of *Punch*, but he was also a straight landscape painter *(Plate 260)*. In *Punch* he illustrates a few Irish subjects like his cartoon on the English contributions to the relief of the Famine done in 1846.[30] One of the finest of the fairy pictures, *The Triumphal Entry, the Fairy Pageant*, was

bought after his death by his brother for the National Gallery of Ireland. Another, *Under the Dock Leaves: an Autumnal Evening's Dream* (Victoria and Albert Museum) is a brilliant study of the dappled light of a woodland glade combined with a fairy progress, less obvious than in some of his works and thus more to modern taste.[31] We illustrate *The Witch (Plate 261)*, a very immediate and lively watercolour with crayon, which shows him at his least sentimental though there are "little folk" in the background. Fairy pictures were a popular genre in Victorian times, usually of much more mawkish sentiment than in Doyle's work.

260
RICHARD DOYLE
*Isel Hall, Cumberland,
1879*
*(National Gallery of
Ireland)*

261
RICHARD DOYLE
The Witch
*(Huntingdon Library,
San Marino)*

One of the influences on them was *Fairy Legends* by the Cork writer, Thomas Crofton Croker, published in 1825, which we mentioned earlier as it influenced Maclise.

From an Irish point of view, the youngest son, Charles Altamont Doyle (1832–93), now famous as the father of Sir Arthur Conan Doyle, is the most interesting. He was, in both his writings and drawings, sympathetic to Irish nationalism, as can be seen in his drawing of a High Cross in memory of Lord Edward FitzGerald[32]. Though an amateur, he was a fine watercolourist and it is tempting to suggest that his *Bank Holiday (Plate 262)* represents an Irish fair such as the one held at Donnybrook, near Dublin. This has an element of caricature but is a lively, colourful scene. It is sad to record that he went mad and spent some years in the Montrose Royal Lunatic Asylum in Edinburgh, which he ironically called "Sunnyside." Both Charles and Richard have at times a nonsense element in their work which links with that of Edward Lear.

Other members of the family, notably the sisters, also drew in a comic vein. A number of sketches[33] by Sylvia Doyle, such as a watercolour of a Dublin horse-drawn bus *(Plate 263)* with caricatured figures sitting on

top and another of a carriage upsetting an apple-woman, show Sylvia's quick-witted style. These came from a large collection of her drawings and sketches showing the high life in which she moved.

262 (Right)
CHARLES ALTAMONT DOYLE
A Bank Holiday, probably Donnybrook Fair
(National Gallery of Ireland)

263 (Top)
SYLVIA DOYLE
A Dublin Horse-drawn Bus

CHAPTER ELEVEN

MOSTLY PRIMITIVES AND AMATEURS

One of the fascinations of watercolours is the work of primitive artists who, in most cases, will have had little or no training but whose charm and verve rises above their lack of technical skill. Upper-class children were taught to draw, paint, play a musical instrument and dance. A record of this is in the account book dating between 1771 and 1785 of the Rt. Hon William Brownlow of Lurgan, who brought his family during "Parliament winters" to their Dublin House in Merrion Square.[1] He notes on 19 January 1773, "A month's Drawing for Letitia £2.2.9d." Later the name of the master appears as Mr Warren, whose wife was also paid to teach the children dancing. This must have been the John Warren recorded in Strickland between 1768 and 1777 as a painter in crayons and watercolours and a Dublin Society Schools pupil.

An excellent example from this background is George Edward Pakenham (1717–68), the brother of the first Lord Longford, who later became a Hamburg merchant in London. In 1737 he travelled, aged twenty, to Germany, first to Dresden and then to Potsdam. There he drew King Frederick William III reviewing his giant Grenadiers in three rows *(Plate 264)*. Two of the Grenadiers – 7 ft 2 ins and 7 ft 4 ins without shoes – were Irish, and Pakenham met them to hear their histories. He returned to Ireland in September 1738 and drew the "Lovell Pacquet boat" off the Welsh coast and "the Dublin yatch." In Dublin he carefully maps out the mouth of the Liffey and the Mole at Ringsend, drawing all the shipping and houses with their Dutch gables. Constantia Maxwell has quoted extensively from his journal[2] and reproduces the view of

his carriage and four on the fine road to Mullingar with two farms with crops and stock on either side, and another of his brother's house, Pakenham Hall, with a lively fox hunt in the foreground. He describes his brother's extensive improvements, cut banks, avenues and long canal.

Though many amateur pictures were drawn by sons and daughters of the households, others may well be by local schoolmasters, coach painters or estate surveyors. Such drawings often appear in the vignettes of survey maps. They also have a more important role as valuable topographical records of the town and country of Ireland going back to the second quarter of the eighteenth century.

One of the earliest is a bird's eye view of the town of Clones in Co. Monaghan *(Plate 265)*, dated 1741, by an unknown artist. This shows its church, its square with high cross, its slated houses, the remains of the castle bawn, the ruined round tower, the surrounding countryside with tilled fields, woods, a carriage and four that contrasts with a farm cart and finally, on the horizon, a very well-preserved motte. A very similar watercolour of Montalto, Co. Down *(Plate 266)*, shows Lord Moira's seat with its new plantings. It is dedicated to the Earl by his most humble servant "M [Matthew] Wren." It is just possible that these two drawings are by the same hand, though the artist of Montalto clearly loved smoking chimneys and they do not appear in the view of Clones. They are the equivalent in watercolour of the great oil painting of Stradbally Hall and gardens.[3] The artist, Wren, is almost certainly one of the map-maker John Rocque's assistants.

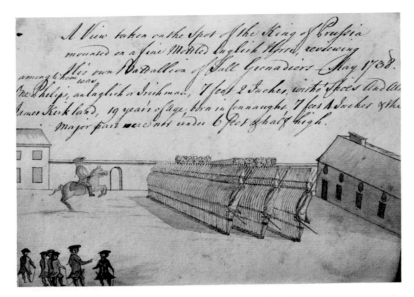

264 (Top)
GEORGE EDWARD
PAKENHAM
*The King of Prussia
reviewing his Giant
Grenadiers, 1737-38*

265 (Above)
UNKNOWN ARTIST
*A view of Clones,
Co. Monaghan, 1741*
(National Library of
Ireland)

266 (Right)
MATTHEW WREN
Montalto, Co. Down

abbey, its adjacent buildings and its surrounding battlemented walls. Marshall knew more about perspective but did not include people, so that *Howth* has far less general interest. A later eighteenth century *View of Enniscorthy taken from the Rising Ground above the Mall (Plate 268)* is indistinctly signed "R French(?)" and graphically shows the river with its shipping, the old bridge and the dominating castle keep with its towers and bartizan. A more professional town view is that of *Enniskillen from the Fort hill (Plate 269)* which is proudly signed by William Clarke and done in 1787 for Doctor Smyth. The charm of this watercolour lies in the delineation of every house and monument – even the castle is brought into view, despite the fact that it could not be seen from this vantage point. All the architectural features are numbered with an accompanying key and one must imagine that it was made for engraving.

Horse breeding and horse racing were very much part of Irish life then as now, and it has always been surprising to us that so few horse pictures by Irish artists survive in any medium. Daniel Quigley was probably the best-known Irish horse painter in oils in the eighteenth century. Much of his work derives, or is copied, from the Englishman James Seymour, and a watercolour reflecting the influence of these artists in the Mellon Collection at Yale is entitled *The Portraiture of Othello the Property of Mr Prior late S[r] Ralph Gores. Taken from the life (Plate 270)* and goes on to list the horse's wins. It is unsigned and probably by an Irish artist, possibly a sketch

Another of the same genre is signed and dated "Marshall del[t] 1745," and entitled *A Prospect of Howth, from a Mount to the East (Plate 267)*. This feebler, but less primitive, drawing shows the harbour and roofless

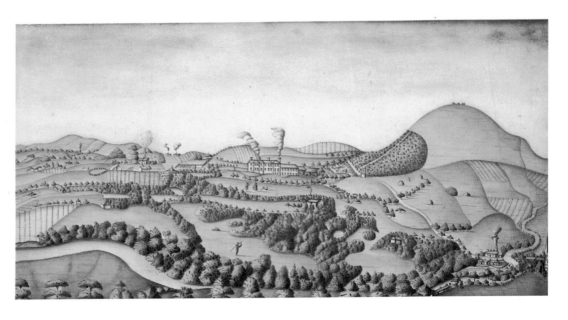

by Quigley, and is striking with its silhouetted outline.

In contrast to the world of the racetrack, betting and silver two-handled trophies is the particularly spectacular naïve painting of the Methodist, *George Whitefield preaching in the timber yard at Lurgan, 12 July 1751 (Plate 271)*,[4] which is by the woollen draper William Miller (d. 1779). It is one of Ireland's most original primitives and, as John Hewitt[5] has commented, it reminds one of New England work, and shows Whitefield with Geneva bands and squinting eyes towering over a crowd of often grotesque, bonneted women and barefaced men said to have been likenesses of Lurgan citizens. The artist has cut round some of the heads, which gives the composition a three-dimensional, collage effect. Above in the sky is a lengthy inscription in Miltonic blank verse, possibly Miller's own composition.

An anonymous painting entitled *Lord Kingsborough's Lake (Plate 272)* (Lough Key, Co. Roscommon), probably dates between 1766 and 1768, when the Kingsborough peerage was briefly recreated. It has been suggested that this most professional of amateur paintings is by Lady Andover, a friend of Mrs Delany, and a sister of the third Earl of Aylesford. She came from an artistic family, but we have no evidence that she was in Ireland. It is tempting to see it as a product of the Dublin Society Schools with its links with Barralet and its general resemblance of composition and figures to George Mullins

and Thomas Roberts. It also has echoes of Thomas Sandby.

The line between professionals and amateurs can be slight, and William Osborne

267 (Top)
MARSHALL
A Prospect of Howth, Co. Dublin, from a Mount to the East, 1745
(National Library of Ireland)

268 (Above)
R. FRENCH
A view of Enniscorthy, Co. Wexford

269 (Left)
WILLIAM CLARKE
Enniskillen from the Fort Hill, Co. Fermanagh, 1787

270
UNKNOWN ARTIST,
POSSIBLY DANIEL
QUIGLEY
Othello
*(Yale Center for British Art,
Paul Mellon Collection)*

271
WILLIAM MILLER
*George Whitefield
preaching in the timber
yard at Lurgan, 1751*
(Ulster Museum)

Hamilton's watercolours are an example of high-quality work. We have no idea of how he was trained, but his three views of Lota, the mansion newly built by Davis Ducart for the Cork-born burgher Robert Rogers, all date about 1772 and show his highly skilled painting. The first *(Plate 273)*, dated 1772, is a panoramic view of the house set in its

272
UNKNOWN ARTIST
*Lord Kingsborough's
Lake, Rockingham,
Co. Roscommon*

273
WILLIAM OSBORNE
HAMILTON
Lota, Co. Cork, c.1772

274
CATHERINE
BORTHWICK
*Kilkenny on the Nore,
the Ormonde Castle*

plantations, with a masterly display of ship-ping in the river Lee in front and old Black-rock Castle with its eighteenth-century domed gazebo in the left foreground. The second gives a more detailed closeup of the house, with Ducart's architecture clearly portrayed and a chaise and numerous visitors riding and walking in the grounds. The third is a view from the house, signed and inscribed "View from Lota demesne... the little island and sun lodge... Passage in the dis-tance." These must be among the most delightfully arcadian views of an eighteenth-century Irish estate.

Returning to castles and leaping some de-cades, *Kilkenny on the Nore, the Ormonde Cas-tle (Plate 274)* was the subject of Catherine

275

H. PRESTON
*Gormanstown Castle,
Co. Meath*

primitive genre as late as 1806, when he painted his *East View of Ardmore* (National Library of Ireland). He came from Dublin and might well have drawn the vignettes in maps or such other decoration.

The nineteenth century spawned a plethora of good amateurs. A good example of topography is the *View of the Main Street of Kells (Plate 276)*[6] by a painter who signs "E.W." It is dated July 1810. The artist may well have been trained, as he understands perspective and the varied architecture, including a house with its Dutch gable, a fortified tower house and the village inn, which are all well differentiated. It also shows the British military presence on guard outside their sentry boxes. It is a most charming and informative town view. The topographical delination of Irish towns is rarer than one might expect but an excellent and detailed example is the anonymous *View of Newry (Plate 277)* drawn in the 1850s, which shows plainly the influence of Burgess. Visitors were inclined towards this genre, and there is a fine purply evening view of Drogheda seen through the Boyne Viaduct *(Plate 278)* of 1878 by Henry George Roper-Curzon, seventeenth Baron Teynham (1822–92).

Despite the length of this chapter we can only touch on a small number of amateurs; there were enormous numbers of them. Two

Borthwick's watercolour done around 1800, with the river figuring prominently in the foreground and people fishing, promenading and boating. *Gormanston Castle (Plate 275)* was primitively depicted by a member of the Preston family, possibly a daughter of the eleventh Viscount, and is signed and dated indistinctly "H. Preston 179?." A coach is arriving and the building is shown in its medieval and seventeenth-century guise before the whole place was romantically transformed into a great baronial pile in Regency times. Charles Haliday was working in this

276

E.W.
*View of the Main Street
of Kells, Co. Meath,
1810*

277
UNKNOWN ARTIST
A view of Newry,
Co. Down

who drew and painted in Russia are amusing. John Joshua Proby, first Earl of Carysfort (1751–1828), was active in Irish and English politics and a friend of Lord Charlemont and Henry Grattan. He went as Minister to Berlin from 1800 to 1802, and while there visited St. Petersburg, where he

executed a number of amateurish but unusual watercolours of Russian characters such as two White Russian nobles, a "Patriach of Imeretia" and Cossacks marching *(Plate 279)*. The other amateur who visited Russia, also artistically weak but fascinating, was Martha Wilmot, the daughter of an

278
LORD TEYNHAM
The Boyne Viaduct,
Drogheda, Co. Lough,
1878

279
LORD CARYSFORT
Cossacks Marching

Great [by Falconet]. The base was dragged across the swamps of Finland by a "mammoth orchestration of manpower"[7] reminiscent of the building of the pyramids.

Maria Edgeworth is, of course, so well known today for her novels that it is worth noting that, like all her family and her stepmother's family, the Beauforts, she also drew. We have already mentioned her stepuncle, William Louis Beaufort (Chapter 3), and a sketchbook of antiquities and genre scenes by his sister Louisa Beaufort survives in Trinity College, Dublin.[8] Their brother Francis, later a distinguished Admiral and member of the Royal Society, was also very interested in painting and drew with neat precision. There is a view of *Collon village (Plate 280)*, 1821, showing the church designed by his father, Daniel Augustus, after King's College Chapel, Cambridge. The rest of his career is discussed in Chapter 13. It is worth noting that he visited art exhibitions both in London and Dublin and wrote to Ireland about them, in his letters to his family, including the Edgeworths.

Maria Edgeworth was most interested in genre painting, particularly David Wilkie and Nathaniel Grogan, two of whose works

English army officer living in Glanmire. She lived for some five years with the Princess Dashkoff in Russia in St. Petersburg, in Moscow and in her country estate, Troitskoye from 1803 to 1808. Her watercolours are a historical record of great interest and show various aspects of Russian life down to a watercolour of Peter the Great's watch. She seems to have copied paintings of earlier events like *The Transporting of the Granite Base for the Equestrian Statue of Peter the*

280

FRANCIS BEAUFORT
Collon village,
Co. Louth, 1821

she mentions in her letters.[9] The two Grogan paintings were the *Country Schoolmaster* and *The Wake*, both from the Listowel Collection. Her own sketches are totally incompetent but very amusing; one, for instance, shows her digging into the very top of her clothes cupboard and in the next she is seen falling as the ladder breaks in half.[10] She went to France in 1802 with a family party including her half-sister, Charlotte, who drew far better than Maria. A particularly interesting sketch done by Charlotte in Paris is of Madame Recamier visiting the aged dramatist and critic, Jean François de Laharpe *(Plate 281)*, who died in that year. Maria describes the scene, which took place on 10 January 1803:

> He lives in a wretched house, and we went up dirty stairs, through dirty passages, where I wondered how fine ladies' trains and noses could go and we were received in a dark, small den by the philosopher . . . he was in a dirty reddish nightgown, and a very dirty nightcap bound round the forehead with a superlatively dirty chocolate-coloured ribbon. Madame Recamier, the beautiful, the elegant, robed in white satin trimmed with white fur, seated herself on the elbow of his armchair, and besought him to repeat his verses. Charlotte has drawn a picture of this scene."[11]

After these dramatic events in France we return to the quieter world of Irish and English fashionable life with a correspondent of Maria's, Catherine Maria Dawson, later Countess of Charleville (1762–1851) whose sensitive studies of oak trees in the great park at Charleville are worth recording. Her most ambitious surviving painting is a gouache, *A view of Bangor with the late 18th century Gothick Penrhyn Castle, Wales*,[12] presumably painted after her son became M.P. for Penrhyn. Lady Morgan, who was a close friend, wrote imploring her for a picture. "I have my boudoir full of the offerings of foreign artists; but nothing of nature, of Irish talent,"[13] an example of how people collected their friends' paintings. Lady Charleville was described as "Irish and not exactly the sort that pleased . . . but after many years' acquaintance the excellence of her heart, her sense, her wit, and friendship, has compleatly attached us to her for her own sake . . . She is

in love with her lord . . . They are very rich, tolerably recherché in London, and want no help in worldly affairs."[14]

Artistic talent ran in the family and her granddaughter, Lady Beaujolais Eleanora Catherine Bury (d.1903), did a series of competent, if pedantic, interiors of Charleville Castle in 1844. They are a valuable record of an early Victorian interior. A much more exciting interior dated 1837 is of the drawing room at the old house at Adare, Co. Limerick *(Plate 282)*. It is a fascinating study of Regency draped curtains, lacquer furniture and brilliant pink walls; unfortunately we do not know its author.

Neither do we know the name of the student who drew a Dublin drawing room in 1817 *(Plate 283)* when it was being used for an operation. The civilized decoration with a wall hung with pictures, a fine mirror and fashionable curtains accentuates the barbarity of the event – blood everywhere and bowls of it sitting around on the carpet. The inevitable result was the death of the patient two weeks later.

281
CHARLOTTE EDGEWORTH
Madame Recamier and Monsieur de Laharpe, 1803

Less alarming but equally interesting as examples of nineteenth century interiors are the drawings made by Maryanne La Touche (c.1810–70), who drew a series of interiors between 1840 and 1842 of Marlay, her father's house, and Bellevue which belonged to her uncle, Peter La Touche. The drawing room at Bellevue with its empire curtains and its neo-classical ceiling has much of its furniture under casement covers, showing how much care our ancestors took of their possessions.

All of these make sharp and remarkable contrasts with a pencil study by another

282
UNKNOWN ARTIST
The drawing room of the old house at Adare, Co. Limerick, 1837

unknown artist of an ensign's room in the barracks in Omagh *(Plate 284)*, done in 1836. It records all the officer's dress and equipment and a number of his pictures, framed and unframed, hung above the fireplace and about the room.

A diplomat amateur was Sir John Crampton, second Bt. (1805–86), the son of the well-known Dublin surgeon, Sir Philip Crampton, Bt., who was artistic and an intimate of the Beauforts and the Edgeworths. John must have learned to draw extremely competently before he joined the diplomatic corps, as his drawing of St. Petersburg *(Plate 285)*, dated 1830, showing a boat with a group of men talking set against the background of the Peter and Paul fortress, is an assured study. His sense of humour was marked and can be seen in his drawing of the second Earl of Enniskillen playing his harp in his carriage *(Plate 286)* with a procession of his tenantry behind him, dated 1839.[15] His style changes totally, probably as a result of some lessons from David Cox, Junior, so that the sea piece in the Victoria and Albert Museum is almost a pastiche of David Cox, Senior, being a pure watercolour with virtually no outline. However, he later returns to his outline manner, though using a freer, bolder line. His sister Selina was also a watercolourist but of less competence, who frequently visited her brother on his various posts. A humorous example of her work is *The Winds blowing across the Lake at the Tudor Cottage at Lough Bray, Co. Wicklow*

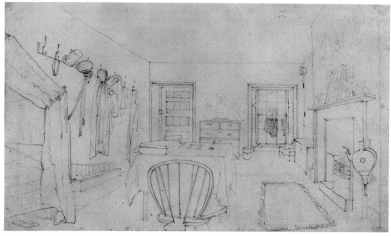

283 (Top)
UNKNOWN ARTIST
An Operation in a Dublin drawing room, 1817
(The Meath Hospital)

284 (Above)
UNKNOWN ARTIST
An Ensign's room in Omagh, Co. Tyrone, 1836

285 (Left)
SIR JOHN CRAMPTON, BT
A scene in St. Petersburg, 1830
(Department of Prints and Drawings, British Museum)

(Plate 287). The cottage had been built for them by their old friend, the architect Sir Richard Morrison.

Morrison's son, William Vitruvius Morrison, was the architect for the mansion built for Crampton's neighbour, Sir George Hodson, Bt. (1806–88). Hodson was an excellent draughtsman, as a drawing of his house, Hollybrook, signed and dated 1857, indicates. Hodson was an amateur architect as well as an oil painter and exhibited at the Royal Hibernian Academy, from 1827 to 1875, mostly views done in Europe. His drawings include a view of the *Seminoff monastery in Moscow*, Rhineland castles, the walls of Seville and a particularly sensitive *View from Sorrento*. His figure studies show

well his soft modelling as in his *Boy with an Oar* (Plate 288). His still lifes in watercolour were exhibited at the end of his life, and one dated 1875 shows that they were competent and painted with *trompe l'œil* effect.

One of the best of the visiting amateurs was the Revd Richard Calvert Jones, who was in Ireland in 1835 to officiate at the wedding of Lord Glengall's daughter at Cahir, Co. Tipperary. He made a tour and did not leave till 1836, making views of shipping as well as country towns such as Cahir and a view of Cahir House with figures chatting in its garden. His study of the backview of an officer of the 15th Hussars, who were posted in Cahir, is superbly informal, showing the jacket of the officer's uniform slung

paint and often to take lessons, as he did in Venice on 14 October 1851, and again in Rome, where he was with the artist, James Swinton, in November 1851 and with William Callow, whose watercolour view of St. Peter's is stylistically close to Dufferin's work. He also copied in both Venice and Florence.

In his family seat, Clandeboye, he was involved in painting stage sets and of course in painting watercolours of local scenery and antiquities and of such events as his own wedding in 1862 *(Plate 290)*. He depicted the children of his tenants all dressed in white strewing rose petals in front of him and his bride, Hariot Rowan Hamilton. He was active as President of the Belfast School of Design from its foundation in 1849 and mentions in his speech on the 26 March

288
SIR GEORGE
HODSON, BT
Boy with an Oar

289
REVD RICHARD
CALVERT JONES
Hussar Officer, c.1835/6

over his shoulder *(Plate 289)*. Jones has become increasingly famous as a pioneer photographer and his work is often mistaken for that of his friend, Fox Talbot.

The best documented of the amateurs is the first Marquess of Dufferin and Ava (1826–1902), whose eminent career as a diplomat, as Governor General of Canada and Viceroy of India is very well known. His Canadian watercolours will be discussed in Chapter 13. His work as an artist has rarely been noticed. He was precocious both as a critic and as a painter. His unpublished diaries tell us a good deal about his artistic career: for instance, he first admires Rubens and Van Dyck in 1839,[16] aged thirteen, and goes on in 1842 to criticize the Royal Academy in London, particularly Maclise. On a second visit he describes Maclise's picture in the following words: "everything is solid nothing clear and transparent or light . . ."[17] Earlier,[18] he had recorded making a copy after Turner.

He was active as an artist by this time, having been taught at Eton by the drawing master, Gordon B. Bradley. He painted his room there and later his rooms at Oxford. He had been sketching in Naples in 1842, and throughout his career he continued to

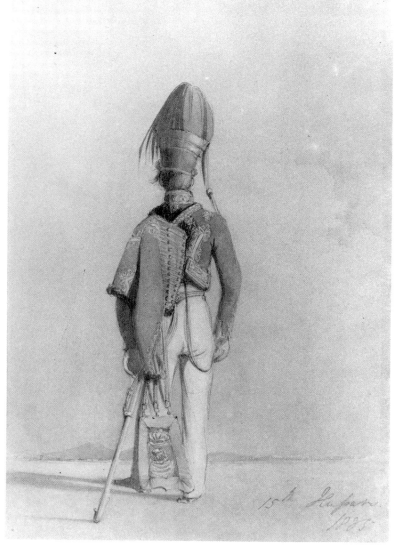

290
MARQUESS OF
DUFFERIN AND AVA
*Lord Dufferin bringing
his bride to Clandeboye,
Co. Down, 1862*
(Dufferin Foundation)

1851 that "they had collected £400 in support of the School,"[19] which was much more than had been collected in Dublin, Cork or Manchester. On his frequent returns to Ireland from his overseas appointments, Dufferin made drawings of the Clandeboye estate he had taken so much care in landscaping with the professional gardener and guidebook writer, James Fraser, mostly in the 1850s. A long panorama from the roof of the house shows the planting and Helen's Tower on the horizon. There is a companion picture looking back from Helen's Tower. He uses vivid colour in his watercolours and simple, strong outlines.

As we have noted, most of the leisured classes, whether male or female, took drawing lessons, and many achieved commendable standards, though they are often important today for what they recorded rather than for their artistic merits. An example of a famous author whose watercolours are known is Oscar Wilde. His blotchy view of Lough Corrib was probably done when he was young, from Moytura, his father, Sir William Wilde's house.

A more consistent practitioner was Vice Admiral Lord Mark Kerr (1776–1840), a younger son of the fifth Marquess of Lothian and married in 1799 to Charlotte, Countess of Antrim in her own right. He was a topographical draughtsman and watercolourist, particularly interested in eccentric garden follies and grotesque "monsters" *(Plate 291)* dressed as human beings. He was precursor of Edward Lear. He made a personal illustrated logbook when on the ship *HMS Lion* from 27 September 1792 to 9 September 1794, which took Earl Macartney and Thomas Hickey to China. It is replete with shore lines and a series of buildings and landscapes in China. His landscape views of seats, such as Belvoir, Lord Dungannon's house near Belfast in its woods, is inscribed "drawn by father, Lord Mark Kerr in 1805." He was also an amusing caricaturist and probably learned the basis of his art when he was in the navy.

Another Northerner, but one of professional competence is the architecturally minded clergyman, the Revd Narcissus Batt (1824?–98), who was a pupil of Andrew Nicholl. Ten volumes of his enormously interesting architectural drawings belong to the Ulster Museum and include such important examples as the drawing of the nave of Christchurch Cathedral, Dublin, made before its alteration. Though most of his pen and ink drawings are not of Irish buildings, *The Interior of the Chapel at Ferns Castle,*

1833, is an outstanding example. Martyn Anglesea says of it: "He perfected a sensitive way of hatching to express the texture of dressed stone work."[20] A relative, Mrs Batt, did many watercolours in the North including Purdysburn House, The Batts' Belfast home.

John Arthur, second Lord Bloomfield (1802–79) and son of one of the Prince Regent's Irish cronies, is another example of one of these interesting recorders. A watercolour sketchbook of his appeared on the Dublin art market a few years ago, showing many Tipperary houses including Bloomfield Lodge, where he was born, and Loughton, where he lived. One of the most interesting was the view of Mitchelstown Castle, Co. Cork (now demolished), showing its entrance by the beautiful eighteenth-century Kingston College. They all date from the late 1830s.

These views of houses and seats remind us that in Jane Austen's *Emma,* Mr Dixon, the Irish landowner, who was wooing Miss Campbell, sent drawings by himself of Bally-craig, which the chattering Miss Bates described as being a beautiful place: "Jane has heard a great deal of its beauty; from Mr Dixon I mean – I do not know that she ever heard about it from anybody else; but it was very natural, you know, that he should like to speak of his own place while he was paying his addresses . . ."[21]

Prospective governesses, as well as prospective wives, were sometimes sent views. An example dating from 1812 was of Mrs Honnor sending a view of Lee Mount to her proposed governess, Elizabeth Fenwick, who wrote:

> I was shown a fine view of Lee Mount. It stands on the side of a Hill, sheltered to the North by a wood. The grounds slope down to a river, on the other side of which rises an abrupt precipice, crowned with the ruins of a fine old Castle. The background, of a range of Mountains, shuts in the whole. In a painting it is romantic & picturesque in the extreme."[22]

Miss Fenwick took the post, and her letters from Lee Mount are a fascinating record of the Jane Austen-like country life in Ireland in the early nineteenth century, in contrast to her later adventures in Barbados, New

York and Connecticut. We have met with the younger Grogan as being art master to this family in Chapter 5, and it is interesting that Lee Mount still survives, just outside Cork at Carrigrohan.

A lady of remarkable interest and talent was Mary Ward, née King (1827–69), who married a younger son of Lord Bangor and lived at Ballylin, Co. Offaly. She painted a watercolour of the avenue *(Plate 292)* there on 24 September 1858. She was a notable Irish naturalist and astronomer and, as Owen

291
LORD MARK KERR
"To Bed... To Bed, To Bed Shakespear [sic],*"*
1827

292
MARY WARD
The Avenue at Ballylin, Co. Offaly, 1858

Harry claims, "Ireland's first lady of the Microscope."[23] She was also an author of a number of important scientific works, including one on the natterjack toad, 1864. We are not concerned with her scientific drawings, but her topographical views show her good rendering of architecture but sometimes very weak handling of trees and shrubs. Many watercolours by her hang in Castleward, Co. Down (National Trust), her husband's home. She met with a tragic end, run over by her cousin Lord Rosse's steam carriage.

His sister, Lady Alicia Parsons (1815–85), was also an artist. She drew views in Birr, and her sketchbooks include a number of the denizens of the town, officers of the garrison, local ladies and elderly gentlemen walking in the Mall, many with witty soubriquets. Perhaps her most unusual works are her naïve view of the *Harbour at Kingstown* and *A Scene on the Packet Boat* in the Irish Sea in the mid 1860s. She eloped to Gretna Green in 1837 and married the son,

Edward, of Queen Victoria's dreaded Sir John Conroy.[24]

An interesting Irishwoman, Mary Boyle (c.1800–69), married in 1817 the Revd Christopher Lovett Darby from Leap Castle and lived at Kells Priory, Co. Kilkenny. Her brother-in-law was John James Hornby, the rector of Winwick Lancashire, the parish near Knowsley, the Earl of Derby's seat. During a visit there she met Edward Lear, who was working for the Earl, and he was the principal influence on her work, which is, strangely, most readily seen now in the Indianapolis Museum of Art.[25] Her landscapes are influenced by Lear with their strong lines, distant horizons and a great sense of space. She painted in Ireland, landscapes and subjects such as the *Interior of Holy Cross Abbey* and *Flood Hall* near Jerpoint, but also in England, Sussex and the Lake District as well as Lancashire. She went on a European holiday in 1850 to France, Belgium and down the Rhine to Switzerland. Whether she met Lear on his

293
LOUISA PAYNE
GALLWAY
The Long Gallery at Adare, Co. Limerick, c.1867

visits to Ireland is not known, but he visited and drew in Ireland on more than one occasion, for the first time in 1835. His chalk drawings made in Co. Wicklow accentuate the distant coastal scene and contrast the simplicity of the outline of the Sugar Loaf mountain with the outlines of a foreground fir tree.

Louisa Payne Gallway (d.1872) was born at Adare, sometime in the second decade of the century, the daughter of General Sir William Payne Gallway and his wife, Lady Harriet Quin, daughter of the first Earl of Dunraven. Some of her watercolours, which are weak enough in technique, are set in a screen which is still in the family's possession. They include a wide variety of subjects, ranging from a study of Irish peasant girls to landscape views in Ireland and especially of Adare with its ruined abbeys and castle. The screen, which was a gift to her cousin Augusta Vivian, was entitled *Memoirs of Old Haunts and Happy Days* and dated 1867. The most interesting watercolour is the interior of the Long Gallery in the recently rebuilt Adare Manor *(Plate 293)*, showing the family in their domestic life.

A figure we have already met is Catherine Isabella Osborne of Newtown Anner, the mother of Lady Blake (see Chapter 7). She was a keen sketcher and a series of her sketchbooks survive at Myrtle Grove. They were done on her country house visits and include notes and sketches, made in the 1860s, of practically every country house in Northern Ireland. An amusing touch was the sketch entitled *A Memory of a Perfectly Sleepless Night* showing a sketch of her

baldaquined bed at Strawberry Hill on 8 July 1871.

Watercolours such as these and others we have mentioned are extremely important for the restoration of the rooms of the past. Outdoor activities are also recorded, as in the charming watercolour of gentlemen picnicking while out shooting on Gibson's Bog under the Devil's Bit, Co. Tipperary *(Plate 294)*. This is reputedly by Emily Rachel Gibson, a Tucker from Trematon Castle, Cornwall, who married in 1868, William Gibson of Rockforest, Co. Tipperary.

Mary Herbert[26] (1817–93), the wife of Henry Arthur Herbert of Muckross, who was a Balfour from Whittinghame in Scotland, continued the Herbert tradition (see Chapter 5) of recording and creating picturesque buildings and landscapes around Muckross House, Killarney *(Plate 295)*, between 1843 and Queen Victoria's visit in 1861. Her own landscapes, which began as rather fussy studies, are simplified with experience till her late work depicts with real talent the hazy blues and greens of Killarney's unmatchable landscape and lakes. A close contemporary and an Englishwoman who married an Irishman is Louisa Ann Stuart (1818–91), who came to Ireland on her marriage in 1842 to the third Marquess of Waterford, the notorious sportsman. She lived at Curraghmore until the death of her husband in 1859. She was a pupil of Ruskin and professional in quality, moving in the circle of Watts and Burne-Jones. Apart from her cartoons for stained glass windows in the church at Clonegan, few of her Irish watercolours are known, though sketchbooks

295
MARY HERBERT
Killarney Lake from
Muckross, Co. Kerry

survive in the Waterford family collection. A good example of an Irish subject is the richly coloured scene, entitled *Kinahan's Whiskey (Plate 296)*, showing two pathetic children watching their parents carousing inside the whiskey store.

Her brother-in-law, who became the

fourth Marquess, married in 1843 Christiana Leslie of Glaslough, the sister of the artist Sir John Leslie (1822–1916). Lady Waterford and Sir John were close friends and shared a passion for painting, which he studied after he left the army in 1850. In 1853 when he exhibited *Children, They have*

296
LADY WATERFORD
Kinahan's Whiskey

297
SIR JOHN LESLIE, Bt.
View of Florence

Nailed Him to the Cross[27] in the Royal Academy, he was a fully professional, near Pre-Raphaelite painter. However, he took further lessons in Dusseldorf in 1856 and in Rome with Richard Buckner, the portrait painter. Some watercolour sketches such as his panoramic *View of Florence (Plate 297)* survive from his Italian period at Glaslough and show him to have been a competent watercolourist.

Moving from high life to low life far away in Listowel, Co. Kerry, is a very rare depiction of a local squire being entertained in a shebeen *(Plate 298)*, painted about 1842 by a Bridget Maria FitzGerald (1817–1905), a member of a minor gentry family living in Listowel, related to the Knights of Kerry. She must have seen Grogan's pictures or prints of them and possibly engravings of interiors by Wilkie, which were well known. Her manner, though very primitive, is expressive, and the watercolour exudes bustling vitality; there is music provided by a Scotch piper, cards played in the background, the squire, looking somewhat worse for wear, slumped in his chair, not

298
BRIDGET MARIA
FITZGERALD
*A Shebeen, Listowel,
Co. Kerry, c.1842*
*(On loan to the Listowel
Library)*

299
SAMUEL WATSON
The Irish Jig, 1845

300
CAPTAIN WILLIAMS
In Days of Yore, 1839
(National Library of Ireland)

to mention gossiping shoppers and a pig eating from a creel of potatoes.

A watercolour by Sir Lucius O'Brien, who rebuilt Dromoland Castle, should be noted here as it depicts "below stairs," the laundry at Dromoland, and is an illustration for one of O'Brien's unpublished doggerel poems in which a phantom appears at the door. Sir Lucius was a cousin of the O'Briens discussed in Chapter 13, who were painting both in Canada and in New Zealand.

These naïves form a particularly interesting contrast with a grisaille watercolour by the artist Samuel Watson (1818–67?), a Cork illustrator who is probably best known for his booklet, *Historic Furniture of Ireland*, 1853, designed and lithographed for Arthur Jones and Son, the cabinet-makers. Although he is a trained artist, we feel that it is sensible to include Watson at this point as his watercolour *The Irish Jig* (Plate 299), which was exhibited at the Royal Hibernian Academy in 1845, is another folk piece and thus particularly valuable. It is a signed and dated work and shows another shebeen, with lively dancing figures, political discussions over rival newspapers by the hearth, fighting figures and, of the greatest interest, beautifully depicted details of domestic utensils. In its careful, smooth professionalism, it is entirely different from Miss FitzGerald's robust amateur attempt.

Urban peasant sketches by Captain Williams, who is little known, include one signed and dated "Captain Williams del Dublin 1839," which shows a decrepit cab with a cadaverous horse and an Irish driver with apelike features. This typical caricature has immense vitality and is entitled *In Days of Yore (Plate 300)*. Another, a sketch of *Mick Fagan, the Stage Coachman* in livery, smoking his pipe, is dated Dublin Castle 1 Jan 1856. These drawings illustrate the English attitude to Irish peasants,[28] one of disdain and ridicule. The use of simian features for the Irish is a well-known feature of English political caricatures.

Unfortunately, it is rather shameful to find an Irishman, Lord Gerald FitzGerald (1821–86), taking up this derogatory tone in depicting fair scenes and on the race course. He was better known as an etcher than a watercolourist. His family included three other amateurs: his mother, Charlotte Augusta, Duchess of Leinster (1793–1859); his cousin, Frances Charlotte FitzGerald de Ros (d. 1851); and her daughter, Olivia Cecilia (d. 1885), who was an amusing and authentic portrayer of high life.[29]

To return to topography, we must briefly consider an amusing, if frankly bad, artist, William Greenlees, whose main importance is as a recorder of long-vanished houses. No information is known about him, but as many of his subjects are Northern, he may

have come from Ulster. A typical example of his work is his view of *Vice-Regal Lodge, Phoenix Park, Dublin (Plate 301)*, dated 16 December 1838. The foreground is awash with military activity, citizens on horseback, running deer and factory-like chimney smoke.

A contrasting unknown artist drew a most minutely observed view of *Killeavy Castle, Co. Down (Plate 302)*, with its elaborate gardens which include a grotto, an obelisk and a fountain, high above Newry. This is a combination of careful drawing and ludicrous naïvety of conception.

301
WILLIAM GREENLEES
Vice-Regal Lodge, Phoenix Park, Dublin, 1838

302
UNKNOWN ARTIST
Killeavy Castle, Co. Down
(Armagh County Museum)

215

303
JOHN E. BOSANQUET
*Sunville, North Circular
Road, Limerick*
(Limerick Museum)

A somewhat naïve performer, described by Strickland as being "slovenly and of little merit," is J.E. Bosanquet (fl.1854–61), who came from Cork and worked as a photographer. His drawings are valuable records of the townscape of Cork and are filled with incident. One of his country house views of Castle Kevin, Co. Cork, shows the artist with his portfolio arriving at the front of the house. We illustrate a prosperous merchant's villa, *Sunville (Plate 303)*, on the North Circular road, Limerick, with its rockery, croquet lawn and greenhouse.

Two amateurs whose quality is higher are Louisa Tenison of Kilronan Castle, Co. Roscommon, and Dacre Mervyn Hamilton of Cornacassa, Co. Monaghan. Louisa's precise drawing of Montreux *(Plate 304)* is

304
LOUISA TENISON
Montreux

typical of the Victorian lady while Hamilton's *View of the Temple of Diana at Nîmes (Plate 305)* is a far more professional work. He exhibited in the Irish Fine Art Society, which was one of the precursors of the Watercolour Society. The Nîmes drawing shows his competence at architecture and his ability to handle light and shade. His daughter, Lady Bangor, was also a competent watercolourist.

The end of the century is so full of amateurs that it is impossible to discuss them all. One can mention as typical examples Mrs Coralie de Burgh (1880–1959) and Mrs Gilliland (fl.1892–1939). The most famous of all was William Percy French (1854–1920), always known as Percy French, that uproariously funny writer of popular songs, mostly Irish, who entertained at least two generations of Irish, English and American audiences. It is not surprising that he made a lot of caricatures. He had been trained as an engineer in Trinity College and started life as a drainage engineer in Co. Cavan, an occupation which naturally invoked an amusing, popular song, "William, Inspector of Drains."

French was a prolific watercolourist, painting sketches wherever he went. He nearly always used a blotchy, pure watercolour technique but wrote on 17 July 1901 in *The Tatler* an article on *How I make Smoke Pictures, with a piece of porcelain, a match and a candle.*[30] Although most of his work is straight landscape *(Plate 306)*, he occasionally painted in towns, and his charming view of the side of the Museum Building in Trinity College is an example of this aspect of his work and shows the influence of Rose Barton. Most of his landscapes have an airy, atmospheric quality, redolent of our bogs and humid climate.

A number of amateurs congregated in Cork, which was the second most important artistic centre in Ireland. James Beale (1798–1879) was one of these. He was a shipbuilder who commissioned, in 1837, the *Sirius*, the first steamship to make the Atlantic crossing. Before these shipping activities he had travelled extensively in Italy, Norway and Morocco, where he painted numerous watercolours. A letter written from the North African coast in 1832 shows him working: "I finished

between breakfast and dinner today a sepia light and shadow drawing of a thunderstorm off the bay of Tangiers, coast of Africa, with an Algerian pirate in the fore-sea and the Atlas mountains in the distance. I took the outline from nature and was in a thunderstorm very near where I took the sketch from."[31] *A Storm off the Bay of Tangiers* is a tumultuous essay in sail, sea and mountain peaks, and another of *Torc Waterfall* (O'Sullivan's Cascade) has the same sinuous and cursive line. In contrast, *Isole Madre Lago Maggiore* is all peace and tranquillity (all, Crawford Art Gallery, Cork). A relative of his partner R.J. Lecky, Susan Lecky (1837–96), was an excellent draughtswoman and did some fine studies in Valentia, Co. Kerry, near where she lived, from about 1863, at Ballinskelligs Abbey (Crawford Art Gallery, Cork). She also worked as

305
DACRE MERVYN
HAMILTON
Temple of Diana at Nîmes

306
PERCY FRENCH
*In County Donegal,
Ireland*

a botanical painter and was known as a plantswoman.

Joseph Stafford Gibson (1837–1919) was more interesting. Apparently he was born to a family that lived much in Spain, having become fascinated by that country when fighting in Wellington's Peninsular campaign. Gibson presented an enormous portfolio of watercolours to the Crawford Art Gallery in 1919. These probably represented his life's work, and very fine they are too. They are unfortunately totally unknown today, as they were during his lifetime, since he never exhibited. He travelled widely on the continent, as they contain drawings, not just from Spain but from France and Germany and one watercolour of Kensington Gardens. There are none of Ireland, despite the fact that he was a native of Kilmurry, Co. Cork.

On his occasional trips to Ireland, he visited the Headmaster of the Cork School of Art, James Brenan, for help and encouragement, and he finally bequeathed to the School his coin collection, his Spanish ceramics and his silver ware as well as his watercolours and, most importantly, a sum of £14,790 "for the furthering of Art in the City of his boyhood."[32] This formed the Gibson Bequest, which was used to buy pictures for the Crawford Art Gallery.

The watercolours themselves are truly remarkable and vary from the delicacy of his foliage in pictures of the Forest of Compiegne, 1869, or Nogent sur Maine, 1872, to the abstract Glacier de Bossons, Chamonix, 1876, and the extraordinary verve of his series of alleyways with their overhanging roofs, shadows, and searing light, which he did in towns in Spain later in his career, from 1898 to 1907.

We must mention that though most of the amateurs we have discussed worked too early to learn from them, Vere Foster's ten books of instructions on Watercolour Painting were of considerable influence after they came out, in the last third of the nineteenth century. They were published in Belfast and he employed excellent artists to make the copy drawings. The books gave detailed instructions on all the materials required, from paper to pencils, rubbers, brushes, palettes, etc. His first *Drawing Copy Book for National Schools* was published in 1868 and, surprisingly, his *Advanced Watercolour Drawing Book* came out in 1873, some ten years before *Simpler Lessons in Watercolour*, 1883/84. Books on flower painting, marine painting, landscapes, trees and coastal scenery followed hard on each other's heels. They were approved by the Education Department and praised to the hilt by *The Graphic* who said, "If any parent who reads these lines has a boy or girl who wishes to learn how to be an artist, let us boldly recommend Vere Foster's Drawing Book. It is not only the cheapest, but by far the best we have seen."[33] They were among the most influential artistic products to come out of Ireland.

We might wind up this chapter with a figure typical of many an army officer and amateur. He sums up the sophistication and cosmopolitan qualities of many Irish families who lived on the continent. Ireland with its agrarian woes must have seemed a sad place to retire to, and the sunnier atmosphere and climate of Italy beckoned. An example was Colonel Robert Goff (1837–1922), who in his later life is best known as an etcher, though he was a watercolourist and illustrated his wife's books on Florence and Assisi. He peopled his views with impressionistic figures, though the architecture remains solidly portrayed. They vary from a Whistlerian image of *Charing Cross Bridge* (Plate 307) on a wet evening to the warmth of a street in Cannes with its cafés and shops.

This amateur work varies enormously in quality from the naïves of Greenlees to the professionalism of the Pro-consul Lord Dufferin, but all of them give us vivid insights into the life and *mœurs* of their period. They should not be disregarded.

307
COLONEL ROBERT GOFF
Charing Cross Bridge, London
(Bristol Museum and Art Gallery)

308
FANNY CURREY
*The West Gate at
Clonmel, Co. Tipperary,
on market day, 1889*

309
HELEN O'HARA
Sea piece

CHAPTER TWELVE

THE WATERCOLOUR SOCIETIES
AND THE LADY ARTISTS

The last thirty years of the nineteenth century saw the establishment of various sketching clubs in Ireland which eventually became the Watercolour Society of Ireland.[1] According to Strickland, there had been an isolated exhibition of watercolours in 1823, though no record of this exists. It seems, surprisingly, given the popularity of the medium, to have led nowhere. The Royal Hibernian Academy relegated all but a few watercolours to an ill-lit back room, and this must have annoyed women exhibitors as the preponderance of their work was in that medium. The English watercolourists had organized themselves in 1804, so that it is even stranger that it was not till 1870 that a group of ladies in Lismore and Clonmel founded their society, the Irish Amateur Drawing Society, for the "mutual improvement in painting and drawing and the cultivation of a taste for art."

Their number included the redoubtable Miss Fanny Currey (d. 1912), Baroness Pauline Prochazka (d. 1928), Miss Harriet Keane (d. 1920), Miss Frances Keane (d. 1917), Miss Henrietta Phipps and Miss F. Musgrave (d. 1918), all from nearby landed families. The Society's first exhibitions were held in 1871, and from then on regularly till 1891 in various provincial centres in Ireland, and annually from 1877 in Dublin. A summary of the catalogue of the third exhibition held in 1872 in Carlow and two laudatory reviews of it have been published indicating that the exhibitions achieved some success.[2] The Society changed its name to the Irish Fine Art Society in 1878 and finally to the Watercolour Society of Ireland in its Belfast exhibition of 1887/8.

Miss Currey was renowned as a grower of daffodils and owned the Warren Nursery in Lismore, which was famed for its daffodil varieties, so it is not surprising that many of her paintings were flower pieces. Until recently, however, nothing by her was known to us except some envelopes decorated when she was a girl.[3] A charming watercolour of Clonmel *(Plate 308)*, dated 1889, was recently found in the collection of her friend and neighbour, Lady Blake of Myrtle Grove in Youghal, which shows the West Gate on market day. It is a freely worked picture, demonstrating that she knew about the recent developments in painting. Gifford Lewis says she worked as a journalist.[4] She had many influential friends like the Osborne girls from Newtown Anner who were to become the Duchess of St. Albans and Lady Blake (see Chapter 7) and Edith Somerville, well known for her writing as well as her painting. It was, no doubt, partly due to these friends that her efforts for the watercolour painters were so successful. Edith Somerville wrote to Violet Martin on 3 May 1888: "Fanny Currey has written to me to meet her in town before the 14th, as she wants to talk about Picture shows and the like."[5]

Miss Currey gave her address in the Royal Hibernian Academy as The Mall House, Lismore, from 1882 to 1896 when she stopped exhibiting with them; in 1898 she was joined by Helen O'Hara (fl.1881–1919), who gave this address in exhibitions from then on. Nothing is known of Helen O'Hara's training but a watercolour dated 1882 by her is known. She came of the Co. Antrim family and taught painting in her early years. The Ulster Museum's *Evening*, which is a seascape with two gulls, was

310
HARRIET E. KEANE
The Bluebell Wood

probably painted in Portstewart, where she lived for some time. It is very competent and professional. Other sea pieces *(Plate 309)* are known; one on the Dublin art market shows a dramatic storm scene with billowing spray, rain clouds and a steamer labouring away in the distance. Not much of her work has emerged as yet, though Martyn Anglesea has seen a McCloy-like early work, and some pastoral scenes are known, including the quietly assured and undated *A Mountain Stream*, an autumnal study of bracken, moor and pine trees with a rushing stream as its high point. Miss Harriet Keane's style is somewhat similar as can be seen in her delicately painted *Bluebell Wood (Plate 310)*. Some of her paintings, from the titles in the Royal Hibernian Academy, indicate that Helen O'Hara was influenced by Mildred Anne Butler, with whom she corresponded. A *View on the River Blackwater (Plate 311)* is the most detailed, delicate essay, in shades of green and white, showing her masterly talents and that at her best she was as good as Mildred Anne Butler or Rose Barton.

In Dublin the ladies organized themselves in 1872 under a Miss Deane in the Ladies Sketching Club, and in the following year kindly allowed gentlemen to become members. Miss Deane was superseded as Secretary in 1874 by Miss Mary Kate Benson

(fl.1874–d.1921), so that the two societies were generally known as Miss Currey's and Miss Benson's.

The gentlemen had not remained entirely idle and had formed the Dublin Sketching Club, with Alexander Williams as Secretary in 1874. We discuss this later in Chapter 14; it was an entirely different type of group with meetings once a week where they drew a set subject. They had numerous outings and convivial social evenings. A humorous caricature by Frances Nugent, entitled *Souvenir de Castle Connell (Plate 312)* shows a group of three ladies and one diminutive gentleman, feverishly sketching away on the Shannon bank. A great number of professional artists joined the Dublin Sketching Club and, though ladies had been honorary members from the early 1880s, in 1888 Miss Benson's Ladies Sketching Club amalgamated with them.

Another club was formed in Queenstown (Cobh), Cork, in the early 1890s, of which Beatrice Gubbins was later Secretary, and in Belfast the Ramblers Club[6] was founded in 1879. All these societies helped to disseminate watercolour painting in Ireland and made for a very lively artistic scene towards the end of the century. For women it was a triumphal period, as many young ladies who would never have been permitted to attend a

311
HELEN O'HARA
*View on the River
Blackwater, near
Lismore, Co. Waterford*

university were allowed to study at professional art schools. Some, like Mildred Anne Butler, actually seem to have gone on their own. She went to London and Newlyn, though Edith Somerville was accompanied by several members of her family when she first went to Paris. There had been numerous lady amateurs painting in Ireland throughout the century, but in the 1880s several achieved professional status though they still lived at home and were financially independent. The work of Fanny Currey, for instance, by the late 1880s was considered so highly that she "could not be considered an Amateur in any sense of the word save one, that she is not dependent upon the pursuit of Art for a livelihood."[7]

The oldest of the group of lady artists was Rose Barton (1856–1929), the daughter of a lawyer with a fine country house at Rochestown, Co. Tipperary. Unfortunately her father died in 1874, the year she made her social debut at the Viceregal court in Dublin. It has been conjectured[8] that she had a disastrous love affair and the combination of this and the death of her father resulted in her going, in 1875, on a visit to Brussels with her mother and sister, where she learned painting and drawing. Afterwards they went on to Geneva. Sometime later Rose worked in London under the

landscape painter Paul Naftel and was in Paris in the early 1880s, where she studied under Henri Gervex. She may have been contemporary there with Jacques Émile Blanche, whose style is closely reminiscent of Rose Barton's in its subtle, impressionistic mood. She had exhibited *Dead Game* as early as 1878 in the Royal Hibernian Academy, but her subjects change in 1883 to more typical atmospheric-sounding scenes like her picture entitled *Winter*. Though much of her later life was spent living in London, she kept in close contact with her Irish friends

312
FRANCIS NUGENT
*"Souvenir de Castle
Connell," Co. Limerick,
1905*

and relatives. She exhibited at the Royal Academy for the first time in 1884 and was a regular exhibitor at the Watercolour Society of Ireland. She became an Associate of the Old Watercolour Society in London in 1893 and later, in 1911, was the first woman member of the Society to show over seventy paintings. Many of her watercolours are of Dublin and London because she illustrated two books, *Picturesque Dublin, Old and New*, 1898, and *Familiar London* in 1904 for which she also wrote the text.

Rose had a real feeling for weather, especially the foggy atmosphere of London with its glimmering street lamps, rain-washed streets and busy thoroughfares. In a letter to her friend Mildred Anne Butler written in

1924, depressed by being unable to paint because of ill health, she says, "Unfortunately all the effects my soul loves mean more or less bad weather and I have a beloved dragon of a nurse who lives with me and prevents me doing anything rash."[9] Her figures are good and full of character if sometimes sentimental, but her beautiful, Whistlerian, muted colours as in her *View of the Custom House (Plate 313)* never fail to express the season and the time of day.

Her subjects are straightforward everyday scenes. Her rather rare beach scene, *On Yarmouth Sands*, 1893 *(Plate 314)*,[10] she exchanged for a picture of peacocks by Mildred Anne Butler. The picture is remarkably Boudin-like, pale and shimmering in

313
ROSE BARTON
The Custom House, Dublin

summer sunlight, and it is a reflection of her French training which clearly pleased her, as she gave it to her artist friend. Unlike most Irish women painters, Rose Barton had a sentimental streak and painted children beautifully, as in *Here we dance Lubin, Lubin (Plate 315)*. *The Turkey Girl (Plate 316)* is another genre subject in which she handles the different textures of grass, feathers and flowers with great skill. She had a social conscience like may of her contemporaries as can be seen in her sombre interior entitled *The Treasure of the Humble (Plate 317)*.

Though only two years younger than Rose Barton, Mildred Anne Butler (1858–1941) is a later developer. In 1878, the year Rose Barton first exhibited at the Royal Hibernian Academy, Mildred's drawings are schoolgirl in style, copying romantic subjects, bulls fighting, army and hunting scenes, with a tight dry brush. They show little promise and it was only while working from about 1883 to 1885 under Paul Naftel that her talent blossomed. He may possibly have been known to her family as he had taught Rose Barton a few years earlier and he had worked in Ireland about 1860–1. Mildred Anne prized four watercolours by Naftel and always said that it was from him that her first real understanding came.[11] Her tuition was by post; she seems to have sent Naftel a portfolio of drawings and watercolours once a month and these were returned annotated with constructive criticism. He thought a great deal of her and felt

314
ROSE BARTON
On Yarmouth Sands,
1893

that the change in her work and perception had been enormous in the three years he taught her. Her interest in animal painting, which can be seen from her earliest works, must have led her to the studio of William Frank Calderon, well known for this genre, who founded a school of animal painting in 1894 where such artists as Munnings and Lionel Edwards were later to study.

In July 1894 she was in correspondence with Luke Fildes and Stanhope Forbes over suitable lodgings in Newlyn,[12] where she went with May Guinness, another Irish artist, to study under the Limerick-born painter, Norman Garstin. She spent two summers in Newlyn in 1894 and 1895, and she was influenced by Garstin and Forbes. From them she must have heard about the impressionists, as Garstin had written about Manet and knew Degas.

315
ROSE BARTON
"Here we dance Lubin,
Lubin"

This period saw Mildred develop her final style, broad washes, strong use of colour and great understanding of sunlight and shadows. Despite the titles of her pictures, she is rarely sentimental and if one compares her work with that of many of her contemporaries like Helen Allingham and Maud Naftel, whom she must have known, she keeps her subjects simple, uncluttered and direct. She does not paint pretty peasants in English villages because she lived in Kilmurry *(Plate 318)*, a large, but unpretentious, country house and farm *(Plate 319)* in Co. Kilkenny, in a deeply rural setting *(Plate 320)*, green and lush.

Most of her work was done there though she travelled to the continent regularly and to England frequently, where she exhibited in shows which travelled round provincial centres. She also exhibited abroad, in France and Japan; and in 1911, the Grand Duke of Hesse bought two of her pictures in an exhibition sent to Darmstadt. Her other royal patrons were Queen Alexandra and Queen Mary, for whom she painted a tiny picture for her doll's house. In 1896 her work *The Morning Bath* was bought for the Chantrey Bequest (Tate Gallery), the first work by a woman artist bought by them, and in the same year she became an Associate of the

316 (Facing Page)
ROSE BARTON
The Turkey Girl

317
ROSE BARTON
The Treasure of the Humble

Royal Society of Painters in Watercolours. She was only made a full member in 1937, after she had given up painting due to arthritis.

Though from her sketchbooks Mildred seems to have painted a great deal in the open air *(Plate 321)*, much work was done in the studio from detailed notes taken on the spot, supplementing her small, quick drawings. She made full-scale charcoal cartoons for her major watercolours, many of which survive, obviously because correction in this medium is nearly impossible. Moreover, she

318
MILDRED ANNE
BUTLER
*A Window at Kilmurray,
Co. Kilkenny*

319 (Facing Page)
MILDRED ANNE
BUTLER
Steam Threshing

320 MILDRED ANN BUTLER *The Orchard*

321 MILDRED ANNE BUTLER *The Artist Painting*

paid great attention to realistic detail. In 1888 and again in 1900 there are letters from Mr G. Picard, a London taxidermist, specifying the prices for stuffing a selection of ordinary birds. Clearly she found stuffed specimens necessary alongside her own observation. She also used photography in the case of the steam train and for many of her animals. The photograph of her painting tethered cows *(Plate 322)* outside is an amusing sidelight on her problems. In an undated letter from a friend, Lucy Guinness, who lived near Newcastle-upon-Tyne, Mildred is asked to stay to study a splendid array of crows' nests beside the railway near Chester-Le-Street. Mrs Guinness says, "It would be rather jumpy with the trains tearing by every few minutes,"[13] but nonetheless she clearly felt Mildred would surmount all obstacles to study the nests close at hand.

The set pieces of animals and birds like *And straight against that Great Array Went Forth the Valiant Three (Plate 323)* seem to become less frequent after the First World War, and her luscious studies of the gardens at Kilmurry with its opulent borders and superb trees become her main subjects from the war years onwards. The flower pictures understandably became very popular and were her principal exhibits towards the end of her career, though they are repetitive and sometimes even garish. The war and her arthritis must have curtailed her travelling, though she painted particularly charming scenes of children on the beach at the seaside in Ireland, at Tramore, in 1917, 1918 and 1919.

Although the nostalgia of Edwardian country house life, with its apparently endless summer days *(Plate 324)*, unhurried beauty and peace, haunts most of her work, it is not for that that she is renowned, but as a highly competent artist in watercolour. A great revival of interest in her pictures has recently taken place since her studio, which remained nearly intact, was sold from Kilmurry in 1981.[14] In her day, Mildred received remarkable critical acclaim on both sides of the Irish Sea, and a perspicacious critic in the *Athenaeum* of 5th May 1897 sums up her style aptly:

> The young lady knows how to look at her subjects with the eyes of a well-trained

artist; she can make good pictures out of simple and indeed trivial material; and all her . . . contributions are extremely interesting and even beautiful, although there is not a shred of story, anecdote, incident or an atom of pathos beyond that which always attends really artistic representations of homely nature . . . These pictures command attention by the massing and breadth of their chiaroscuro, and the solid way in which they have been handled.[15]

Mildred Anne Butler's exact contemporary from Castletownshend, in West Cork, Edith Somerville (1858–1949), developed more quickly and spent a term in the South Kensington School of Art in 1877 when she was only nineteen. Her parents were nervous about her studying on the continent but allowed her to spend two terms with private masters in Dusseldorf in 1881/82, where her cousin, Egerton Coghill, was studying. In 1884, her mother, her eldest brother, a cousin and a friend all accompanied her to Paris, though they couldn't stand the boarding houses, and soon retreated to Ireland. In Paris she studied with Colarossi *(Plate 325)* over many years, staying for short periods

from time to time; much later, in 1894 and 1895, she worked under Délécluze. These escapes from the fun and headaches of life at Drishane, her home in West Cork, were clearly essential to her.

Edith may have seen herself as an oil painter, but it is as an illustrator of articles and books written by herself and Violet Martin that one thinks of her today. She developed a somewhat caricatural style of black

322
Photograph of Mildred Anne Butler painting tethered cows

323
MILDRED ANNE BUTLER
The Valiant Three, 1893 (National Gallery of Ireland)

324
MILDRED ANNE
BUTLER
*Cows in a buttercup
field*

and white drawing and also a sensitive use of wash in silhouette, as in *Children of the Captivity*. Her feeling for countryfolk is melancholy and her character studies sombre, revealing her compassion for the rigours of the life of the Irish peasant. In contrast, her highly witty illustrations of the hunting field for the *World of the Irish RM* and her drawings of studio life in Paris are lighthearted and done with a swift, instant vision which echoes her remark that "I was taught in Paris

that it was the first impression that mattered . . . paint rapidly so as to keep it fresh."[16]

After the highly professional careers of Mildred Anne Butler and Edith Somerville, the life of Beatrice Gubbins[17] (1878–1944), whose home – where many of her watercolours are now exhibited – was the Palladian House, Dunkathel, Co. Cork, is clearly that of a talented amateur. Little is known about her training, though it is thought that she went to the Crawford School of Art in Cork

325
EDITH SOMERVILLE
*Study at Colarossi's
School, Paris*

326
BEATRICE GUBBINS
*Study of a courtyard
with barrel*

where one sister did attend in 1885. She lived at home all her life but travelled extensively in Europe, particularly Paris, and North Africa. She was a keen motorist from the early years of the century and in 1931 flew to Algeria from London. From the early 1900s till the outbreak of the Second World War, she was Secretary of the Queenstown Sketching Club, a club which was rigorous in the criticism it made of members' work. This was circulated under pseudonyms, and many of her surviving watercolours still have the criticisms of other members attached.

Beatrice's subject matter is varied – domestic scenes *(Plate 326)*, landscapes and still lifes. Her work includes watercolours done in Devonshire during the First World War, as well as street scenes and figure studies done in Morocco, which she visited in 1929. She has some of the features of both Mildred Anne and Edith – the loose washes of the former, the silhouette of the latter – but her composition is rarely as tight as their professional work.

Lady Dobbin[18] (1868–c.1955) was another Cork amateur, the wife of a successful tobacco manufacturer. She was the daughter of a Bristol solicitor and presumably was trained in England before coming to Cork on her marriage in 1887, though she is said to have been taught by Harry Scully. She exhibited at the Royal Hibernian Academy from 1894 to 1947, watercolour landscapes, flower pieces and portraits. A number of Cork views such as the tower of St. Anne's, Shandon *(Plate 327)*, done in simple

327
LADY DOBBIN
*St. Anne's, Shandon,
Cork
(Crawford Municipal Art
Gallery, Cork)*

328
HARRIET OSBORNE
O'HAGAN
*Portrait of her sister,
Eugenie.*
*(National Gallery of
Ireland)*

Colville,[20] who started exhibiting in 1892 in the Watercolour Society's exhibitions and continued to do so till her death in 1953. She lived in Baily, Howth, and her straightforward landscapes and town views were justifiably popular.

Gladys Wynne (1878–1968) was another Anglo-Irish lady and, though brought up in Killarney, lived in Glendalough form 1907. She was educated in Florence and Rome but her painting belies this. It is homely, and her Irish village street, with thatched cottages and a hint of the modern world with the large parked car, is typical of her rural idylls. She handled paint with considerable competence.

There were a number of pastellists among the women painters, of whom Harriet Osborne O'Hagan[21] (1830–1921) was one of the earliest. First a pupil of the Dublin artist, George Sharp, she went to Paris about 1866 and remained there for most of the rest of her life. She studied with numerous artists, including Couture, and became a teacher, allegedly opening the first academy of women artists in Paris. Her deeply romantic style is shown in her charcoal drawing of her sister Eugenie *(Plate 328)* where the eyes dominate the delicate, sensitive face.

washes, can be seen in the Crawford Art Gallery in Cork. Her work is very atmospheric and she enjoyed painting half lights as in *Afterglow*, showing a glamorous 1920s group lingering in a garden in the twilight. She was also influenced by both Rose Barton and Mildred Anne Butler.

Another artist who was influenced by these two is Rosalie Franks[19] (fl.1921–9), about whom little is known except that she once exhibited at the Royal Hibernian Academy, in 1928, and regularly at the Irish Watercolour Society. She lived in Malahide and painted there a great deal.

A prolific watercolourist was Helen

In contrast, Harriet Hockley Townshend[22] (1877–1941) uses pastel in a more forthright manner. Her *Winter* (Castletown House) of 1911 is a boldly drawn portrait of a fashionably dressed young woman swathed in furs and a muff. As usual, nothing is known of her training, though she spent some time at the Metropolitan School of Art in 1910 and was affected by the all-pervading influence of Orpen.

Josephine Webb[23] (1853–1924), the daughter of a Dublin outfitter, had the luck to be well educated at Alexandra College and the Queen's Institute before she went to the Académie Julian, where she was a contemporary of Sarah Purser. Josephine Webb exhibited regularly in Dublin and her pensive pastel of Dora Sigerson, the poet, is in the National Gallery of Ireland.

Jessie Douglas[24] (1893–1928), from Belfast, is a livelier artist, whose fresh watercolour portrait *Cherry Ripe* makes one pleased that more of her work is appearing. She taught Jane Service Workman[25] (1873–1943), who married James Yeames, the

329
SARAH PURSER
*Portrait of John Butler
Yeats*

nephew of the well-known English painter W.F. Yeames. Miss Workman's charming *Ombre et Lumière* shows a brightly lit room through a door which illuminates the tea table set in the dark foreground. There are regrettably far too few interiors in Irish painting, though, again, Mildred Anne Butler practised this genre with considerable success.

The number of women artists at this period is quite remarkable and they cannot all be mentioned. Many of them concentrated on oils, as did Sarah Purser[26] (1848–1943), but she has to be discussed because of her remarkable and influential career. Like most women artists, she came of an upper middle class family, her father being an unsuccessful industrialist while two of her brothers were very well known Trinity College academics. Because of her father's financial collapse in 1873, Sarah had no money, and she lived in Paris for six months on thirty pounds, attending the Académie Julian in 1878/9. This clearly affected her lifetime concern with making money and no doubt gave her the strength of personality to become a great patron of the arts, who created the revival of stained glass art in Ireland nearly single-handed. She was also Dublin's wittiest and most vitriolic artistic hostess. Her charcoal and pencil nude studies done in Paris, some of which are in the National Gallery of Ireland, are remarkably strong drawings, and her later pastel portraits, such as the one of her nephew Frank,[27] are good, competent, unpretentious exercises. Her pencil self-portrait, like many of her drawings, is clearly much influenced by John Butler Yeats and is a penetrating study. We include her portrait of him *(Plate 329)*. Her small landscape watercolours show the influence of Nathaniel Hone.

Mary Swanzy[28] (1882–1978) was a younger oil painter who, however, did a considerable number of drawings. Her early training was with Mary Manning, who ran an art school popular with upper class Dubliners and had herself been educated in Paris. Later Swanzy trained in Paris under Délécluze, at the Grande Chaumière and at Colarossi's, and possibly briefly in Matisse's atelier. She was aware, as none of the others were, of the most recent developments in painting, such as the work of Degas, Cézanne, Gauguin, Matisse and Picasso. This shows up more in her oils than in her crayons, which tend to be lively and instantaneous, such as her series done in Czechoslovakia[29] when she was doing relief work at the end of the First World War. Later her work in Samoa and Honolulu is notable. She created shapes in blocks, and, though her drawings remain realist, in her oils she moves towards Cubism.

Three of Ireland's most famous women artists, Wilhelmina Geddes (1887–1955), Evie Hone (1894–1955) and Mainie Jellett (1897–1944), all worked in watercolour or gouache, though the first two are remembered principally as stained glass artists and the third for her oils. Geddes used watercolour and pencil more for studies for her glass and for illustrations and rarely as an end in itself. The other two are really outside the scope of this book as they are the founders of Ireland's modern movement.

330
MAINIE JELLETT
The Life class in the Westminster School of Art, London

With a whole generation of women behind them, they were able to strike out on brave new paths. They were perhaps, partly because of their financial independence, far more adventurous than the male artists of their time; even so outstanding a master as Orpen was conservative in contrast. Mainie Jellett,[30] perhaps the finer painter of the two, studied first in Dublin and then in London under Sickert at the Westminster School of Art *(Plate 330)* and finally in Paris under Lhôte and Gleizes. Her outstanding pencil nudes *(Plate 331)* done in her student days make a sound basis for her later abstract experiments. Unfortunately, Evie Hone's[31] early work in the Byam Shaw School in London and under Sickert and Meninsky is unknown to us, and her work in Paris, where

she stayed with Jellett, had already taken on the full influence of Cubism as had her friends. But as we are not concerned with the modern movement in this book, we must sadly leave these celebrated artists.

To conclude this catalogue of women in Irish art of the late Victorian and Edwardian era, we must admit to leaving out many an interesting name, as women's art flowered in the twentieth century. The art of the relatively leisured lives of Mildred Anne Butler, Rose Barton and their contemporaries – though one must remember most of them were active in running farms or growing daffodils and in teaching, as well as in their art – contrasts with the grit and innovation of the women of the twentieth century who set a standard for all Ireland.

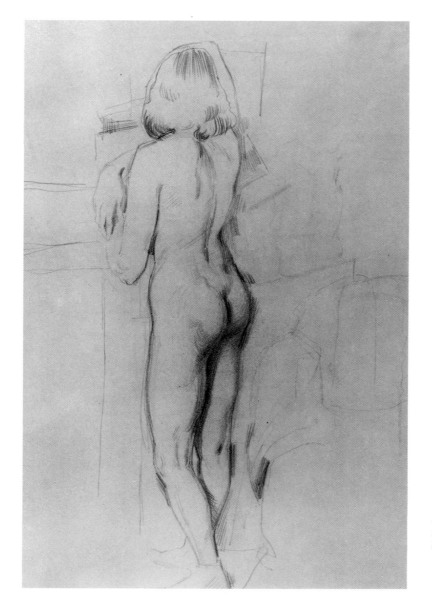

331
MAINIE JELLETT
Nude

CHAPTER THIRTEEN

THE IRISH IN AMERICA
AND THE COLONIES

We have already discussed a few artists with Irish connections who flourished in America, namely, John White, Henrietta Dering Johnston, John James Barralet and Nathaniel Grogan. Barralet, as we wrote in Chapter 4, spent the latter part of his career in America where he was highly important for his landscapes, decorative drawings and engravings. The Irish miniaturist Walter Robertson (c. 1750–1802), a Dublin Society Schools product, who went to America with Gilbert Stuart, lodged with Barralet in Philadelphia and painted a miniature of Washington for which Barralet provided embellishments.[1]

A few other miniaturists, such as Lawrence Sully (1769–1803/4) and John Ramage (fl.1763–d.1802), also had American careers. Sully was the elder brother of the famous portrait painter, Thomas Sully, and was born in Kilkenny and trained in England. John Ramage[2] entered the Dublin Society Schools in 1763 and is recorded painting in Halifax, Nova Scotia, from 1772 to 1774 and then in Boston. He led a lively life, including a bigamous marriage, not to mention time in a debtors' jail. As well as miniatures he is said to have drawn pastel portraits,[3] which is extremely likely given his training, and to have worked as a goldsmith. His most famous miniature is of George Washington, done in 1789 in New York, for which he made the chased gold frame.[4] It was magnanimous of Washington to employ him, as he had fought throughout the War of Independence as an officer in the Royal Irish Volunteers, a regiment formed by Irish merchants in Boston to fight the Americans. In New York he was very successful, a great beau and considered the best artist working

there. An engraving or fine ink drawing of the head of a man was recently found in Dublin and may date from the brief period he worked in Dublin before going to Canada. Fleeing from his creditors in 1802, he finally returned to Montreal where, in an obituary, he was described as "Limner being a wandering Portraitist."[5]

Very few amateur artists from Ireland worked in the American colonies, though Guy Johnson[6] (c.1740–88) was an exception. He came to America when he was about sixteen to assist his future father-in-law, Sir William Johnson (1715–74), of Johnson Hall in Upper New York State, who was the Secretary and Deputy Agent for Indian Affairs during the French and Indian Wars. Sir William himself was a military draughtsman; an engraved *View of Niagara Fort*, inscribed "taken by Sir William Johnson on the 25th July 1759," further mentioned that it was "drawn on the Spot in 1758." This engraving, showing the battlemented fort and strong house on the shores of Lake Ontario, was published in the *Royal Magazine*. Guy's only surviving work is a well-known view of Fort Johnson, "drawn on the spot by Mr Guy Johnson in Oct 1759."[7]

Isaac Weld (1774–1856) is a more interesting artist. He attended Samuel Whyte's school in Grafton St., Dublin, and then went adventuring in America and Canada in the wilderness with Indian guides, escaping shipwreck and other disasters. He also got to know George Washington at Mount Vernon and moved in the best circles. Weld illustrated his own book, *Travels through the States of North America and the Provinces of Upper and Lower Canada, during the years 1795, 1796, 1797.*[8] Sadly, none of the

332
CHARLES CROMWELL
INGHAM
*Warrior at the Last
Judgement*
*(New-York Historical
Society)*

original watercolour views survive, though a copy after *A View of the Hudson River*[9] is in the New-York Historical Society. Except in the United States, this book was enormously popular, being translated into French, German and Dutch. Weld returned to Ireland disillusioned by his travels in America, "finding the society less than ideal and the scenery not as grand as he had expected."[10] In 1807 he published his popular guide to Killarney. Later he became Secretary to the Dublin Society, making the speech at a Distribution of Premiums at the Schools in 1842 (see Chapter 4), in which he estimated that ten thousand artists and craftsmen had passed through the Schools since their foundation nearly a century earlier.[11]

A prize-winning product of the Schools who occasionally worked as a miniaturist was Charles Cromwell Ingham,[12] (1796–1863), who also studied under William Cuming and exhibited in Dublin both before and after he went to America in 1816. One of the first artists to exhibit at the American Academy of Fine Arts, founded in New York in 1816, he was also a member of the New

York Drawing Association and a founder and Vice President of the National Academy of Design. Ingham was a popular painter, specializing in sentimental portraits of girls and women with all the elaborate trappings of costume, coiffeurs and flowers. He is known, too, for subject pictures which included Fuseli-like watercolours, such as his *Warrior at the Last Judgement (Plate 332)*,[13] a sepia now in the New-York Historical Society. He was instrumental in establishing the Artists' Sketch Club in 1829 and was its first President. He was also involved in its reorganization in 1847 when it became the famous Century Association, New York's most intellectual and learned gentlemen's club. He was a vital figure in social and artistic circles in New York.[14]

The best-known and perhaps the most interesting Irish artist in the United States at this period was William Guy Wall[15] (1792–after 1862). By the time he arrived in New York from Dublin in 1818, Wall was a fully trained artist and had an immediate success with his far-famed *Hudson River Portfolio*, a series of twenty hand-coloured aquatints after watercolours which he published between 1820 and 1825 and reprinted in 1828. They were so popular that they were even regularly reproduced on Staffordshire pottery[16] and have been described by I.N.P. Stokes as the "finest collection of New York State views ever published."[17] A large number of the watercolours are now in the New-York Historical Society's collection[18] and in the Metropolitan Museum of Art *(Plates 333 and 334)*. In style they look back at artists like Thomas Sautell Roberts, Gaspar Gabrielli and Oben, whose work he would have known as a young man, rather than to Sandby, as has been suggested.[19]

Strickland does not mention that he went to the Schools but he must have been taught in Dublin. It is worth recording that Wall's engraver, John Rubens Smith, claims to have taught him the proper watercolour technique, but this sounds like sour grapes as Smith was removed from his job as engraver of the Hudson River Portfolio and replaced by John Hill.[20] William Dunlap, who wrote a *History of the Art of Design* published in 1834, describes Wall's technique as follows: "Mr Wall's practice of late is to color all his drawings from nature on the spot 'the only way' he says, 'to copy nature truly'."[21] Donald Shelley describes Wall's use of watercolour,[22] noting his unerring rendering of light and shade and his colours adapted from nature, consisting mainly of blues, greens and browns receding into the distance and giving an illusion of atmospheric perspective which very much reflects his Irish background. This is evident in his *View of the Hudson River and New York from Weehawk* (Metropolitan Museum of Art).

The Hudson River watercolours are somewhat old-fashioned: they are formally composed with carefully placed figures but have a fresh and glimmering quality of woods and water. He handles the tumult of waterfalls sometimes uneasily, but his sheets of still water are depicted with great limpidity. As they measure fifty to seventy-five centimetres (twenty to thirty inches) or more

across, it is unlikely that Wall did in fact colour them outside, as has been suggested. In the engravings there are alterations from the watercolours and they lack the delicacy of the originals.

Wall exhibited at the American Academy of Fine Arts[23] from the moment he arrived in New York, possibly Irish subjects, as one was of ruins. He became one of the first members of the National Academy of Design in New York and exhibited there from 1826 to 1837. He also exhibited at the Pennsylvania Academy and the Boston Athenaeum. He was a member of the Sketch Club, which his fellow countryman, Ingham, had helped to found. It is pleasant to record that that great statesman and man of taste, Thomas Jefferson, was an admirer of Wall's work and that in about 1826 he had offered Wall the situation of Teacher of Drawing

333
WILLIAM GUY WALL
View of the Hudson River
(Metropolitan Museum of Art, The Edward C. Arnold Collection)

and Painting at the University of Virginia, which he had helped to found the year before. Wall declined, as it was not a professorship, but nevertheless this was a great accolade.[24]

Wall also worked in oils. He returned to Dublin in 1837 where he exhibited at the Royal Hibernian Academy and in 1847 became President of the Royal Irish Art Union. But he went back to New York about 1856 and finally returned in 1862 to Dublin, where it is presumed he died. Though he exhibited watercolours as well as oils in the RHA, few Irish scenes survive. They include an oil of the Dargle valley, taken from the same spot that Barret and Barralet had used in the previous century. This has recently been on the New York art market as "Catskill Scenery." An interesting sideline illustrating the lengths to which artists had to go to earn a living at this period is his connection with "Master Hubard,"[25] an infant prodigy in scissor work with whom Wall exhibited pictures and for whom Wall painted backgrounds in an undated exhibition in Galway. He had a son, William Archibald Wall, born in New York in 1828, who worked as an artist not only in the United States but also in Ireland and England, where he died sometime after 1875.

334
WILLIAM GUY WALL
The Bay of New York taken from Brooklyn Heights
(Metropolitan Museum of Art, The Edward C. Arnold Collection)

335
WILLIAM CRAIG
Alice Falls
(Museum of Fine Arts,
Boston, M. & M. Karolik
Collection)

The Dublin-born William Craig (1829–75) was educated in the Dublin Society Schools and worked till 1862 in Ireland, exhibiting picturesque views and ruins in watercolours at the Royal Hibernian Academy. There are two examples of his work in the National Gallery of Ireland, one, *Kingstown Harbour and Killiney Hill Obelisk from Carrickmines,* signed and dated 1849, with the word "Pupil" added. This is a pale imitation of the work of Petrie, with naïve figures, including a peasant girl carrying sticks. The other, *Dublin from Three Rock Mountain,* 1854, shows a marked improvement and the influence of Faulkner. In 1863 Craig went to the United States, where he became one of the eleven original members of the American Society of Painters in Watercolour founded in 1866. He seems to have been quite successful exhibiting Irish as well as American views *(Plate 335).* One entitled *Fort Lafayette, New York Harbour*[26] is in the New-York Historical Society and is dated 1875, the year he was drowned in Lake George.

Some of these Irish artists arrived in America quite young, such as Edward Gay (1837–1928) and William James Hennessy (1839–1917), but as they received their artistic training in America we are not concerned with them here. The same applies to painters usually associated with oils, such as Thomas Hovenden (1840–95), even though he had been trained in the School of Art in his native city, Cork.[27]

Irish artists reached Canada almost as early as the other American colonies: John Ramage, whose American career we have outlined, was first in Halifax in 1772. As one might expect, it was in the area of surveying, map-making and fortifications that we find them first. They were frequently soldiers who would have had some training in mechanical but not figure drawing, in which they are amateurs.

One of the earliest was Henry Hamilton, who died in the West Indies in 1796 as Governor of Bermuda and Antigua. Nothing is known about his early years, except that he was Irish and enlisted in the British army in 1754 when he would no doubt have been quite young. Drawings, including Forts at Beausejour and Lawrence, both dated 1755, are in the map room of the British Library.[28] These are neatly executed and precise drawings, totally factual and most competent. They have the appearance of maps even to the inscription on a floating ribbon above Fort Beausejour. Hamilton's distinguished military career included the Seven Years War

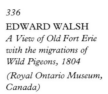

336
EDWARD WALSH
*A View of Old Fort Erie
with the migrations of
Wild Pigeons, 1804*
*(Royal Ontario Museum,
Canada)*

in North America, when he was taken prisoner, but later he held the Lieutenant Governorships of Detroit and Quebec. Further drawings by him are in Canadian collections.

Another army painter was Edward Walsh (1756–1832),[29] from Waterford, who trained late in life as a surgeon in Glasgow, obtaining his degree in 1791 when he became an army surgeon in Ireland. He was in Ireland throughout the 1798 uprising, but then went to Holland and as a result of that campaign published a book[30] in 1800 which included engravings after his drawings. In 1803 he was sent to Canada, where a number of watercolours survive from his various postings which included Montreal in 1806, when he painted his view of that city[31] through a screen of well-handled trees; the whole reminds us of the Dublin Society Schools eighteenth–century style. His masterpiece, done in1804 when he was posted at various places on the border as part of the defence of Canada against American encroachment, shows *A View of Old Fort Erie with the migrations of Wild Pigeons (Plate 336)*. This is much more naïve than the Montreal view but has infinite charm, showing the now extinct sight of the migrations of pigeons darkening the sky of his frigidly blue watercolour. During his Canadian travels he collected much material on the Indians, their customs and language. He returned to

Waterford about 1808 and was active in publishing and in literary circles in Ireland though he remained in the army, fighting at Waterloo.

William Eagar (c.1796–1839) had an entirely different style. He came from Ireland, possibly a member of the Kerry gentry family, and it is not known where he was educated, though Italy has been suggested. To us he has a distinct stylistic link with Samuel Frederick Brocas, and he certainly knew the work of his Dublin contemporaries. He emigrated to St. John's, Newfoundland, sometime before 1819.[32] When he was in St John's he painted portraits as well as teaching. He moved to Halifax, Nova Scotia, in 1834 as its greater wealth and sophistication gave him a better income for his growing family.

Eagar's views, many of which were engraved, vary from large landscapes of untamed countryside to others which are as much genre scenes as landscapes. His work is an important record of Halifax buildings and streetscapes in his day. His somewhat naïve manner is very lively and is perhaps best seen in his view of the *Market Wharf and Ferry Landing, Halifax (Plate 337)*, with all the stalls, fishwives, and poultry and other dealers.[33]

Eagar published a book entitled *Landscape Illustrations of Nova Scotia,* which

337
WILLIAM EAGAR
*Market Wharf and Ferry
Landing, Halifax, Nova
Scotia*
*(Royal Ontario Museum,
Canada)*

appeared in five or six parts[34] and for which
the prospectus was issued in 1836. A catalogue survives of a loan exhibition[35] which he
assembled and exhibited at Cochran's buildings in Halifax in 1838, which must be one
of the earliest such shows in Canada.
Though most of the pictures were by other
artists and old masters he included a few of
his own and some by his pupils.

Other Irish artists in Canada were
Richard Dillon (c.1740–1827) and Robert
Auchmaty Sproule (1799–1845) (back endpaper) who were both important topographical watercolourists in Montreal. Indeed in
the nineteenth century, it is notable that
some of Canada's best-known painters were
Irish-born or of Irish parentage, but because
they were educated in Canada we do not
intend to discuss them at length. They
include Paul Kane[36] (1810–71), who was
born in Mallow and went to Canada when
he was about nine; he is famous for his paintings of Indians and the West. Lucius
Richard O'Brien[37] (1832–1900) was born in
Canada, a cousin of the Inchiquin family.
His father was a pioneer founder of Shanty
Bay, Ontario, which was his birthplace. He
worked as an architect and engineer but is
best known for his landscapes and as the first
President of the Royal Canadian Academy
founded in 1880.

Only recently has George Russell Dartnell (1798–1878) been discovered to be

Irish, from Rathkeale in Co. Limerick. He
trained as a surgeon in Ireland and took up
this profession in the army in 1820. Like so
many of our imperial wanderers, he painted
in several continents – in the Mediterranean;
in India; in England and Ireland; and in
Ceylon, where he painted his pet elephant[38]
in 1825 with two sloth bears and a monkey,
all of whom appear in his quarters, the elephant bringing in the kettle for tea. He was
posted for some nine years to Canada. His
early medical training in Cork was at a time
when that city was founding a number of
learned institutions, and from a later drawing of the *South Gate Bridge, Cork (Plate 338)*[39]
of 1834 it is clear that he was familiar with
paintings by Nathaniel Grogan. Although

338
GEORGE RUSSELL
DARTNELL
*The South Gate Bridge,
Cork, 1834*

339
GEORGE RUSSELL
DARTNELL
*The Ice Shove at
Montreal, 1836*
*(Royal Ontario Museum,
Canada)*

Grogan had died in 1806, his work was around and had also been engraved. But Dartnell obviously never had a formal artistic education and his watercolours to the end have an amateur look about them, despite their charm and fluency. He is basically a landscape painter though he occasionally sketched American Indians.

One of Dartnell's finest drawings is of the *Barracks at Penetanguishene Harbour*, 1837,[40]

where he was posted for some time. It is a calm, pellucid study of water and the sun breaking through dark rain clouds. His ice and snow scenes are also among his best and he was clearly fascinated by the power of the ice, as in his *Ice Shove at Montreal (Plate 339)*[41] of 1836 which is a beautiful tonal watercolour.

Before his retirement in England he was promoted to the position of Deputy Inspector

340
ROBERT HOOD
*The Hudson Bay Company
Ships, the Prince of
Wales and Eddystone
bartering with the
Eskimos..., 1819*
*(National Archives of
Canada)*

341
ROBERT HOOD
Building Fort Enterprise on the Winter River, Northwest Territories, 1820

(National Archives of Canada)

of Hospitals and he spent many years working in the military lunatic asylum, Great Yarmouth. After his retirement he continued this interest as he opened a private clinic. He painted till the end of his days and often visited his home country.

Dartnell's interest in the Canadian winter leads us to mention the three Irish naval artists who painted in the Arctic. Of these the earliest was Robert Hood (c.1795–1821), who may have come from Portarlington[42] but was certainly born in Ireland, though later his father was a clergyman at Bury in Lancashire. His Irish connections are strengthened by the fact that a collection of his bird paintings and his journal were found in the early 1970s in the attic of a coach house at Birch Grove in Tipperary which belonged to the Birch family, descendants of his sister.[43] He cannot have had much artistic training in Ireland as he joined the navy as a first-class boy volunteer in 1809, aged fourteen, though he may, like Francis Beaufort, whom we discuss later in this chapter, have gone to a school in Dublin which trained boys for the navy and army. As a midshipman he was a member of the first overland Arctic expedition made by Sir John Franklin in 1819–21.

Hood's watercolours of the Arctic are of the first rank and indicate that he must have studied art at some time. Despite the superb detail of humans, animals and birds, these landscapes and icy seascapes have tremendous depth and solidity and give a masterly impression of the ominous silence and cold of the Arctic. They include shipping scenes such as *The Hudson's Bay Company Ships . . . bartering with the Eskimos off the Upper Savage Islands . . .* , 1819 *(Plate 340)*, which includes a naked Eskimo, who has just sold all his clothes, in a canoe! The scene of *The Trout Fall and portage at the Trout River . . .* , 1819 (W.H. Coverdale Collection, Public Archives of Canada), is a lonely landscape showing the wilderness with its white water and the natural forest, while man taming this is depicted in *Building Fort Enterprise on the Winter River, Northwest Territories, 1820 (Plate 341).*[44] Hood was also a masterly painter of birds which he saw on the Arctic expedition, and often worked under very difficult circumstances, when his pens and brushes became frozen. They show again that he was no beginner at the art. Tragically, he died aged about twenty-five, shot by an Indian.[45] Sir John Franklin wrote:

> After our usual supper of singed skin and bone soup, Dr Richardson acquainted me with the afflicting circumstances attending the death of Mr Hood [who, on the verge of starvation, had been shot by the interpreter, Michel] . . . His scientific observations together with his maps and drawings . . . evince a variety of talent, which,

342
JAMES DUNCAN
St. Antoine Hall,
Montreal, 1850
(Royal Ontario Museum,
Canada)

had his life been spared, must have rendered him a distinguished ornament to his profession.[46]

The other two were nothing like so memorable. One was William Henry James Browne[47] (d.1872), the son of the harbour master in Dublin who joined the navy and went on the Ross expedition to the Arctic (1848–9) and again on *HMS Resolute* in 1850–1. He was a fine watercolour painter and, when wintering in the Arctic, a scene painter in the Royal Arctic Theatre; he later painted an Arctic panorama in London. The third Irishman was George Frederick Mecham,[48] born in Queenstown (Cobh) in 1828, who died in Honolulu in 1858. He acted in the Royal Arctic Theatre when Browne was painting sets in 1850/1 and was on *HMS Resolute* in 1852–4. He was a painter of topographical views.

James Duncan[49] (1806–81), who came from Coleraine and emigrated about 1825, probably studied in Belfast before he left, though there is no record of this. He is well known for his panoramic canvas of Montreal and his views of Quebec, his streetscenes and landscapes, snow scenes and waterfalls, mostly painted in watercolour. He worked for the *Illustrated London News* and the *Canadian Illustrated News* as well as teaching

drawing in Montreal. His soft style and his interest in buildings and gardens are particularly well shown in his watercolour of *St. Antoine Hall, Montreal (Plate 342)* dated 1850. It shows a classical villa of a well-to-do Canadian, set in its garden with many of the plants in pots ready to be removed in the winter to the extensive greenhouses in the background. Duncan's figure style in his pencil drawings is reminiscent of the work of the Brocas family, as is the subject of some of them, including *The Celebrated Blind Fiddler, Montreal (Plate 343)*. His watercolour groups have more emphasis on solidity. They are important records of Montreal social life.[50]

Sir Richard George Augustus Levinge (1811–84),[51] a baronet from Westmeath, was commissioned in the army in 1828, was posted to St. John in New Brunswick in 1835 and was in Canada for five years. During this time in St. John, he painted two charming views of sleighing which indicate the relaxed and convivial social life that the officers enjoyed in Canadian garrisons. One is a static view of the meeting of the Sleigh Club[52] (Royal Ontario Museum), in front of the barracks, with officer dandies and their friends arriving for a social event. He was interested in Indians and painted a number of lively watercolours of them hunting.

343
JAMES DUNCAN
The Celebrated Blind Fiddler, Montreal
(Royal Ontario Museum, Canada)

These and other Canadian scenes were included in a Toronto sale in 1969.[53] In 1836 he made an adventurous trip down the Ohio and Mississippi rivers to the Red River, a major tributary of the Mississippi, and travelled as far as Alexandria, Louisiana. Here he came across "the ruffians who composed the invading army to Texas."[54] His book based on his adventures and intended as a guide to sportsmen, *Echoes from the Backwoods*, was illustrated by him and published in 1846. He painted a splendid work of the paddle steamer on which he travelled, the *Ouishita (Plate 344)*[55] which makes a great contrast with his free sketches clearly done on site. Some of these have great zest, like *Treeing a Bear (Plate 345)*[56] which shows two figures in a canoe beating a large bear up a

344
SIR RICHARD G.A. LEVINGE, Bt.
The Paddle Steamer, Ouishita
(Amon Carter Museum, Fort Worth)

247

345
SIR RICHARD G.A.
LEVINGE, Bt.
Treeing a Bear
*(Royal Ontario Museum,
Canada)*

water-girt dead tree. For an artist with no formal training in figure painting as far as is known, his work is very remarkable. Levinge's brother, Major George Charles Rawdon Levinge (1812–54), was also an accomplished draughtsman, who sadly died en route to the Crimea.

Two more artists tell us a lot about Canadian life: one is a professional, William Armstrong (1822–1914), and the other a talented amateur, the famous Viceroy, the Marquess of Dufferin and Ava, whom we

have already mentioned in Chapter 11. These will complete this Canadian survey.

Armstrong,[57] who was born in Dublin the son of a general, was taught in the Dublin Society Architecture School where he won a prize for architectural drawing. Then he worked on both the Irish and English railways before emigrating in 1850, making his headquarters in Toronto where in that year he is listed in the Toronto Directory as "an artist and civil engineer." Though for twenty-six years he taught drawing in the Toronto Normal School and the Technical and Collegiate Schools, he found time to work for the Canadian Pacific Railway, which took him to western Canada. One of his most attractive drawings is a watercolour showing passengers, including an Indian, waiting for a train *(Plate 346)* under a sign saying *"Railway Going West."*[58] This includes a group having tea on a big packing case.

Armstrong exhibited works in many shows in Ontario and also in Paris in 1855 and in the Dublin International Exhibition of 1865. The latter included twenty-eight watercolours of Canada from Ontario to Vancouver Island, portraits of twenty-seven Indian chiefs and photographs of Lake

346
WILLIAM ARMSTRONG
Railway Going West
*(Royal Ontario Museum,
Canada)*

Superior.[59] He had many of his sketches reproduced in periodicals. He was particularly proud of his watercolour of *The Arrival of the Prince of Wales in Toronto*, which was the high point of his journalistic work.

More interesting however, are Armstrong's scenes of the West, including the vivid *Mr and Mrs St. John Running the Rapids, Sturgeon River* (Royal Ontario Museum), 1871,[60] where he conveys extremely well the movement and force of the billowing water around the Indian canoe. His fluent brushwork is seen here at its best, but his most dramatic picture *(Plate 347)* is of a *Blackfoot*

Indian Encampment, Foothills of the Rocky Mountains.[61] The Indian tents with their amazingly shaped open tops and the lively depiction of the Indians in the camp in the foreground make a remarkable contrast set against the icy mountains and the cold sky. Most of these drawings were obviously worked up in the studio, as much sketchier work which was probably done on sight still exists.

Lord Dufferin's painting makes a considerable contrast, though much of the subject matter is similar to Armstrong's. As we have said, he probably had no other training in art

347
WILLIAM ARMSTRONG
Blackfoot Indian
Encampment, Foothills
of the Rocky Mountains
(Royal Ontario Museum,
Canada)

348
MARQUESS OF
DUFFERIN AND AVA
Interior of the Dufferins'
fishing cabin on the
St. John River, New
Brunswick
(The Dufferin Foundation)

than what he would have had at Eton under the art master, Gordon B. Bradley, and brief spells of tuition when on the continent, but certainly by the time he was in Canada as Governor General between 1872 and 1878 he had become very proficient. His style is gentle and precise, at its best in a domestic scene, like the interior of the Dufferins' fishing cabin on the St. John river, New Brunswick[62] *(Plate 348)*. In this charming watercolour Lady Dufferin can be seen through the open door sitting reading a paper while someone's legs loom up to her left propped high on the veranda column. Others show canoeing, a paddle steamer, waterfalls and above all else a splendid drawing of a *Waterspout on the prairies in Saskatchewan (Plate 349)*, with brilliant effects of cloud and

349
MARQUESS OF
DUFFERIN AND AVA
Waterspout on the prairies
in Saskatchewan
(The Dufferin Foundation)

lightning suffusing the whole with a lurid atmospheric impression. Lord Dufferin also painted when he was Viceroy of India but these drawings have not yet come to light.

Turning to other countries which were colonized by the British, we find that in all of them the Irish provided artists, whether military men or, as in Australia, convicts, surveyors, engineers and explorers – as well, of course, as the women who went with them and painted domestic scenes, flowers, butterflies and other subjects, a number of whom we have already discussed in Chapter 7. Most of the painters were competent amateurs, quite different from the stream of highly professional British artists who went to India in the eighteenth and early nineteenth centuries. Apart from Thomas Hickey (see Chapter 4), the only other Irishmen in that group were three miniaturists, an area of art outside the scope of this book.

However, it is worth noting that of these, Walter Robertson (d. 1801) had come on from America where he had worked for a few years, and John Camillus Hone (d. 1836), son of Nathaniel Hone, advertised himself in the *Calcutta Gazette* in 1785 as "offering to teach drawing and painting."[63] Hone was in India between 1782 and 1790, and, as he was not a success, he returned to Ireland.

The third was Samuel Andrews (c. 1767–1807), who went to Madras in 1791, and sometime between 1794 and 1798 visited Fort Marlborough, Bencoolen, West Sumatra.[64] He is the only Irishman whom we have found painting in this area, where he made a series of eight aquatints which were published by William Marsden in 1799. The set includes several shore scenes as well as views of buildings, including one of *Government House and Council House*. He was in England in 1795 but returned to India and died at Patna in 1807. Presumably he must have made many landscape watercolours besides his portrait work, which is mostly in grisaille.

A typical example of the peripatetic Irishman is Walter Synnot (1773–1851), a younger son of a distinguished landed family from Ballymoyer, Co. Armagh. He and his brother and sister are the subjects of the splendid Joseph Wright of Derby conversation piece of 1781 now in the National Gallery of Victoria, Melbourne.[65] Synnot

had served in Newfoundland, Nova Scotia and Jamaica, and, retiring from the army, he emigrated to South Africa in 1820. He returned for five years to Ireland and set sail again in 1836 for Van Diemen's Land (Tasmania), where he lived in Launceston. He was an amateur landscape painter: examples are the view of his home, Ballymoyer, taken in 1819, and another of Tinderbox Bay in Tasmania[66] (both National Gallery of Victoria). When he was in South Africa he painted native plants, and a volume of botanical interest is now in the Baillieu Library, University of Melbourne.

Admiral Sir Francis Beaufort (1774–1857), Synott's almost exact contemporary, was a naval officer renowned as Hydrographer

350
CAPTAIN HENRY BUTLER
Scenery of the Guarapiche River, 1843

of the British Navy between 1829 and 1855, who helped to perfect the famous Admiralty charts and is now known to every yachtsman as giving his name to the international scale of wind force. We mentioned him earlier (Chapter 11) as the son of Daniel Augustus Beaufort and closely connected with the Edgeworths whom we have often mentioned, so it is not surprising that he was a fine draughtsman. As we have noted when discussing his brother William (Chapter 3) and his sister Fanny (Chapter 7), he was taught when in Bristol in 1782 by Nicholas Pocock and a Miss Simmonds and later probably when in Dublin at David Bates's Military and Marine Academy about 1784.[67] Everywhere he sailed he was involved in charting and always drew anything of interest he saw. He worked around the world

351
JAMES WALLIS
*Collage representing
his life*

Later he used the format of this log as the basis of a book he published in 1841, written and illustrated by himself, entitled *South African Sketches: Illustrative of the Wild Life of a Hunter on the Frontier of the Cape Colony.* These illustrations, mostly of animals, are lively and colourful and indicate that he must have had some training, probably in the army. His later work done in the West Indies, Grenada, Tobago and Venezuela emphasizes a totally different and more sinister atmosphere. These drawings are creepy, bizarre and flamboyant *(Plate 350)* – full of snakes, crocodiles and other tropical denizens, with exotic, vegetal effects.[70]

James Wallis (1785?–1858),[71] from Cork, who became an army officer, ensign in 1803 and major in the 46th regiment, is yet another of these military travellers. He arrived in Sydney in 1814 where he was commandant at Newcastle, New South Wales, working on the building of Christ Church with the convicts, Joseph Lycett and James Clohasy, an Irish stonemason who drew the first plan. Wallis is best known today for his engravings for his book,[72] *An Historical Account of the Colony of New South Wales*, published in London in 1821. Though these were formerly thought to have been drawn by Lycett, an original watercolour of the *View of the Hawkesbury river and the Blue Mountains from Windsor*,[73] signed by Wallis, has now confirmed that he was the artist. It is interesting to point out that he drew "the closed valley" of Vaucluse where his fellow Corkman, convict and notorious abductor, Sir Henry Brown Hayes, built his villa. Wallis was not impressed by the untouched beauties of the wilderness and hoped to see them turned into "the cheerful village, the busy town and the crowded city."[74]

As an army officer Wallis travelled extensively and left an amusing and touching record of his life in a watercolour collage *(Plate 351)* which forms the frontispiece of an album of his sketches given to his greatniece, Mary Hilton. This collage shows an urn out of which appears, painted on a flap, a weeping willow composed of the names of many of his dead fellow officers. Below the urn, an oval vignette encloses symbols from Wallis's life including the mountains of both the Cape of Good Hope and South America, the

from the River Plate in South America, the Dutch East Indies and China to his most famous work on the coast of Turkey, which resulted in his book *Karamania*,[68] as well as in Europe. Through his diaries we can follow his travels and the sketches which he included. A panorama of the Bombay waterfront done in 1806 is a remarkable record of all the architecture found there.[69] His subjects vary from collieries to Lichfield Cathedral, from Irish villages to newly discovered antiquities in Turkey.

Another Irishman who worked in Cape Colony was Captain Henry Butler (1805–81), of the 59th regiment, grandson of the eleventh Viscount Mountgarret and father of one of our finest Irish watercolourists, Mildred Anne Butler (see Chapter 12). On his journey on the *Romney* from Cork to the Cape in 1835, he kept a log with drawings and watercolours, landscapes and jungle scenes of Madeira, Brazil and the Cape.

Australian dingo dog, his dead charger, his parrot, his regimental colours and the arms of his native city, Cork.[75] He lived in Cork in the early 1820s, when he filled his garden at Lucyville with plants from the southern hemisphere and probably kept some Australian dogs.[76] Though we may choose one place to discuss the work of these Irishmen, in fact most of them drew in many corners of the Empire.

The situation in Australia was entirely different, as the few artists that emerge included some convicts, most of whom seem to have obtained their "ticket of leave" fairly quickly. Apart from the watercolourists, there were a number of oil painters, including the portraitist James Anderson (fl.1852–72), from Belfast; the portrait and scene-painter J.T. Dennis (fl.1838–70); the scene-painter William Duke (1815–53), from Cork, whose splendid whaling pieces brought him considerable fame; the engraver W. Kellett Baker;[77] and Captain Otway, who was almost certainly Irish and whose delightful "Charley spearing Kangaroos" was painted in 1847.[78]

One of the earliest and most interesting Irish artists in Australia was Richard Browne (1776–1824), who has recently been identified as the Irish convict of the same name, who was transported to Australia in 1811 and lived till 1816 in Newcastle, New South Wales. Besides a couple of engraved, topographical drawings of that outlying settlement made in 1813, he painted the plates for the so-called "Skottowe" manuscript, being "Select specimens from Nature of the Birds Animals etc etc of New South Wales."[79] These show that he must have had some training in his native Dublin, and it has been suggested[80] that he was a relative of the distinguished Irish natural historian, Dr Patrick Browne of Co. Mayo, who had compiled various Irish floras.[81] The Skottowe watercolours are bright in colour and the birds *(Plate 352)* are reminiscent of the work of Samuel Dixon.

Browne was more famous in his day for his drawings of aborigines[82] fishing, fighting, dancing in corroborees which, despite an element of caricature, were regarded by his contemporaries as accurate ethnography

352
RICHARD BROWNE
The Lyre Bird
(Mitchell Library, State Library of New South Wales)

and attempted to show the aborigines as untainted by the Westerners. He repeated them on a number of occasions and was an extremely popular artist in Sydney.

Another fascinating case was the Irish convict Samuel Clayton (fl.1793–d.1853), who was transported in 1816 to Sydney and, though not given his "ticket of leave" till 1824, advertised in the *Sydney Gazette* in 1817 that he took likenesses either in full or in profile. Later he advertised that he gave instruction in ornamental painting and drawing as well as in engraving and miniature painting, and he is also known to have made silhouettes. According to Strickland, who was not conversant with his Australian career,[83] he was the eldest son of the Dublin engraver Benjamin Clayton (c. 1754–1814), who taught him his trade as an engraver, and he was the brother of Benjamin and Robert Clayton who both also worked in the same field in Dublin. Strickland tells us that the illustrations in the 1793–4 volume of *Anthologia Hibernica* were by Samuel Clayton after William Beauford, but he knew no more about his subsequent career.

Only a year after his arrival in Sydney, in 1817, Clayton engraved the first bank notes issued by the newly founded Bank of New South Wales, but he is now best known for his engraving on silver, such as the double-handled Irish cup for the Hyde Park Race of 1819, and for several commemorative trowels, such as the one used by Governor Macquarie to lay the first stone of the first Catholic chapel in Sydney in 1821.[84] Although he advertised in 1818 that he had "a variety of jewellery and silver work on hand," the most recent authorities do not think he was a silversmith. Unfortunately none of his paintings appears to have survived. His ne'er-do-well brother Robert joined him and worked with him in Australia.

Loetitia Casey, née Gardiner,[85] (c. 1819–63) was an Irish immigrant who went with her father, a captain in the 8th Dublin Foot, to Van Diemen's Land in 1835 and drew domestic scenes of life in New Norfolk and in Hobart. Her work is now to be found in the Museum in Launceston, Tasmania.

Adam Gustavus Ball (1821–82), born in Dublin and educated in Trinity College as an engineer, went to Sydney in 1839, where he worked for eight years as a civil engineer. In 1847 he went overland to Adelaide and is noted for his sketches in the bush of camp scenes, kangaroo hunting and mustering of cattle. His brother, J.T. Ball, became the Lord Chancellor of Ireland, but Adam remained in Australia. His work has been described as "all executed with verve in a

353
JAMES GLEN WILSON
Fijian and Tongese Canoes at Levuka, 1855

bold, free style"[86] and can now be seen in the Art Gallery in Adelaide.

A Young Irelander who was transported in 1849 was William Paul Dowling (d. 1877), who became a portrait painter and lithographer in Hobart, interestingly using crayon in his portrait of Mary Marguerite Allport.[87] In 1859 he moved to Launceston, where he worked as a photographer, handtinting his prints.

Artists who travelled in the South Seas include the little known Frederick Fowler,[88] who exhibited Irish views in Melbourne in 1852 and 1862 as well as watercolours of Fiji, Tonga and Samoa; and Patrick Joseph Hogan (c. 1805–1878),[89] a surveyor who had trained in the Royal Hibernian Academy Schools and started work in Auckland, New Zealand, in 1849. He taught drawing as well as surveying and in 1858 went on to Sydney, where he worked as a government surveyor as well as an artist. His surviving New Zealand watercolours show his work as varying from the naïve to his competent views of Auckland done in 1852, now known to us from lithographs.

The most important of the South Seas travellers was James Glen Wilson[90] (1827–63). His best-known works are oils in the Ulster Museum and in the collection of the Harbour Commissioners, Belfast. These include *The Emigrant Ship*, 1852, and a view of the *Belfast Ferry Steps, Donegall Quay*, 1851. He was probably born in Co. Down into a family of independent means and may have been trained in the Belfast School of Design in the early 1850s. However, the competence of the two pictures just mentioned indicates that he must have received instruction earlier elsewhere, as an artist at that period would certainly have started his artistic training in his teens. In 1852 Wilson joined the Royal Navy's hydrographic survey ship *HMS Herald*, as "artist borne as clerk," drawing and photographing throughout the voyage. The ship proceeded via South America, where he drew watercolours of society in Rio de Janeiro, and South Africa to Australia, reaching Sydney in 1853. Based there, *HMS Herald* continued through the Western Pacific, visiting other islands, Tonga, Fiji *(Plate 353)* and the New Hebrides.

Wilson left the expedition before its return to England in 1861, as he took up an appointment in March 1859 as a Surveyor with the New South Wales Department of Lands. He eventually settled in Molong, where he died aged thirty-six. The majority of his surviving work, except his two Belfast oils and a Sydney Harbour view,[91] which is known in two versions, are watercolours or drawings, done when he was either in the navy or travelling as a surveyor. They are extremely varied in subject matter, from drawings of the survey ship done in considerable detail, to sketches of trees with creeping plants on Lord Howe Island. Two scenes on Fiji show women drying palm leaves in front of their village houses and two armed native men squatting under a tree; only the men are fully finished. He also recorded the birds and fishes he saw, and the domestic objects *(Plate 354)* and warriors' weapons on all the islands he visited. The highly detailed draughtsmanship Wilson displays is unique among Irish emigrés and may be explained by the needs of his cartographic work, where exactitude is an essential. His fine pencil line and precision of detail could be compared with English contemporaries and would surely have been admired by Ruskin. He is a brilliant recorder of facts; he never lets his imagination or his emotions intrude.

A link between Australia and New Zealand is the career of George O'Brien[92] (1821–88). He was born in Co. Clare, the

354
JAMES GLEN WILSON
Three Baskets

355
GEORGE O'BRIEN
Dunedin from the Junction,
1869
(Otago Early Settlers'
Museum)

son of Admiral O'Brien, and the grandson of Sir Lucius O'Brien of Dromoland which made him a cousin of the famous rebel William Smith O'Brien, who was in Australia when George arrived, although there seems to have been no communication between them. He was a cousin of the Lucius Richard O'Brien whom we have already mentioned, in Canada. George O'Brien is first safely documented in 1851 in Melbourne, where he worked as a draughtsman in the Surveyor General's office. There are two drawings of Melbourne showing the town in 1839 and 1840 which seem to indicate that O'Brien reached Australia earlier in his teens, but as there are no records of him before 1851 it is now thought that the drawings were commissioned retrospectively. He did not remain in the Surveyor General's office for long but practised as an architect and surveyor. There is a series of very fine drawings, many dated which continue till 1863, of Melbourne and its vicinity in the La Trobe Library and the National Gallery of Victoria in Melbourne. His panoramic *View of Melbourne and Williamstown in 1862* foreshadows his New Zealand work. He exhibited at the Victorian Industrial Society a *View of Florence and the Arno* in 1858, which suggests that he returned home if only briefly.

At the moment there is no evidence where O'Brien was taught. It seems likely, however, that if he went out at about the age of thirty, he must have been trained in England or Ireland and probably as an architect. His later architectural watercolour drawings were done in New Zealand, where he is first recorded in 1863. He settled there with his wife and growing family in Dunedin but he

travelled, painting in the North Island and Auckland. In Dunedin *(Plate 355)* he continued as a surveyor and civil engineer and also taught drawing.

From our point of view it is O'Brien's splendid New Zealand watercolours[93] that are of such importance. Many of these are large and convey with great skill the enormous empty spaces *(Plate 356)*, the inlets, mountains and plains of his new country. He paints vegetation with botanical concern and is equally interested in huge drawings of the new towns and settlements set against a blue sea and sky. Many of these panoramas are idealized, arcadian visions and not close to contemporary photographic evidence, yet they include much carefully rendered detail. To us they have something of the quality of Edward Lear, often using his colouring. They are crisp in execution and he uses simple, translucent washes. Many of the smaller pictures are in an oval format and he frequently employs a bird's eye viewpoint which increases the breadth of his vision. O'Brien is uninterested in weather and atmosphere or even mystery; his vision has clarity and simplicity, and a matter-of-fact approach to the industrial development and increasing urbanization of the new colony. These watercolours are among the most impressive we have met with so far in the colonies.

Other Irishmen who painted in New Zealand included John Guise Mitford (1822–54) from Clontarf, Dublin, who settled in New Zealand in 1841 in the Customs Service, working mostly in Auckland. There is an amusing caricature of himself wearing a Maori feather cloak and carrying a spear which includes vignettes of his houses in

Auckland and Wellington. He had a dubious reputation, for when posted to Russell in 1858, he is recorded as having "a great fondness for drink and Maori girls."[94] He used a gentle, atmospheric manner in his watercolours and includes Maori scenes. His watercolour entitled *Tarawera Lake (Plate 357)* of about 1845 includes a Maori fort and is a fine example of his style. Roger Blackley thinks that most of Mitford's known pictures were done on a trip he made into the interior in the summer of 1844/5 and that he may not have painted much later.[95]

Sir William James Tyrone Power (1819–1911), who came of the famous theatrical family from Co. Monaghan, was in New Zealand from 1846, when he was serving with the army, and published in 1849 a book he illustrated himself entitled *Sketches in New Zealand with Pen and Pencil.*

Another army officer whose work is of great interest was Alexander Henry Watkins Grubb (1842–1925), who lived for some years in New Zealand from 1863. He also painted in Ceylon and no doubt in his other postings. He gives us many scenes connected with the Maori wars and he won the New Zealand medal in 1870. His fine view of Trincomalee, Ceylon, done in 1872, shows him to have been advanced in his use of brilliant colour.[96]

The most impressive Irish recorder of the Maori was Richard Aldworth Oliver[97] (1811–89), who came of the Limerick family of Castle Oliver and, like his father, became an admiral. He was surveying in the Pacific between 1847 and 1851, and in 1852 published *A Series of Lithographic Drawings from sketches in New Zealand.* His watercolour landscapes are splendidly atmospheric for an amateur and vary from a French frigate breaking up in a storm to a beautiful calm scene of the palm-fringed Dillon's Bay, which is inscribed ". . . where Williams the missionary was killed and eaten . . ." The Maori scenes include a majestic wooden meeting house and stockade, family groups clad in voluminous capes or playing cards outside a hut *(Plate 358)* while the women work and smoke in the background, and a fascinating view inscribed "Food stage erected for feast by Bay of Islands chiefs. Sept 1849." He was impressed by the beauty of Maori women and half-castes, whom he painted in both native and European dress with very fluent brushwork. Oliver painted wherever he was, and there is a figure study of New Hebridean natives and landscapes done in the West Indies.[98]

So many of the paintings which we have reviewed are invaluable as records of the development and life in these far-flung

356
GEORGE O'BRIEN
*A View from Signal Hill
and Port Chalmers, c.1866*
*(Hocken Library,
University of Otago,
Dunedin)*

357
JOHN GUISE MITFORD
Tarawera Lake, c.1845
*(National Library of
New Zealand, The
AlexanderTurnbull
Library)*

posts of empire, and they are a memorial to the intrepid spirit of adventure and the artistic talents of Irishmen living and working in extremely varied conditions and climates. We have only begun the search for these compatriots, often unknown as Irishmen, partly because they were usually connected with British naval or military forces and therefore in the literature listed as English. We realize that there are many gaps in our knowledge which need to be filled. However, their exotic subject matter gives a startling and unfamiliar facet to Irish painting.

358
RICHARD A. OLIVER
*Maori playing cards in
front of a hut, c.1840*
*(National Library of
Australia)*

THE END OF THE ACADEMIC TRADITION: LATE NINETEENTH AND EARLY TWENTIETH CENTURY LANDSCAPE AND FIGURE PAINTERS

As we have noted, there was enormous interest in watercolour painting in the second half of the nineteenth century, even among oil painters. Among the earliest to emerge was Nathaniel Hone the Younger (1831–1917),[1] who is one of the least-known Barbizon painters despite living there for seventeen years. Though he practised in oil, he created some of the finest watercolours executed in late nineteenth century Ireland. He did not exhibit any of them in the Royal Hibernian Academy but left them, with the oils in his studio, to the National Gallery of Ireland, which is why they are unknown outside Ireland.

Naturally, Hone knew all the Barbizon painters, and some of his watercolours, with their grey, silvery light, owe a considerable dept to Corot, an example being *An Italian Monastery above a Valley* (National Gallery of Ireland). This dates probably to the end of his Barbizon period and is a development from his early French drawings, which are somewhat flatly executed and are muddy in tone. His colour brightens gradually, for instance *A Vine Pergola* (NGI) and his beautiful study of *A House and Salita near Nice* (Plate 359), which perhaps date from his Italian honeymoon in 1872. His travels to Egypt and Greece in 1892 produced many vivid watercolours, which are also notable for their silhouetted composition, for instance, *Palm Trees and Buildings, Egypt* (Plate 360) and *The Acropolis* (NGI).

Hone's late Irish watercolours are rich and strong in colour and have a true sense of distance and space. Apart from working near his home at Malahide (Plate 361) in a flat, pastoral area of Ireland, he frequently visited the West, near Kilkee in Co. Clare, where

the rocks *(Plate 362)*, cliffs and surf were a constant inspiration. One of the difficulties of discussing his late work is that it photographs very badly as it is dependent on fluid brushwork and colour. These later watercolours were clearly an inspiration for his oils.

Walter Osborne[2] (1859–1903) and Frank O'Meara (1853–88) share with Hone a European training. Osborne was the son of the well-known animal painter William Osborne, and was born and bought up in Dublin. After attending the RHA Schools, Osborne went to the School of Art in Antwerp where he had a number of Irish contemporaries. Antwerp was very popular with English and Irish students; in 1881, for instance, there were thirty-eight *Anglais* listed, and forty-three in the next year.[3] These would, of course, have included the Irish. Before the century ended, most Irish artists of consequence had attended Antwerp, including Norman Garstin, J.M. Kavanagh, Nathaniel Hill, Richard Thomas Moynan, Roderic O'Conor, and Dermot O'Brien.[4]

After Antwerp, Osborne went to Brittany in 1882, to Dinard, Quimperlé and Pont Aven, where he worked before the Gauguin circle had established themselves. It was Bastien-Lepage whose *plein-air* realism was the major influence on English and Irish art at this time. Osborne does not appear to have used watercolour in his earliest years; his numerous studies are in pencil, meticulously drawn. He continued to use pencil studies to the end of his life but the later ones are softer, the line meanders freely over the subject and he occasionally combines it with crayon and chalk, as in his portrait of *Margaret Stokes* (National Gallery of Ireland).

359
NATHANIEL HONE
A House and Salita near Nice
(National Gallery of Ireland)

As far as we can judge, it was not until the 1890s that he used watercolour frequently and *When Yellow Leaves . . . (Plate 363)* of 1887 with its impressionistic strokes is still a pastel. Sometimes he works on a large scale as in finished works, but he also uses watercolour for studies as in *Master Aubrey*

Gwynn, 1896 (National Gallery of Ireland). By this time Osborne had settled permanently in Dublin for family reasons and he was an important member of the Dublin artistic scene, which included George Moore, W.B. Yeats, Hugh Lane, Walter Armstrong, Nathaniel Hone, John Hughes,

360
NATHANIEL HONE
Palm Trees and Buildings, Egypt, 1892
(National Gallery of Ireland)

the sculptor, and several other important figures. His large watercolours are few in number and depict mostly figure subjects and not landscapes. He treated them in many ways as he did his oils, with strong brushstrokes and clear colour. The *House-builders (Plate 364)*, showing two children building card houses, and *The Doll's School* (both NGI) are among his finest achievements. In the latter he heightens the watercolour with pastel. An unusual watercolour is the multi-figured *Race-course (Plate 365)* which wittily portrays a scene right out of Somerville and Ross's *Irish RM* books. Whether he would have continued to use the medium and develop it further is speculation, as he died of pneumonia in 1903, aged forty-three.

Another lively watercolourist reflecting Osborne's brushwork is Harry Scully (d.1935) who had studied in the Cork School of Art in 1885 but made his career mainly in Newlyn, France *(Plate 366)* and Holland, ending his days near London. He specialized in rural subjects and church interiors.

Frank O'Meara died even younger than Osborne: he was only thirty-five and, having spent practically all his career in France, in Grez-sur-Loing, he returned to his home-town, Carlow, to die. The fact that he lived abroad means that he was virtually unknown in Ireland and had no influence on Irish art. He is, however, one of the best Irish painters of the century, working mostly in oils. His reputation is based on a handful of works, all

of commanding quality. O'Meara was a typical artist–Bohemian, and the Sargent portrait of him done in 1875 shows his attractive and quizzically cocky expression. William Low painted a word picture of his alternating capricious moods and sensitive temperament as an artist: ". . . superficially he realised fairly well one of the heroes of Charles Lever's novels, gay, witty and insouciant, with a capacity for sudden white anger, . . ." followed by "profuse self-condemnation, warm apologies and humorous excuses for his 'wild Irish' temper."[5]

A sketchbook of O'Meara's early drawings done in Carlow has recently appeared, and at this early stage in his career he used pencil to portray the local scenery in neat fashion *(Plate 367)*. But later he used charcoal as well in such a work as *On the Quays,*

361
NATHANIEL HONE
A Line of Windswept Beeches
(National Gallery of Ireland)

362
NATHANIEL HONE
Rocks at low tide
(National Gallery of Ireland)

363
WALTER OSBORNE
"When Yellow Leaves or none or few do hang upon those Boughs that shake against the cold,"
1887

364
WALTER OSBORNE
House-builders, 1902
(National Gallery of Ireland)

Etaples (Plate 368) of about 1888. This is an interesting asymmetrical drawing with a feeling of softness and silhouette. As Julian Campbell comments, "the picture has an elegant 'art nouveau' flourish."[6] O'Meara shows his usual interest in age and social content with the barefoot girl talking to her elderly companion.

A more adventurous artist than Osborne is Roderic O'Conor (1860–1940), who went to both the Metropolitan and RHA Schools in Dublin and to Antwerp in 1883/4 before studying briefly under Carolus Duran in Paris. He was the eldest son of a Roscommon landed family related to the O'Conor Don, the chief of one of the oldest families in Europe, and this brought with it later in his life the problems of inheritance which undoubtedly marred his artistic career.[7] His next move was to Grez-sur-Loing which, because it was close to Paris, meant that O'Conor was able to keep in touch with the most modern trends in art. Unlike his fellow Irishmen, he may have become acquainted with Van Gogh before he left for Arles, and he was certainly aware of his art. He did not meet Gauguin until considerably later, in 1894, after he had been staying in Pont

Aven for a couple of years. As a result his "great" period derives from the work of Van Gogh and not Gauguin, who was, however, to become an intimate.

In 1893 O'Conor stayed for some months with Seguin at La Pouldu and worked with him on etchings;[8] though O'Conor did not continue to use this medium, they link closely with his only surviving drawings, which are from this date onwards. His crayon studies of Breton peasants *(Plate 369)* have strong outline and character conveyed with simple lines. His landscapes, which are mostly of trees *(Plate 370)*, almost assume a life of their own, dancing and walking on the page, like the occasional drawing of peasants clumping along a road.[9] His enormously exciting art *(Plate 371)* varies from the liveliness of his landscapes to quietly sensitive studies in the Bonnard manner. From his later period, few drawings survive.

Some of O'Conor's most sensitive works were his oil nude studies. It is extremely rare in Ireland till the twentieth century to find the nude used as a subject. We have no Ettys, we have no Leightons with the startling exception of one academic painter from Limerick, St. George Hare (1857–1933), who, though mainly an oil painter and a subject painter at that, exhibited a number of watercolours and pastels, one of which, *The*

366 (Below)
HARRY SCULLY *Continental Street*

Slave Girl (Plate 372), is an outstanding example in the Leighton manner. Hare's paintings exhibited at the Royal Institution included two in 1904, *The Sea People* and *The New Neptune*, which might suggest nude subjects, as does his best-known painting, *Miserere Domine*.[10] While his pastel nude is an excellent study in three dimensions as well as of lighting effects, the only watercolour landscape known to us, *Ladies, Cove, Tramore, Co. Waterford*, is peopled with matchstick figures and is remarkably weak. Though Hare seems to have lived in England, where he had studied at South Kensington, he continued to exhibit in the Royal Hibernian Academy and elsewhere in Ireland.

367
FRANK O'MEARA
Study of a Bridge

368
FRANK O'MEARA
On the Quays, Etaples,
c.1888
(Hugh Lane Municipal
Gallery of Modern Art)

The more humdrum artists who filled the Dublin exhibitions were not at all adventurous. Many of them were represented in Hugh Lane's giant *Exhibition of Irish Painters* held in the Guildhall Art Gallery, London, in 1904, though he was profligate in including many artists who had no connections with Ireland at all, like Charles Shannon, Phil May and Gordon Craig. Hercules Brabazon Brabazon, though of a distinguished Irish family and the owner of Irish property, was included, but he was born in Paris and lived in England. Lane included Walter Osborne, Jack Yeats, Mildred Anne Butler, Rose Barton and William Orpen and

some artists less well known today, Joseph Poole Addey, Philip Homan Miller and Bingham McGuinness, but he left out Bartholomew Colles Watkins and Alexander Williams.

The most distinguished of the minor men is Joseph Poole Addey (fl.1877–1914), who first exhibited at the Royal Hibernian Academy in 1877, giving a Derry address, and he did not move south till 1888. He taught in the School of Art in Derry and exhibits many Donegal and Co. Derry landscapes, but he was also a portrait painter and some of his best watercolours are of figures. A charming

interior, dated 1902, of a woman holding a guitar, seated on a chaise longue in front of a Chinese screen,[11] is one of the first examples in Ireland of the then fashionable chinoiserie. A girl with a parasol *(Plate 373)*,[12] probably a beach scene, is composed of strong, simple colours and forms. His landscape of *Killiney Bay (Plate 374)*, 1898, has the same pure simplicity and is suffused with soft and purply evening light reflected on the sand. He deserves to be better-known.

369 (Above)
RODERIC O'CONOR
Bretonne Assise, c.1893
(Musée de Pont Aven)

370 (Left)
RODERIC O'CONOR
Arbres du Pouldu

371 (Below)
RODERIC O'CONOR
Côtes Bretonne
(Cecil Higgins Art Gallery, Bedford)

A rather older artist, Bartholomew Colles Watkins (1833–91), was a painter of some quality. He came of an artistic family. Two uncles, Bartholomew (1794–after 1864) and George (d. 1840) practised as artists, and Bartholomew also worked as a picture cleaner and dealer both in London and Dublin. There was another nephew, Bartholomew, who helped with the business but died young. Though best known for his oils, Bartholomew Colles Watkins's watercolours are not sketches but finished works and tend to be quiet landscapes with few figures. His fine *Sunset over Clonmacnoise* is a descendant of Petrie's style without the social comment, and it is interesting that he quotes Petrie in his titles,[13] for instance in a painting of Lough Derg. He had been trained at the Royal Dublin Society Schools, and exhibited in London as well as the Royal Hibernian Academy, and though he painted in North Wales, in England and in Norway, most of his work is of Irish beauty spots. His *Hill near Esher (Plate 375)*, a cedar-girt view of

372
ST. GEORGE HARE
The Slave Girl

373
JOSEPH POOLE ADDEY
Girl with a Parasol

English home county landscape, is muted in tone in comparison to his brilliant sunsets.

The dangers landscape painters undertook are illustrated by his own tragic death from pneumonia in 1891. The railways had by this time opened up the furthermost fastnesses of the West of Ireland but they had not reached the coast. As a result, when Watkins was taken ill twenty miles from the rail head, he died before medical help could reach him.

Bingham McGuinness, whose birth date

374
JOSEPH POOLE ADDEY
Killiney Bay,
Co. Dublin, 1898

375
BARTHOLOMEW
COLLES WATKINS
Hill near Esher, 1876
(National Gallery of
Ireland)

is unknown, died in 1928, and is one of the most prolific of Irish Victorian water-colourists. Trained under the architect John Mulvany, he maintained a considerable understanding of architecture throughout his career. He also went to the RHA Schools and to the Dusseldorf academy, exhibiting first at the RHA in 1866. He painted and travelled all over the continent throughout his life. He is a highly competent, if dull, practitioner in the English tradition, deriving ultimately from Bonington through other Englishmen whom he must have known, such as Samuel Prout and James Holland. He was admired in his lifetime, his rich tones and picturesque subjects finding a ready market and critical acclaim. In an unknown newspaper cutting of 1878, he is described as "one of the few Irish painters who does not fear to plunge into rich colour," and it mentions his *Old Houses at Berne*. In another, probably from the *Irish Times* of 17 December 1884, the critic mentions his "sunny radiance in tone, in marked contrast with any other works about them."[14] We illustrate a continental town scene *(Plate 376)*

which shows his thick, peachy tone, and the "sunny radiance" just mentioned, seen here to good advantage.

A figure of some importance in Irish watercolour painting is Alexander Williams[15] (1846–1930), who for some fifty years was Secretary of the Dublin Sketching Club. Born in Drogheda, he was the son of a hatter, to whom he was first apprenticed. With his brothers he then became a taxidermist of some standing, as some of their works were bought by the Natural History Museum. Later in life he also worked as a musician, singing in the Chapel Royal choir and in St. Patrick's Cathedral.

Despite the variety of his occupations he was an unrelenting painter both in oils and watercolour, exhibiting over four hundred and fifty paintings, landscapes and coastal scenes at the Royal Hibernian Academy alone, between 1871 and 1930. Apart from a few evening classes at the Royal Dublin Society, he had no formal artistic training, as his father had been put off by William Brocas's forthright comment, "Make a sweep of him first."[16] Perhaps recognizing his failings,

376
BINGHAM
McGUINNESS
*Continental
Street Scene*

he remarks, in his manuscript autobiography, "How different with me it might have been, had I been taken in hand, and had gone through proper courses of Art Study and my footsteps placed in the right course."[17] Indeed this is very true, as his oils and finished watercolours often suffer from muddy colour and poor composition. He was popular as an illustrator, combining with Stephen Gwynn to produce *Beautiful Ireland*[18] for which he made no less than forty-six watercolours. A number of sketchbooks recently on the Belfast art market show that he was a lively draughtsman with a pleasant use of wash.

Williams was clearly a man of parts, making friends with everybody from grandees like Tom Conolly, with whom he stayed at Castletown and at Cliff House, Belleek, to the Dublin intelligentsia who formed the Sketching Club. He was also adventurous in seeking new areas to paint. For instance, he appears to be one of the earliest to use Achill as a base, for the first time in September 1873. "At that time the Midland Western Railway only reached Westport and I was obliged to start by the night Mail at 8.20pm,"[19] he remarked. After travelling all night, the coach reached Achill the next day at 12.15. We have already mentioned (in Chapter 12) the foundation of the Dublin Sketching Club, with its first meeting held on 20 October 1874. He describes the scene at the second meeting a week later as follows:

> A long table down the centre of the room was prepared for sketching purposes round which the members sat and for two hours worked to illustrate the two subjects chosen for illustration "Sunset" and "Rejection" . . . Time was called by the Hon. Sec. at 10.15, and each member placed his work on a screen where it was criticised by those present . . . A light supper of cheese and bread washed down with ale followed . . .[20]

The first members were not professional artists but they soon joined, and with its regular "most enjoyable 'working' evenings" and its occasional "conversaziones and smoking concerts"[21] and later weekend outings, the Club was enormously popular and held many an informal exhibition.

John Butler Yeats (1839–1922) came from a different background, prosperous and middle class, much closer to Osborne. He is now somewhat overshadowed by his two brilliant sons, the poet and the artist. He started his career as a barrister but gave up a secure professional life to become an artist in 1867, when he went to London to study at Heatherley's. He remained in London till 1902, but visited Ireland frequently.

Yeats was initially influenced by the Pre-Raphaelites and his most famous

377
JOHN BUTLER
YEATS
William Butler Yeats
(National Gallery of Ireland)

watercolour is *Pippa Passes* (National Gallery of Ireland), which is based on a poem by Browning. However, he is much better known for his lovely pencil portrait drawings which do not change in style, but all have a soft, smudgy tonal technique which adds to their romantic appeal. He occasionally did watercolours such as that of his son, William Butler Yeats, which is in a black wash with white highlights. It makes a remarkable contrast with the romantic pencil profile, also of William *(Plate 377)*. The vivacious portrait of Sarah Purser *(Plate 378)* appears as if it were quickly dashed off, though Yeats is known to have been a very slow worker.

He was influenced by such French artists as Fantin Latour and the American, Whistler. His son, W.B. Yeats, said:

> My father began life a Pre-Raphaelite painter; when past thirty he fell under the influence of contemporary French painting. Instead of finishing a picture one square inch at a time, he kept all fluid, every detail dependent upon every other, and remained a poor man to the end of his life . . ."[22]

It seems to us that Whistler, who lived in France for many years but later settled in London, was the most important influence. The lithograph of Mallarmé of 1893 by Whistler, for instance, has obvious links with J.B. Yeats's *Self Portrait* of two years later. Yeats's *A Woman Dozing* is also a Whistlerian study. In 1907 he left for America, where he lived for the remainder of his life and where he became friendly with John Sloan and Robert Henri when he was living at the Petitpas boarding house, which was something of an artistic centre.

His famous son Jack B. Yeats[23] (1871–1957) owes little stylistically to his father, though his *Self-Portrait* of c. 1920 in the National Gallery of Ireland must be a positive remembering of his father's drawings. Born in London, Jack spent much of his childhood in Sligo, where he went to school, staying with his Pollexfen grandparents. Sligo was to be his chief inspiration all his life, and the drawings that he made in his youth in the West were to be the basis for many of his late works. For the first twenty-five years of his career Yeats worked more in watercolour and pen and ink than in oil, largely because he was working as an

illustrator. Indeed, he worked for *Punch* under the pseudonym "W. Bird" from 1910 to 1948. By 1920, however, most of his paintings were in oils. His artistic education was in London, where from 1877 he attended several art schools, the South Kensington, the Chiswick and the Westminster.

The earliest watercolours, dating from 1897, are race course illustrations, an interest maintained throughout his life, as in *The First Time Round (Plate 379)* of 1903, which exhibits all his great vivacity. The drawings done in 1899 on the Norfolk Broads *(Plate 380)* are more unusual in subject but brilliant in their feeling for movement, freshness,

378
JOHN BUTLER YEATS
Sarah Purser

379
JACK B. YEATS
The First Time Round,
1903

limpid light and colour. There are numerous landscape sketches of the Sligo area and of various places in England as well as figure subjects, of which *Memory Harbour (Plate 381)* of 1900 is a good example as a summing up of the romance of his Sligo background. The free wash drawings which he was doing on the Norfolk Broads are uncommon, and later work such as the *Circus Chariot* (National Gallery of Ireland) of around 1910, which has a great sense of speed and even danger, is built up in layers of paint and

is somewhat murky as a result. None of these has the heavy black outline that one often associates with Yeats and that he used on his broadsheets which his sister, Elizabeth, printed. He used the two styles concurrently.

From childhood, he had been collecting old ballad sheets, which he could still pick up in Sligo. He first made similar broadsheets after meeting Pamela Coleman Smith,[24] an American artist and folklorist, in 1900, illustrating poems by his brother, by George Russell (AE) and by John Masefield.

380
JACK B. YEATS
On the Broads, Norfolk,
1899
National Gallery of
Ireland)

381
JACK B. YEATS
Memory Harbour, 1900

The County of Mayo (Plate 382), 1903, is a study of an emigrant and typical of this phase with its black outlines and shading and is based on an earlier watercolour study. Later examples such as *The Country Shop*, 1912, are lighter and sketchier. His pure black and white work done for magazines like *Punch* was superbly described by Sir Kenneth Clark:

> They had none of the tricks of the trade . . . They were, to begin with, frankly illustrations; and the life they illustrated was fierce, feckless and independent, very far from the comfortable bourgeois bohemianism which I, in common with most middle-class Englishmen, supposed to be the artist's lot. These proud angry-looking men, with cloth caps pulled over one eye, those high-stepping horses and stormy ragged race meetings, suggested a way of life in which man was neither an economic criminal with a respect for law and order, nor an aesthetic animal with a respect for learning and the Russian ballet.[25]

This critique of Yeat's black and white work applies as much to the subject matter of his watercolours, and it is typical of his patriotic fervour for Ireland which, however, never spilled over into active republicanism. His individual studies of Irish types, such as *The Rogue* (Hugh Lane Municipal Gallery of

382
JACK B. YEATS
The County of Mayo (The Pirate), 1902/3
(National Gallery of Ireland)

Modern Art), are among his most powerful works and it is interesting that his contemporary and friend, George Russell (AE), in one of his rare drawings, *The Traveller* (Armagh County Museum), attempts similar subject matter with a pedestrian and conservative pen. Nobody could compete with Yeats when he was dealing with Irish life and character.

All these famous names are primarily remembered for their oil paintings but there were, in Dublin and, perhaps, especially in Belfast, many artists who worked as watercolourists and also as illustrators. The Ramblers Sketching Club, which we mentioned

273

383
ANTHONY CAREY
STANNUS
*View of Carrickfergus
Castle, Co. Antrim*

384
JOSEPH WILLIAM
CAREY
View in Scotland, 1885
(Ulster Museum)

in Chapter 12, was founded in 1879 and became the Belfast Art Society in 1890. It was a great stimulus to art in Belfast, and all the artists discussed here were members.

Anthony Carey Stannus (1830–1919) is one of these. He was born in Carrickfergus from a family of architects and builders, one of whom founded the Carrickfergus Literary and Scientific Society.[26] He was educated at the Belfast School of Design and then worked in Belfast and Wales briefly before having an adventurous career in the army of the Emperor Maximilian of Mexico and in South America. He became a correspondent of the *Illustrated London News*, and when he returned he spent much of his time in London, coming back to Belfast in 1882. He was one of the founder members of the Ramblers Sketching Club and its President from 1885 to 1890.

Stannus's early watercolours of Belfast, dating from the 1850s, now in the Harbour Commissioners collection, are invaluable topographical records. One of them, of *Chichester Quay and High Street, Belfast*,[27] is taken from a drawing by T.M. Baines who illustrated, with Petrie and Bartlett, G.M. Wright's *Ireland Illustrated . . .* of 1831. Stannus soon rose above this old-fashioned style and developed into a very sensitive watercolour painter, examples being his interior of a *Woman Weaving*, and a later landscape of *The Haymakers, Warkworth Castle, Northumberland* (both Ulster Museum). They have clarity of vision and, in both, the figures in the foreground are precisely portrayed. A *View of Carrickfergus Castle (Plate 383)* in a rosy haze shows his command of different effects, and his work has been described as being in the post-Turner tradition and reminiscent of Clarkson Stanfield. Martyn Anglesea considered him the "ideal person to stimulate art activity in Belfast."[28]

Other members of the Ramblers Club included Ernest Hanford, who was Secretary for some years until he left for England in 1886, and whose evocative watercolour of the ruins of the stables at Ormeau Park is in the Ulster Museum; and Joseph William Carey (1859–1937) who, like so many Belfast artists, got his early training in the firm of Marcus Ward. Early in his career he worked as an illuminator of addresses and as an illustrator, but he is best-remembered as

385
HUGH THOMPSON
Bringing him to the Point, 1898
(Ulster Museum)

a landscape and seascape painter. He worked widely in Ireland, from Kerry to Donegal, and elsewhere in the British Isles. His carefully painted *View in Scotland*, 1885 *(Plate 384)*, is a typical work and hardly differs from his style in the 1920s and 1930s. Carey is at his best with wild scenery, though his Irish cottages are somewhat banal.

Of the illustrators, far and away the best was Hugh Thomson (1860–1920), who was another luminary of the Belfast Ramblers Club and had been apprenticed to Marcus Ward under John Vinycomb (1833–1928), the head of the artist department, who had an extremely high opinion of Thomson. The firm of Marcus Ward had set up a stationery and lithographic business in Belfast in 1843. They were known worldwide and were very important for Belfast's artists. It was Marcus Ward who took over the printing of Vere Foster's writing, drawing and watercolour copybooks. Thomson went on to work mainly in England,[29] where he became famous illustrating such literary works as *Cranford* and *Pride and Prejudice* for the publisher Macmillan. He took enormous pains to get his period detail correct and studied the collections of interiors, furnishings and costumes at the Victoria and Albert Museum. Extremely prolific, Thomson had a profound understanding of character as can be seen in his *Bringing him to the Point (Plate 385)*, showing a horse being sold to some unfortunate dupe,[30] and in *The Church*, a picture of three clerics in deep conversation walking down a country road, which is an illustration for Stephen Gwynn's *Highways and Byways in Donegal and Antrim*.[31] Thomson illustrated a number of Gwynn's books.

George Morrow (1870–1955) was the best-known of a large family of Belfast artists and illustrators. With his brothers, Albert, Edwin, Jack and Norman, he started his education at the Government School of Design in Belfast. George's black and white

work became well known in *Punch* but he also worked for the theatre and in water-colour and gouache. A strikingly Frenchified composition by Norman Morrow of a man and woman done in gouache (now in the Ulster Museum), with its simplified outline and detail, was influenced by the rising art of the poster so brilliantly associated with Toulouse–Lautrec.

A contemporary black and white illustrator from Wexford was Harry Furniss (1854–1925), one of whose most famous works was *Imitation the Sincerest Form of Flattery*, a

386
WILLIAM CONOR
Gossiping
*(Ulster Folk and
Transport Museum)*

387
PAUL HENRY
The Grand Canal Dock
(National Gallery of
Ireland)

political cartoon showing the imitative
attitudes of party members to their important
colleagues such as Balfour, Gladstone and
Tim Healy on the benches of the House of
Commons. He made it for *Punch* for whom
he worked for fourteen years.[32] An amusing
and typical example of his work is *The First
Plunge*, a cartoon on the opening of the New
Gallery and the aesthetic movement. In
1905 he wrote an admirable book, *How to
Draw in Pen and Ink.*

A feeling for ordinary people is seen in the
work of William Conor (1881–1968) who,
early in his career, despite a visit to Paris in

1912, turned to the "shawlies" and street
corners of Belfast for his subjects. They are
the illustrated equivalents of characters out
of Sean O'Casey's plays. *Gossiping (Plate
386)*, 1910, brilliantly illustrates these
points, and the sure handling of watercolour
of the sentry in his *Fight and Endure*, 1914
(Ulster Museum), shows another, more serious side to his work. They certainly rank him
with Paul Henry, and at times in his understanding of character he almost aspires to
the genius of Jack B. Yeats.

A contemporary of Conor, Paul Henry
(1876–1958) was the son of a fundamentalist

Protestant minister. As a boy, he was impressed by Millet. Around the turn of the century he was sent to study in Paris at the Académie Julien thanks to the generosity of a distant cousin, and when there, he was overwhelmed by the works of Cézanne, Gauguin and Van Gogh. Indeed he said years later, "I would have walked half across Paris to look at a new thing by him [Van Gogh]."[33] He went on to Whistler's Académie Carmen, where he learned, as S.B. Kennedy says, "to modulate close, tonal relationships and to emphasise the abstract qualities of his compositions."[34] Throughout his life he used charcoal for his studies, and as late as the 1920s he drew *The Grand Canal Dock (Plate 387)* in this medium which he particularly liked and which was so perfect for his Whistlerian style. He also painted a number of watercolours, of which *Cloudscape with Bird in a Thorntree (Plate 388)*, though not dated, echoes the works of Whistler, Arthur Rackham and Edmund Dulac and is probably early in date. The charcoal studies of figures in the West of Ireland, where he went to live on Achill in 1911, show the same interest in peasants as Conor showed in his townies. A multitude of sketches of this period are in the National Gallery of Ireland. He is, of course, known so well today for his later art in oils, but his

early watercolours are, like his early oils, so much more moving than his archetypal Irish cottages and turf stacks. His wife, Grace (1868–1953), was also a well-known artist though more famous for her oils.

Another member of the Belfast Ramblers Club, who links the world of Belfast shipbuilding and city worthies to the cosmopolitan scenes of Edwardian society, is Robert Ponsonby Staples (1853–1943), who inherited the family baronetcy when he was eighty. Staples was educated on the continent, starting in Louvain and moving to Paris, Dresden and Brussels. The doors of the London art world were opened to him by a cousin, Sir Coutts Lindsay, who owned the Grosvenor Gallery. His chalk sketches of high society, the Prince of Wales, Lily Langtry, the Randolph Churchills, Sarah Bernhardt and other celebrities flashily evoke the glamorous world of England before 1914.[35] Whether sketching, riding on the Row, boating at Henley or attending Ascot, or depicting the life of the music hall and theatre, he echoes the glib influence of Helleu and constantly reminds one of other artists such as Boudin and Toulouse–Lautrec. Occasionally his watercolours such as the charming *The Three Sisters* of 1911 and *Nora Painting (Plate 389),*[36] have a quiet intimacy, showing the devoted fondness he had for his "chicks," as he called his daughters. Staples returned to Belfast in 1905, many years before he inherited Lissan, where he died, an aged and eccentric figure. He refused to wear shoes, particularly those with rubber soles, as he was concerned that their insulation would cut off the life-giving forces of the earth's magnetic field!

391
SIR WILLIAM ORPEN
Nude Study
(Ulster Museum)

One of the artistic luminaries of the early twentieth century was William Orpen[37] (1878–1931), whose exquisite draughtsmanship was renowned on both sides of the Atlantic. Like most artistic Dubliners, he went to the Metropolitan School of Art but, unlike many, he continued to the Slade School in London where he was a contemporary of Augustus and Gwen John and was taught by Henry Tonks and Wilson Steer, whose friendship was close despite the vital differences in their teaching. Orpen's drawings done in pencil and chalk have a great sense of form created by his delicate and precise line. An excellent example of his use of chalk is an early academic, student work in the National Gallery of Ireland which shows a male nude model and is dated 1897. Later still, using chalk, he developed a softer, warmer and more tonal style, as in the study of his wife and daughter, *Grace and Bunny,* of around 1905, now in the Whitworth Art Gallery, Manchester. His early watercolours are usually studies, such as his *Study for Waiting for the Cue (Plate 390)* and his man and woman on a horse (National Gallery of Ireland) study for his now destroyed *Western Wedding,* 1914.

The most delightful of Orpen's drawings are his rapid sketches often illustrating letters and notes, menus and other ephemera, which show his sense of humour and his own introspective sense of the ridiculous and lack of self-confidence. They occur throughout his career and include many near caricatures like *Lane, throwing a man out of the Abbey* during the *"Playboy* riots" in the Abbey Theatre, or his *Trying the Impossible* which shows him struggling with a huge canvas of a nude woman. The National Gallery of Ireland was presented with an excellent collection of these by Orpen's daughter, Vivienne Graves, whose mother was the artist's great inamorata, Mrs Howard St. George, an American heiress. One of these shows them dining *à deux* at the Berkeley, Mrs St. George wearing a huge hat under the brim of which he sits and talks with a large libation in front of him.

Orpen's drawings were best popularized through the lithographic reproductions of his etchings made for the Goupil Gallery during the period when he spent his summers at Howth, just before the First World

War. These etchings, which include delicate nudes of his models, frequently show him in his characteristic hat. The watercolour drawing for *The Draughtsman and his Model* for one of these etchings is one of his most outstanding works and we illustrate a superb nude study from the back *(Plate 391)*. Self-portraits haunt him throughout his life and occur regularly in characters in his pictures and therefore also in his drawings. The ink self-portrait in the National Gallery of Ireland for *A Young Man from the West*, 1909, has the same pose and grim three-quarters face as *The Dead Ptarmigan* (National Gallery of Ireland), 1909. His biographers, Konody and Dark, talking of his sketchbooks, speak correctly when they note that "Continual practice of drawing . . .

sharpened Orpen's power of observation and gave sureness and authority to his hand."[38]

Orpen was greatly disillusioned by the appalling tragedy of the First World War, and many watercolours occur among his works as a war artist such as *Three Soldiers watching a shell burst (Plate 392)*. Other war drawings, like this one, show his unheroic reaction to the sordid horrors of the battlefield. He frequently painted the flowers that sprouted in the mud of the tragic, war-stricken countryside. His brother, Richard Caulfield Orpen (1863–1938), an architect, was also a good watercolour painter, though sometimes his work is dominated by buildings such as his three drawings of *Dublin Alleyways* (National Gallery of Ireland), which show his sure drawing style. A *View of*

392
SIR WILLIAM ORPEN
Three Soldiers watching a shell burst

Sheephaven Bay is a handsome, airy, light-filled watercolour.[39]

William John Leech (1881–1968), the son of a Trinity College Professor of Law, was another interesting product of the Metropolitan School of Art at this time. Though, like Orpen, primarily an oil painter, he used a lot of watercolour not only for studies but for finished work too. He went to Paris for further education at the Académie Julian, where he was influenced by Jean Paul Laurens and Bouguereau. He spent most of the years from 1903 to 1914 in Concarneau in Brittany, though he visited his family and exhibited in Ireland. After an initial academic "brown" period, by the turn of the century the influence of Whistler had lightened his palette. A review in *The Times* refers to Leech as "an artist who aims at vivid illusion by means of that process of elimination which was practised by Whistler."[40] *Trees in the Snow* and *A Snow Covered Field (Plate 393)* (both National Gallery of Ireland), both of around 1910, show Whistleresque *Japonism* in their linear division, their flatness and asymmetry.

At a group exhibition in the Leinster Lecture Hall in Molesworth Street which included Leech, Casimir Dunin-Markievicz, Constance Gore-Booth, and George Russell (AE) a fellow exhibitioner was Dermot O'Brien, who was an enthusiastic advocate of Leech. O'Brien (1865–1945), who became President of the Royal Hibernian Academy in 1910, was, like Orpen, a product of the Slade School, but he went on to Antwerp and to the Académie Julian, as well as travelling widely on the continent. His main forte is in oil but, like all Slade School pupils, he is an excellent draughtsman, as demonstrated by his studies for *The White Dress* and for *Lennox Robinson* (both National Gallery of Ireland), and his group of *Lady Glenavy and her son Patrick Campbell (Plate 394)*, which dates about 1914. There are many drawings and watercolours, too, of the lush, pastoral countryside near his Co. Limerick home, Cahirmoyle.

As the reader will have observed, we have cut off many of these painters in their youth, but this is because we complete this survey of Irish drawings and watercolours at the beginning of the First World War, and at the waning of the academic tradition. This was a great period for Irish art, which in literature was known as the Irish Renaissance. We omit many a well-known name simply because of their age.

An example is Patrick Tuohy[41] (1894–1930), a pupil of Orpen, by whom we include only the haunting and obsessive watercolour, *The Little Seamstress (Plate 395)*, for which he won the Taylor Award in 1915. In Chapter 12 we have touched on Mainie Jellett, Evie Hone and Wilhelmina Geddes and, as we said then, we sadly omit them as outside our period. Harry Clarke[42] (1899–1931, with his fin-de-siècle drawings showing the influence not only of Beardsley but also of other artists such as Erté and Bakst, was producing drawings, watercolours and illustrations like those for *The Rape of the Lock* (1913), and *The Rime of the Ancient Mariner (Plate 396)*. His wife, Margaret Clarke, a student of Orpen, is also remarkable

393 (Facing Page)
WILLIAM LEECH
A Snow-Covered Field, c.1910
(National Gallery of Ireland)

394
DERMOT O'BRIEN
Lady Glenavy and her son Patrick Campbell, c.1914

396
HARRY CLARKE
*No. 7 from eight
illustrations to* The Rime
of the Ancient Mariner

397
MARGARET CLARKE
Academic Drawing

for her exquisite draughtsmanship *(Plate 397)*. Grace Gifford[43] (1888–1955), whose mischievous caricatures such as *Edward Martyn "having a week of it" in Paris* bear the talents to be expected of a great niece of Frederick William Burton, was another Orpen pupil. His most famous student was John Keating (1889–1977), who was a superb draughtsman, using pencil and chalk rather than watercolour. His love of the West of Ireland and the supposedly simple peasant life together with his nationalistic fervour combined to make him reject modernism.

We could mention other names but in reality we hope we have indicated that art in Ireland moved on from no mean beginnings and has flourished ever since. Unlike England, Ireland produced no major masters of watercolour painting but a great many of the second rank, who are too little-known, and who illustrate the natural beauties of our country. Many others who are virtually unknown throw a considerable light on the social life of Ireland over the last three centuries, and we hope the book may have unveiled many a surprise both in quality and subject matter.

395 (Facing Page)
PATRICK TUOHY *The Little Seamstress, 1915*
(Hugh Lane Municipal Gallery of Modern Art)

NOTES

INTRODUCTION
Pages 9–12

1 David Blayney Brown, *Catalogue of Drawings in the Ashmolean Museum, Oxford by Artists Born Before 1775* (Oxford, 1982).

2 *Tour in England, Ireland, and France, in the years 1828 and 1829*, publ anonymously (London, 1832), vol. 1, p. 242.

3 T. Crofton Croker, *Researches in the South of Ireland* (London, 1824), pp. 29–30.

4 Gordon N. Ray (ed.), *The Letters and Private Papers of William Makepeace Thackeray* (London, 1945), vol II, p. 76, in a letter dated 31 Aug. – 1 Sept. 1842 to Mrs C-S in Paris.

5 A.W. Hutton (ed.), *Arthur Young's Tour in Ireland 1776–1779* (2 vols., London, 1892), vol. 2, p. 131. Scotland's art schools were the closest in the British Isles to the Irish system. See Mungo Campbell, *The Line of Tradition* (Edinburgh, 1993), Catalogue of an exhibition of Scottish Watercolours, pp. 14, 15.

6 See Jeanne Sheehy, *The Discovery of Ireland's Past: The Celtic Revival, 1830–1930* (London, 1980), pp. 17–27.

7 Judy Egerton, *British Watercolours* (London, 1986), p. 4.

8 Anne Crookshank and the Knight of Glin, *The Painters of Ireland* (London, 1978).

CHAPTER 1
Irish Watercolours: the Beginnings
Pages 13–21

1 Walter Scott (ed.), *Lord Somers (ed.), A collection of scarce and valuable Tracts . . .* , 2nd edn. (13 vols., London, 1809–15), vol. 1, includes, starting on p. 558, John Derricke, *Image of Irelande* (London, 1581). The complete set of twelve woodcuts illustrated in the first edition only survive in the copy in the Drummond Collection in the Library of the University of Edinburgh. Some of them are reproduced in many modern histories of Ireland and all in John Small (ed.), John Derricke, *The Image of Irelande* (Edinburgh, 1883).

2 Derricke, *Image of Irelande,* 1809 edn., p. 583.

3 University Library, Ghent, ms. 2466.

4 Preussischer Kunstsammlungen, Kupferstichkabinett, Berlin-Dahlem. See J. M. Massing, "Dürer's *Warriors and Peasants* 1521," *Irish Arts Review Yearbook,* vol. 10 (1994), (pp. 223–6).

5 John T. Gilbert, *Facsimiles of National Manuscripts of Ireland . . .* (London, 1882 and 1884), part IV, 1 and 2.

6 Collection, the Marquess of Salisbury, Hatfield House.

7 G.A. Hayes McCoy, *Ulster and other Irish Maps, c. 1600* (Dublin, 1964).

8 W.A. Wallace, *John White, Thomas Harriot and Walter Ralegh in Ireland* (London, 1985), pp. 6–8.

9 J.H. Andrews, *Irish Maps* (Dublin, 1978), p. 14, illus. 12.

10 Wallace, *John White,* p. 9.

11 J.H. Andrews, *Plantation Acres* (Belfast, 1985) (discuss all these cartographers in detail except for Bartlett).

12 Gilbert Camblin, *The Town in Ulster* (Belfast, 1951), several illustrations.

13 Andrews, *Irish Maps,* illus. 9.

14 Camblin, *Town in Ulster,* plate 11.

15 Brian de Breffini (ed.), *The Irish World* (London, 1977), p. 117.

16 Thomas Morris, *Holy Cross Abbey* (Dublin, 1986), pp. 1–3, illus 2; Denis Murphy (ed.), *Triumphalia Chronologica Monasterii Sanctis Crucis in Hibernia 1640* (Dublin, 1891).

17 Copies in the Genealogical Office and the Gilbert Collection Library. They contain only Dublin church monuments.

18 Anne Crookshank and the Knight of Glin, *Irish Portraits 1660–1860* (London, 1969), catalogue of an exhibition held in Dublin, London and Belfast, 1969–70, illus. p. 10.

19 Walter Strickland, *Dictionary of Irish Artists* (Dublin, 1913), vol. II, pp. 569–76.

20 Rolf Loeber, "Biographical dictionary of engineers in Ireland 1600–1730," *The Irish Sword,* Winter no. 79, vol. XIII, no. 53, p. 283 after "Dartmouth"; Ruth Isobel Ross, "Phillips's Pleasing Prospects,"*Country Life* (4 March 1976), pp. 552–3. A number of his drawings are illustrated in this article.

21 Thomas Dineley, *Observations made on his tour in Ireland and France, 1675–80*, National Library of Ireland ms. no. 392.

22 Richard Tyler, *Francis Place 1647–1728, an exhibition . . . of his work* (London, York and Kenwood House, 1971). This is good biographically but does not contain any Irish drawings though it does include a good bibliography. Many Irish drawings are in the National Gallery of Ireland and in the Victoria and Albert Museum, and two articles on them exist by John Maher, "Francis Place in Dublin," *Journal of the Royal Society of Antiquaries of Ireland* (1932), vol. 62, pp. 1–14 and "Francis Place in Drogheda, Kilkenny and Waterford," *JRSAI* (1934), vol. 64, p. 41 ff. Raymond Gillespie, "Describing Dublin: Francis Place's Visit (1698–1699)," *Visualizing Ireland,* Adele M. Dalsimer (ed.), (Boston and London, 1993), pp. 99–118.

CHAPTER 2
The Early Eighteenth Century
Pages 23–32

1 Anne Crookshank and the Knight of Glin, *Irish Portraits 1660–1860* (London, 1969), catalogue of an exhibition held in Dublin, London and Belfast, 1969–70, no. 12, p. 32.

2 Christie's, London, 24 March 1987, Lot 6.

3 "The notebooks of George Vertue, vol. III," *Walpole Society* XXII (London, 1933–4), notebook 4, p. 99.

4 We are indebted to Nicola Figgis for information on this artist and for obtaining photographs of his Roman drawings. See Nicola Figgis, "Henry Trench . . . Painter and Illustrator," *Irish Arts Review Yearbook 1994,* vol. 10, pp. 217–22.

5 We are indebted to Roger Wilson for identifying the subjects of these drawings.

6 Scottish Record Office, GD 18/4595–4648

7 PR030/24/23/8 Letter from Shaftesbury to Fagan from Naples, 13 Feb. 1712.

8 Edgar Wind, "Shaftesbury as a patron of art," *Journal of the Warburg and Courtauld Institutes,* vol. 2 (1938–9), pp. 185–8.

9 Sheila O'Connell, "Lord Shaftesbury in Naples, 1711–13," *Walpole Society,* vol. 54, 1988 (publ. 1991), p. 162.

10 Ibid., p. 200.

11 Ibid., p. 185 (20 June)

12 Ibid., p. 187 (16 Sept.)

13 British Library additional mss. 47027, f. 18. Information for this and the following footnote kindly communicated to us by Dr Edward McParland.

14 British Library additional mss. 47025, f. 80.

15 Vertue, vol. III, p. 30.

16 *Universal Magazine,* London, Nov. 1748.

17 Michael Wynne, "Thomas Frye c. 1710–62," *Burlington Magazine,* vol. CXIV, no. 827 (Feb. 1972), pp. 79–84.

18 Ibid., p. 80.

19 Benedict Nicholson, *Joseph Wright of Derby,* 2 vols. (London and New York, 1968) pp. 67–8.

20 Whaley Batson, *Henrietta Johnston,* Introduction to the catalogue of an exhibition held in the Museum of Early Southern Decorative Arts, Winston-Salem, North Carolina and the Gibbes Museum of Art, Charleston, South Carolina, Oct. 1991–Feb. 1992, p. 2. This is the most recent catalogue of her work.

21 William A. Shaw (ed.), *Huguenot Society,* vol. XVIII (Lymington, 1911).

22 Lecture given by Martha Severens in connection with the 1991–2 exhibition, see footnote 20.

23 Information kindly communicated by Philip Blake.

24 The quotation was said by Bishop Downes and can be found in Strickland, vol. 1, p. 277. The information about the Digby inventories was kindly given us by Dr T. Barnard.

25 Daphne Foskett, *Dictionary of British Miniature Painters* (London, 1972), vol. 1, p. 277, and vol. 2, plate 311.

26 Batson, *Henrietta Johnston*, p. 8.

27 Ibid., p. 9.

28 Lady Llanover (ed.), *Autobiography and Correspondence of Mary Granville, Mrs Delany* (6 vols. London, 1861). vol. I, p. 316. All three quotes come from a passage in a letter by Mrs Delany, dated 25 Nov. 1731.

29 Ibid., vol. II, p. 412, letter dated 11 Jan. 1745–6.

30 Ibid., vol. II, p. 415, letter dated 25 Jan. 1745–6. The use of the word "egging" is not easily understood. It may mean that they were using glair (prepared white of egg) as the binding medium with their colours instead of gum arabic which would have been more commonplace.

31 Ibid., vol. II, p. 592, letter dated 22 Sept. 1750.

32 Public Record Office of Northern Ireland ms. no. D 562/342.

33 Michael Clarke, *The Tempting Prospect* (London, 1981), pp. 14–17.

34 Sothebys, 8 October 1993, Lot 742.

35 John Turpin, *A School of Art in Dublin since the Eighteenth Century* (to be published in Dublin, 1994), p. 65.

36 Alan Joseph Bliss (ed.), *A Dialogue in Hibernian Stile between A and B . . .*, vol 6 of *Irish Writing from the Age of Swift* (Dublin, 1977), p. 66.

37 These pamphlets were both published in 1751.

38 Lady Llanover (ed.), *Mrs Delany*, vol. III, p. 17.

39 Apart from the work edited by Lady Llanover, there is now a new edition of Mrs Delany's Irish letters entitled *Letters from Georgian Ireland*, Angelique Day (ed.), (Belfast, 1991). There is also a biography by Ruth Hayden, *Mrs Delany: her life and her flowers*, 2nd edn. (London 1992).

40 Lady Llanover (ed.), *Mrs Delany*, vol. I, p. 283.

41 Ibid., frontispiece.

42 Such as Stalker and Parker's *Treatise of Japanning . . .* (Oxford, 1688), and *The Ladies Amusement* (c. 1760). Mrs Delany mentions her interest in letters to her sister, 9 Sept. 1729 and 13 July 1731, in Lady Llanover (ed.), vol. I, pp. 213 and 285.

43 This pastel is after the Rosalba self-portrait in the Galleria dell'Accademia, Venice. The inscription on the back reads, "Rosalba after an original done by herself by Mary Pendarves 1739." This was covered by a Dublin concert programme and a label which read ". . . copied from an original of her own painting by Mrs Delany – whilst a Widow after the death of Mr Pendarves. Bequeathed by Harriet Port [her great niece] Septr 1824 to her niece Frances Bunsen."

44 Martyn Anglesea and John Preston, "A Philosophical Landscape . . .," *Art History*, 3:3 (Sept. 1980), p. 252.

45 One set is in the Ulster Museum, Belfast; the other is in a private collection in Ireland.

46 Lady Llanover (ed.), *Mrs Delany*, vol. iii, p. 521, letter dated 8 Oct. 1758.

CHAPTER 3
The Antiquarians
Pages 33–46

1 G.F. Mitchell and H.M. Parke, "The Giant Deer in Ireland," *Proceedings of the Royal Irish Academy*, LII:B (1949), p. 294, plate XVII; Stuart Piggott, *Ruins in a Landscape. Essays in Antiquarianism* (Edinburgh, 1976), pp. 10, 11 and illus. 2.

2 A letter from Loftus to Robert Cecil about the deer's head and antlers is dated 27 Sept. 1597, *Calendar of State Papers relating to Ireland 1596–7*, PRO 1893, p. 406.

3 K. Theodore Hoppen, *The Common Scientist in the Seventeenth Century. A Study of the Dublin Philosophical Society 1683–1708* (London, 1970).

4 J.G. Simms, *William Molyneux of Dublin*, P.H. Kelly (ed.), (Dublin 1982); T. O'Raifeartaigh (ed.), *Royal Irish Academy: a Bicentennial History 1785–1985* (Dublin, 1985) pp. 2, 3.

5 Michael Herity, *Irish Passage Graves*, (Dublin, 1974), p. 8.

6 Ibid., p. 9.

7 Michael McCarthy, *The Origins of the Gothic Revival* (New Haven and London, 1987), pp. 45, 46; Edward Malins and the Knight of Glin, *Lost Demesnes* (London, 1976), pp. 118–21; James Howley, *The Follies and Garden Buildings of Ireland* (New Haven and London, 1993), pp. 183–5, 198–200, 209 for Tollymore. For Wright in general see Chapters 3, 7 and 11.

8 Herity, *Irish Passage Graves*, pp. 12–13.

9 McCarthy, *The Origins of the Gothic Revival*, pp. 42–8.

10 Thomas Wright, *Louthiana: or an Introduction to the Antiquities of Ireland*, (London, 1748).

11 Hoppen, p. 140. One of these is illustrated in Martyn Anglesea and John Preston, "A philosophical landscape: Susanna Drury and the Giant's Causeway," *Art History*, 3:3 (Sept. 1980), pl. 16.

12 Anglesea and Preston, "A Philosophical Landscape," p. 257.

13 Charles Smith, *The Ancient and Present State of the County of Cork* (2 vols., Dublin, 1750), vol. 1, pp. 146–7.

14 Herity, *Irish Passage Graves*, p. 12.

15 Christine Casey, "Miscellanea Structura Curiosa," *Irish Arts Review*, Year Book, 1991, pp. 85–91; and Howley, *Follies and Garden Buildings*, pp. 31–2 and 218–19.

16 Francis Grose, *Antiquities of Ireland* (2 vols, London, 1791–5), vol. 2, p. 58. The two following illustrations are of Burnt Court.

17 Liam Price (ed.), *An Eighteenth Century Antiquary . . . Austin Cooper . . .* (Dublin, 1942), p. 21. See also Richard A. Cooper, "Genealogical notes on the Austin Cooper Family in Ireland 1660–1960," *The Irish Genealogist*, vol. 3, no. 9 (Oct 1964), pp. 351–95, with particular reference to pp. 353–4. Some of the Cooper Collection is still owned by the family but other items are in the Royal Irish Academy.

18 Anne Crookshank and the Knight of Glin, *The Painters of Ireland* (London, 1978), pp. 55–61.

19 C.E.F. Trench, "William Burton Conyngham (1733–96)," *Journal of the Royal Society of Antiquaries of Ireland*, 115 (1985), pp. 40–61.

20 T. O'Raifeartaigh (ed.) *Royal Irish Academy*, p. 7.

21 Ronald Lightbown,"18th and 19th century visitors – part II," *Old Kilkenny Review* (second series 3:2, 1985), pp. 161–73.

22 James N. Brewer, *The Beauties of Ireland*, (2 vols., London, 1825), vol. 1, pp. 482–3.

23 Much of our information on Tarrant comes from Emer Singleton, "Charles Tarrant, surveyor, architect, artist and cartographer. (1730–1818)," *Old Bray Journal*, 1:5 (Dec. 1991), pp. 7–15.

24 Trench, *Conyngham*, p.46. The subject of the Batalha trip by Conyngham, Tarrant and Colonel Brougham is being researched by Professor Michael McCarthy.

25 James Cavanah Murphy, *Plans, elevations . . . of the church of Batalha . . .* (London, 1795).

26 Kilruddery mss., by courtesy of the Earl of Meath.

27 Peter Harbison, *Beranger's Views of Ireland* (Dublin, 1991), 24 engraved views; Francis Grose, *Antiquities*, vol. 2, p. 15.

28 Daniel Charles Grose, *The Antiquities of Ireland*, Roger Stalley (ed.), (Dublin, 1992).

29 Patricia Boyne, *John O'Donovan (1806–61) a biography* (Kilkenny, 1987), pp. 43–4.

30 Trench, *Conyngham*, p. 45.

31 John Andrews, *Plantation Acres* (Omagh, 1985), illus. p. 155, pp. 156–72.

32 Canon C.C. Ellison, *The Hopeful Traveller, the Life and Times of Daniel Augustus Beaufort . . .* (Kilkenny, 1987), pp. 33 and 41. Pocock charged six guineas for eight lessons, a high price but at least three children were involved. The book mentions all the members of the artistic Beaufort family and is illustrated.

33 George Harding, *Two Tours of Ireland in the years 1792–3*, ms. Lough Fea, Shirley Papers, p. 109, taken from a transcript by Edward McParland. See also Edward McParland, "Emo Court, Co. Leix –," *Country Life* (23 May 1974), p. 1276.

34 Julian Faigan, *Paul Sandby Drawings* (City of Hamilton Art Gallery), (Sydney, 1981).

35 Harding, *Two Tours*, p. 109.

36 James Gandon, Jr., and Thomas J. Mulvany, *The Life of James Gandon*, Maurice Craig (ed.), (London, 1969), p. 49.

37 Malins and Glin, *Lost Demesnes*, p. 82.

38 Mrs Godfrey Clarke, *Gleanings from an Old Portfolio* (3 vols., Edinburgh, 1895), vol. 1, p. 53.

39 Harding, *Two Tours*, p. 109.

CHAPTER 4
The Dublin Society Schools
Pages 47–75

1 George Berkeley, *The Querist* (2 parts, Dublin, 1725 [1735]–36), pt. 1, p. 15, q. 71.

2 "The Notebooks of George Vertue," vol. III, *Walpole Society*, XXII (London, 1933–4), p. 98.

3 John Turpin, "School of Ornament in the Dublin Society in the Eighteenth century," *Journal of the Royal Society of Antiquaries of Ireland*, 116 (1986), pp. 38–50; John Turpin, "French Influence on Eighteenth-Century Art Education in Dublin," *Eighteenth-Century Ireland*, vol. 5 (1990), pp. 105–16 and John Turpin, "Irish Art and Design Education from Eighteenth century to the Present," *Irish Arts Review Yearbook*, vol. 10 (1994), pp. 209–16. Another article on the early French influence on Irish art is Anne Crookshank, "The Conversation Piece," *Decantations A Tribute to Maurice Craig* (Dublin, 1992), pp. 16–20.

4 William Carey, *Some Memoirs of the Patronage and Progress of the Fine Arts in England and Ireland* (London, 1826), pp. 183–4.

5 Thomas James Mulvany, "Memoirs of Native Artists No. 1–Mr Francis R. West," *The Citizen*, no. XXIV, (Oct. 1841), p. 206.

6 Anthony Pasquin (i.e. John Williams), *Memoirs of the Royal Academicians and an Authentic History of the Artists of Ireland* (London, 1796), reprinted with an introduction by R.W. Lightbown (London, 1970), p. 17.

7 John O'Keeffe, *Recollections of the Life of John O'Keeffe, written by himself* (2 vols., London, 1826) vol. 1, p. 2.

8 Carey, *Some Memoirs*, pp. 187–8.

9 Robina Napier(ed.) *Johnstoniana, Anecdotes of the Late Samuel Johnston Lld...* (London, 1884), pp. 223–4. We are grateful to Ronald Lightbown for bringing this book to our attention.

10 Carey, *Some Memoirs*, pp. 183–4.

11 Sir Vere Hunt, *Journals*. Typescript in the possession of Mid-Western Archives, The Granary, Limerick, no pagination.

12 *Report of the first public Distribution of Premiums, Royal Dublin Society* (Dublin, 1843), p. 10.

13 *An Essay on Perfecting the Fine Arts in Great Britain and Ireland*, printed by William Sleator (Dublin, 1767), p. 39.

14 Carey, *Some Memoirs*, p. 188. For French influence, see John Turpin in *Eighteenth-Century Ireland*, note 3.

15 Dorothea Herbert, *Retrospections of Dorothea Herbert 1770–89* (London, 1929), vol. 1, p. 45.

16 George Breeze, *Society of Artists in Ireland. Index of Exhibits 1765–80* (Dublin, 1985), p. 23. For information on Praval see Rudger Joppien and Bernard Smith, *The Art of Captain Cook's Voyages* (New Haven and London 1985), vol. 1, pp. 56–9, illus. He is identified as the Chas Provall who was taken on the *Endeavour* as a supernumerary in Batavia on 19 Dec. 1770. Due to the illness and death of the official draughtsmen, Praval, who was an indifferent artist, seems to have been used by Banks.

17 Christine Casey, "Books and builders...," unpublished Ph.D. thesis, Trinity College, Dublin, 1991.

18 J.H. Andrews, *Irish Maps*, Irish Heritage Series, no. 18 (Dublin, 1978), p. 15. See also A. Stuart Mason and John Bensusan-Butt, "P.B. Scalé: Surveyor in Ireland, Gentleman of Essex," *Proceedings of the Huguenot Society*, XXIV:6 (1988), pp. 508–18.

19 James Williamson, *Autobiography* (1819). Information from Michael Ludgrove, late of Christie's of London. Collection Ulster Museum. See also J.H. Andrews, "Surveyors and Surveying in James Williamson's autobiography," *Familia*, vol. 2, no. 7, 1991, pp. 7–11.

20 Gottfried Küttner, *Briefe uber Irland* (Leipzig, 1785), p. 60. We are grateful to Mrs Mia Craig for her translation.

21 Iolo Williams, *Early English Water-colours* (London, 1952. Reprint, Bath 1970), p. 43.

22 H.L. Mallalieu, *Understanding Watercolours* (Woodbridge, 1985), p. 90.

23 Patricia Butler, *Three Hundred Years of Irish Watercolours and Drawings* (London, 1990), illus. p. 54.

24 *Universal Magazine*, vol. III (London, Nov. 1748).

25 Edmund Burke, *A Philosophical Enquiry into the Origin of our Ideas of the Sublime and the Beautiful* (London, 1767). We have used the edition by J.T. Boulton (London, 1958), p. 82.

26 Pierpont Morgan Library, New York.

27 Pasquin, *Memoirs of the RAs*, p. 41; Rudger Joppien and Bernard Smith, *The Art of Captain Cook's Voyages*, vol. 1, p. 73 and illus. between pp. 82 and 200.

28 Mrs Godfrey Clark, *Gleanings from an Old Portfolio*, Edinburgh 1985, vol. 1, pp. 251–2.

29 Martyn Anglesea, *Portraits and Prospects*. Catalogue of an exhibition of watercolours from the Ulster Museum in association with the Smithsonian Institution (Belfast, 1989), p. 38; and Martyn Anglesea, "John James Barralet: a drawing master at Glenarm Castle in the late 18th century," *The Glynns* (Belfast, 1991), vol. 19, p. 5. Also Robert L. Raley, "John James Barralet in Dublin and Philadelphia," *Irish Art Review* (Autumn, 1985), 2:3, p. 19.

30 William Dunlap, *A History of the Rise and Progress of the Arts of Design in the United States* (3 vols., 1834), vol. 2, pp. 42–5, quoted from Phoebe Lloyd Jacobs, *John James Barralet and the Apotheosis of George Washington, Winterthur Portfolio 12* (Charlottesville, 1977), p. 118. For further information see "Philadelphia's Irish legacy" (Robert Raley), *The 1984 Antiques Show* (Philadelphia, 1984), pp. 47–54.

31 Edward Nygren with Bruce Robertson and other authors, *Views and Visions: American Landscape before 1830* (Washington, Corcoran Gallery of Art, 1986), p. 233.

32 We are indebted to James Holloway of the Scottish National Portrait Gallery for information on this picture.

33 Williams, *Early English Watercolours*, pl. 127.

34 Also brought to our attention by James Holloway.

35 Sotheby's, 16 July 1987, Lot 51.

36 Professor Michael McCarthy (University College, Dublin), "Beyond the Grand Tour, Anglo Irish Travellers to Greece and the Levant 1740–50," unpublished lecture (1992), typescript p. 10. Another account of Dalton's life, by Francis Russell, will appear in the forthcoming *Mellon Dictionary of British Artists in Italy*.

37 J. Gandon and T.J. Mulvany, *The Life of James Gandon Esq* (Dublin, 1846), p. 210.

38 Quoted by McCarthy, "Beyond the Grand Tour," p. 10. Eileen Harris in *British Architectural Books and Writers, 1556–1785* (Cambridge, 1990), pp. 173–5, discusses the problems of Dalton's *Antiquities*.

39 McCarthy, "Beyond the Grand Tour," p. 10.

40 Ibid., p. 10.

41 W.B. Stanford and E.J. Finopoulos (eds.), *The Travels of Lord Charlemont in Greece and Turkey 1749* (London, 1984), p. 66.

42 Francis Hardy, *Memoirs of... James Caulfield, Earl of Charlemont...* (London, 1810), p. 11.

43 McCarthy, "Beyond the Grand Tour," pp. 11 and 12.

44 Pasquin, *Memoirs of the RAs*, p.51, under "Rogers."

45 O'Keeffe, *Recollections*, vol. 1, p. 2.

46 Ibid., p. 209.

47 Pasquin, *Memoirs of the RAs*, p. 18.

48 Michael Wynne, "An influence on Robert Healy," *Burlington Magazine*, CXVIII; 879 (June 1976), p. 413, pls. 95–7 and 100–5.

49 Ibid., pl. 105.

50 O'Keeffe, *Recollections*, vol. 1, p. 28.

51 Judy Egerton, *George Stubbs 1724–1806*, Catalogue of an exhibition, Tate Gallery and Yale Center for British Art, London (1984–5), no. 28, pp. 52–3.

52 *The Public Monitor or New Freeman's Journal* (Dublin), 27 March 1773.

53 Patrick Montague-Smith, "The Dexters of Dublin and Annfield, Co. Kildare," *The Irish Ancestor*, II: 1 (1970), pp. 342, illus.

54 W.B. Sarsfield Taylor, *The Origin, Progress, and Present Condition of the Fine Arts in Great Britain and Ireland* (2 vols, London, 1841), vol. II, pp. 285.

55 Sotheby's, 21 Nov. 1985, Lot 67.

56 Mildred Archer, *India and British Portraiture 1780–1825* (London, 1979), pp. 204–33, illus. p. 220. Also George Breeze, "Letter to the editor: Hickey portraits," *Apollo* (Jan. 1976), p. 79.

57 Christie's, 17 Nov. 1987, Lot 129.

58 Kenneth Garlick and Angus McIntyre (eds.), *The Diary of Joseph Farington* (New Haven and London, 1978), vol. I, p. 282.

59 O'Keeffe, *Recollections*, vol. I, p. 12.

60 John Turpin, "The School of Ornament of the Dublin Society in the 18th century," *Journal of the Royal Society of Antiquaries of Ireland*, 116 (1986), pp. 40–3. Turpin's account differs from Strickland's and is no doubt more precise in dating.

61 Dublin Society Minutes, 9 Dec. 1756.

62 Thomas James Mulvany, "Hugh Douglas Hamilton," *Dublin Monthly Magazine*, Jan.–June 1842, p. 68.

63 Ibid., pp. 68–9.

64 National Library of Wales, Wynnstay mss., Box 115/21, no. 43.

65 *English Drawings, 1990*, exhibition catalogue, Hazlitt, Gooden and Fox, p. 78.

66 Sotheby's, Oct. 1991, Lot 67.

67 Christie's, 30 June 1981, Lot 34.

68 For his cut paper work see, W.A. Thorp, "The Art of the Cut Paper-cutter," (*Country Life*, 10 July 1943), pp. 194–6; Edward A. McGuire, "Pastel portrait painting in Ireland in the XVIII century," *The Connoisseur*, 103 (Jan. 1939), pp. 12 and 13; National Gallery of Ireland, *Acquisitions 1984–6*, p. 45 and illus. p. 46.

69 Homan Potterton, "A commonplace practitioner in painting and in etching: Charles Exshaw." *The Connoisseur*, CLXXXVII: 754 (Dec. 1974), pp. 269–73.

CHAPTER 5
Genre and Landscape
Pages 77–98

1 H.L. Mallalieu, *The Dictionary of British Watercolour Artists up to 1920* (2 vols., Woodbridge, 1976), vol. 1, p. 191; and there are further details of Nixon's life in Martyn Anglesea, *Portraits and Prospects*, catalogue of an exhibition of watercolours from the Ulster Museum in association with the Smithsonian Institution (Belfast, 1989), p. 30.

2 Henry Angelo, *Reminiscences of Him with Memoirs of his Late Father and Friends*, (2 vols., London, 1828–30), vol. 1, pp. 208–12.

3 Ibid., p. 335.

4 Anglesea, *Portraits and Prospects*, p. 30.

5 Anthony Pasquin, (i.e. John Williams), *Memoirs of the Royal Academicians and an Authentic History of the Artists of Ireland* (London, 1796). Reprinted with an introduction by R.W. Lightbown (London, 1970), p. 53.

6 Peter Murray, *Illustrated Summary Catalogue of the Crawford Art Gallery* (Cork, 1992), p. 174.

7 The most important of these is "Gleanings on Old Cork Artists," *Journal of the Cork Historical and Archaeological Society* (vol. VI, 2nd series, 1900), pp. 106–8.

8 A.F. Wedd, *The Fate of the Fenwicks*

1798–1828 (London 1927), p. 117.

9 Most writers on watercolour painters, including J.L. Roget, *History of the Old Watercolour Society* (London, 1891), vol. 1, p. 173, agree with M. Hardie, *Watercolour Painting in Britain* (3 vols., 1967–9), vol. 2, p. 133. Stanley William Fisher, however, in his *Dictionary of Watercolour Painters 1750–1900* (London, 1972), says he was "Irish by birth."

10 Iolo Williams, *Early English Watercolours . . .* (London, 1952), pp. 223–4.

11 Anne Crookshank and The Knight of Glin, *The Painters of Ireland* (London, 1978), p. 134.

12 This group of Ashford drawings was on the Dublin art market in the 1970s accompanied by a sheet of paper with Ashford's signature on it.

13 Edward Malins and The Knight of Glin, *Lost Demesnes* (London, 1976), pp. 132 and 135.

14 Crookshank and Glin, *Painters of Ireland*, p. 136.

15 Andrew Wilton and Anne Lyles, *The Great Age of British Watercolours 1750–1880*, catalogue of an exhibition at the Royal Academy, London, and the National Gallery of Art, Washington (1993), pl. 55, no. 232.

16 Andrew Wilton, *British Watercolours 1750–1850*, (Oxford, 1977) p. 28.

17 George Holmes, *Sketches of some of the Southern Counties of Ireland . . .* (London, 1801), p. 120.

18 Daniel Augustus Beaufort, "Tour of Kerry," *Journal of the Kerry Archaeological and History Society*, 18 (1985), p. 193.

19 Alexander Hamilton, ms. diaries of A.H. 1793–1807, Hamwood collection. Entries for 10 and 11 Sept. 1804.

20 Wilton, *British Watercolours*, p. 57.

21 Ibid., p. 57.

22 Unknown Diarist, Royal Irish Academy ms. 24K 14/15, (2 vols., 1801–3), vol. 2, p. 113.

23 Leger Galleries, London, exhibition of *English Watercolours* 10 Nov.–24 Dec. 1980, no. 35.

24 Unknown Diarist, vol. 2, pp. 113–14.

25 H.L. Mallalieu, *Understanding Watercolours* (Woodbridge, 1985), p. 109.

26 Christie's, Dublin, *John Chambers Collection*, 9 Dec. 1992, Lot 365.

27 Michael Wynne, "Lord Charlemont's Album," *Irish Georgian Society*, XXI:1–2, (Jan.–June 1978), pp. 1–6.

28 Unknown Diarist, vol. 1, pp. 258–9.

29 Anglesea, *Portraits and Prospects*, pp. 54–5, no. 25.

30 Anne Martha Rowan et al., *The Architecture of Sir Richard and W.V. Morrison* (Dublin, 1989).

31 Ann M. Stewart, *Irish Art Loan Exhibitions 1765–1927* (Dublin, 1990), vol. 1, pp. 282–4.

32 J.H. Roget, *History of the Old Watercolour Society* (2 vols., London, 1891), vol. 1, p. 289.

33 Ibid., vol. 1, p. 159.

34 H.L. Mallalieu, "Francis Nicholson,"

Watercolours and Drawings, IV:3 (Summer, 1989), pp. 15–8, fig. 7.

35 T. Crofton Croker, *Researches in the South of Ireland* (London, 1824), pp. 32–3.

36 Mallalieu, *Understanding Watercolours*, p. 189.

37 Patricia Butler, *Irish Watercolours and Drawings* (London, 1990), illus. p. 68 (incorrectly called *Castles on the Liffey* in the Victoria and Albert Museum).

38 Vivien Igoe and Frederick O'Dwyer, "Early views of the Royal Hospital Kilmainham," *Irish Arts Review Yearbook*, Dublin (1988), illus. pp. 82–3.

39 Roget, *History of the O.W.S.*, vol. 1, p. 162.

40 The latest information on James Malton is in the introductions by the Knight of Glin and Maurice Craig to the reprints of Malton's *Dublin* of 1799 (Dublin, 1978), and Malton's *Dublin Views in Colour* (Dublin 1981).

41 Sacheverell Sitwell, *Narrative Pictures: English genre and its painters: with notes on the illustrations by Michael Sevier* (London, 1937), pp. 51–2.

CHAPTER 6
Subject Pictures
Pages 99–107

1 William Pressly, *The Life and Art of James Barry* (New Haven and London, 1981).

2 William Pressly, *James Barry The Artist as Hero* (Tate Gallery Catalogue, 1983).

3 W. Pressly, *Life and Art of Barry*, p. 195.

4 George Breeze, *The Society of Artists in Ireland* (Dublin, 1985), p. 9

5 Ibid., pp. 27–8: Tresham's Roman career is discussed in Nicola Figgis, "Irish Portrait and Subject Painters in Rome 1750–1800," *Irish Arts Review, Yearbook* (1988), pp. 128–32.

6 Information from Eyre and Hobhouse Ltd., London.

7 Nancy L. Pressly, *The Fuseli Circle in Rome*, catalogue of an exhibition held in the Yale Center for British Art, 1979, no. 106, p. 105.

8 Ibid., p. 79, footnote 2: A manuscript list of British artists in Rome, covering the period 1753–5, by Richard Hayward, is in the British Museum Printroom.

9 Ibid., p. 79. Nancy Pressly's note is the source of most of our information on Durno.

10 Peter Murray, *Illustrated Summary Catalogue of the Crawford Municpal Art Gallery* (Cork, 1992) contains the most recent summary and discussion of his work.

11 *Dublin University Magazine* XXV (March 1945), p. 339.

12 Ibid., p. 339.

13 These drawings are in the Crawford Art Gallery, Cork, whose Curator, Peter Murray, kindly brought them to our attention.

14 *The Cork Constitution*, 24 May 1828, p. 2, col. 2.

CHAPTER 7
Still Life and Flower Painting
Pages 109–124

1 "The notebooks of George Vertue," vol. III, *Walpole Society*, XXII (London, 1933–4), p. 122.

2 Sir William Gilbey in his *Animal Painters of England from 1650* (London, 1900), vol. 1, pp. 102–3, gives the date of 1680, but no evidence to support his claim; however, it was accepted by Dudley Snelgrove.

3 Sotheby's, Madrid, 27 Feb 1985. Brought to our attention by Dr Jane Fenlon.

4 These twelve engravings each included a number of birds, fifty-eight species in all.

5 Iolo Williams, *Early English Watercolours* (London, 1952), p. 27.

6 John Murdoch, *Forty British watercolours from the Victoria and Albert Museum* (London, 1977), no. 1.

7 Ada Leask, "Samuel Dixon," *Irish Georgian Society*, XVIII:4 (Oct.–Dec. 1975), p. 131.

8 His work was first researched by Strickland and then exhaustively by Ada Leask in two articles in the *Irish Georgian Society Bulletin*, XVIII:4 (7 Oct.1975), pp. 110–36 and XXIII:1 and 2 (Jan.–June 1980), pp. 1–32.

9 Ada K. Longfield (Ada Leask), "William Kilburn (1745–1818) and his Book of Designs," *Irish Georgian Society* XXIV:1 and 3 (Jan.–June 1981), p. 1.

10 Ibid. A great many designs are illustrated in this article.

11 Ruth Hayden, *Mrs Delany: her life and flowers* (London, 1980). The chapter entitled "Flower collage: a new art," pp. 130–60, includes many illustrations. The methods employed by Mrs Delany are described on pp. 132–3. A painter whom Mrs Delany considered to be "unrivalled" in her paintings of flowers and insects was Dorothea Forth. She was a neighbour who married the Hon. Revd Francis Hamilton in 1733.

12 Alfred Friendly, *Beaufort of the Admiralty, the Life of Sir Francis Beaufort 1774–1857* (London, 1977), p. 21. We are grateful to Dr Robert Wark for information on the Huntingdon Library holdings.

13 Canon C.C. Ellison, *The Hopeful Traveller* (Kilkenny, 1987), pp. 33 and 41 and Trinity College, Dublin, ms. 4031, folio 165, for her London visit.

14 Robert Nash and Helen Ross, *Dr. Robert Templeton . . . Naturalist and Artist*, Catalogue of an exhibition, Ulster Museum, Belfast, 1980.

15 Ibid., p. 1.

16 Burke's *Landed Gentry of Great Britain and Ireland*, 1868 edn.

17 Peter Murray, *Illustrated Summary Catalogue of The Crawford Municipal Art Gallery . . .* (Cork, 1992), p. 208.

18 Ibid., p. 211.

19 Ibid., p. 216

20 Ibid., p. 229.

21 Richard Dunscombe Parker, *Birds of Ireland*, Martyn Anglesea (ed.), (Belfast, 1984).

22 *Irish Woman Artists from the Eighteenth Century to the Present Day*, Wanda Ryan-Smolin (ed.), catalogue of an exhibition at the National Gallery of Ireland, Hugh Lane Municipal Gallery and Douglas Hyde Gallery, July–Aug. 1987 (Dublin, 1987), pp. 186 and 94, no. 29.

23 C.V. Ellwood and J.M.V. Harvey, "Lady Blake," *Bulletin of the British Museum Historical Series*, 18:2, (29 Nov. 1990), pp. 145–202.

24 "Our Governor's wife as Naturalist," article from a woman's magazine (c. 1886) found in a scrapbook at her home at Myrtle Grove.

25 *Tuam Herald*, 10 February 1894.

26 Brendan Noon et al., *A Vision of Eden, the Life of Marianne North* (London, 1980).

27 *Irish Women Artists*, p. 193.

28 Patricia Butler, *Three Hundred Years of Irish Watercolours and Drawings* (London, 1990), illus. p. 82.

29 Konrad Oberhuber and William W Robinson, *Master Drawings and Watercolours The Hofer Collection*, catalogue of an exhibition, Fogg Art Museum, Cambridge, Mass. (1984), cover illus., pp. 53–4 and plates 45a and b.

CHAPTER 8
The Early Nineteenth Century
Pages 125–156

1 John O'Keeffe, *Recollections of the Life of John O'Keeffe. Written by Himself* (2 vols., London, 1826), vol. 1, p. 133.

2 Anthony Pasquin (i.e. John Williams), *Memoirs of the Royal Academicians and an Authentic History of the Artists of Ireland* (London, 1796). Reprinted with an introduction by R.W. Lightbown (London, 1970), p. 41.

3 Published in Naples, 1791–5.

4 Ian Jenkins, "Adam Buck and the vogue for Greek vases," *Burlington Magazine* CXXX: 1023 (June 1988), pp. 448–55; and Celina Fox (ed.), *London – World City 1800–1840)* (New Haven and London, 1992), pp. 146–7.

5 Martyn Anglesea, *Portraits and Prospects*, catalogue of an exhibition of watercolours from the Ulster Museum, in association with the Smithsonian Institution (Belfast 1989), no. 21, pp. 42 and 43.

6 London, 1836.

7 Unknown Diarist, Royal Irish Academy ms. 24K 14/15, 2 vols., vol. i, p. 255, dated 6 July 1801.

8 G.H.R. Tillotson, *Fan Kwae Picture . . .* (London, 1987), p. 2; and Patrick Conner, *George Chinnery 1774–1852* (Woodbridge, 1993), p. 31. The latter book has a chapter on Chinnery in Ireland, pp. 31–46 and 292–3.

9 Unknown Diarist, pp. 252–3, dated 6 July 1801.

10 H. and S. Berry-Hill, *George Chinnery, 1774–1852* (Leigh-on-Sea, 1963), plate 7.

11 The Holmes watercolour is bound into the James George Robertson album of Kilkenny material in the Royal Society of Antiquaries of Ireland.

12 Arts Council of Great Britain, *An Exhibition of Watercolours and Drawings by John Harden* (Bristol, 1951).

13 Daphne Foskett, *John Harden of Brathay Hall 1777–1847* (Kendal, 1974).

14 Michael Quane, "Tour of Ireland by John Harden in 1797," *Journal of the Cork Historical and Archaeological Society*, 1953–5, LVIII: 187, pp. 26–32 and 188, pp. 81–90; LVIX:189, pp. 34–41, and 190, pp. 69–77; LX:191, pp. 14–21, and 192, pp. 80–7. These articles comprise Harden's Irish Journal; the original manuscript is in the Royal Irish Academy.

15 George Holmes, *Sketches of some of the Southern Counties of Ireland . . .* (London, 1801), p. 3.

16 Foskett, *Harden*, plate vii, nos. 23–4.

17 Ibid., p. 45.

18 Mrs G.H. Bell, *The Hamwood Papers* (London, 1930), p. 331.

19 Ibid., opp. p. 26.

20 Ibid., pp. 332–3.

21 The only copy of this pamphlet that we know of is in a private collection in Ireland.

22 Ibid.

23 Anne Crookshank and the Knight of Glin, *The Painters of Ireland* (London, 1978), illus. p. 174.

24 *Irish Women Artists from the Eighteenth Century to the Present Day*, catalogue of an exhibition at the National Gallery of Ireland, Hugh Lane Municipal Gallery and Douglas Hyde Gallery, July–August 1987 (Dublin, 1987), illus. p. 85.

25 William Allen was Dublin's leading art suppliers from 1781 to 1870. The address was 88 Dame Street from 1781 to 1786, moving to 32 Dame Street, 1787–1832 and finally to Westland Row.

26 Crookshank and Glin, *Painters of Ireland*, illus. p. 181.

27 We are indebted to Mrs Marie Davis for bringing this picture to our attention and for other information about the school.

28 William Grattan, *Patronage Analysed* (Dublin, 1818). It was addressed to the Royal Irish Institution for the Encouragement of the Fine Arts in Ireland.

29 Paul Caffrey, "Sampson Towgood Roch, miniaturist," *Irish Arts Review*, 3:4 (1986), pp. 14–20, illus. pp. 16 and 17; Rosemary ffolliott, "Provincial Town Life in Munster," *The Irish Ancestor*, V:1 (1973), pp. 37–52, cover illustration and plates 2 and 3. These two articles illustrate different drawings from Roch's sketchbook as do William Nolan and Thomas P. Power (eds.), *Waterford History and Society* (Dublin, 1992).

30 John Turpin, "The Dublin School of Landscape and Ornament 1800–1854," *Irish Arts Review*, 3:2 (Summer 1986), p. 49. For additional information about the Brocas family see P.J. Raftery, "The Brocas Family, Notable Dublin Artists," *Dublin Historical Record*, XVII:1 (Dec 1961), pp. 25–34.

31 Crookshank and Glin, *The Painters of Ireland*, illus. p. 184.

32 *Irish Women Artists*, p. 88, no. 16.

33 Francis Greenacre, *The Bristol School of Artists . . .*, catalogue of an exhibition, City Art Gallery, Bristol (Nov 1973), pp. 269–73, illus. p. 271. The quote by Cumberland is on p. 269 and he spells the artist's name "Cassin."

34 Francis Goodwin, *Rural Architecture* (2 vols., London, 1835), vol. II, plates 31–4.

35 Ibid., vol. II, p. 40.

36 James Stevens Curl, *Moneymore and Draperstown* (Belfast, Ulster Architectural Heritage Society, 1979), which is well illustrated.

37 *Catalogue of Paintings: Exhibiting several fine Works, by the Old Masters And a Collection of Pictures* by the Artists and Amateurs of Limerick (1821).

38 Ibid., p. iv.

39 Crookshank and Glin, *Painters of Ireland*, illus., pp. 198–9.

40 Michael Wynne, "James Hore, Gentleman View–Painter," *Irish Arts Review*, 2:1 (Spring 1985), pp. 38–42: See also Wynne, *Studies*, vol. 65 (Spring 1976), pp. 46–51, illus. and vol. 68 (Winter 1979), pp. 291–3.

41 Michael Wynne, "The Gondo Tunnel on the Simplon Pass c. 1829," *Irish Arts Review Yearbook* (1992), pp. 220–1.

42 Information kindly given by Mrs Cynthia O'Connor.

43 Robert Day, "Sketches of Cork in 1838 by William Roe," *Journal of the Cork Historical and Archaeological Society*, series 2, vol. VIII (1902), pp. 150–4; "William Roe: views of Cork and its environs 1837–9," *Capuchin Annual* (1941), pp. 158–70, illus.

44 Peter Murray, *Illustrated Summary Catalogue of the Crawford Municipal Art Gallery, Cork* (1992), pp. 215–16.

45 Ibid., p. 216.

46 Ann M. Stewart, *Irish Art Loan Exhibition 1765–1927* (Dublin, 1990), pp. 8–9.

47 Formerly private collection Co. Tipperary.

48 Crookshank and Glin, *Painters of Ireland*, illus. p. 183.

49 Ibid., illus. p. 182.

50 Cyril Barrett, "Michael Angelo Hayes RHA and the Galloping Horse," *The Arts in Ireland*, 1:3 (Dublin 1972/3), pp. 42–7.

51 Crookshank and Glin, *Painters of Ireland*, illus. p. 210. Here the work was attributed incorrectly by us to Petrie.

52 Cyril Barrett, Introduction to the Rosc *Exhibition of Irish Art in the Nineteenth Century*, held in Cork, 1971, p. 8.

53 Martin Archer Shee, *The Life of Sir Martin Archer Shee* (2 vols., London, 1860), vol. 1, pp. 159–60.

54 William Makepeace Thackeray, *The Irish Sketchbook* (London, 1842; edition used, Belfast and London, 1985), p. 21.

55 *Barney Bryan's Sketchbook*, published in Exeter, no date, includes reproductions after twenty-five drawings, signed "RRS."

56 Paul Caffrey, "Samuel Lover's Achievement as a Painter," *Irish Arts Review*, 3:1 (Spring 1986), p. 53.

57 Jane MacFarlane, Trinity College Dublin, 1976, unpublished BA thesis, entitled "Sir Frederick William Burton RHA (1816–1900): his life and work." She quotes from a letter dated 26 Sept 1838 transcribed by Margaret Stokes and used by Miss Stokes in her draft biography of F.W. Burton, which is now in the National Gallery of Ireland archive.

CHAPTER 9
The Romantic Period: Landscape and Topography
Pages 157–174

1 John Hutchinson, *James Arthur O'Connor*, catalogue of an exhibition at the National Gallery of Ireland (Dublin, 1985), p. 84.

2 Francis Greenacre, *Francis Danby*, catalogue of an exhibition, Tate Gallery, London, in association with the City of Bristol Museums and Art Gallery (London, 1988), p. 78, illus. 1.

3 Martyn Anglesea, *Portraits and Prospects*, catalogue of an exhibition, Ulster Museum in association with the Smithsonian Institution (Belfast, 1989), p. 70, no. 35.

4 Hutchinson, *O'Connor*, p. 85.

5 Greenacre, *Danby*, p. 135, no. 83

6 Patricia Butler, *Three Hundred Years of Irish Watercolours and Drawings* (London, 1990), illus. p. 57.

7 Ibid. These are illustrated p. 14, no. 100 and pp. 146–7, nos. 109 and 110.

8 Ibid., pp. 29–30.

9 Ibid., p. 9.

10 Ibid., pp. 120–1, no. 50.

11 National Library of Ireland ms. 789 no. 46. This letter and the next two footnotes are quoted in Peter Murray, "George Petrie," unpublished thesis, (Trinity College, Dublin, 1980).

12 William Stokes, *George Petrie* (London, 1868), p. 27.

13 National Library of Ireland ms. 789, no. 66.

14 Stokes, *Petrie*, p. 395.

15 Ibid., p. 11.

16 Ibid., p. 21.

17 W.M. Thackeray, *The Irish Sketchbook, 1842* (London, 1843), Belfast and Dover, New Hampshire edn. (1985), pp. 21–2.

18 Petra Coffey, "George Victor Dunoyer, 1817–69," *Sheet Lines*, the Journal of the Charles Close Society, University of Exeter, no. 35, Jan. 1993, pp. 15–25. The author is writing a book on this artist. See also Jean Archer, "Geological Artistry . . .," *Visualizing Ireland*, Adele M. Dalsimer (ed.), (Boston and London, 1993), pp. 133–44.

19 Many drawings for Hall's *Ireland* are in the National Library of Ireland.

20 Alma Brooke-Tyrell, "Mr Howis the artist of Jervis Street 1804–82," *Dublin Historical Record*, XXXII:1 (Dec. 1978), pp. 27–38.

21 *The Proceedings and Transactions of the Kilkenny and South East of Ireland Archaeological Society*, vol. III, 1854–5 (Dublin, 1856), pp. 417–19. On 7 Nov. 1855 O'Neill sent a translation of the inscriptions on The Cross of Cong which points out the errors in a similar translation made by Petrie.

22 Henry O'Neill, *The Fine Arts and Ancient Civilisation of Ancient Ireland* (London, 1863) and *The Round Towers of Ireland, part the first, containing descriptions of the four round towers in the county Dublin* (Dublin, 1877).

23 Anglesea, *Portraits and Prospects*, pp. 82–3, no. 40.

24 Ibid., p. 78.

25 Martyn Anglesea, "Andrew Nicholl and his Patrons in Ireland and Ceylon," vol. 71, *Studies* (Summer 1982) p. 134.

26 Published Dublin, 1835 and illustrated by Petrie, Nicholl and O'Neill.

27 Anglesea, "Andrew Nicholl," p. 147.

28 Martyn Anglesea, *James Moore* (Belfast, 1973) p. 19, no. 383, also *GPA Irish Arts Review Yearbook 1991–2*, p. 269.

29 Ibid., cat. no. 20, illus. p. 24.

30 Ibid., p. 5.

31 Mr and Mrs S.C. Hall, *Ireland: its scenery; character . . .* (London, 1841–3), 3 vols.

32 Christie's Sale, Castletown, 29 May 1980, Lots 53–61.

33 Ibid. and *Jeremiah Hodges Mulcahy . . .*, catalogue of an exhibition, Cynthia O'Connor Gallery, Dublin, Aug. 1980.

34 Many of these are in the National Gallery of Ireland.

35 ms. in private collection.

36 Michael Clarke, *The Tempting Prospect* (London, 1981), pp.16–17.

CHAPTER 10
The Victorians
Pages 175–194

1 A. Rorimer, *Drawings by William Mulready*, catalogue of an exhibition, Victoria and Albert Museum, (London, 1972); and Marcia Pointon, *Mulready*, catalogue of an exhibition, Victoria and Albert Museum, (London, 1986), also in National Gallery of Ireland and Ulster Museum, Belfast 1986–7.

2 Pointon, *Mulready*, p.18.

3 Included in a volume, National Library of Ireland ms. TX 1979, p. 29 of illustrations, for Hall's *Ireland*. One of a number of such illustrations used in the issue "The Irish Abroad," of *Ireland of the Welcomes*, (July–Aug. 1992). For further information about Croker see Peter Murray, *Illustrated Summary Catalogue of the Crawford Municipal Art Gallery* (Cork, 1992) p. 195 and in this book under Francis Nicholson, Chapter 5.

4 Richard Ormond and John Turpin, *Daniel Maclise*, exhibition catalogue, (London and Dublin, 1972), p. 20, no. 1, illus.

5 Ibid., no. 11.

6 Ibid., no. 35.

7 Ibid., no. 34, illus.

8 Ibid., pp.108–13, illus.

9 Ibid., p. 100, no. 105, illus.

10 Elizabeth Butler, *From Sketch-book and Diary* (London, 1909), pp. 3–27 and plates 2–6.

11 Margaret Stokes's unpublished notes for a biography of Burton, National Gallery of Ireland archives.

12 Gordon S. Haight, *The Letters of George Eliot* (9 vols., New Haven and London, 1954–79), vol. IV, p. 147, in a letter dated 30 April 1864 to Sara Sophia Hennell.

13 *The Times*, 25 April 1864. A modern interpretation can be found in Pamela Berger, "The Historical, the Sacred, the Romantic . . .," *Visualizing Ireland*, Adele M. Dalsimer (ed.), (Boston and London, 1993), pp. 71–88.

14 Letter to Robert Callwell, dated 1840, transcribed in Margaret Stokes's notes for Burton's biography, National Gallery of Ireland archives.

15 In a notebook of transcribed notes by Margaret Stokes after Burton, dated 1835–57, pp. 8–11, and in a list of colours, p. 2, National Gallery of Ireland archives.

16 The Dublin Society had been given the title Royal by George IV in 1820.

17 Christie's, 9 Feb. 1988, Lot 48.

18 *Proceedings of the Royal Dublin Society*, vol. LXXXI (Dublin, 1845), p. lii.

19 Sotheby's, 20 July 1978, Lot 216.

20 Murray, *Cork Catalogue*, p. 214. For his Dublin work see Nancy Netzer, "Picturing an Exhibition . . .," Dalsimer (ed.), *Visualizing Ireland*, pp. 89–98.

21 Forrest Reid, *Illustrators of the Sixties* (London, 1928), pp. 255–6.

22 Eileen Black, *Samuel McCloy (1831–1904)* catalogue of an exhibition in the Lisburn Museum (1981–2).

23 Ibid., no. 52.

24 We are grateful to the Gloucester Art Gallery for their help in connection with John Kemp.

25 Murray, *Cork Catalogue*, p. 182.

26 Obituary in the *Halifax Courier*, 22 Feb. 1890, kindly sent to us by M.E. Corbett of the Calderdale Libraries, Halifax.

27 Murray, *Cork Catalogue*, p. 255.

28 *Richard Doyle and his family*, Victoria and Albert Museum exhibition catalogue (London, 1983), and Celina Fox (ed.), *London: World-City 1800–40* (New Haven and London, 1992), p. 596, no. 674.

29 *Proceedings of the Royal Dublin Society*, vol. LXXXI, Dublin 1845, p. lvi.

30 *Richard Doyle and his family*, Victoria and Albert Museum exhibition catalogue, 1983, illus. pp. 31–2.

31 Patricia Butler, *Irish Watercolours and Drawings* (London, 1990), plates 111 and 108.

32 Michael Doyle, *The Doyle Diary* (London, 1978), illus, p. 21 and pp. VI and VII.

33 Alistair Mathews, *Drawings and Watercolours*, cat. 79, no. 133, (Bournemouth, spring 1972) includes numerous drawings.

CHAPTER 11
Mostly Primitives and Amateurs
Pages 195–219

1 PRONI ms. no. D1928/A/I/9.

2 ms. notebook, Tullynally Castle; Constantia Maxwell, *Country and Town under the Georges* (London, 1940), pp. 60–3, and plates facing pp. 32, 48, and 292.

3 Anne Crookshank and the Knight of Glin, *The Painters of Ireland* (London, 1978), illus. p. 55, no. 38. For John Rocque see Chapter 4.

4 Martyn Anglesea, *Portraits and Prospects*, catalogue of an exhibition of watercolours from the Ulster Museum in association with the Smithsonian Institution, Belfast, 1989, pp. 2 and 3.

5 John Hewitt, *Art in Ulster* (Belfast, 1977), pp. 174–5.

6 Angret Simms with Katharine Simms, *Kells* (Royal Irish Academy, Dublin, 1990).

7 Diana Scarisbrick, "Companion to a Russian Princess," *Country Life*, vol. 169, no. 4351 (8 Jan. 1981), p. 76–8; *Irish Women Artists*, catalogue of an exhibition at the National Gallery of Ireland, Hugh Lane Municipal Gallery, and the Douglas Hyde Gallery, July–Aug. 1987 (Dublin, 1987), p. 194. Martha Wilmot's own diaries were published by the Marchioness of Londonderry and H. Montgomery Hyde, introduction and notes, *The Russian Journal of Martha and Catherine Wilmot, 1803–8 . . .* (2 vols., London, 1934).

8 Trinity College, Dublin ms. 8264. Louisa Beaufort entitled this sketchbook "Scraps to amuse my dear Admiral from LCB." It is dated the year of her brother's death, 1857. Canon C.C. Ellison, *The Hopeful Traveller, the Life and Times of Daniel Augustus Beaufort* (Kilkenny, 1987). This has illustrations by both Louisa and Francis opposite, p. 102 and p. 51 respectively.

9 Christina Colvin (ed.) *Maria Edgeworth, Letters from England* (Oxford, 1972), p. 358.

10 Christina Colvin, "Maria Edgeworth's Bedroom," *Country Life* 161; 4149 (6 Jan. 1977), p. 47.

11 Augustus Hare (ed.), *Life and Letters of Maria Edgeworth* (2 vols., London, 1884), vol. 1, p. 125.

12 *Irish Women Artists*, pp. 90 and 154–5.

13 Ibid., p. 154.

14 Ibid., p. 155.

15 See also H.L. Mallalieu, *A Dictionary of British Watercolour Artists up to 1920* (2 vols., Woodbridge, 1979), vol. II, p. 350, where he illustrates *A St. Petersburg driver asleep*.

16 Unpublished Diaries of the Marquess of Dufferin and Ava, Clandeboye, Co. Down, p. 3, entry dated 9 June 1839.

17 Ibid., p. 26, entry dated 22 May 1842.

18 Ibid., entry for 11 Apr. 1842.

19 Conversazione and Annual Report of the Belfast School of Design (Belfast, 1852).

20 Martyn Anglesea, "Sketches of a Victorian Vicar: Narcissus Batt, 1824(?) 98," *Ulster Genealogical and Historical Guild Newsletter*, 1:9 (1983), p. 285. The article, pp. 282–9, is well illustrated.

21 Jane Austen, *Emma*, edition Zodiac Press (London, 1978), pp. 119–20.

22 A.F. Wedd, *The Fate of the Fenwicks, letters to Mary Hayes, 1798–1828* (London, 1927), pp. 85–6.

23 Owen Harry, *Mary Ward* (Birr, 1991).

24 *Irish Women Artists*, pp. 180 and 92–3.

25 Martin F. Krause, Jnr. *Catalogue of British Drawings and Watercolours 1775–1925*, Indianapolis Museum of Art, (1980); and *Irish Women Artists*, p. 158.

26 *Irish Women Artists*, pp. 92 and 168.

27 Crookshank and Glin, *Painters of Ireland*, p. 230, illus. no. 53.

28 L. Perry Curtis, *Apes and Angels, The Irishman in Victorian Caricature* (Newton Abbot, 1971), where the problem is discussed.

29 *Irish Women Artists*, pp. 88, 89 and 185; and for Olivia de Ros, Mark Girouard, *Life in the English Country House* (New Haven and London, 1978), pls. 132, 143 and 144.

30 Alan Tongue, *A Picture of Percy French* (Antrim, 1990), p. 40, where this is reproduced.

31 Murray *Cork Catalogue*, p. 169.

32 Ibid., p. 9.

33 This quote from *The Graphic* appears on the back of the booklets.

CHAPTER 12
The Watercolour Societies and the Lady Artists
Pages 221–236

1 The most complete account of the development of these amateur societies is the unpublished BA thesis by Shirley Armstrong Duffy, (Trinity College, Dublin, 1984).

2 Oliver Snoddy, "An unlisted item of Carlow Printing," *Carloviana* (Carlow, 1969), pp. 8–11 and 22. Baroness Prochazka's scrap-book with cuttings of these exhibitions and of critiques of them has recently been found at her old home, Lyrath, Co. Kilkenny.

3 Mark Girouard, "Stamped, Addressed and Illustrated," *Country Life* (30 July 1970), pp. 290–1.

4 Gifford Lewis, *The Selected Letters of Somerville and Ross* (London, 1989), p. xxiv.

5 Ibid., p. 73.

6 Martyn Anglesea, *Royal Ulster Academy of Arts* (Lisburn, 1981), pp. 7–25.

7 *Irish Women Artists*, catalogue of an exhibition at the National Gallery of Ireland, the Hugh Lane Municipal Gallery, the Douglas Hyde Gallery, 1987, (Dublin 1987), p. 158.

8 Raymond Brooke, *The Brimming River* (Dublin, 1961), p. 84. See also Vera Kreilkamp, "Going to the Levée . . .," *Visualizing Ireland*, Adele M. Dalsimer (ed.), pp. 37–54.

9 Letter belonging to the authors.

10 Christie's, London, 20 Oct. 1981, Lot 187.

11 Information from the family.

12 Letter belonging to the authors.

13 Ibid.

14 Christie's, London, 13 Oct. 1981.

15 The information on Mildred Anne Butler comes from the exhibition catalogue by the authors held in 1981 in Kilkenny, Dublin and Christie's, London, and from Anne Crookshank, *Mildred Anne Butler* (Dublin, 1992). See also Kristin Morrison, "Ancient Rubbish . . .," Dalsimer (ed.), *Visualizing Ireland*, pp. 23–36.

16 Gifford Lewis, *Edith Somerville and Martin Ross* (London, 1985), p. 85.

17 Peter Murray, *Illustrated Summary Catalogue of the Crawford Municipal Art Gallery, Cork* (Cork, 1992), p. 174; and *Irish Women Artists*, p. 164.

18 *Irish Women Artists*, p. 159.

19 Ibid., p. 162.

20 Ibid., p. 156.

21 Ibid., pp. 93–4 and 180.

22 Ibid., p. 190.

23 Ibid., p. 192–3.

24 Ibid., pp. 118–19 and 159–60.

25 Ibid., pp. 106 and 194.

26 John O'Grady, "Sarah Purser," unpublished Ph.D. thesis (University College, Dublin, 1974); Mary Brennan Holohan, "Sarah Purser," unpublished BA thesis (Trinity College, Dublin, 1989); *Irish Women Artists*, p. 182.

27 Cyril Barrett, *Irish Art of the 19th Century*, catalogue of the 1971 Cork Rosc exhibition (Cork, 1971), p. 69, no. 123.

28 Fionnuala Brennan, *Mary Swanzy*, catalogue of an exhibition at the Pyms Gallery, London (Nov.–Dec. 1989).

29 Julian Campbell, *Mary Swanzy*, catalogue of an exhibition at the Pyms Gallery, London (Autumn 1986), and Fionnuala Brennan, *Mary Swanzy*, both well illustrated with oils as well as drawings.

30 Bruce Arnold, *Mainie Jellet and the Modern Movement in Ireland* (New Haven and London, 1991); Daire O'Connell, *Mainie Jellett*, catalogue of an exhibition at the Irish Museum of Modern Art (Dublin, 1991).

31 As Evie Hone turned to stained glass in the 1930s, no serious study of her painting career has yet been published. However, see Stella Frost (ed.), *A Tribute to Evie Hone and Mainie Jellett* (Dublin, 1957) and S.B. Kennedy, *Irish Art and Modernism, 1880–1950* (Belfast, 1991).

CHAPTER 13
The Irish in America and the Colonies
Pages 237–258

1 Dale T. Johnson, *American Portrait Miniatures in the Manney Collection*, Metropolitan Museum of Art (New York, 1990), pp. 186–7.

2 Johnson, *American Portrait Miniatures*, pp. 181–4.

3. Daphne Foskett, *A Dictionary of British Miniature Painters* (2 vols., London, 1972), vol. 1, p. 461.

4 Christie's, London, *Fine Picture Miniatures*, 7 Nov. 1988, Lot 53.

5 J. Russell Harper, *Painting in Canada a History* 2nd edn. (Toronto, 1978), pp. 92–3 and 425.

6. Ibid., pp. 115–16.

7 Earl Thomas, *Sir John Johnson, Loyalist Baronet* (Toronto and Reading, 1986), for the background of the Johnsons; George C. Groce and David H. Wallace, *The New-York Historical Society's Dictionary of Artists in America 1564–1860* (New Haven and London, 1957).

8 Published London, 1799.

9 Richard J. Koke, compiler, *A Catalogue of the Collection including Historical Narrative and Marine Art* (New-York Historical Society, 1982), pp. 257–8.

10 Edward J. Nygren with Bruce Robertson, *Views and Visions: American Landscape before 1830* (Washington, 1986), p. 302.

11 *Report of the first public Distribution of Premiums, Royal Dublin Society* (Dublin, 1843), p. 10.

12 Koke, *New-York Hist. Soc. Catalogue*, pp. 217–19; and *Artists by Themselves: Artists' Portraits from the National Academy of Design* (New York, 1983), p. 64; Johnson, *American Portrait Miniatures*, pp. 139–41.

13 Richard J. Koke, *New-York Hist. Soc. Catalogue*, pp. 218–19.

14 Albert Ten Eyck Gardener, "Ingham in Manhattan," *Metropolitan Museum Bulletin* X:9 (May 1952), pp. 245–53.

15 His life is written in William Dunlap, *History of the Rise and Progress of the Art of Design in the United States* (New York, 1834), 3rd edn. (3 vols, Boston, 1918), vol. 3, pp. 103–4.

16 Donald A Shelley, "William Guy Wall and his watercolours for the Hudson River Portfolio," *New-York Historical Society Quarterly*, vol. XXXI (Jan.–Oct., 1947), (New York, 1948), p. 26.

17 Edwin Wolf, 2nd, and Marie Elena Korey, *Quarter of a Millenium The Library Company of Philadelphia 1731–1981 . . .* (Philadelphia, 1981), p. 202.

18 Koke, *New-York Hist. Soc. Catalogue*, pp. 224–35.

19 Victor Koshkin–Youritzin, *American Watercolours from the Metropolitan Museum of Art* (New York, 1991), p. 15. Several of Wall's watercolours are reproduced in this catalogue, plates 22–5.

20 Nygren with Robertson, *Views and Visions*, pp. 300–2.

21 Dunlap, *History of Design in the United States*, vol. 3, pp. 103–4.

22 Shelley, "William Guy Wall," pp. 35–8.

23 Nygren with Robertson, *Views and Visions*, pp. 300–1.

24 William Dunlap, *History of Design in United States*, vol. 3, p. 103; and Theodore E. Stebbings, Jr., *American Master Drawings and Watercolours* (New Haven, 1976), pp. 114–15.

25 Sue McKechnie, *British Silhouette Artists and their Work 1760–1860* (London, 1978), pp. 236–46. William James Hubard (1806–62) was in Ireland in 1823–4 and left from Dublin for the United States in 1824; it was during Wall's period in Ireland (1837–56) that the Galway exhibition took place.

26 Koke, *New-York Hist. Soc. Catalogue*, vol. 1, p. 224 and for other examples see *M. and M. Karolik Collection of American Paintings 1815–65* (Cambridge, Mass., 1949), p. 119.

27 Peter Murray, *Illustrated Summary Catalogue of the Crawford Municipal Art Gallery, Cork* (Cork, 1992), pp. 213, 237.

28 Roy Strong, *A Pageant of Canada*, catalogue of an exhibition held in Ottawa 1967, pp. 122, 124 and illus. pp. 123 and 125.

29 W. Martha E. Cooke, *W.H. Coverdale Collection of Canadian Paintings, Watercolours, and Drawings* (Ottawa, 1983), pp. 200, 202 and figs. 399 and 399d.

30 Edward Walsh, *A Narrative of the Expedition to Holland, in the Autumn of the Year 1799; illustrated with a Map of North Holland and Seven Views of the Principal Places Occupied by the British Forces* (London, 1800).

31 Mary Allodi, *Canadian Watercolours and Drawings in the Royal Ontario Museum* (2 vols., Toronto, 1974), vol. 2, no. 1606.

32 Mary Sparling, *Great Expectations The European Vision in Nova Scotia 1749–1848*, catalogue of an exhibition held in Halifax, Toronto and Montreal (1980–1), pp. 38–43.

33 Allodi, *Canadian Watercolours*, vol. 1, plates 738–42.

34 F. St. George Spendlove, *The Faces of Early Canada* (Toronto, 1958) pp. 32–3.

35 Mary Sparling, *Great Expectations*, pp. 81–4.

36 J. Russell Harper, *Painting in Canada*, pp. 115, 120–3 and 418.

37 Harper, *Painting in Canada*, pp. 194 and 423.

38 Honor De Pencier, *Posted to Canada* (Toronto, 1987), p. 26, fig. 2.

39 Ibid., plate 16 and p. 99.

40 Ibid., plate 58 and p. 12.

41 Ibid., plate 21 and p. 10

42 Cooke, *Coverdale Collection*, p. 122. The entry on Hood begins on p. 120.

43 Stuart Houston, "Birds by Hood," *The Beaver Magazine of the North* (Summer 1974), p. 4.

44 These are all illustrated in Cooke, *Coverdale Collection*, nos. 285, 287 and 290.

45 Harper, *Painting in Canada*, p. 132.

46 Houston, "Birds by Hood," p. 7, where he quotes from John Franklin, *Narrative of a Journey to the Shores of the Polar Sea*.

47 Harper, *Painting in Canada*, p. 133 and p. 407.

48 J. Russell Harper, *Early Painters and Engravers in Canada* (Toronto, 1970), p. 120.

49 Harper, *Painting in Canada*, pp. 105–6 and p. 410; for further information and illustrations see Cooke, *Coverdale Collection*, pp. 64–8 and figs. 152–65.

50 Allodi, *Canadian Watercolours*, vol. 1, nos. 677, 678; and the Duncan sketchbook, nos. 691–726.

51 Harper, *Painting in Canada*, pp. 54 and 419.

52 Allodi, *Canadian Watercolours*, vol. 2, plate 1365.

53 Sotheby and Co. (Canada) Ltd., sale catalogue, Toronto, 22–23 Apr. 1969, Lots 35–50.

54 Ron Tyler, *Visions of America* (London, 1983), p. 201.

55 Amon Carter Museum, Fort Worth; and Tyler, *Visions of America*, p. 104.

56 Allodi, *Canadian Watercolours*, vol. 2, plate 1368.

57 For further information see Cooke, *Coverdale Collection*, pp. 4–7, figs. 2–9; Allodi, *Canadian Watercolours*, vol. 1, nos. 6–51. See also *Canada in the Nineteenth Century: the Bert and Barbara Stitt Family Collection*, catalogue, Art Gallery Hamilton (1984), p. 35.

58 Allodi, *Canadian Watercolours*, vol. 1, plate 8.

59 *Dublin International Exhibition*, 1865, descriptive catalogue (London, 1866), p. 332.

60 M. Allodi, *Canadian Watercolours*, vol. 1, plate 17.

61 Ibid., plate 35.

62 Strong, *Pageant of Canada*, p. 269, no. 235. For further works Ibid., pp. 268–9.

63 Mildred Archer, *India and British Portraiture* (London, 1979), p. 403.

64 John Bastin and Pauline Rohatgi, *Prints of S.E. Asia in the India Office Library* (London, HMSO, 1979), p. 200 and illus. pp. 68–83; Daphne Foskett, *Dictionary of British Miniature Painters* (2 vols., London, 1972), vol. I, p. 139 and illus., vol. II plate 3.

65 Dr Emma Devapriam, "The Synnot children by Joseph Wright of Derby," *Art Bulletin of Victoria*, 26 (1986), pp. 15–21.

66 Ibid., illus. p. 17.

67 Canon C.C. Ellison, *The Hopeful Traveller* (Kilkenny, 1987), pp. 33 and 41.

68 London, 1817.

69 Alfred Friendly, *Beaufort of the Admiralty* (London, 1977), pp. 156–7.

70 Christie's, London, 13 Oct. 1981, Lots 176–88; most are illustrated in the catalogue.

71 Australian Dictionary of National Biography (2 vols., Melbourne, 1966–7), vol. 2, p. 568.

72 Four of these are illustrated in Tim McCormack et al., *First Views of Australia 1788–1815* (Sydney, 1987), pp. 186–9. Page 279 includes a biography of Wallis.

73 Ibid., p. 279 and Christie's, South Kensington, *Pictures, Drawings and Watercolours . . . of . . . Australasian interest*, 28 May 1987, Lot no. 219, illus. For further Wallis watercolours see Ibid. Lots 220–3, one of which is of Rostellan, Co. Cork.

74 Tim Bonyhady, *Images in Opposition Australian Landscape Painting 1801–90*, (Melbourne, 1985), p. 60.

75 Christie's, South Kensington, 25 May 1989, Lot 161, also information from David Mitchell of Toronto.

76 We are grateful to Robert Kearns and to David Mitchell, both of Toronto.

77 Joan Kerr (ed.), *Dictionary of Australian Artists*, vol. 1 (University of Sydney, 1984).

78 Patricia R. MacDonald and Barry Pearce, *The Artist and the Patron, Aspects of Colonial Art in New South Wales* (Sydney, 1988), illus. p. 103.

79 Tim Bonyhady et al., *The Skottowe Manuscript a commentary* (Chippendale, Australia, 1988).

80 Kerr (ed.), *Dictionary*, pp. 104–6.

81 E. Charles Nelson and Eileen M. McCracken, *The Brightest Jewel* (Kilkenny, 1987), p. 21.

82 Sotheby's, Sydney, 29 Oct 1987, Lots 130–82.

83 Kerr (ed.), *Dictionary*, pp. 157–8.

84 *Australian Antiques* (Sydney, 1977), p. 64 and illus. p. 68.

85 Kerr (ed.), *Dictionary*, pp. 136–7.

86 Ibid., p. 48.

87 Ibid., p. 213.

88 Ibid., p. 259.

89 Ibid., p. 360.

90 All the information on James Glen Wilson comes from the writings of Eileen Black of the Ulster Museum whose most comprehensive article is "James Glen Wilson (1827–63): an Irish artist in Australia," *Familia, Ulster Genealogical Review*, 2:3 (1987), pp. 37–46. Her most recent article on Wilson is "James Glen Wilson," *Irish Arts Review* (1990–1), pp. 99–102.

91 Macdonald and Pearce, *The Artist and the Patron*, pp. 109–10.

92 Roger Collins and Peter Entwhistle, *Pavilioned in Splendour* (Dunedin Public Art Gallery 1986); and Una Platts, *Nineteenth Century New Zealand Artists* (Christchurch, 1979), pp. 183–4.

93 Many are illustrated in Collins and Entwhistle, *Pavilioned in Splendour*.

94 Roger Blackley, "J. Guise Mitford," *Art of New Zealand 27* (1983), pp. 46–9.

95 Ibid., p. 47.

96 Geoffrey Watkins Grubb *The Grubbs of Tipperary* (Cork, 1972), plate XXXII.

97 Platts, *Nineteenth Century New Zealand Artists*, p. 185 and information from John Stacpoole, Auckland.

98 A collection of his work is in the Turnbull Library in Wellington and others in the Nan Kivell collection, National Library of Australia, Canberra. A large number were sold by McArthur and Co. in Auckland, 20 Oct. 1983. The catalogue included a biography.

CHAPTER 14
Late Nineteenth and Early Twentieth Century Landscape and Figure Painters
Pages 259–285

1 Julian Campbell, *Nathaniel Hone*, catalogue of an exhibition held in the National Gallery of Ireland (Dublin, 1991).

2 Jeanne Sheehy, *Walter Osborne*, (Ballycotton, 1974).

3 Ibid., p. 15.

4 Julian Campbell, *The Irish Impressionists*, catalogue of an exhibition held in the National Gallery of Ireland, (Dublin, 1984).

5 William Low, *A Chronicle of Friendships 1873–1900* (London, 1908), pp. 66–7.

6 Julian Campbell, *Frank O'Meara and his Contemporaries*, catalogue of an exhibition held in the Hugh Lane Municipal Gallery of Modern Art, Dublin, The Crawford Art Gallery, Cork, and the Ulster Museum, Belfast (Dublin, 1989), p. 49.

7 Roy Johnston, *Roderic O'Conor*, unpublished Ph.D. thesis, (Trinity College, Dublin, 1991)

8 Roy Johnston, *Roderic O'Conor*, catalogue of an exhibition, Barbican Art Gallery, London, and Ulster Museum, Belfast (1985), illus. pp. 100–12.

9 Ibid., pp. 114–18.

10 Anne Crookshank and the Knight of Glin, *The Painters of Ireland* (London, 1978), illus. p. 250.

11 Gorry Gallery exhibition catalogue (16–19 Oct. 1987), no. 41, illus. p. 8.

12 Gorry Gallery exhibition catalogue, (Apr.–May 1986), no. 41, illus. 13.

13 Ann M. Stewart, *Royal Hibernian Academy of Arts* (3 vols., Dublin 1990), vol. III, p. 251.

14 Quotations kindly given us by Shirley Armstrong Duffy.

15 Gordon T. Ledbetter, "Alexander Williams 1846–1930: Sidelights on a Victorian Painter," *The Irish Ancestor*, no. 2 (1975), pp. 83–90.

16 ms. Autobiography of Alexander Williams, private collection, vol., 1, p. 98.

17 Ibid., p. 119.

18 *Beautiful Ireland*, described by Stephen Gwynn, illustrations by Alexander Williams (4 vols., London, 1911–12).

19 ms. *Autobiography of Alexander Williams*, vol. 1, p. 129.

20 Ibid., p. 138.

21 Ibid., p. 138.

22 Quoted from W.B. Yeats, *Autobiographies* in Fintan Cullen and William M. Murphy, *The Drawings of John Butler Yeats*, catalogue of an exhibition, Albany Institute of History of Art (Albany, 1987), p. 17.

23 Hilary Pyle, *Jack B. Yeats* (London, 1970).

24 Hilary Pyle, *Jack B. Yeats in the National Gallery of Ireland* (Dublin, 1986), p.8, and Hilary Pyle, *Jack B. Yeats His Watercolours, Drawings and Pastels* (Dublin, 1993), p. 24, and for the entry for the *County of Mayo*, p. 114. Adele M. Dalsimer, "The Irish Peasant Had All His Heart . . .," Adele M. Dalsimer (ed.), *Visualizing Ireland* (Boston and London, 1993), pp. 201–30.

25 Kenneth Clark, introduction to the catalogue of an exhibition *Jack B. Yeats 1870–1957*, Toronto (1971), and quoted in *Jack B. Yeats 1871–1957, a centenary exhibition*, 1971–2. catalogue of an exhibition held in Dublin, Belfast and New York (Dublin, 1971), pp. 11–12.

26 Eileen Black, *Paintings, Sculptures and Bronzes in the collection of the Belfast Harbour Commissioners* (Belfast, 1983), p .41.

27 Ibid., illus p. 103, no. 51.

28 Martyn Anglesea, *The Royal Ulster Academy of Art* (Belfast, 1981), p. 12.

29 Mrs J. Comyns–Carr, *Reminiscences* (London, 1925), pp. 69–71 includes further information on this artist.

30 See *A Concise Catalogue of the Drawings, Paintings and Sculptures in the Ulster Museum* (Belfast, 1986), p. 167, no. 1140, where it is said to be an illustration for *An Irish Horse Fair 1898* by Stephen Gwynn.

31 Stephen Gwynn, *Highways and Byways in Donegal and Antrim* (London and New York, 1899).

32 Partricia Butler, *Three Hundred Years of Irish Watercolours and Drawings* (London, 1990), p. 119, illus. no. 127. See also Harry Furniss, *Confessions of a Caricaturist* (2 vols., London, 1901).

33 George Dawson, Introduction to the catalogue of an exhibition, *Paul Henry*, Trinity College, Dublin, and Ulster Museum (Dublin, 1973), p. 3.

34 S.B. Kennedy, *Paul Henry* (Dublin, 1991), p. 11.

35 *A Spice of Life*, exhibition catalogue, David Messum Gallery (London, Nov.–Dec. 1991).

36 Ibid., no. 26, illus.

37 Bruce Arnold, *Orpen Mirror to an Age* (London, 1981).

38 P.G. Konody and Sydney Dark, *Sir William Orpen Artist and Man* (London, 1932).

39 See J. Crampton Walker, *Irish Life and Landscape* (Dublin and Cork, c. 1925), illus.

40 *The Times*, 20 April 1912, p. 4.

41 Rosemarie Mulcahy, "Patrick Tuohy 1894–1930," *GPA Irish Arts Review Yearbook* (1989–90), pp. 107–18.

42 Nicola Gordon Bowe, *Harry Clarke* (Dublin, 1989).

43 Butler, *Irish Watercolours*, p. 123.

Trade card of John Melchior Barralet, 1777 (Dyfed Archives, Derwydd Collection). See text pp. 53–8.

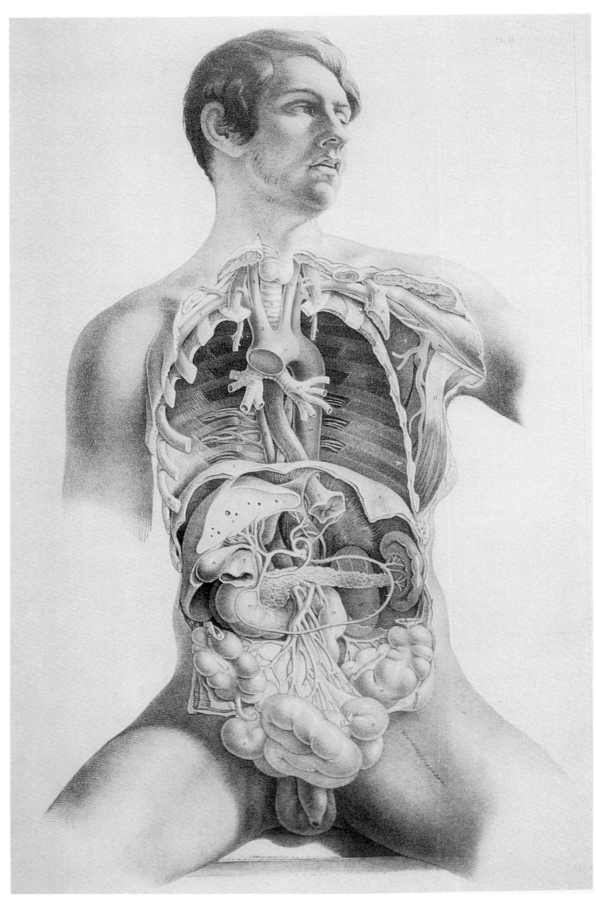

398 JOSEPH MACLISE *Anatomical Drawing, 1851 (Royal College of Surgeons in Ireland)*

WATERCOLOUR ARTISTS WHO WORKED IN IRELAND

This checklist is not meant to supersede such important Dictionaries as those by Strickland and Mallalieu. Its virtue is that it mentions a number of minor artists previously unrecorded as well as the important artists.

A

Addey, Joseph Poole, fl. 1877–1914
First Headmaster Londonderry School of Art 1875–87. Exh. RHA 1877–1914. Exh. Dublin Sketching Club from 1886; Ramblers Club from 1891 and in WCI. See text p. 265.

Aglio, Agostino, 1777–1857 *Visitor*
Italian settled in England 1803. Must have visited Ireland before exhibiting a view of Killarney, 1818, and publishing *Twelve Pictures of Killarney*, 1820. Still painting views of Killarney 1842.

Aitken, James Alfred, RWS, RHA, 1846–97 *Visitor*
B. Edinburgh but went as a child to Dublin where he studied in the RDS schools. Exh. RHA 1865–91. Returned to Scotland 1872.

Alday, Paul, fl. 1809–27
Amateur landscape watercolourist. Exh. RHA 1826–7 and ISA 1809. Owned a music shop. No works now known.

Alexander, Douglas, ARHA, 1871–1945
Marine and landscape painter mostly working in the West of Ireland. Exh. RHA 1935 and 1938.

Allen, Joshua, fl. 1887–1921
Only known by thirty drawings of *Vanishing Dublin* (NGI), signed and dated 1888.

Allingham, Helen née Paterson, RWS, 1848–1926 *Visitor*
Married the Irish poet, William Allingham, 1874, and visited Co. Donegal after her husband's death.

Alpenny (Halfpenny), Joseph Samuel, 1787–1858
B. Ireland, trained London, 1804 premium Soc. of Arts. Painted portraits, figures, and history pieces mostly in watercolour, occasionally oil. Went to Waterford 1810 and started exhibiting in Dublin, where he lived 1812–24. Returned to London where he lived till he died. Exh. RA 1805–8 and 1825–53. Published *New Drawing Book of Rustic Figures* 1825. See text p. 150.

Alpenny (Halfpenny), William, fl. 1739
Architectural drawings of Waterford 1739.

Andrews, Anna, fl. 1851
There is a pencil drawing heightened with white, of *Ballycraigy Waterfall* (UM), dated 1851.

Andrews, Samuel, c. 1767–1807
Worked in India and the East Indies from 1791, landscapes and portraits. See text p. 251.

Annesley, Lady Mabel, 1881–1959
B. Co. Down where she lived till she emigrated to New Zealand in 1941. Best known for her woodcuts though she painted watercolours (UM).

Anson, Charles, fl. 1875–93, *Visitor*
Exh. NWS *The Village of Shanganagh . . .* 1886.

Archdeakon, T., second half of eighteenth century
Antiquarian draughtsman, worked with Beranger (q.v.) (works in NLI and BM).

Arden, Margaret, Lady, née Wilson, m. 1787–d.1851 *Visitor*
A watercolour of *Castletown Roche, 1790* is known.

Armstrong, Robert, fl.1835–57
Architectural and archaeological draughtsman. Master of the endowed school of Raheny. Author of *Fingal: Scenes and sketches illustrative of the History, Antiquities, Topography and Statistics,* Dublin, 1835. Exh: RA 1848–57 (works in NLI).

Armstrong, William, 1822–1914
Civil engineer, draughtsman, photographer. Born in Dublin, where he studied art and won prize for architectural drawing. Apprenticed as engineer on English and Irish railways. Emigrated to Toronto, 1851, and worked on Canadian railways. Turned to full-time painting in 1880s. Taught drawing in Toronto Normal School. Died in Toronto. See text pp. 248–9.

Ashford, William, 1746–1824
B. Birmingham but spent career from 1764 in Ireland becoming first Pres. of the RHA. Best known for his oils. See text pp. 81–2.

Ashworth, Thomas, fl. 1794
Copies after Austin Cooper and others exist in RIA.

Atkinson, George, 1880–1941
Cork-born, he trained at the Royal College of Art, London, and travelled widely on the continent. When he returned to Ireland he lived in Dublin, taught at and became Director of the National College of Art and exhibited at the RHA and elsewhere. Though most interested in the Arts and Crafts, he painted many landscapes and portraits working in oils, pencil, watercolour and as an etcher.

Atkinson, George Mounsey Wheatley, c. 1806–84
B. Cobh, an amateur marine painter who started his career as a ship's carpenter. By 1842 he was exhibiting in the RHA. Both his *Visit of the Queen and Prince Albert to Queenstown in 1849* and his *Sketches in Norway . . . 1852* were lithographed. Exh. RHA 1842–5, 1879. Most of his works are in oils. His children were all artists, the eldest George Mounsey, d.1908, was born in Cobh, interested in Irish archaeology, taught art and examined at South Kensington. Exh. London 1859–68; RHA 1872–3. The second son, Richard Peterson, c. 1856–82, who was also born in Cobh, painted landscapes and marines. The third son, Robert, also painted marines while his daughter, Sarah, fl. 1880–1915, later Mrs. H.E. Dobbs m. 1885, became an art teacher in Dublin and exh. RHA 1880–84 (works in Crawford Art Gallery, Cork).

Aylmer, Thomas Brabazon, 1806–57
B. Limerick, topographical landscape painter in oils and watercolour. Travelled widely in Belgium, England, Germany and Italy. Lived in London from 1834, later in Tunbridge Wells and Weston-super-Mare, 1849, and finally in Bath. He also drew in the Bristol area. Exh. London 1834–56. Illus. and wrote articles in Art Journal, 1853.

B

Badge, Thomas, c. 1782–1841
B. Dublin, educ. D. S. schools, awarded medals for drawing 1798–9. Exh. Dublin 1812 and 1819. Topographical landscape painter but mostly worked as an engraver.

Bailward, Miss M.B. *Visitor*
Exh. NWS 1890, scenes of Co. Waterford.

Ball, Adam Gustavus 1821–82
B. Dublin, settled Australia. See text pp. 254–5.

Barber, Rupert, fl. 1736–c. 1772
Best known as an enamel miniaturist; also worked in pastel and chalk and occasionally oil, mostly painting portraits. A fine drawing, *The Beggar of Dublin*, signed and dated 1744, is in the New Orleans Museum of Art.

Baring, Ann, fl. 1791 *Visitor*
Amateur landscape painter in oils and watercolours, d. of John Baring (1730–1816). Known to have worked in Ireland.

Baring, Lady Emma, fl. 1888–1933 *Visitor*
Amateur, d. of the first Earl of Northbrook, m. in 1890, Col. the Hon. Sir Henry G.L. Crichton, third son of the third Earl of Erne. Exh. NWS 1888, *Bear Rock-Coast of Donegal, Ireland* and 1890 *Tramore, Ireland.*

Barker, Robert, 1739–1806
B. Kells, Co. Meath practised in Dublin and later Edinburgh as portrait and miniature painter but best known for his panoramas with which he was assisted by his son Henry Aston Barker. His first, of Edinburgh, was exhibited there and also in London where he settled. He produced numerous panoramas, the Thames . . .; Brighton; Windsor; Margate; Malta; Gibralter and Paris. His son, Henry Aston Barker, c. 1774–1856, visited Ireland and exhibited in Dublin 1823–4.

Barker, Thomas of Bath, 1769–1847 *Visitor*
A watercolour of Killarney (BM) indicates he either visited Ireland or copied from others.

Barnard, Revd William Henry, 1767–1818
B. Co. Derry or Co. Donegal, grandson of Bishop of Derry, pupil of Malchair. Amateur, lived England, graduated Oxford 1797, travelled widely. Irish drawings include Dublin (1788), Antrim Coast (1792), Bray (1795). His son Lieut. Gen. Henry William Barnard also painted. See text p. 91.

Barralet, John James, c. 1747–1815
B. Dublin. Studied DSS, won premium 1764. Worked with Grose (q.v.), Beranger (q.v.) and for Crow St. Theatre. Exh. London 1770–80; ISA 1780. See text pp. 53–8.

Barralet, John Melchior, c. 1750–c. 1787
B. Dublin, brother of John James Barralet (q.v.). Exh. London 1774–87. See text p. 58.

Barret, George, 1732–84
B. Dublin, son of clothier. Studied at DSS. Landscape painter. See text pp. 51–3.

Barret, George the Younger, 1767–1842 *Visitor*
The son of George Barret (q.v.). He visited Ireland in 1804 and probably on other occasions, as he exhibited Irish views in 1814, 1815 and 1838. See text p. 85

Barry, James, 1741–1806
Born Cork. Subject picture painter. See text pp. 99.

Barry, Moyra A., 1886–1960
B. Dublin, educ. RHA schools and won the Taylor prize; continued in the Slade School, before going to Ecuador to teach. On her return to Dublin she exh. RHA 1908–58 and in the Watercolour Society. She painted a wide range of subjects but preferred flower painting.

Barry, Redmond, fl. 1800
Known only by landscape watercolour of Ross Castle, Kerry. Signed and dated 1800 (NGI).

Bartlett, Richard, late fifteenth-early sixteenth century *Visitor*
Topographer and map-maker. See text, p. 13.

Bartlett, William Henry, 1858–1932 *Visitor*
A genre painter, active from c. 1874. Exh. RHA 1897 and 1905; West of Ireland subjects at Grosvenor Gallery 1882 and 1886; Donegal subjects 1905; Also in Ireland 1911.

Barton, Rose Maynard, 1856–1929
B. Dublin, Exh. RHA 1878–1918. See text pp. 223–5.

Batt, Elizabeth Hannah, b. c. 1818
Amateur landscape watercolourist, d. of Thomas Batt of Rathmullen, Co. Donegal, m. 1846, Caesar Otway (1809–67).

Batt, Revd Narcissus George, c. 1824–98
Amateur draughtsman, drew topographical subjects. See text pp. 208–9.

Battersby, Mary, fl. 1804–41
Flower and bird painter. See text pp. 116–17.

Baxter, W.G., c. 1855–88
B. Ireland, educ. in an architect's office, Manchester, worked in London as a comic artist in "Judy." Produced drawings for Ally Sloper's *Half Holiday* 1884–6.

Baynes, Thomas Mann, fl. 1794–1854 *Visitor*
Worked for J. Davies's *Ireland Illustrated* 1832. Watercolour for his view of High Street, Belfast in Huntingdon Museum, Calif. Exh. London 1820.

Beale, James, 1798–1879
Amateur, b. Cork, a pioneer in steamship travel, he visited Norway, Italy, Morocco (1832) and no doubt many other places, sketching all the time. See text p. 217.

Beauford, William H., 1735–1819
B. Ireland, amateur antiquarian draughtsman and landscape painter. Toured South of Ireland in 1786 with Ledwich and in 1787, Carlow and Wicklow. Work engraved in Ledwich's *Antiquities of Ireland*, 1790 and other publications. See text pp. 43, 44.

Beaufort, Revd Daniel Augustus, 1739–1821
B. London, son of Huguenot refugees, brought up in Ireland where his father was a clergyman. He is renowned as a map-maker, his *New Map of Ireland*, 1792, being the most famous. See text pp. 84–5.

Beaufort, Frances Anne (Fanny), see under Edgeworth, Frances.

Beaufort, Francis, 1774–1857
B. England, son of Daniel Augustus (q.v.). Educated in Ireland. Amateur watercolourist, joined the Royal Navy becoming Rear-Admiral. Travelled on duty widely, sketching all the time; was in the Far East, Argentina 1807, Canada 1809, and surveyed the coast of Asia Minor in 1810, publishing his account, illustrated by himself in 1817, under the title, *Karamania*. Many of his drawings are in the collection of the Huntingdon Library in California. See text pp. 251–2.

Beaufort, Louisa, 1781–1867
Daughter of Daniel Augustus (q.v.) who travelled with him frequently and was an amateur watercolourist. In 1827, she published an *Essay upon the State of Architecture and Antiquities previous to the landing of the Anglo-Normans in Ireland*, which she illustrated and which won her honorary membership of the RIA. A small sketchbook is in TCD.

Beaufort, the Revd William Louis, 1771–1849
Amateur topographical landscape painter, son of Daniel Augustus (q.v.). Was educated in O'Brien's Art School in Dublin. See text p. 44.

Bedingfield, Philip, d. 1897 *Visitor*
Amateur, artillery officer becomes Major-General. Exh. RA 1853. Travelled to China 1857, then to Canada. In Ireland 1863. See text p. 173.

Beechey, Rear-Admiral Richard Brydges, RN, 1808–95 *Visitor*
B. London, amateur watercolourist and oil painter, son of the portrait painter Sir William Beechey. In Ireland for a long time from 1835, firstly surveying the mouth of the Shannon and the West Coast, later, from 1864, living in Monkstown and Dublin. About 1877 lived in Plymouth. Exh. RHA 1842–94; London 1832–77.

Bennet, William, 1811–71 *Visitor*
Exh. Irish views in NWS in 1855–6 and 1861.

Benson, Charlotte E, 1846–93
Amateur, b. Dublin, educ. RDS Schools, exh. RHA 1873–91, in the WSI, 1879 and 1882, and the Dublin Sketching Club, 1888–92. Travelled widely in Ireland and also visited India, 1887, Europe and England.

Benson, Mary Kate, fl. 1874–d. 1921
Sister of above, educ. in England under Herkomer and Calderon and in Paris under Lazare. Exh. RHA 1873–1906. Travelled widely on the continent and in England and Ireland. Secretary of the Ladies Sketching Club, 1874. See text p. 222.

Bentley, Charles, 1806–54 *Visitor*
A marine painter. Exhibited Irish seascapes and landscapes regularly from 1838.

Beranger, Gabriel, 1729–1817
B. Rotterdam, settled in Dublin 1750. Topographical draughtsman and antiquarian. First tour through Ireland in 1773, Co. Wicklow; 1779 in the West with Bigari (q.v.); 1780 with J.J. Barralet (q.v.) in Wexford and Wicklow; 1781, in Dundalk. Also did pastel portraits, silhouettes and bird paintings. See text pp. 39–40.

Bermingham, Nathaniel, fl. 1735–74
B. Ireland, apprenticed to a herald-painter. Working in Dublin from 1740 as a paper cutter of portraits and coats of arms, also a pastellist whose few surviving works are ovals, the heads in profile. From 1744 in London. Exh. London 1774.

Bernard, Margaret, fl. 1885–6 *Visitor*
Exh. NWS 1885, view in County Mayo.

Bigari, Angelo Maria, fl. 1772–9 *Visitor*
B. Bologna, came to Ireland c. 1772 employed as scene painter. In 1777, sent work to Soc. of Artists exhibition included landscapes and genre scenes. Accompanied Beranger (q.v.) to West of Ireland drawing antiquities. Many works engraved in Grose's *Antiquities* which indicate he travelled widely in Ireland. May have left Ireland in 1779. See text pp. 39, 40–1.

Bindon, Francis, c. 1700–65
Gentleman architect and painter, only known drawing a portrait of Swift, 1735, (NGI).

Black, James, fl. 1813
An Armagh artist of small oval watercolour portraits and oil landscapes.

Blake, Lady, see under Osborne, Edith.

Blakey, Nicholas, fl. 1747–d. 1778
An Irishman, early career unknown. By 1747 living in Paris where he died in 1778. He certainly spent many years in England as well as France, as he was involved in illustration as well as painting portraits in oils. He illustrated Hanway's *Travels in Persia*, 1753, and worked with Hayman on illustrations of English history publ. in 1778. His beautiful drawing style is markedly rococo and he may have been trained in France. See text pp. 24–5.

Blaymire, Jonas, fl. 1733–63
B. Ireland, a surveyor and measurer who made topographical drawings of Irish cathedrals for Walter Harris's edition of Ware's works. Two views of St. Patrick's Cathedral, Dublin, survive.

Bloomfield, John, second Lord Bloomfield, 1802–79
Amateur. See text p. 209.

Bolton, Charles Newport, 1816–84
B. Ireland. Amateur draughtsman of landscapes and topographical views widely ranging in Ireland, Wales and Scotland. Two volumes of views of Killarney and views of the River Suir were published and exhibited. Exh. RHA 1845–6.

Bolton, John Nunn, 1869–1909
B. Dublin, educ. Metropolitan School of Art and RHA. Won Taylor Prize, 1892. Painted landscapes in both oil and watercolour. Lived for sometime in Warwick and taught in Leamington School of Art. Exh. RHA 1890–1909.

Booth, William Joseph, 1795/6–1871 *Visitor*
An architect who worked as Surveyor for the Draper's Company 1822–54 in Ulster. Excellent topographical watercolourist. See text, pp. 144–5.

Borthwick, Catherine, mid-eighteenth century
An amateur who painted a view of Kilkenny Castle. See text pp. 199–200.

Bosanquet, John Claude, fl. 1872–3.
Son of J.E. Bosanquet (q.v.), painted landscapes. Exh. RHA 1872–3.

Bosanquet, John E., fl. 1854–61
A Cork photographer who painted local views mostly in watercolour. Exh. RHA 1854–61. See text p. 216.

Bourke, E., fl. 1850
One work in pencil of Duleek Abbey, signed and dated 1850, is known.

Bourne, Magdalene Dysart, fl. 1900
Amateur; watercolour of New Abbey, Kilcullen, dated 1901, is known.

Bouvier, Auguste Jules, 1827–81 *Visitor*
A Colleen carrying a Jug, was on the London art market recently.

Boyle, James, fl. 1832
Employed as a Civil Assistant sketcher in the Ordnance Survey. Began Oct. 1832 and worked in Hill drawing in Cos. Antrim and Derry.

Boyne, John, B., 1750–1810
B. Co. Down, went to London as a child; apprenticed to the engraver, William Byrne; worked as a strolling player and from 1781 as a drawing master. Style varies from lively genre to theatrical portraits, illustrations, and caricatures. Exh. London 1788–1809. See text pp. 77–8.

Boys, Thomas Shotter, 1803–74 *Visitor*
Exh. NWS 1886 *The Slate Quarries near Newtown Anner, Ireland.*

Bradford, Benjamin, early nineteenth century
Drawings included in Daniel Grose's *Antiquities of Ireland*. See text p. 43.

Branegan, J.F., fl. 1841–88
Probably Irish. Marine painter in Dublin 1841 but travelled widely later in British Isles, Isle of Man, Scotland 1857, Norfolk 1871, Rochester, London. Exh. London 1871–88.

Brennan, Michael George, 1839–71
B. Castlebar, Co. Mayo, educ. DSS and the RHA and RA schools. Worked for *Fun* and *Punch* but in early 1860s left to live in Italy, dying on a visit to Algeria. Painted landscapes, genre scenes, mostly in oils. Exh. RHA 1868–73; London 1865–72.

Bridgford, Thomas, 1812–78, RHA
B. Lancashire, came to Ireland c. 1817–18, where he lived except between 1834 and 1844, when he was in London. Studied at RDS schools; exh. London 1835–44; RHA 1827–34 and 1841–79; RHA 1851, taught drawing; known for small watercolour and chalk portraits. See text pp. 153–4.

Brocas, Henry, 1762–1837
B. Dublin, self-taught landscape painter, caricaturist and engraver. Exh. in Dublin from 1800. In 1801 became Master of the Landscape and Ornament School of the Dublin Society Schools. The father of four painters, James Henry, c. 1790–1846; Samuel Frederick, c. 1792–1847; William, c. 1794–1868; Henry, c. 1798–1873. The work of this family is discussed in the text on pp. 137–44.

Brocas, James, 1754–80
Brother of Henry Brocas (q.v.). Portrait painter in oils, crayons and miniatures. Educ. Dublin Society Schools.

Brooke, Henry, 1738–1806
B. Dublin, painter of history pieces and religious subjects. He worked and exhibited in London and Dublin. An important sketchbook by him is in the NGI. See text p. 74.

Brooke, William Henry, ARHA, 1772–1860
B. Dublin, son of the above; studied under Henry Drummond and lived mostly in England; signed drawings from 1786; worked also in oil. Illustrator of books from landscape and mythology to Moore's *Melodies* and Carleton's *Traits and Stories of the Irish Peasantry*. Frequently etched his own work. Exh. London 1810–26; RHA 1827–46; made ARHA 1828. See text pp. 95–6.

Browne, James Denis Howe, b. 1827
Amateur traveller in Europe and Asia Minor, where he painted. Grandson of the second Earl of Altamont. Lived at Claremont House, Co. Mayo. His view of Mont Blanc was lithographed.

Browne, Richard, 1776–1824
B. Ireland, famous for watercolours of Australian animals and birds. See text pp.253–4.

Browne, William Henry James, d. 1872
Amateur; naval officer; travelled to Fiji islands and the Arctic. See text p. 246.

Brunton, William, 1833–78
Illustrator, b. Dublin, educ. RDS schools from 1847. Worked mainly in black and white, in London illustrating comic magazines and books.

Buck, Adam, 1759–1833
B. Cork, apparently self-taught, worked as a portrait watercolourist and miniature painter. Exh. Parliament House Dublin 1802; London 1795–1833. See text pp. 125–6.

Buck, Frederick, 1771–c. 1840
B. Cork, younger brother of Adam Buck (q.v.). Educ. Dublin Society Schools. Worked mostly as a miniature painter.

Buckley, C.F., fl. 1841–69
Thought to have come from Cork. Lived London. Travelled widely in British Isles; Irish examples are known. Exh. landscapes, London 1841–69.

Buckley, J.E., fl. 1835–73
Possibly the John Buckley, Cork painter c. 1835, mentioned in Strickland as painting portraits, landscapes and miniatures. In 1843 was living in London with C.F. Buckley (q.v), presumably his brother. Exh. RHA 1860; London 1843–61.

Buckley, William, fl. 1840–5
Perhaps a relation of C.F. and J.E. Buckley, as he

painted with C.F. in England. Exh. London 1840–5.

Bulwer, Revd James, 1794–1879 *Visitor*
Amateur, in Ireland 1823–33 when Perpetual Curate of Booterstown, Dublin, and may have visited later as he married an Irish girl. Was honorary member of the RHA and Cork Soc. for Promoting Fine Arts in 1833. Exh. RHA 1830.

Burbidge, Frederick William, 1847–1905 *Visitor*
Came to Ireland 1879 as Curator of the Trinity College Botanic Gardens. A flower painter who travelled worldwide and published his work in botanical magazines. In 1873 he wrote and illustrated *The Art of Botanical Drawing*.

Burges, William, ARA, 1827–81 *Visitor*
Architect and fine draughtsman. In Ireland in connection with the building of St. Finbarr's Cathedral, Cork, which he designed, 1865–76.

Burgess, James Howard, 1817–90
B. North of Ireland, landscape, genre painter. Worked for many publications including Hall's *Ireland* 1841. He also painted in England, Scotland and North Wales (1871). Also worked in oils. Exh. RHA 1830–80. See text p. 170.

Burgess, John of Leamington, 1814–74 *Visitor*
A view of Glenarm Castle, Co. Antrim, sold in Sothebys 28.4.83, Lot 252.

Burton, Sir Frederick William, RHA, FSA, LL.D, HRWS, 1816–1900
B. Corofin, came to Dublin as a child. Taught drawing by Brocas brothers. Exh. RHA 1832–61; London 1842–82. See text pp. 179–83.

Bury, Lady Beaujolais Eleanora Catherine, d. 1903
Amateur known for her interesting interiors of Charleville Castle, 1844. See text p. 203.

Bushe, Letitia, fl. 1731–57
Daughter of Arthur Bushe of Dangan, Co. Kilkenny. See text pp. 27–30.

Butler, Elizabeth Southerden, Lady, née Thompson, 1846–1933 *Visitor*
Famous as oil painter of battle scenes. Came to Ireland for honeymoon after marriage, 1877, to Lt. Gen. Sir W.F. Butler. Publ. (London, 1909) *From Sketch-book and Diary* which includes plates of some of her Irish sketches. See text p. 179.

Butler, Emma, fl. 1881–95
Amateur landscape watercolourist and etcher. Travelled in France, Belgium, Austria and Italy.

Butler, Mildred Anne, RWS, 1858–1941
B. Kilkenny. See text pp. 225–31.

Butler, Patrick Henry, 1805–81
B. Kilkenny. Amateur landscape and genre painter, father of Mildred Anne Butler (q.v.). See text p. 252.

Butts, John, c. 1728–65
B. Cork, pupil of Rogers, landscape painter who also worked as scene and sign painter. Moved to Dublin c. 1757. Master of James Barry. See text pp. 61–2.

Byrne, Patrick, J., 1783–1864
An architect who made watercolours of Dublin streets and interiors. Member Royal Institute of Architects and RHA. Exh. RHA 1861–4.

C

Callow, William, RWS, 1812–1908 *Visitor*
A watercolour of *The Lodge, Virginia, Co. Cavan* is known.

Calvert, Frederick, fl. 1807–30
B. Cork, landscape painter who worked for engravers. There is an aquatint *Parliament Bridge, Cork* 1807. Went to England, publ. views

of Tintern Abbey, Staffordshire and Shropshire. Travelled widely in England. Publ. 1815, *Lessons on Landscape Colouring, Shadowing and Pencilling*. Exh. Dublin 1812 and 1815 and RHA 1834.

Calvin, F., nineteenth century
Landscape artist. Watercolour of *North Gate Bridge, Cork*.

Campbell, Cecilia Margaret, 1791–1857
Taught by her father, John Henry Campbell (q.v.), m. 1826 George Nairn. Painted landscapes in both oils and watercolour; exh. in Dublin from 1809 and RHA from 1826–51. See text p. 90.

Campbell, John Henry, 1757–1828
Landscape painter; studied Dublin Society Schools. Exh. RHA 1826 and 1828. See text pp. 89–91.

Campion, George Bryant, 1796–1870 *Visitor*
Exhibited NWS landscape, genre watercolours with Irish titles 1842–64 usually of Tipperary, Killarney or Cork.

Carey, Lt., 17th Light Dragoons, fl. 1792 *Visitor*
See text pp. 96–7.

Carey, John, c. 1860–1943
Painter of genre watercolours in Belfast. Brother of Joseph William (q.v.).

Carey, Joseph William, 1859–1937
B. Belfast, trained at Marcus Ward & Co. Opened his own business with Richard Thompson producing illuminated addresses, books, illustrations, etc. Painted landscapes and seascapes in oil and watercolour. Exh. RHA 1915–35. See text p. 275.

Carlow, Viscount, see under Portarlington, first Earl of

Carr, Sir John, 1772–1832 *Visitor*
A barrister who became a travel book writer. *The Stranger in Ireland*, 1806 was written and illustrated by himself, following a trip to Ireland.

Carver, Robert, fl. 1750–91
B. Dublin, taught by his father and Robert West. His main career was as a scene painter in Crow St and later Drury Lane and Covent Garden. Exh. several watercolour landscapes as well as oils in the ISA 1765–8. When in London, 1765–90, he became President in 1778 of the Incorporated Society of Artists.

Carysfort, John Joshua Proby, first Earl of, 1751–1828
Amateur artist. See text p. 202.

Casey, Loetitia, née Gardiner, c. 1819–63
Amateur draughtswoman, worked in Australia. See text p. 254.

Casey, William Linnaeus, 1835–70
B. Cork, studied Cork School of Design. Taught in Limerick School of Art; later went to London; obtained Art Master's Certificate at the Nat. Art Training School 1858. Taught the royal children and at the St. Martin's Lane Academy. Painted portrait and genre subjects in watercolour.

Cashin, Edward, fl. 1823–6
B. Ireland; only work in Bristol known. See text p. 144.

Catterson Smith the Elder, Stephen, PRHA 1806–72
English, spent career in Ireland. See text p. 153.

Caulfield, Mrs, fl. c. 1778
An amateur painter in watercolour, oil and needlework. Mentioned by the Revd J. Campbell in his *Philosophical Survey of the South of Ireland* 1778, as a flower, bird and genre painter.

Chaigneau, Thomas Henry T., c. 1760–92
B. probably Dublin, entered DSS 1776. Landscape and architectural watercolourist. Visited England. Probably the Theophilus Chaigneau brother of the Secretary of the Dublin Society, 1780. Peter Chaigneau. Exh. ISA 1777 and 1780.

Chalmers, J., fl. 1801–20
Landscape and scene painter working in Dublin c. 1801. Later worked in the Cork theatre and in 1819 taught in the Cork Institution. Exh. Cork Society for the Promotion of the Fine Arts.

Charleville, Catherine Maria, Countess of Charleville, 1762–1851
B. Catherine Dawson, educ. Dublin and Toulouse and married the first Earl of Charleville in 1798. An amateur of good quality, a landscape painter who sometimes used gouache. See text p. 203.

Chase, John, 1810–79 *Visitor*
Exhibited NWS topographical landscapes with Irish titles in 1865 (Cork), Kilcrea Priory 1867 and 1872, Killarney 1873. Exh. RHA 1858. His wife, Mary Ann, also exhibited a view of Killarney in 1834 in the NWS.

Chatterton, Henrietta, Lady, née Iremonger, 1806–76
B. in England, came to Ireland on her marriage in 1824 to Sir William Chatterton, Bt., of Castle Mahon, Co. Cork. Wrote, illustrated and published *Rambles in the South of Ireland during the year 1838* and *Home Sketches and Foreign Recollections, 1841.*

Chearnly, Anthony, fl. 1740–c. 1785
Irish antiquarian draughtsman. See text pp. 34–7.

Chearnly, Samuel, d. 1746
Brother of Anthony (q.v.). See text p. 34.

Chinnery, George, 1774–1852 *Visitor*
English by birth, lived in Ireland 1795–1802. See text pp. 127–8.

Clarke, Harry, 1889–1931
Most famous as a stained glass artist, but equally brilliant as an illustrator of books and a designer. See text p. 283.

Clarke, Margaret, née Crilley 1888–1961
A pupil of the Metropolitan School of Art Dublin and a meticulous draughtswoman. Later m. to Harry Clarke (q.v.). See text pp. 283–5.

Clarke, William, fl. 1787
Amateur, known for a view of Enniskillen. See text p. 196.

Clayton, Samuel, fl. 1793–1853
Irish, deported to Australia. See text p. 254.

Cocking, Thomas, fl. c. 1783–91 *Visitor*
The servant of Francis Grose (q.v.), with whom he came to Ireland in 1791. See text p. 41.

Coghill, Sir Egerton Bushe, 5th Bt., 1853–1921
Lived in Castletownshend, Co. Cork. Attended the Academy of Art in Dusseldorf. He was best known for his oil paintings and photography but exhibited some watercolour sketches in the RHA. Exh. RHA 1882–1919.

Cole, William Philip, RBA, RCA, 1884–1964 *Visitor*
English landscape and portrait painter, stained glass artist. An Irish work, *Rock of Cashel*, dated 1934, exists.

Collier, Thomas Frederick, fl. 1848–88
Admitted RDS schools 1848, prize winner. Painted landscapes, flowers and outdoor still lives. Travelled in England and Scotland. Exh. RHA 1850–60 and 1888; London 1856–60. See text pp. 188–9.

Collins, Charles, c. 1680–1744
Probably Irish: recorded as such in *Dublin Evening Post*, 4 May 1786. Painter in oil, watercolour and body colour, of still life, flowers and birds. See text p. 109.

Colomb, Wellington, 1827–95
Irish-born, amateur landscape painter, oils and watercolourist. Joined the Royal Irish Constabulary stationed at Killarney. Exh: RHA 1848–51, 1858–9, 1862 and 1879; London 1865–7.

Colquhoun, Miss Annie Trew, fl. 1890–3
Lived in Buncrana, Co. Donegal, amateur watercolourist. Exh. landscapes and genre in the RI (NWS) 1890, 1892–3 and Ramblers 1892–3.

Colville, Helen, d. 1953
A Dubliner, she lived in Howth and started exhibiting in 1892 in the Watercolour Society of Ireland, also RHA (oils and watercolours) 1920–47. Also exh. England. Landscapes were her favourite subject matter. See text p. 234.

Comerford, John, c. 1770–1832
B. Kilkenny; worked mainly as a miniaturist but also in oils. See text p. 128.

Connolly, John, early nineteenth century
Landscape painter in watercolour; also produced lithographs.

Conor, William, 1881–1968
B. Belfast, best known as an oil painter of portraits and genre subjects. Exh. RHA 1918–68. See text pp. 277.

Conyngham, William Burton, 1733–96
Better known as a patron of the arts and a collector of antiquarian watercolours, but he is recorded as sketching when touring in Spain and Portugal. See text pp. 37–9.

Cook, Ebenezer Wake, 1843–1926
May have been a visitor; a watercolour of Spike Island, Co. Cork was recently on Dublin market.

Cook, Samuel, 1806–59 *Visitor*
1849 visited Ireland. Exhibited Irish scenes NWS 1850. Known for interiors of Lismore Castle.

Cooley, Thomas, ARHA, 1795–1873
B. Dublin, grandson of architect of same name; he was deaf and dumb, trained in Dublin, made his career in both capitals. In London c. 1810; 1813; 1817–23; 1829–46; and Dublin in between and from 1846 to his death. Worked as an oil portrait painter, but left pencil and pen and ink drawings of genre subjects. Exh. RA, 1813–46; RHA, 1826–56 which are probably all oils. See text p. 132.

Cooper, Austin, FSA, 1759–1830
B. Killenure Castle, Tipperary. See text pp. 35–7.

Cornish, Hubert, c. 1770–1832 *Visitor*
A view of Blarney Castle, 1809, is known.

Coulter, William Alexander, 1849–1936
B. Glenariff, Co. Antrim. Started life as a sailor but settled in San Francisco about 1869 where apart from numerous oils he drew many sketches in pen and ink working for the local newspaper. Exh. first in 1874 at the San Francisco Art Association. He travelled for two years in Europe but returned to San Francisco in 1880. In 1882 he was in Hawaii sketching and in 1896 joined the staff of the San Francisco Call. He had a great love of detail. He held many one-man shows.

Craig, William, 1829–75
B. Dublin, studied RDS schools from 1847. 1863 went to US. Exh. RHA, 1847–62. See text p. 241.

Cramer, A., fl. 1814
Watercolour of Drumcondra Bridge 1814 (NGI).

Crampton, Sir John, 2nd Bt., 1805–86
B. Dublin, diplomat and amateur watercolour painter. Posted to Turin 1826, St. Petersburg 1828–34; Brussels 1834–9; Vienna 1839–44; Berne 1844–5; Washington, 1845–56; Hanover 1857; St. Petersburg 1858–60; Madrid 1860–9; 1869 (after retirement) lived in Bray. See text p. 205.

Crampton, Selina, 1806–76
B. Dublin, amateur watercolourist, sister of Sir John Crampton (q.v.) See text pp. 205–6.

Craven, W., *Visitor?*
Painted a view of Killiney Bay (not topographically accurate).

Cregan, Martin, PRHA 1788–1870
An oil painter who did some chalk and wash portraits. Exh. RHA 1826–59.

Creswick, Thomas, RA, 1811–69 *Visitor*
Visited Ireland 1837 and possibly at other times; work included in Hall's *Ireland* 1842–3 and Ritchie Heath's *Ireland* 1837–8. Exh. Irish subjects London 1836–9; RHA 1842–6.

Crilley, Margaret, see under Clarke, Margaret

Croker, Thomas Crofton, 1798–1854
B. Cork; an amateur draughtsman who exh. in Cork in 1817. Known principally as an antiquarian and writer. His *Fairy Legends and Traditions in the South of Ireland*, 1825, was his most famous and influential book. Went to live in London 1818 but returned frequently to his native city and was a patron of Irish artists in London. In 1830 m. Marianne Nicholson, d. of Francis Nicholson (q. v.). See text pp. 95–6.

Crone, Robert, c. 1718–79
B. Dublin, trained Dublin Society Schools and under Robert Hunter and Philip Hussey, who sent him to Rome 1760. See text pp. 58–9.

Crookshank, Miss T.C., first half nineteenth century
Amateur draughtswoman. Known by pencil drawings, including one of Castle Caulfield, Armagh Museum.

Crosby, Charles James, 1809–90 *Visitor*
An inland revenue official who retired to Ireland and painted small watercolours and drawings.

Crowley, Nicholas Joseph, RHA, 1819–57
B. Dublin; studied Dublin Society Schools and in RHA. An original member of the Association of Artists in Belfast, founded 1836. Exh. RHA 1829–58 where he exhibited some watercolours; London 1835–58. Best known as an oil painter.

Cruickshank, Robert, 1789–1856 *Visitor*
A watercolour entitled *The Irish Schoolmaster*, is owned by the Huntingdon Museum, California. He may not have visited Ireland. His brother George illustrated the *Irish Rebellion*.

Cuitt, George, 1779–1854 *Visitor*
He was born and died in Yorkshire though he lived in Chester between 1804 and 1820 and is known as a landscape painter and etcher. A drawing of Molesworth Street, Dublin, dated 1820, is known.

Cullen, John, 1761–1825/30
B. Dublin, studied Dublin Society Schools and later pupil of H.D. Hamilton (q.v.). He made crayon and wash oval portraits and practised as a miniaturist. Exh. Dublin 1800–17. See text p. 72.

Currey, Fanny W., fl. 1858–d. 1912
B. Lismore, d. of Francis Edmond Currey, agent to the Devonshire estate and a fine early photographer. Fanny was a founder member in Lismore, 1870, of the Irish Amateur Drawing Society, now Watercolour Society of Ireland. She also exhibited in the Grosvenor Gallery, London, 1880–9 and the Royal Institution, 1883–96. Travelled France 1879; North Wales; Holland c. 1883; possibly Tangiers c. 1888 and in the south of England. See text pp. 221, 223.

D

Dalton, Richard, 1715–91
Probably b. in Bologna. Said by James Gandon to be Irish and educ. by Robert West (q. v.). See text pp. 60–1.

Danby, Francis, ARA, 1793–1861
B. Co. Wexford, studied at Dublin Society Schools. Spent most of his career in England. Exh. RHA 1844–56; RA 1820–60. See text pp. 157–8. Two of his sons, James Francis, 1816–75, and Thomas, 1817–18, occasionally exhibited in the

RHA and James Francis may have visited Ireland as he exhibited some Irish subjects. Thomas, however, is better known as a watercolourist.

Darby, Mary, c. 1800–69
Amateur watercolourist, the wife of a clergyman in Kells, Co. Kilkenny. Painted landscape views near her home and in England, Sussex 1844; Lancaster 1847, Lake District 1848/9 and in 1850 went to France, Belgium, Luxembourg and down the Rhine to Switzerland. See text pp. 210–11.

Dartnell, George Russell, 1798–1878
B. Co. Limerick, a surgeon in the British army, he was stationed in many parts of the world including Canada. See text pp. 243–5.

Davie, George S., fl. 1872
A landscape painter who worked near Cork.

Davis, William, 1821–72
B. Leixlip, made his career in Liverpool. See text p. 192.

Dawson, see under Portarlington, first Earl of.

Dean, Hugh Primrose, fl. 1758–84
From Co. Down; made his career mostly in England and Italy. See text p. 222.

Deane, Miss, fl. 1847–74
A naïve drawing of a farmyard scene, dated 1847, is known and is probably by the same Miss Deane who founded the Ladies Sketching Club in 1872 in Dublin. See text p. 222.

Deane, Sir Thomas Manly, 1851–1933
A Cork architect, son of Sir Thomas Newenham Deane (q. v.); a sketchbook (NGI) shows his pencil drawings. See text p. 145.

Deane, Sir Thomas Newenham, RHA, 1828–1900
An architect from Cork who painted landscape and genre watercolours. Exh. RHA 1863–98; London 1853.

Deane, Zachariah, fl. 1753–8
A copyist of Dixon's flower and bird pictures. See text p. 111.

De Burgh, Coralie Helen, 1880–1959
Amateur watercolourist, portraits, landscapes, etc.

Delacherois, J., mid-nineteenth century
Member of the Co. Down family. An amateur, sketches using mostly pencil.

Delacour, F.J., fl. 1830
Painting landscapes in the Cork district in the Nicholson manner. There is also one done near Plymouth. There was a family of Delacours living near Mallow so that he may be Irish and so may be a B. Delacour, fl. 1818–43, who painted groups and portraits in the Buck manner exh. in London 1818–43. Strickland mentions a W. Delacour, fl. 1753 in Dublin who painted miniatures.

Delany, Mrs, née Granville, 1700–88 *Visitor*
B. England. First married, aged 17, to Alexander Pendarves, who died 1724. Visited Ireland first in 1731 and then lived there from 1743 to 1768 during her marriage to Patrick Delany, Dean of Down. Their house at Delville outside Dublin was the centre of a literary and artistic coterie which included Dean Swift. See text pp. 27–32, 112–14.

De Lanauze, Alexander, c. 1704–67
A portrait painter who is recorded on 15 May 1739 as taking "a little sketch of Croagh Patrick and Nephin, exactly as those mountains appear." This pencil sketch survives in Armagh Public Library among the papers of the Physico–Historical Society, G11.23. Perhaps the earliest record of sketching from nature in Ireland in modern times. (Information kindly supplied by Dr T. Barnard.)

Delrenne, Edmond, fl. 1915–16 *Visitor*
Belgian. Painted a watercolour of O'Connell Street, Dublin immediately after the rising in 1916. Exh. RHA 1915–16.

Dering, Henrietta, c. 1674–1728/9
A Huguenot refugee whose interesting career spans the Atlantic. Known also under her married name Johnston. See text pp. 26–7

De Rienzy, Thomas, first half nineteenth century.
An army officer, member of the de Rienzy family, Clobeman Hall, Co. Carlow. Drew and painted a ms album entitled *Sketches from nature taken in England, Ireland and Jersey* between Sept. 1821 and Oct. 1825. See text p. 173.

De Ros, Baroness Olivia Cecilia, d. 1885
Amateur draughtswoman, genre subject matter. Her mother, Frances Charlotte FitzGerald de Ros, d. 1851, was also an amateur artist. See text p. 215.

Derricke, John, fl. 1581 *Visitor*
Published *Image of Irelande*, 1581. See text p. 13.

Dibden, Thomas Colman, 1810–93 *Visitor*
Started as a clerk in GPO, London. Exh. RHA 1843–87 but no Irish views.

Digby, Simon, Bishop of Elphin, fl. 1668–1720
A miniaturist who is recorded as painting watercolours and by whom a pastel portrait of the first Duke of Ormond survives. He worked as a picture restorer and his daughters were also artists (Inchiquin Mss, no. 2621, where in a letter from William Butler to Sir Donat O'Brien, Newmarket, 2 May 1711, he writes, "The Duchess of Ormonde lately sent his Grace's picture to the old bishop [Simon Digby] to be repaired. He returned it 'amended,' and two nice new copies in return. Whereof she sent pencils and rules to the young damsels who as it is believed will exceed their father in that particular." (Information kindly supplied by Dr T. Barnard). See text p. 26.

Dillon, Frank, RA, 1823–1909 *Visitor*
NWS, exhibited an Irish scene, *A Street in Galway*, in 1887. Exh. oils of oriental subjects RHA 1856–1904.

Dillon, Richard, c. 1740–c. 1827
An amateur topographical artist who lived and drew for some years in Montreal where he had a Coffee House. Went to Canada c. 1780 where he is said to have been valet to the Irish Administrator and Governor, Sir Guy Carleton. He is probably Irish and this supposition is strengthened by the fact that John Nixon (text pp. 77) stayed with him on his business trip to Montreal in 1804. See *Early Plans and Views of Montreal*, exhibition catalogue, McCord Museum of Canadian History 1992.

Dineley, Thomas, fl. 1681 *Visitor*
A barrister who visited Ireland 1681, travelling from Dublin to Carlow, Kilkenny, Limerick, Bunratty, Youghal and Cork, and illustrated his diary with naïve sketches (NLI). See text pp. 18–21.

Dixon, Samuel, fl. 1748–69
B. Dublin; perhaps studied under Robert West and in the Dublin Society Schools. Exhibited at the Irish Society of Artists in 1768 on his return from a visit to London, where he had held an exhibition of his work. See text pp. 109–14.

Dobbin, Lady, née Kate Wise, 1868–1955
B. Bristol, but made her career in Ireland after her marriage in 1887. Amateur artist mostly of watercolours. Exh. RHA 1894–1947. See text pp. 233–4.

Douglas, Allen Edmund, 1835–94
B. Clones, amateur, worked as a doctor and painted as a relaxation. Lived for twenty-five years in Warrenpoint and painted the Mourne Mountains.

Douglas, Jessie, fl. 1893–d. 1928
A Belfast artist first exh. with the Belfast Art Society in 1893. Travelled abroad. See text p. 234.

Douglas, John, fl. c. 1845
Portrait painter in Belfast; also painted watercolour portraits.

Dowling, William Paul, d. 1877
Worked in Australia as a portrait painter and later photographer. Sometimes used crayons. See text p. 255.

Doyle, Charles Altamont, 1832–93
Son of John Doyle (q.v.), b. in London and spent most of his career in Scotland. See text p. 194.

Doyle, Henry Edward, CB, RHA, 1827–92
B. Dublin, studied Dublin Society Schools. Early career spent in London working as a draughtsman, wood engraver and illustrator of books and magazines (*Punch* and *Fun*). Returned to Dublin c. 1864 and became Director of the NGI in 1869 till his death. Painted watercolour, charcoal and pencil portraits and religious subjects. Exh. RHA 1870–84; London 1858. See text p. 192.

Doyle, James William Edmund, 1822–92
Son of John Doyle (q.v.) b. in London, began his career as a painter but turned to historical research.

Doyle, John, 1797–1868
B. Dublin, studied in the Dublin Society Schools and later under Gabrielli and John Comerford. Settling in London c. 1821, gained fame as a political caricaturist using the *nom de plume* "HB." He was the father and grandfather of famous writers and artists. See text p. 192–3.

Doyle, Richard "Dicky," 1824–83
B. London, taught drawing by his father, John Doyle (q.v.). 1843 began contributing to *Punch* and designed its cover. He left in 1850 and became a book illustrator. Always painted watercolours and concentrated later in his career on fairy themes. Exh. London 1868–83. See text pp. 193–4.

Doyle, Sylvia, mid nineteenth century
Daughter of John and sister of Charles, Henry, James and Richard Doyle (qq.v.). Was an accomplished, satirical draughtswoman. See text p. 194.

Drury, Susanna, fl. 1733–70
Little is known about her family. She married after 1758 a Mr Warter and was dead when he sold his collection before going abroad; it was advertised in Faulkner's *Dublin Journal*, 6–8 April 1776. In this her famous gouaches of the Giant's Causeway are mentioned in connection with her miniaturist brother, Francis (Franklin), d. 1771, who may have accompanied her there and also painted the Causeway. He might be responsible for the drawing of which the line engraving is in the King's maps in the BM. See text p. 32.

Dubois, Edward, early nineteenth century
Published in 1807, *My Pocket Book*, a burlesque on Sir J. Carr's (q.v.) *The Stranger in Ireland*.

Dufferin and Ava, Frederick Temple Blackwood, first Marquess of, 1826–1902
B. Florence but returned at an early age to Clandeboye, Co. Down. An amateur watercolourist: landscapes and genre scenes. His illustrious career took him all over the world though he died in Ireland. See text pp. 207–8, 249–51.

Duggan, Patrick, fl. 1815–20
B. Ireland, studied Dublin Society Schools, winning prizes. His landscape drawings are engraved in Hardiman's *History of Galway*, 1820, and in the *Memoirs of the Family of Grace*. No works now known.

Duncan, James, 1806–81
B. in Coleraine. Went to Canada 1825. Professional artist, painting in oil and watercolour. Known for views of Montreal area. Illustrator for newspapers and taught drawing at various Montreal schools. Exh. Canada 1865–81. See text p. 246.

Dundee, Capt W., fl. 1817 *Visitor*
Army officer, 62nd regiment, painted landscapes in Co. Longford and Co. Fermanagh 1817. Painted a view of Limerick.

Dunoyer, George Victor, 1817–69
B. Dublin. He was a member of the RIA from 1859 and of the Kilkenny Archaeological Society, and he worked for the Geological Survey of Ireland for some twenty years. His drawings and watercolours include, landscape, fish, fruit, genre, etc. A very prolific artist who travelled all over Ireland. Exh. RHA 1841–63. See text pp. 121–2, 163–4.

Durno, James, c. 1745–95
Made his career in England and Italy. See text p. 102.

E

Eagar, William, c. 1796–1839
B. in Ireland, emigrated to Newfoundland, 1830 and went on to Halifax, Nova Scotia in 1834. Had many of his views published as lithographs in both England and America. See text pp. 242–3.

Edgeworth, Charlotte, 1783–1807
Half sister of Maria Edgeworth (q.v.); was a competent artist. See text p. 203.

Edgeworth, Frances, 1769–1865
B. daughter of Daniel Augustus Beaufort (q.v.), m. Richard Lovell Edgeworth, 1798. A watercolourist of quality who was noted for her flower painting. See text p. 114.

Edgeworth, Maria, 1768–1849
Notable as a writer, she was also an amateur artist of amusing if weak quality. See text pp. 202–3.

Edridge, E.L., early nineteenth century *Visitor*
Drawing of Kingstown, dated 1831 is known.

Egan, J., fl. 1841
From Clonmel. Worked for Hall's *Ireland*; especially involved in the Kilkenny area.

Ellis, John, c. 1705–1776
Botanical artist. Drawings in Linnean Soc., London.

Ellis, John, fl. 1767–1812
B. Dublin, educ. Dublin Society Schools, exh. indian-ink drawings in Society of Artists 1767 and 1768. Also worked in gouache. Was a scene painter in London, and in Dublin opened in 1792 a "Museum" where he exhibited works of art.

Elmore, Alfred, RA, 1815–81
B. Clonakilty, Co. Cork; went to England about 1827 to study and made his career there. Famous as a subject picture painter, he was also renowned for his watercolours. Became honorary RHA 1878.

Ennis, Jacob, 1728–70
Educ. Dublin Society Schools, and in the Accademia de San Luca, Rome. See text p. 100.

Enniskillen, William Willoughby, 3rd Earl of, 1807–86
Amateur; studied drawing under Henry Bright, a noted teacher in London.

Evans, William, 1788–1877 *Visitor*
Exhibited Connemara Views from 1836 and Killarney and Lismore from 1840.

Exshaw, Charles, fl. 1747–71
B. Dublin; pupil of Francis Bindon; went to Rome and Paris 1747–55; won prizes. Returned to Ireland. Exh. Irish Society of Artists 1764. See text p. 74.

F

Fahey, James, RI, NWS, 1804–85 *Visitor*
Exh. NWS 1840 Killmallock and Killarney; 1863, 1868 and 1871 Co. Antrim views and antiquities; RHA 1845–7.

Fairholt, Frederick William, 1814–66 *Visitor*
Well-known illustrator. Worked for Hall's *Ireland*.

Farington, Joseph, RA, FSA, 1747–1821 *Visitor*
A dated work "Mussenden Temple, Co. Down [sic] 1808," is known.

Farmer, Henry George, 1848–1900
Sergeant-Major of the Depot of the Leinster Regiment at Crinkle. Three watercolours by him are known. He may have been a visitor.

Faulkner, John, RHA, fl. 1848–90
B. Ireland, studied at RDS schools from 1848. Exh. regularly 1852–70 and again 1880–7 in RHA; oils and watercolours. See text pp. 183–5.

Ferguson, Samuel, 1810–86
B. Belfast, architectural draughtsman and sketcher of nature. Toured continent 1845–6. Close friend of Sir Frederick William Burton and acquainted with Petrie (qq. v.).

Firminger, Revd Thomas Augustus Charles, 1812–84 *Visitor*
Exh. NWS 1838 views of Killarney, Kilmallock and Glendalough; 1839 Killarney and Kilmallock; 1840 Waterford; 1841 Cashel.

Fisher, Sir George Bulteel, 1764–1834 *Visitor*
Amateur painter. Signed watercolours of Lismore Castle, dated 1794, exist in the Huntingdon Museum, California.

Fisher, Jonathan, fl. 1763–1809
B. Dublin, started life as a woollen draper and may have studied painting in London. He was back in Dublin by 1763 when he won a Dublin Society premium for landscape. He won another in 1768. Exh. Irish Society Artists and other exhibitions 1765–1801. His topographical landscapes were engraved. He issued a series on Killarney, 1770; Carlingford, 1772; and 60 plates of the Scenery of Ireland from 1796. See text pp. 46, 88–9.

FitzGerald, Bridget Maria, 1817–1905
Amateur artist. See text pp. 213–14.

FitzGerald, Lord Gerald, 1821–86
Amateur draughtsman, illustrator and member of the Junior etching club. See text p. 215.

Fitzgerald, J., fl. 1796
A view of old St. Finbarr's, Cork, engraved 1796 after a drawing by Fitzgerald in the Irish Architectural Archive.

Fitzgerald, John Austen, 1832–1906
Exh. RHA 1860, 1888 and 1897–8. Works rare and mostly of fairy and dream subjects.

Fitzgerald, Robert David, 1830–92
B. Tralee and went to Australia 1856 becoming in due course Deputy Surveyor-General, New South Wales. Notable for his ornithological drawings and his interest in ferns and orchids, publishing the first volume of *Australian Orchids* in 1875, the second being published posthumously in 1882.

Fitzpatrick, Thomas, 1860–1912
B. Cork, apprenticed to a Cork painter. Illustrator and cartoonist for *The Weekly Freeman, Weekly National Press* and the *Leprechaun*, which he founded in 1905. Also painted in oil and watercolour. Lived in Dublin most of his life though he spent a couple of years in London. His daughter Mary assisted him with illuminated addresses.

Ford, James, fl. 1772–c. 1812
Studied at the Dublin Society Schools from 1772, winning a prize. He worked largely as an engraver for the Society's publications and other books.

Forde, Samuel, 1805–28
B. Cork, studied in Cork Academy under J. Chalmers (q.v.). Forde painted religious and literary subjects, one in "distemper." Also employed in decorative work. See text pp. 102–6.

Forrest, Charles, fl. 1765–80
B. Ireland; studied Dublin Society Schools from 1765, winning a premium. See text pp. 64–5.

Forrester, James, c. 1730–76
B. Ireland; studied D.S. Schools 1747–52, winning premiums and prizes. Left for Rome where he was living when he died. See text p. 59.

Forster, John, fl. 1773–94
A drawing of *Ballinsnave Castle, Co. Roscommon,* 1794 is known. Probably the same man as the John Forster 1773–80, mentioned in Strickland's Dictionary who exhibited in the Society of Artists and was according to Pasquin educated in Paris.

Forster, Thomas, b. c. 1677, fl. 1690–1713 *Visitor*
Miniature painter who used plumbago and may have visited Ireland. See text p. 26.

Forth, Dorothea, fl. 1731–59, m. 1733 the Hon Revd Francis Hamilton
D. and co-heiress of James Forth of Redwood, King's Co. Her "paintings of flowers and insects are unrivalled" according to Mrs Delany, 25 Nov. 1731. Her work is unknown. See text p. 290, chapter 7, note 11.

Fowler, Frederick, fl. 1852–62
Exh. Irish views in Melbourne 1852–62 and also views of the South Sea islands. See text p. 255.

Franklin, John, fl. 1819–61
B. Ireland, educ. RDS 1819. Went to England c. 1829 and exh. London between 1830 and 1861. Illustrator, Hall's *Ireland* 1841; W. Harrison Ainsworth's *Old St Pauls* and W. Carleton's *Irish Peasantry* 1852, and worked for the *Art Journal* 1850. Exh. RHA 1826–8, 1842, landscapes and subject pictures, many in watercolour.

Franks, Rosalie, fl. c. 1921–9
Dublin artist, exh. Irish Watercolour Society from 1921 and RHA 1928. She travelled extensively on the continent and in style is clearly influenced by Rose Barton (q.v.). See text p. 234.

Fraser, Charles, *Visitor* first half nineteenth century
A Scottish artist, nephew of Alexander Fraser (1786–1865). Both were friends of Jeremiah Hodges Mulcahy (q.v.) and must have visited him in Limerick about 1857 as work by them of Ireland is known from that date.

Fremantle, Elizabeth, Lady, née Nugent, d. 1874 *Visitor*
Amateur watercolourist, m. 1824. View of the Curragh Camp, Co. Kildare known.

French? R., second half of eighteenth century
The signature on a *View of Enniscorthy* can be read as above. See text p. 196.

French, William Percy, 1854–1920
B. Cloonyquin, educ. TCD as an engineer. Worked with Cavan Board of Works till mid–1880s. Then started to compose, arrange folk music and paint; also worked as an entertainer. Mostly painted landscapes in Ireland but also worked on the continent. Exh. RHA 1891–1901. See text p. 217.

Fripp, Alfred Downing, RWS, 1822–95 *Visitor*
Grandson of Nicholas Pocock (q.v.), visited Ireland c.1844/5. *Galway Bay,* 1845 and *Clonmacnois,* 1846 are known. Illus. book on Clonmacnois 1846. Exh. RHA 1844–53. His brother George A. Fripp, 1813–96, also a watercolourist, visited Ireland with F. Goodall and F.W. Topham (qq.v.).

Frye, Thomas, 1710–62
An oil painter and mezzotint engraver who also used pastel, crayon and watercolours for portraits. Lived in England from c. 1730. Exh. London 1760–61. See text pp. 25–6.

Furniss, Harry, 1854–1925
B. Wexford, a black and white illustrator. Settled in London in 1873; contributed to principal newspapers and magazines in England and America. Joined *Punch* 1880. Later toured America, Canada and Australia. Many publ. Exh. London 1875–88. See text pp. 276–7.

G

Gabrielli, Gaspar, fl. 1805–30 *Visitor*
A Roman artist who came to Ireland with Lord Cloncurry in 1805, returning to Italy in 1819. Though mostly employed as a decorative landscape painter in Lyons House and elsewhere, Gabrielli painted landscapes in oils and watercolours and also made etchings. Few Irish watercolours are known. See text pp. 93–4.

Gandon, James, FSA, 1743–1823.
The famous architect occasionally painted watercolours in the manner of Malton. Few works are known and are of architectural interest. His son James Gandon II also used watercolours. Exh. RHA 1827–8 and 1837–8.

Gardiner, William Nelson, 1766–1814
B. Dublin, studied Dublin Society Schools 1781–4, winning a medal. Went to London and worked as a portrait painter, actor, scene painter and silhouette drawer, and engraver. After a visit to Dublin he returned to England, taking a degree at Cambridge, finally returning to painting subject pictures and portraits in oil and watercolour. In 1801, due to failing sight, he became a bookseller. Exh. London 1787–93.

Gardner, William Biscombe, 1847–1919 *Visitor*
Exh. Wicklow views in NWS, 1884 and Grosvenor Gallery 1885.

Garstin, Norman, 1847–1926
An Irish painter who settled in Newlyn, Cornwall. He painted a number of watercolours, landscape and genre though his main work is in oil. Exh. RHA 1883–1916; London 1882–93.

Garvey, Edmund, RA, d. 1813
B. Ireland. In England by 1769 when given a premium by the Society of Arts in London for landscape. Won another in 1771. Visited Italy and Switzerland, returning to Bath, and finally lived in London from 1778. Exh. London 1767–1809. Worked in watercolour and oils.

Gastineau, Henry, c. 1791–1876 *Visitor*
Exhibited Irish views from 1838, Counties Antrim, Down, Meath, Dublin and Wicklow, and, in 1844, Killarney. Exh. RHA 1838. His wife also painted.

Gaye, Howard, fl. 1877–1891
A drawing of Arklow dated 1887 is known.

Geddes, Wilhelmina Margaret, 1887–1955
Studied Belfast School of Art from 1903, and in 1910 attended Orpen's classes in the Metropolitan School, Dublin. Though famous for her stained glass she designed posters, bookjackets and illustrated books using watercolour for a large proportion of her work. Lived in London for much of her career. See text p. 235.

Gernon, Vincent (de), 1856–c. 1921
B. Dublin. Won the Taylor Scholarship 1879 and 1880. He had studied in Antwerp from 1877 and later went on to Paris, working under Carolus Duran. He travelled widely on the continent and lived for many years in America but ended his days in Dun Laoghaire. He exhibited in the RHA intermittently from 1877 to 1909.

Gethin, Percy Francis, 1875–1916.
B. Holywell, Co. Sligo. Studied in Paris and taught art in London and Liverpool. Exh. RHA 1900–17.

Gibbs, Robert, fl. 1808–16
Nothing is known certainly about this artist but he may have come from Derry, though he lived in Cork. First recorded c. 1810, painting portraits. He did numerous pen and watercolour drawings in grisaille of the Kilkenny area probably for the architect William Robertson. He worked widely in Southern Ireland and stylistically looks as though he was a pupil of G. Holmes. See text pp. 129–30.

Gibson, Emily Rachel, née Tucker, fl. 1868
Amateur, Englishwoman, m. William Gibson of Rockforest, Co. Tipperary. See text p. 211.

Gibson, Joseph Stafford, 1837–1919
From Kilmurray, Co. Cork but lived most of his life in Spain and travelled widely on the continent. See text p. 218.

Gifford, Grace, 1888–1955
A Dublin-born great niece of Sir F.W. Burton (q.v.), she trained under Orpen in the Metropolitan School of Art. Best remembered for her caricatures in pen and ink of Irish personalities which she published in three collections in 1919, 1929, and 1930. She was a committed member of Sinn Fein and took an active part in the republican movement from c. 1916–22. See text p. 285.

Gilbert, John, 1846–1915
Cork watercolour painter. Exh. RHA 1885–1915. Involved in arranging exhibitions in Cork in the 1880's and in writing.

Giles, James William, RSA, 1801–70 *Visitor*
Fine watercolours of Powerscourt House, 1857.

Gilliland, Ann Moore, née Hignett,
fl. 1892–1939
English by birth, she married into a Derry family in 1892. Her competence as a watercolourist indicates that she was a trained artist.

Gilpin, William Sawrey, 1762–1843 *Visitor*
Exhibited views of the Killarney area between 1805 and 1811. See text p. 85.

Gleeson, Evelyn, 1855–1944
Though of English birth she spent most of her career in Ireland. Educ. in London and Paris, she was a committed Suffragette, and returned to Ireland to found the Dun Emer Guild in Dundrum between 1902 and 1904. She used pastel for her portraits, and watercolours for her landscapes and still lifes.

Godfrey, Sir John Fermor, 4th Bt, 1828–1900
Amateur. Famous for his hunt at Kilcoleman Abbey, Co. Kerry, and his humorous hunting sketches.

Goff, Col. Robert Charles, 1837–1922
B. Dublin, amateur watercolourist and etcher, learning the latter technique in the early 1870s. His career in the army took him to the Crimea, Ceylon, Malta and England, returning in 1878. Subsequently he lived in London and Brighton, moving to Florence c. 1900 and finally to Switzerland c. 1914. He travelled continually and his work reflects his interest in architecture and people. See text p. 219.

Gonne, Mrs Anne, 1816–after 1853 *Visitor*
English, came to Ireland on marriage 1840 to the engraver, Henry Gonne. Worked as a flower painter and teacher.

Goodall, Frederick, RA, 1822–1904 *Visitor*
Visited Ireland with F.W. Topham (q.v.), G.A. Fripp (q.v.).

Goodall, J. Edward, fl. 1877–91 *Visitor*
Exh. NWS *A Weaver's Home, Co. Galway* in 1886.

Goodwin, Francis, 1784–1835 *Visitor*
The architect of Lissadell, Co. Sligo, who visited Ireland in 1834 in connection with this work. See text p. 144.

Graham, Henry, fl. 1768–1808
B. Ireland; studied Dublin Society Schools 1768 and later under Jonathan Fisher (q.v.), for whom he worked for years as an assistant. Painted landscapes and invented a box of watercolours, for which he won a medal from the Dublin Society in 1782. Exh. Irish Society of Arts 1777 and 1780. No works now known.

Grattan, George, 1787–1819
B. Dublin, educ. Dublin Society Schools, medal winner. Worked in watercolour and crayon, painting portraits, genre and landscape. Later work in oil, painting history pieces and genre scenes. Influenced by Morland. Exh. Dublin 1801–13; London 1812. See text pp. 135–6.

Grattan, William, c. 1792—c. 1821
Younger brother of George Grattan (q.v.), studied at Dublin Society Schools, where he won medals. Exh. in Dublin 1809–16. Met with little success and wrote a pamphlet, 1818, which he concludes by saying, "The painters of this country, owing to the great want of patronage, are obliged to desert the higher walks of the profession for whatever employment in the arts the fleeting taste of the moment may proffer." See text pp. 135–6.

Gray, Paul Mary, 1842–66
B. Dublin, took up drawing and painting fairly late, exhibiting in the RHA watercolours and oils from 1861 to 1863. He then went to London and spent a hectic three years illustrating books and magazines before his early death at the age of 24.

Green, The Revd William Spotswood,
1847–1919
B. Youghal. A mountaineer, marine and fisheries expert and amateur artist whose watercolours of his climbing expeditions to New Zealand, where he made the first ascent of Mount Cook in 1882, to Canada, and the Alps are of great interest. He also drew in Ireland. He published and illustrated several books including *The High Alps of New Zealand*, London, 1883. There is a short biography of Green in R.L. Praeger, *The Way that I Went*, Dublin and London, 1937, pp. 344–7.

Greenlees, William, fl. 1838–9
An amateur who is known to have worked in Dublin, Co. Tyrone, Armagh, Fermanagh, Cavan, Meath and Down, painting towns, villages and country houses. Exh. RHA 1860–86. See text p. 215.

Gregory, Robert, 1881–1918
Son of Lady Gregory of Coole Park. His portrait drawings in chalk are sensitive and of high quality.

Grierson, Charles McIver, 1864–1939
B. Cork, educated Plymouth and lived for many years in London, returning to Sligo by 1900. Painted watercolour literary and genre scenes, pastel and black and white. Elected RI 1892. Exh. RI 1899–1901; RHA 1886–1925.

Grogan, Nathaniel, c. 1740–1807
B. Cork. His early career was in the army and included a visit to America. He appears to have been self-taught and became a very fine artist. His sons Nathaniel and Joseph worked in his manner; their dates are unknown. Exh. London, 1782, and may have visited there. See text pp. 78–80.

Grose, Daniel Charles, c. 1760–1838
Nephew of Francis Grose (q.v.), on whose death in 1791 he took over and completed with Edward Ledwich the *Antiquities of Ireland*. He settled in Ireland, dying in Carrick-on-Shannon. See text pp. 41–3.

Grose, Capt. Francis, FSA, 1731–91 *Visitor*
A topographical draughtsman who came to Dublin shortly before his death in May 1791 to prepare the *Antiquities of Ireland* in the same manner as his earlier publications of the *Antiquities of Scotland*, etc. Exh. London 1767–77. See text pp. 40, 43.

Groves, William, fl. 1836
Employed as a Civil Assistant Sketcher in the Ordnance Survey. Began August 1836 working in the Survey section in Co. Leitrim.

Grubb, Alexander Henry Watkins, 1842–1925
A member of the Co. Tipperary family, his army career took him ultimately to New Zealand, where he lived for some years after 1863. See text p. 257.

Gubbins, Beatrice, 1878–1944
A Cork amateur artist of high quality. See text pp. 232–3.

Guinness, May, 1863–1955
B. Dublin. Family commitments prevented her studying art seriously till c. 1905–7 when she went to Paris and worked under Van Dongen, and later Lhote. She worked in both oils and watercolour. Exh. RHA 1897–1911.

Guirl, James A., fl. 1861.
B. Ireland, fought in American Civil War in Twenty-second Indiana Volunteers and provided drawings for *Harper's Weekly*. Known to be Irish as an Irishwoman in St. Louis gave him a "tin cupfull of good old rye" because of their common nationality. Catalogue of *M. and M. Karolik Collection of American Watercolours and Drawings 1800–75*, Boston, vol. II, 1962, pp. 69, 70.

H

Hackett, John B., fl. 1819
Employed as a Civil Assistant sketcher by the Ordnance Survey. Began work in 1829 in the Geological Section in Co. Derry.

Hagen, Johann Van der, see under Van der Hagen, William.

Halfpenny, Joseph S., see under Alpenny, Joseph Samuel

Halfpenny, William, see under Alpenny, William

Haliday, Charles, fl. 1806
Amateur topographical draughtsman. One work of Ardmore known, signed "Chas Haliday Dublin," 1806. See text p. 200.

Hall, George Lothian, 1825–88 *Visitor*
Painted landscape and coastal scenes. Visited Ireland 1856.

Hamerton, Robert Jacob, fl. 1830–91
An illustrator on staff of *Punch*. May have come from Longford, where he is said to have taught in a school when aged 14. In London by 1831. Exh. domestic "subjects" RHA 1844; London 1831–58. Also did watercolour landscapes and crayon portraits.

Hamilton, Caroline, née Tighe, 1777–1861
Lady amateur. Drew genre subjects, usually interiors in grisaille. Has a strong sense of ironic humour, influenced by Hogarth. Painted in England as well as Ireland. See text pp. 132–3.

Hamilton, Dacre Mervyn, 1837–99
An amateur from Cornacassa House, Co. Monaghan. See text pp. 216–17.

Hamilton, Gustavus, 1739–75
B. Ireland, educ. DSS and apprenticed to Samuel Dixon (q.v.). Became a miniaturist, but watercolour flower paintings and pastel portraits exist.

Hamilton, Henry, d. 1796
Joined British army 1754. Much of life spent in the West Indies and North America. See text pp. 241–2.

Hamilton, Hugh Douglas, 1739–1809
B. Dublin, educ. Dublin Society Schools 1756, a prize winner. Went to London 1764, where his oval pastel portraits were very popular. 1778 travelled to Italy where he lived till 1791 and earned his living mostly with pastel portraits of grand tourists. He returned to Dublin and his later work is usually in oil. Exh. London 1762–75 and Dublin 1769–71 and 1800–4. See text pp. 66–72.

Hamilton, John, fl. 1767–85.
B. Dublin, went early to England, where in 1767–77 he exhibited at the Incorporated Society of Artists, of which he became Vice President. Worked for Francis Grose (q.v.) for Grose's book *Ancient Armour and Weapons*, 1785.

Hamilton, William Osborne, fl. 1772
Known by three views of Lota, Cork, one dated 1772. See text pp. 197–9.

Hanford, Ernest, fl. 1886.
Secretary of the Belfast Ramblers Club. See text p. 275.

Hanlon, Daniel, 1819–1901
B. Cabinteely, an amateur flower and landscape

---

watercolourist who worked in an architect's office and went to London 1850, working for the London Health Authority. Painted England, Ireland and Scotland.

Harden, John, 1772–1847
B. Borrisoleigh, Co. Tipperary, an amateur painter of genre scenes and landscape. See text pp. 130–2.

Harding, Edward J., 1804–70
B. Cork, worked as a portrait painter in oils, watercolour and miniature. Exh. Cork 1852.

Harding, James Duffield, OWS, 1797–1863
Visitor
A pencil drawing of Dun Laoghaire is known, signed and dated 1810. Exh. RHA 1843, 1850 and 1860–1.

Hardwick, William Noble, NWS, 1805–65
Visitor
A pupil of Turner who lived in Bath from 1838. Exh. views of Killarney in NWS 1854–5.

Hare, St. George, RI, 1857–1933
B. Limerick, studied under N.A. Brophy and at South Kensington 1875. Work in oil, watercolour and crayon included landscapes, portraits, genre, subject pictures including oriental. Exh. RHA 1881–1916; widely in London, 1880–93 and at the NWS 1896–1904. See text pp. 263–4.

Hargitt, Edward, RI, 1835–95 *Visitor*
Scottish watercolourist. Probably visited Ireland more than once; a drawing of Enniskerry 1857 exists and he exhibited views of Killarney and Kerry NWS 1892–3. Exh. RHA 1854 and 1861–2.

Harlow, George Henry, 1787–1819 *Visitor*
A London portrait painter said to have visited Ireland in 1803.

Harrington, Elizabeth, Countess of,
c. 1819–1912
B. in Switzerland, the daughter of Robert de Pearsall; m. 1839 the seventh Earl of Harrington. An amateur who spent much of her life in Ireland and was a friend of the Duchess of Leinster (q.v.).

Harrison, Sarah Cecilia, c. 1864–1941
B. Co. Down, educated at Metropolitan School of Art, Dublin, and lived and worked in Dublin as a portrait painter mostly in oils but also in watercolours and pencil. Landscape sketches are also known. Exh. RHA 1889–1933; London 1889–92.

Hartland, Henry Albert, 1840–93
B. Mallow, studied at Cork School of Art. Went to Wales 1870 and Liverpool 1871 where he remained for most of his life, visiting London in 1887 for two years. Also lived briefly in Huddersfield and occasionally visited Ireland. Painted landscapes Ireland, Wales and England. Exh. RHA 1865, 1870 and 1878–9; London 1868–89. See text pp. 191–2.

Harvey, William Henry, 1811–66
Professional botanist who drew his own illustrations. See text p. 122.

Hassell, John, 1767–1825 *Visitor*
An engraver, writer and drawing master who painted *An extensive view of Tarbert, Co. Kerry* in 1795.

Hastings, J., 1841–2
An amateur topographical draughtsman. Sketches of the Shannon, the Shannon Estuary and Limerick exist, dated 1841/2 (NLI). Exh. RHA 1842.

Haverty, Joseph Patrick, RHA, 1794–1864
B. Galway. Most of his works are in oils. RHA 1829. Lived in Dublin, Limerick and London at various times. Exh. RHA 1826–66; London 1835–58. A watercolour of his famous *Limerick Piper* is known.

Hayes, Claude, RI, 1852–1922
B. Dublin, son of Edwin Hayes (q.v.). Landscape

---

watercolourist. His career largely spent out of Ireland which he left c. 1867. Trained RA schools and Antwerp. Elected RI 1886. Exhibited regularly in all main London exhibitions 1873–93; RHA 1874–84.

Hayes, Edward, RHA, 1797–1864
B. Co. Tipperary, studied Dublin Society Schools and under J.S. Alpenny (q.v.). Worked principally as a watercolour portrait painter and occasionally as a miniaturist. Landscapes are known in both oil and watercolours. Taught drawing when young in Clonmel, Kilkenny and Waterford. Exhibited regularly at the RHA 1830–64. See text p. 150.

Hayes, Edwin, RHA, RI, 1820–1904
B. Bristol, came to Dublin c. 1833 and trained in Dublin Society Schools. A marine painter, he worked first from a boat sailing between Dublin and Cork and later went as a steward to America and back. 1842–52 lived in Dublin. 1852 moved to London and worked as a scene painter. Exh. in BI from 1854 and RA from 1855 and in the NWS, of which he became an Associate 1860 and member 1863. 1871 made RHA. Irish subjects occur rarely after 1869. Exh. RHA 1842–1904. See text p. 185.

Hayes, Michael Angelo, RHA, 1820–77
B. Waterford, son of Edward (q.v.), who taught him. Lived and worked from time to time in England. First exhibited 1837 RHA and specialized in Horse and Military subjects, though also painted landscape and genre. Exh. with NWS 1849–56 and in 1858 and 1860. RHA 1837–76; London 1845–77. See text pp. 150–3.

Hayward, John Samuel, 1778–1822 *Visitor*
English amateur. Visited Ireland 1805, Dublin, Counties Wicklow and Kildare. See text p. 86.

Head, Sir Francis Bond, 1st Bt, 1793–1875
Visitor
Wrote and illustrated a guide book entitled *A Fortnight in Ireland*, London 1852.

Healy, Michael Joseph, 1873–1941
An Irish stained glass artist who sketched chiefly figures, in watercolour.

Healy, Robert, 1743–71
Studied Dublin Society Schools; noted for his small portraits in grisaille pastel and his genre scenes. See text pp. 62–4.

Healy, William, fl. c. 1769–74.
Younger brother of the above, studied Dublin Society Schools. Worked in his brother's manner and held an exhibition of copies after him in 1774.

Henry, Paul, RHA, 1876–1958
An Irish oil landscape painter who made numerous sketches of Irish people, scenes and landscapes. Exh. RHA 1910–59. See text pp. 277–9.

Hensley, Revd Charles, fl. 1833–9
An amateur topographical draughtsman who worked around Dublin and in Counties Waterford, Carlow, Tipperary and Kilkenny.

Herbert, James Dowling, 1762/3–1837
B. Dublin. His real name was Dowling; he adopted Herbert first as a stage name and then permanently. Educated Dublin Society Schools 1779 and then under Robert Home. Practised as a portrait painter in Dublin, Cork, Bath and London working in oil, crayon and watercolours. He wrote, acted and painted stage scenery. His small pencil and watercolour portraits are usually whole-length with elongated limbs. Exh. RHA 1835–6; London 1832–5.

Herbert, Mary, née Balfour, 1817–93
B. Whittinghame, East Lothian, Scotland. No formal training. In 1837 m. Henry Arthur Herbert of Muckross, Co. Kerry. A painter of romantic, landscape watercolours. See text p. 211.

Hickey, Thomas, c. 1741–1824
B. Dublin, educated Dublin Society Schools 1753–56, winning several prizes. His charcoal and pastel portraits date from 1758 before his trip to

Italy in 1767. Worked in Bath 1778; set out for India 1780; early 1780s Lisbon; 1784 arrived India; 1792 returned London; went on Lord Macartney's expedition; 1796 Dublin; 1798 went to Madras staying till death except for two visits to Calcutta 1807, 1812. He returned to his early pastel style in his last years. Whole-length portrait drawings and sketches of his Chinese visit exist. Exhibited Irish Society of Artists, 1768–70; RA, 1772–92. See text pp. 65–6.

Hill, Henry, fl. 1830–40
A Cork architect. See text p. 144.

Hill, Nathaniel, RHA, 1861–1934
B. Drogheda, educ. Metropolitan School of Art 1877–80 and Antwerp 1881–4, winning prizes in both schools and the Taylor Scholarship in 1883 and 1884. Worked Brittany 1883/4, England 1884/5 (North Littleton in Worcestershire), Walberswick and Rye 1885 and again later; returned to Ireland. In 1903 went to live in Herefordshire, moving later to Bettys-y-Coed in N. Wales where he lived till his death. Worked more in watercolour later in life. A charcoal portrait of Walter Osborne is in the NGI. Exh. RHA 1880–95 and Dublin Art Club; London 1886–93.

Hinchey (Hinchy), William James, 1829–93
B. Ireland, educated TCD. Involved in Fenian riots 1850 and went to Paris to study art. Finally settled in St. Louis, Missouri. Worked as a portrait painter, an altarpiece painter and a teacher. One of his portraits is in the Boston Museum of Fine Arts, Karolik Collection.

Hincks, William, fl. 1773–97
B. Waterford, apprenticed to blacksmith; self-taught. Exh. mostly portraits Dublin 1773–80 in Irish Society of Artists and elsewhere works in oils and crayons as well as miniatures. Went to London 1780, where he died sometime after 1797. Worked as an illustrator (*Tristram Shandy*) and exhibited at RA. His most famous works, twelve views of the linen industry, were engraved and published in London 1782. See text p.73.

Hoare, Sir Richard Colt, 2nd Bt., FRS, FSA, 1758–1838 *Visitor*
Amateur; his book of drawings of his Irish tour in 1807 survives in the RIA. See text p. 46.

Hodgson, Edward, FSA, 1719–94
B. Dublin, worked in London at first as a fruit and flower painter in chalk and watercolour, later also in oils. Did some academic drawings. He was Treasurer of the Associated Artists of Great Britain. Exh. London 1763–88.

Hodson, Sir George Frederick, 3rd Bt, HRHA, 1806–88
B. Bray, amateur landscape and figure painter. Apart from the Irish subjects he drew and painted much on the continent. His first visit to Italy was in 1830. He also visited Spain (1845), Austria and Germany (1855/6), Russia and Sweden (1857 and 1859), Turkey. Exh. RHA 1827–75. See text p. 206.

Hofland, Thomas Christopher, 1777–1843, *Visitor*
A painter who exhibited at the RA 1798–42 and published in 1839 *The British Angler's Manual*, which included a section on Ireland. He visited Ireland to draw the illustrations.

Hogan, Patrick Joseph, c. 1805–78
Trained in the RHA Schools but made his career in New Zealand and Australia. See text p. 255.

Holmes, George, fl. 1789–c. 1843
B. Ireland, educ. Dublin Society Schools, winning prize 1789. Topographical watercolourist. Went to London c. 1799 exhibiting RA 1799 and 1802. Usually said to have died 1804, but a drawing in Bristol is signed and dated 1809 and he may be the George Holmes who exhibited RHA 1841 and 1843, sending from a Plymouth address. See text pp. 128–32.

Holmes, Sophia, fl. 1883–93
Exhibited from Dublin addresses in London including NWS 1886–93, mostly flower paintings. Exh. RHA 1883–91.

Hone, Evie, 1894–1955
Stained glass artist who painted a number of pictures in gouache and was a descendant of the well known painter family. See text pp. 235–6.

Hone, John Camillus, d. 1836
Son of Nathaniel Hone, the eighteenth century portrait painter, and ancestor of Nathaniel the Younger. Miniaturist who advertised himself as teaching drawing and painting, *Calcutta Gazette*, 1785. See text p. 251.

Hone, Nathaniel the Younger, RHA, 1831–1917
B. Dublin, educ. as an engineer; took up painting 1853 when he went to study with A. Yvon in Paris and later with Couture. Turned to landscape c. 1856/7, living at Barbizon; later, from the mid '60s, in Fontainebleau. C.1870 spent 18 months in Italy. Returned to live in Ireland 1872. Travelled widely, Brittany and Normandy c. 1867, Holland, Turkey, Greece and Egypt 1892 and frequently to England (especially east coast) and to France. His watercolours, immediate and fresh, are among his best work. Exh. RHA 1862–1917. See text p. 259.

Hood, Robert, c. 1795–1821
Irish naval officer who painted fine watercolours of birds and sketches of arctic exploration. See text pp. 122, 245–6.

Hore, James, fl. 1829–37
A gentleman amateur first recorded in 1829 Rome and touring in Italy. There is also a drawing from Corfu. Later his topographical oils of Dublin exhibited RA 1837. See text pp. 147–8.

Howard, Hugh, 1675–1738
Chalk portraits and pen drawings are known by this portrait painter in oils. See text p. 23.

Howis, William, 1804–82
B. Co. Waterford, educ. RDS 1821 winning prizes in 1823 and 1826. Worked as a landscape painter in oils mostly in the Dublin area. Exh. RHA 1828–63. Numerous drawings in the NGI. See text p. 165.

Howis, William Jr, 1827–57
B. Dublin, educ. RDS, worked as a landscape painter, though pencil portraits are known. In 1844 obtained premium from Royal Irish Art Union for twelve etched landscapes. Exh. RHA 1846–56. Numerous drawings in the NGI. See text p. 165.

Hubard, William James, 1806–62 *Visitor*
A child prodigy, noted for his cut paper work. In Ireland in 1823–4, when he left for the US. Must have been in Ireland at a later date as William Guy Wall (q. v.) was involved with him in an exhibition in Galway sometime after 1837. See text p. 240.

Hughes, John, RHA, 1865–1941
A sculptor who occasionally made crayon portrait drawings.

Hull, Fred William, 1867–1953
B. Drogheda, a Belfast businessman who took up painting in the late 1890s, studying under George Trobridge (q.v.) and David Gould. A member Belfast Art Society 1902. Painted views near Belfast. Exh. RHA 1903–30 and Liverpool.

Hulley, H., fl. 1783–95 *Visitor*
Came to Dublin from Bath c. 1787 and is recorded in Dublin in the 1790s and in Coleraine 1789. Painted watercolour and oil landscapes.

Hume, Revd John, c. 1743–1818
Topographical painter, amateur, probably of Irish origin as he exchanged a benefice in the South of England to become Dean of Derry, 1783. See text p. 44.

Hutchins, Ellen, 1785–1815
An amateur, botanical painter.

I

Ingham, Charles Cromwell, 1796–1863
Studied Dublin Society Schools and under William Cuming, went to the US 1816. See text p. 238.

J

Jacob, Alice, 1862–1921
Trained Metropolitan School of Art, Dublin, and taught in both Dublin and Cork. She designed lace but is best remembered for her botanical drawings done at Glasnevin from 1907 to 1920.

Jellett, Mainie, 1897–1944
Studied in the Metropolitan School of Art, Dublin, under Orpen before going to London, where she worked under Sickert in the Westminster School of Art and finally to Paris where Andre Lhote and Albert Gleizes were her teachers. She often used gouache and watercolour. See text pp. 235–6.

Jervas, Charles, c. 1675–1739
B. Shinrone, Co. Offaly, educ. in Kneller's studio academy and in Rome. He lived most of his life in London, becoming Painter to George II in 1727. He used pastel and pencil as well as oils. See text p. 23.

Jobling, Joseph Middleton, ANWS, 1831–84 *Visitor*
London artist Exh. views of Galway in NWS, 1869.

Jobson, Francis, fl. c. 1600 *Visitor*
Map-maker. See text p. 14.

John, Augustus E., ARA, 1878–1961 *Visitor*
The English artist, well-known for his drawings, Augustus John visited Ireland frequently in the decade before 1916 when his famous cartoon of Galway (Tate Gallery) was painted.

Johnson, Alfred George, fl. 1842–72
B. Ireland, educ. RDS exhibiting oils and watercolours at RHA 1842–72. Worked as draughtsman in the Ordnance Survey.

Johnson, Guy, c. 1740–88
Amateur topographical draughtsman, son-in-law of Sir William Johnson (q.v.). See text p. 273.

Johnson, H.V., twentieth century
Three drawings dated 1904 and 1905, connected with the founding of the Municpal Gallery by Hugh Lane, exist in the NGI.

Johnson, Sir William, 1st Bt., 1715–74
Amateur topographical draughtsman. See text p. 237.

Johnston, Henrietta Dering, see under Dering.

Jones, Capt Edward, fl. 1836–49
Travelled extensively in Ireland painting topographical views in Counties Limerick, Wicklow, Dublin and Donegal. Most works dated 1836, but one 1849. Worked for the *Dublin Penny Journal*.

Jones, George Robert, 1786–1869 *Visitor*
A London born painter. Visited Ireland between 1800 and 1810, making drawings in Counties Kerry, Cork, and Dublin.

Jones, Revd Richard Calvert, 1804–77 *Visitor*
Painted in Counties Cork, Tipperary, Kerry and Dublin. See text pp. 206–7.

Jones, Sir Thomas Alfred, PRHA, c. 1823–93
B. Dublin, educ. RDS 1833 and attended TCD 1842. Then travelled in Europe 1846–9. A portrait painter in oils who began his career working in watercolours and pastel, painting subjects and portraits. PRHA 1869. Exh. RHA 1841–93; London 1872–9. See text p. 185.

Jones, William, fl. 1699 *Visitor*
Probably a visitor. Worked as assistant to Edward Lhuyd. See text p. 33.

Joy, Arthur, c. 1808–52
B. Dublin, studied Dublin Society Schools. RHA 1837, in which year he went to London. Exh. RHA 1830–52; London 1838.

K

Kane, Paul, 1810–71
B. Mallow, went to Toronto c. 1819. Studied art with Fr. Drury. Travelled to Europe in 1841, visiting France and England. Returned to the US 1843; toured Canada 1845–9. See text p. 243.

Keane, Harriet Edith, d. 1920
With her sister, Frances Annie, d. 1917, she was one of the foundresses of the Irish Amateur Drawing Society which became the Watercolour Society of Ireland. Both sisters, daughters of Sir John Keane, third Bart., lived at Glensheelin near Cappoquin. See text p. 221.

Kelly, Elizabeth, née Tighe, late eighteenth and early nineteenth century
Amateur watercolourist. Sister of Caroline Hamilton (q.v.). See text pp. 133–4.

Kemp, John, 1833–1923
Studied at the Cork School of Art and then at the RA before making his career in Gloucester. Exh. London 1870–89. See text p. 189.

Kendrick, Matthew, RHA, c. 1797–1874
B. Dublin, started life as a seaman only studying in the Dublin Society Schools 1825, becoming a marine painter. RHA 1850. Between 1840 and 1848 lived and exhibited in London. He painted usually in oils but watercolours are known. Exh. RHA 1827–71.

Ker, Sophia, early nineteenth century
Amateur watercolourist member of the Ker family of Co. Down; granddaughter of Francesco Guardi.

Kerr, Lord Mark Robert, RN, 1776–1840
M. 1799 Charlotte, Countess of Antrim in her own right. A naval officer who illustrated his log books. See text p. 208.

Kilburn, William, 1745–1818
Botanical illustrator and designer of fabrics. See text pp. 111–12.

King, B., fl. 1812
Pencil landscape draughtsman. Worked Co. Dublin.

King, Capt John Duncan, 1789–1863
B. Ireland; entered army 1806. He took up watercolour painting while in the army. Studied under Lawrence and Horace Vernet. Painted landscapes in many places in Ireland and on the continent in Spain, France, Portugal, Switzerland and Germany. In 1852 appointed a military Knight in Windsor, where he later died. Exh. RHA 1828; London 1824–58.

Kirchhoffer, Henry, 1781–1860
B. Dublin, educ. Dublin Society Schools, 1797. Worked as painter in Cork and was on committee of Cork exhibition 1816, in which year he returned to Dublin. There he exhibited, becoming a founder RHA 1826. Went to London 1835; at one time lived in Brighton. Visited Edinburgh. Painted watercolour portraits and miniatures, small lengths, landscapes, figure subjects, animals and flower pieces. Occasionally worked in oils. Exh. RHA 1826–34; London 1837–43. See text p. 94.

Kirwan, William Bourke, c. 1814– after 1852.
B. Dublin, pupil of R.D. Bowyer. Exhibited miniatures and genre scenes in watercolour in RHA 1835–46. Worked for engravers as a medical draughtsman and a restorer. Tried for murder of his wife 1852, sentenced to transportation for life and said to have died in America.

Knapton, Lady, née Brownlow, mid-eighteenth century
Amateur watercolourist. See text pp. 27–8.

Knight, John Baverstock, 1785–1859 *Visitor*
Visited Co. Antrim coast and drew in Cushendun. His Irish works are not dated. See text p. 97.

Kniveton, William, fl. 1802–20
Landscape painter exhibited Dublin 1802 and 1804 watercolour views of Killarney and Donegal.

L

Lansdowne, Louisa, Marchioness of, née Fox-Strangways, m. 1808–d. 1851 *Visitor*
Amateur. Visited Ireland on several occasions; sketched in many counties including Kerry, Waterford and Down 1809, 1817 and 1823.

Laporte, George Henry, NWS, 1799–1873 *Visitor*
Son of John Laporte (q.v.). Exhibited a history piece of *William III at the Battle of the Boyne* in the NWS in 1865; exh. London 1821–73.

Laporte, John, 1761–1839 *Visitor*
A pupil of J.M. Barralet (q.v.); exhibited watercolours of Killarney and Kerry in the NWS 1833–4. Exh. London 1779–1835. See text p. 53.

Latham, Oliver Matthew, fl. 1844–60
An amateur; studied Dublin Society Schools and then entered the army, from which he retired in 1860. He worked in watercolour, exhibiting RHA 1849. His work is mostly landscapes but he drew incidents in the Crimean War in which he served. Strickland gives his death date as 1860, but it may have been a little later.

La Touche, Maryanne, c. 1810–70
An amateur, fifth daughter of Col. David La Touche of Marley. She died unmarried. Drew a remarkable series of interiors of various La Touche houses including Bellevue and Marley executed in the early 1840s. See text p. 204.

Lawless, Matthew James, 1837–64
B. Dublin; educ. at the Langham school, London. Apart from his numerous oil paintings of historical and genre subjects, he was a prolific illustrator of books and magazines. He painted a number of watercolours. Exh. London 1857–63.

Lawrence, George, c. 1758–1802
Painter of miniatures and small oval watercolour portraits in the manner of Hugh Douglas Hamilton.

Lecky, Susan, 1837–96
A landscape and botanical painter who lived in Co. Kerry. See text pp. 217–18.

Leech, John, 1817–64 *Visitor*
Well-known English illustrator especially of the hunting field. Illustrated Samuel Hole's *A Little Tour in Ireland*, 1859, and visited Ireland to make his illustrations.

Leech, William John, RHA, 1881–1968
An oil painter who also used watercolour frequently. Exh. RHA 1899–1969. See text p. 283.

Leinster, Charlotte Augusta, Duchess of, 1793–1859
Daughter of the third Earl of Harrington. Amateur painter of genre and landscape who encouraged a group of artistic ladies at Carton.

Lemercier, Harriet and Marguerite, see under Osborne O'Hagan, Harriet

Lennox, E.J., nineteenth century *Visitor*
An English artist who painted a view in Co. Clare in 1856.

Lens, Peter Paul, first half eighteenth century *Visitor*
Visited Dublin c. 1737. Though a miniaturist, he is likely, like other members of his family, to have drawn watercolour landscapes.

Leslie, Sir John, 1st Bt., 1822–1916
Amateur painter. Studied in the Dusseldorf

Academy in 1856 and under Richard Buckner in Rome. Landscape and genre watercolours survive. See text pp. 212–13.

Levinge, Sir Richard George Augustus, 7th Bt, 1811–84
Amateur, exh. RHA 1871–2. During his army career painted much in Canada and US. See text pp. 246–8.

Ligar, Charles W., fl. 1829
Employed as a Civil Assistant sketcher by the Ordnance Survey. Began work in 1829 Hill Drawing in Counties Antrim and Derry.

Locke, J., fl. 1837–40
Drew coastal scenes in the West of Ireland and Kerry.

Loftie, James, fl. 1855.
A genre drawing by this otherwise unknown artist is in the NGI.

Lover, Samuel, RHA, 1797–1868
B. Dublin, largely self-taught. Exhibiting in Dublin from 1817 and at the RHA from 1826. Became RHA 1829. He worked much of his time in London, exhibiting at the RA from 1832. A miniaturist, musician, novelist, illustrator and theatrical entertainer. Visited America 1846–8. His watercolours include portraits, landscapes, and town views. See text pp. 155–6.

Low, William, fl. 1840–62
Miniaturist and flower painter; worked in Dublin and Belfast.

Lumley, Arthur, 1837–1912
B. Dublin, where he had his early education. Went to New York c. 1857 and studied in the National Academy of Design. During the American Civil War became an artist correspondent for many magazines and continued as an illustrator after the war. A founder member in 1876 of the American Society of Painters in Watercolours. *Catalogue of the M. and M. Karolik Collection of American Watercolours and Drawings 1800–1875*. Boston Museum of Fine Arts, 1962, Vol. I, p. 223, and Vol. II, p. 76.

Luttrell (Lutterell), Edward, c. 1650–1710
Crayon painter and mezzotint engraver. It is now thought not to be a member of the Irish family of Luttrell and may never have worked here. His crayon portraits are done on paper but sometimes on a roughened copper plate. See text p. 26.

M

McC., Alicia, E., fl. 1829–39
Amateur, painted views of houses and villages in Co. Down and Co. Wicklow between 1829 and 1839.

McCloy, Mrs E.L., née Harris, fl. 1853, still alive in 1913.
B. Waterford, married Samuel McCloy (q.v.) and worked as a portrait artist especially of children, in oil and watercolour.

McCloy, Samuel, 1831–1904
B. Lisburn, studied in the School of Design, Belfast and worked for a firm of engravers before going to study in the Central School, London. About 1853 he was appointed Master of the Waterford School of Art, returning to Belfast about 1874; finally went to live in London in 1881. Though he painted in oils, exhibiting RHA 1862–82 and London 1859–91, his best work is in watercolour. These vary from portraits and landscapes to genre scenes and *trompe l'œil* still lifes. See text pp. 122, 188.

McConnell, William, 1833–67
An Irishman and self-taught draughtsman whose illustrations and cartoons appeared in *Punch* (from 1852), the *Illustrated Times, London Society* and numerous children's books published by Routledge in the 1860s.

McDermott, ?, fl. 1753
One of the imitators of Samuel Dixon (q.v.). See text p. 111.

McDonald, Daniel, 1821–53
B. Cork, son of an artist (James McDaniel, exh. RHA 1832), noted early for his pen and ink portraits and caricatures and published illustrations at the age of 13 in 1833. A sketch, c. 1847, of a famine picture by him survives. This, entitled *An Irish Peasant Family discovering the Blight of their Store*, was exhibited in the British Institution in 1847. Exh. RHA 1842–4 and in London, where he had gone to live in 1845 and where he showed portrait drawings.

McGann, James, fl. 1832
Employed as a Civil Assistant Sketcher by the Ordnance Survey. Began work in October 1832 as a "Hill Drawer."

McGoogan, Archie, fl. 1888–1929
A landscape watercolourist and oil painter working in the Dublin area. He was a member of the Dublin Sketching Club. Exh. RHA 1888–1929.

McGuinness, Bingham, RHA, fl. 1866–d. 1928
B. probably Dublin. He became President of the Dublin Sketching Club. He made regular visits to the continent, including the Netherlands, Germany, Italy, Switzerland and France. He also travelled widely in the British Isles and towards the end of his life had an address in London as well as Dublin. He was known for his one-man shows in London and Dublin. Exh. RHA 1866–1926; London 1882–92. See text pp. 267–8.

Machell, Christopher, 1747–1827 *Visitor*
Amateur, army officer, Lt-Col 15th regiment of Foot. He seems to have spent an extended visit or several visits in the east of Ireland painting watercolours from the Giant's Causeway to Co. Wicklow, though most are of the Dublin area. They date in the following years: 1784–5, 1787 and 1789 and 1804. See text p. 97.

McKenzie, Charles, fl. 1769–1801
Educ. Dublin Society Schools, 1769. Painted landscapes in oil and watercolour. Exh. at Parliament House, Dublin, 1801.

McKewan, David Hall, NWS, 1817–73 *Visitor*
Exh. views in NWS of Co. Down 1864–6, 1868–73.

Maclise, Daniel, RHA, RA, 1806–70
B. Cork, known primarily as an oil painter but worked in pencil and watercolour throughout his career. See text pp. 175–7.

Maclise, Joseph, c. 1815–80
Younger brother of Daniel Maclise (q.v.), trained as a surgeon and published and illustrated in 1851 *Surgical Anatomy* as well as illustrating Richard Quain's *The Anatomy of the Arteries of the Human Body*, 1844. His works are illustrated in *The Anatomy Lesson: Art and Medicine*, catalogue of an exhibition held in the NGI (1992), pp. 72–7.

MacManus, Henry M., RHA, 1810–1878
May have come from Monaghan, where he was living in 1835. He was in London from 1837 to 1844, and from 1845 till 1849 was Headmaster of the Glasgow School of Design. In 1849 till his retirement in 1863 he was Headmaster of the School of Design formed by the government out of the old Dublin Society Schools. He was a member from 1836 of the Belfast Association of Artists. Though much of his work was in oil, he painted watercolour portraits early in his career and topographical views. Exh. RHA 1835–77; London 1839–43. See text p. 164.

McTaggart, William, RSA, RSW, 1835–1910 *Visitor*
Scottish visitor to Dublin 1852–59 during his holidays. Exh. RHA 1854–1901.

Maguire, Joseph Neale, fl. 1752
A draughtsman engaged in heraldry which often included lively depictions of musicians in the borders.

Mahoney, James, ARHA, 1810–79
B. Cork, studied in Rome and travelled in Italy and France before 1842. After 1846 on the continent including Spain. In Ireland 1842–6 and 1853–9, when he settled in London. His watercolours vary from landscape and townscape to subject pictures and illustrations. Exh. RHA 1842–59; RA 1866–78 and NWS, of which he became an associate in 1867. He is well known for his illustrations of the famine which appeared in the *Illustrated London News*. His later work as an illustrator of magazines and of books has become confused by the similar work and similar signature used by his younger namesake listed below. See text pp. 185–8.

Mahony, James, 1847–79
A self-taught Cork boy who was assisted by the engraver Edward Whymper and later illustrated magazines and books in London. As he used a very similar signature to the above, it has not yet proved possible to disentangle their work. See text pp. 187–8.

Maisey, Thomas, 1787–1840 *Visitor*
English visitor. Exh. views in NWS of Dromana, Co. Waterford and the surrounding district in 1832, 1836 and 1838.

Malton, James, c. 1766–1803 *Visitor*
Came to Dublin with his father, Thomas (q.v.) in 1785, leaving in 1791. Produced the finest topographical views of Dublin ever made in watercolour and gouache which were published as engravings between 1792 and 1799. He exhibited views of Dublin in the RA 1790–1800. Other drawings include two of Irish country houses (V&A). See text pp. 97–8.

Malton, Thomas, 1726–1808 *Visitor*
Arrived in Dublin, in 1785 where he taught perspective and stayed until his death. A few drawings by him of Ireland are known. He was the father of James Malton (q.v.).

Mannin, James, d. 1779 *Visitor*
A French or Italian visitor who made his career in Ireland. Painted landscapes and flower pieces and designed the President's Chair for the Dublin Society. Exh. Irish Society of Artists, 1765–73. It is impossible to judge how many of these works were in watercolour. He was a master in the Dublin Society Schools. See text p. 49.

Manning, May d. 1930
B. Dublin, studied in Paris and ran an important school in Dublin where artists like Swanzy (q.v.) and Jellett (q.v.) were pupils.

Markievicz, Constance, née Gore-Booth, 1868–1927
Studied at the Slade School and later at the Académie Julian in Paris. Her charcoal portraits show soft modelling and a blurred outline.

Marshall, fl. 1745
A topographical view of Howth, dated Oct. 1745, is known. See text p. 196.

Martin, C., fl. 1844 *Visitor*
A portrait of Lady Morgan, 1844, is now in the BM.

Mathew, C.H., fl. 1820–30
A view of Thomastown exists and the artist was probably an amateur and a member of the famous family of Mathew who lived in Thomastown and were descended from the step-brother of the first Duke of Ormond and included the great Father Mathew.

May, Capt. Walter M., 1831–96 *Visitor*
English amateur, exhibiting a view of Co. Donegal in NWS 1890.

Mecham, George Frederick, 1828–58
Cork-born, he joined the navy and painted in various parts of the world including the Arctic. See text p. 246.

Melville, Harden Sidney, fl. 1847–81 *Visitor*
English visitor; a drawing of the Father Mathew memorial in Cork, dated 1863, exists in the BM.

Miller, George B., fl. 1815–19 *Visitor*
An Englishman. Taught by Barker of Bath but lived in Ireland (Kilkenny 1815, Dublin 1817–19) for some years. He taught and exhibited in Dublin 1815, 1817 and 1819. See text pp. 145–6.

Miller, Philip Homan, fl. 1880–1928
Lived much of his life in London; travelled in US and elsewhere. Worked in oils and watercolours. Exh. RHA a wide variety of subjects including landscapes, portraits and subject pictures.

Miller, William, fl. 1751–d. 1779
Lived in Lurgan, Co. Armagh. A naïve amateur, who painted flowers and portraits in glass and a famous work of Whitefield preaching in Lurgan. See text p. 197.

Milliken, Richard Alfred, 1767–1815
Amateur, a lawyer who was involved with the arts in Cork and also founded with his sister *The Casket or Hesperian Magazine*, 1797–8. He painted watercolours taking lessons from Francis Nicholson and an exhibition of twenty-two of his pictures was held in Cork in 1816.

Mitchell, Philip, 1814–96 *Visitor*
Exh. views of Donegal 1884–5 at the RI.

Mitchell, Thomas, mid-eighteenth century *Visitor*
A watercolour, *View near the Boyne*, has recently been on the art market. Went to Killarney with Berkeley in 1750.

Mitford, John Guise, 1822–54
B. Clontarf, settled in New Zealand 1841. See text pp. 256–7.

Molloy, Joseph, 1798–1877
B. Belfast, where he taught from 1830 to 70. A topographical watercolourist of houses and villages, he also painted sea pieces and travelled to the South of England.

Monsell, Diana, mid-nineteenth century
Flower painter. An album by her is in the NGI. It dates before 1885.

Montgomery, Lady Charlotte, d. 1906 *Visitor*
D. of the second Earl of Powis, m. 1846 Hugh Montgomery of Grey Abbey, taught by Peter de Wint and painted views of Co. Down and Strangford Lough.

Moore, Revd Charles, late eighteenth century
Amateur topographer, father of Sir John Moore of Corunna fame. Two drawings by him are included in Daniel Grose's *Antiquities*. See text p. 43.

Moore, James, HRHA, 1819–83
B. Belfast, amateur watercolourist who was educated as a doctor in Edinburgh and practised medicine throughout his career. He drew from student days; studied under Andrew Nicholl (q.v.). Exh. RHA 1840–83. See text pp. 169–70.

Morrison, William Vitruvius, 1794–1838
An architect who was a fine watercolourist. See text p. 144.

Morrow, Albert George, 1863–1927; **George,** 1870–1955; **Norman,** 1879–1917; **Edwin A.,** fl 1903–9; **Jack,** fl. 1912–after 1925.
Five of the eight sons of George Morrow of Co. Down. Mostly worked as black and white illustrators for magazines, George being famous for his *Punch* contributions. See text p. 276.

Moynan, Richard Thomas, RHA, 1856–1906
Educ. RDS, RHA schools and Paris. His watercolours are mostly sketches for oils but include a number of portraits and some landscapes. Exh. RHA 1880–1903.

Mulcahy, Jeremiah Hodges, RHA, 1804–89
B. Limerick, best known as an oil painter, but made many pen and wash and watercolour drawings, usually of landscapes in Ireland. Exh. RHA 1843–78; London 1852. A large collection of his drawings are in the NGI. See text pp. 170–1.

Mulligan, William A., d. 1919
Headmaster of the Crawford Municipal School of Art, Cork; probably appointed in 1890 after J. Brenan, the previous Headmaster, left for Dublin. Given the subject matter of his early exhibits at the RHA, he may have been living in Yorkshire; and given the prices, a number of them, if not all, were watercolours. Exh. RHA, 1890–1916.

Mulready, William, RA, 1786–1863
B. Ennis, but went to London with his family at the age of five. Best-known as an oil painter but his drawings, mostly figures and genre scenes, are of high quality. He also made pastel landscape studies. Exh. RHA 1852.

Mulrenin, Bernard, 1803–68
From Co. Sligo. He worked mostly as a miniaturist, but a charcoal and wash portrait and another in ink are owned by the NGI.

Mulvany, George Francis, RHA, 1809–65
B. Dublin, son of the artist Thomas James Mulvany (q.v.). Educ. at the RHA schools and became keeper of the RHA 1845 and founder Director of the NGI in 1862. Though principally an oil painter he made many small chalk or pencil and watercolour portraits, exhibiting them in the RHA 1827–68. Exh. London 1836–39.

Mulvany, John George, RHA, c. 1766–1838
Elder brother of Thomas James Mulvany (q.v.). Studied Dublin Society Schools, winning medals 1782 and 1786. Taught most of his life and exhibited landscape and genre scenes, some in watercolour.

Mulvany, Patrick, fl. 1796
Two signed watercolours of Downpatrick Cathedral are known, dated 1796(BM). They are in the Malton manner.

Mulvany, Thomas James, RHA, 1779–1845
A painter whom Strickland considers a good draughtsman. Noted for his articles on Irish artists in the *Citizen*, and for his editorship of *The Life Of James Gandon*.

Murphy, Dennis Brownell, c. 1755–1842
B. Dublin, studied Dublin Society Schools and became a prominent miniaturist in England, which he visited on serval occasions before settling there in 1798. He is known to have painted landscape watercolours when he visited the Lake District with John Harden (q.v.) in 1798, though these are now lost.

Murphy, James Cavanah, 1760–1814
Educ. Dublin Society Schools 1775. An architectural draughtsman best known for *Plans, Elevations, . . . of the church of Batalha*, 1795. He also contributed to Grose's *Antiquities*, 1791. Other topographical views are known. See text pp. 39–40.

Murphy, John Ross, 1827–92
Spent his early life as a sailor though always painted. Took lessons from Clarkson Stanfield and others, and painted with Edwin Hayes (q.v.) and John Faulkner (q.v.) Most of his works are sea pieces and coastal scenes around Ireland, though he also visited Killarney and Scotland. Exh. RHA 1873–84.

Murphy, Samuel J., late nineteenth century
Watercolourist based at the School of Art, Waterford. Exh. RHA 1883–4.

N

Naftel, Paul Jacob, 1817–91 *Visitor*
Visited Ireland probably about 1860–1. Teacher of Rose Barton (q.v.) and Mildred Anne Butler (q.v.).

Nairn, Cecilia Margaret, née Campbell, 1791–1857
B. Dublin, daughter of John Henry Campbell (q.v.), wife of George Nairn, the horse painter. Taught by her father, she exhibited landscapes

working in both oil and watercolour. Exh. at Dublin 1809 and 1821; RHA 1826–47, principally views of Killarney and Wicklow. She died in England.

Nattes, John Claude, 1765–1822
Possibly Irish by birth, taught by H.P. Dean (q.v.) and became a founder member of the OWS in 1804. Painted in Ireland certainly in 1801, 1807 and 1811, when he was in Gosford, Co. Armagh. Most of his other landscapes are of places in or near Dublin, though he also visited Counties Carlow, Down, Louth, and Kerry. Published several books and painted in France. Exh. RA 1781–1814. See text pp. 80–1.

Nesfield, William Andrews, 1793–1881 *Visitor*
An army officer who, on his retirement, became a landcape painter. He was in Ireland on several occasions exhibiting views of Co. Cork and of Killarney from 1841, and in 1850 a view of the Giant's Causeway.

Newell, Revd Robert Hassell, 1778–1852
An amateur, known to have worked in Counties Wicklow, Limerick, Monaghan, Roscommon, Carlow and Laois, painting landscapes.

Newenham, Robert O'Callaghan, 1770–1849
B. Dublin, amateur landscape topographical draughtsman. Painted all over Ireland during his tours as Supt. Gen. of Barracks in Ireland. From 1826 his works were engraved and appeared in numbers but were all finally published in two volumes in 1830 as *Picturesque Views of the Antiquities of Ireland . . .* A founder in 1816 of The Cork Society for Promoting the Fine Arts.

Newman, J.E., fl. 1846–51
Lived in Dublin. His only known works are carefully detailed drawings of interiors treated as still life (Fogg Art Museum, Cambridge, Mass.). See text pp. 122–4.

Newton, Anne Henrietta, d. 1927
One of the founders of the Irish Amateur Drawing Society, later The Watercolour Society of Ireland. M. 1871 William M. Veseym. Two sisters, Adeline Sarah, m. 1876 Arthur Gordon, d. 1879, and Maria Charlotte Augusta, d. 1888 (appears to have been called Emily), also painted.

Newton, Henry, fl. 1844–56 *Visitor*
Settled in Dublin and exhibited RHA 1847–56. Apart from views near Dublin he painted in the Glens of Antrim. See text p. 185.

Nicholl, Andrew, RHA, 1804–86
B. Belfast, brother of William (q.v.) who encouraged him to draw and paint from childhood. Apprenticed to a Belfast printer 1822–9. Famous for his landscapes and flower pieces. Made illustrations, mostly of antiquities, for the *Dublin Penny Journal* and later worked for Hall's *Ireland*. He taught drawing in Dublin. Exh. RA 1849 onwards, RHA 1832–86. See text pp. 166–9.

Nicholl, William, 1794–1840
B. Belfast, brother of Andrew (q.v.). Amateur landscape watercolourist and founder member of the Belfast Association of Artists, 1836. Exh. RHA 1832–5.

Nicholson, Alfred, 1788–1833 *Visitor*
Son of Francis (q.v.), lived in Ireland 1813–17 and visited again in 1821. See text p. 95.

Nicholson, Francis, 1753–1844 *Visitor*
An English watercolourist who painted a number of Irish views in the early nineteenth century. Almost certainly in Ireland in 1821 and at other earlier dates. See text pp. 94–5.

Nicol, Erskine, 1825–1904 *Visitor*
Scottish visitor, better known as an oil painter of genre scenes, but also painted watercolour portraits, genre subjects and landscapes. He visited Ireland 1846–50 working for the Science and Art Dept. and returned on regular visits afterwards. See text p. 178.

Nixon, John, c. 1750–1818 *Visitor*
The son of Robert Nixon, who traded with Ireland and had property in Scotland. An amateur who was certainly in Ireland 1783, 1785, 1790, 1791 and 1798, for which there are dated drawings. He covered a wide range of places, from Derry to the Causeway, Belturbet and Blarney Castle, as well as the usual southern views including Dublin, Wicklow, Cork and Carlow. He contributed to Grose's *Antiquities*. At one time he was Secretary of the Beef Steak Club in London. See text p. 77.

Noblett, Henry John, 1812–after 1844
B. Cork, landscape painter in oil and watercolour, lived in London 1831–5, exhibiting London 1832–5, and he was a member of the NWS. Most of his exhibits were views of Killarney. He returned to Cork in 1835, worked for Hall's *Ireland* 1841 and exhibited RHA 1844. His death date is unknown. He used his second name, John.

Noel, Amelia, fl. 1795–1804 *Visitor*
English watercolourist who visited Dublin in 1810 and exhibited with the Soc. of Artists in Hawkins Street.

Noel, Louisa, fl. 1807–63
B. London, daughter of Amelia Noel (q.v.). M. c. 1807 John Ball of Dublin, exhibited landscapes and portraits in Dublin 1809–11. She taught oils, watercolours and crayons. Widowed in 1810 she left Ireland briefly c. 1812, returning to Co. Limerick on marriage to Michael Furnell of Cahirelly Castle, Co. Limerick.

Nugent, Frances, fl. 1905
Amateur watercolourist known by one watercolour of a group of painters working at Castleconnell on the Shannon, dated 9th-16th Sept. 1905. See text p. 312.

O

O'Brien, George, 1821–88
B. Co. Clare, settled in New Zealand. See text pp. 255–6.

O'Brien, James George, called Oben, fl. 1779–after 1819
B. Dublin, studied Dublin Society Schools, winning medal for landscape 1779. Exh. Soc. of Artists 1780 and contributed to Grose's *Antiquities*. Lived in London for a few years from 1798 but exh. in Dublin 1801 as Oben. He left Ireland 1809 and exh. RA, Irish views, Kilkenny and Wicklow and around Dublin 1810–16. His death date is not known. See text pp. 91–3.

O'Connor, James Arthur, 1792–1841
B. Dublin, possibly attended the Dublin Society Schools. Better known as an oil painter of landscapes but made drawings and watercolours on sketching tours which are the basis of his oils. Exh. RHA 1830–43; London 1822–40. See text p. 157.

O'Connor, John, ARHA, 1830–89
B. Co. Derry, best known as a scene painter but also exh. oils and watercolours, mostly topographical or architectural scenes. He left Ireland in 1848 after working in Belfast and Dublin theatres and touring companies and at one time, 1845–8, made silhouettes. He returned in 1849 to make a diorama of Queen Victoria's visit and later made many drawings of ceremonial occasions. Exh. RA from 1853 and RHA from 1875. His watercolours, which include interiors as well as landscapes, are detailed and of high quality.

O'Conor, Roderic, 1860–1940
B. Co. Roscommon, educ. Dublin, Antwerp and Paris. Worked most of his career in Paris but frequently visited Brittany. Better known as an oil painter but his watercolours and chalk drawings show the same strength of brushstrokes and marked feeling for pattern. They are usually in monochrome. See text pp. 262–3.

O'Hara, Helen, fl. 1881–1919
B. Northern Ireland, probably Portstewart. She was living in Belfast in 1897 but moved in 1898 to Fanny Currey's (q.v.) house in Lismore. Exh. RHA 1881–92, in Belfast Art Societies and in Watercolour Societies in Ireland and England. See text pp. 221–2.

O'Hea, John Fergus, 1850–1922
A cartoonist, in black and white and colour, who worked for Dublin magazines.

O'Keeffe, Daniel, 1740–87
B. Dublin, studied Dublin Society Schools, winning several prizes. Worked for Samuel Dixon (q.v.); was in London by 1762 painting miniatures. Exh. London 1769–86. He also painted flower pieces in watercolour. See text p. 111.

O'Keeffe, John, 1747–1833
B. Dublin, brother of Daniel (q.v.). Studied Dublin Society Schools, winning a prize 1764. In 1767 exh. watercolours of birds and flowers at Irish Society of Artists. Later he worked as an actor and playwright but continued to paint and draw landscapes when on tour, and some portrait watercolours. His eyesight began to fade in 1779 and he went blind in 1797. See text pp. 62,125.

O'Kelly, Aloysius, 1850–1928
B. Dublin, educ. Metropolitan School of Art and later École des Beaux-Arts Paris; c. 1875 visited Brittany. Lived in London 1876–92, working on the staff of the *Illustrated London News*. Exh. oils and watercolours including 3 in the NWS in 1894. He is best-known for *plein air* and figure subjects though he also painted oriental scenes (including watercolour). Exh. RHA 1878–95. He went to America before 1909 where he exh. and became a member of the New York Watercolor Club.

Oliver, Richard Aldworth, 1811–89
Came from Co. Limerick. His work as a Surveyor took him to the Pacific. See text p. 257.

O'Meara, Frank, 1853–88
B. Co. Carlow. Studied under Carolus Duran 1873, later living at Grez and associating with Barbizon painters. Exh. RHA 1879. See text pp. 259, 261–2.

O'Neal, Jeffrey Hamet, fl. c. 1763–72
Of Irish birth but lived in London, where he worked as a japanner and also as a miniaturist, and painted landscapes and conversation pieces rather in the manner of Nixon (q.v.). Exh. Society of Artists, London 1765–6 and 1772. See text p. 62.

O'Neill, Henry, ARHA, 1798–1880
B. Clonmel, studied Dublin Society Schools, winning several prizes. Apart from a brief stay in London 1847, he lived in Dublin. Exh. RHA from 1837. See text pp. 165–6.

Orpen, Richard Caulfield, RHA, RA, 1863–1938
Brother of William Orpen (q.v.). Worked as a solicitor and architect. In his youth did some illustrations for Dublin magazines. Watercolour landscapes and a few portraits were his chief work. Exh. RHA 1888–1938.

Orpen, William, RHA, ARA, 1878–1931
B. Dublin, educ. Metropolitan School of Art and the Slade School, London. Though best-known as an oil painter of portraits, Orpen was a superb draughtsman. Mainly used black and red chalk or ink on paper, though often also watercolour. These were frequently finished works and not just sketches. Exh. 1901–33. See text pp. 280–3.

Osborne, Catherine Isabella, d. 1880
B. Newtown Anner: d. of Sir Thomas Osborne, 9th Bt, m. 1844 Ralph Bernal. Amateur who sketched in England and Ireland. Mother of Edith Osborne (q.v.). See text p. 211.

Osborne, Edith, Lady Blake, 1845–1926
B. Newtown Anner, amateur watercolourist, mostly scenes from local life, and famous for her flower painting done travelling with her husband, who was in the colonial service. See text pp. 119–21.

Osborne, Walter, RHA, 1859–1903
B. Dublin, educ. Metropolitan School of Art, Dublin, and Antwerp. Best known as a portrait and landscape painter in oil. Most of his watercolour and chalk drawings are studies but he exhibited some at the RHA 1877–1904 and was a member of the Dublin Sketching Club. See text pp. 259–61.

Osborne O'Hagan, Harriet, 1830–1921 *Visitor*
B. Dublin. Pupil of George Sharp and on his advice went to Paris c. 1866, where she studied under several artists, including Couture, probably in the 1870s. She was a teacher herself and worked in both oil and charcoal. Most of her work is portraiture but she also painted landscapes. Her daughter, Marguerite Lemercier O'Hagan, 1859–after 1925, was also an artist and used pastel and charcoal for her landscapes and portraits. See text p. 234.

Ouseley, W., fl. 1790
Views of antiquities in Counties Longford, Mayo and Galway.

P

Pack, Christopher Faithful, 1750–1840 *Visitor*
Came to Ireland in 1787, recommended by Reynolds to the Lord Lieutenant, Duke of Rutland, as a portrait painter. Returned to London in 1796. He came back to Dublin in 1802 becoming a drawing master and Pres. of the Dublin Soc. of Art 1812 and Vice Pres. of the Hibernian Soc. of Artists 1814. On March 21 1821 he sold his collection of pictures, including many of his own works, and finally returned to London. Though he always worked as a portraitist in oils from his first visit, he travelled extensively in Ireland from Kerry to the Giant's Causeway and in Connemara, making careful topographical watercolours which he exhibited both in Dublin and in London.

Pain, George Richard, 1793–1838
English Architect who made his career in Ireland, brother of James (c. 1777–1877). See text p. 106.

Pakenham, George Edward, 1717–68
Amateur; brother of the first Lord Longford, he became a Hamburg merchant. See text p. 195.

Parker, Richard Dunscombe, c. 1805–81
B. Cork, a naturalist famous for his bird paintings. See text pp. 117–18.

Parkinson, Christopher, fl. 1797
Probably Irish, known only by a watercolour dated 1797 after a Barralet engraving of a Military Parade on Leinster Lawn.

Parris, Edmund Thomas, 1793–1873 *Visitor*
Certainly in Ireland 1833 and 1847, staying in Johnstown Castle, Co. Wexford. He made landscape watercolours and studies of peasants as well as decorating interiors of the house.

Pars, William, 1742–82 *Visitor*
Made an extensive tour of Ireland with Lord Palmerston in 1771 visiting Co. Carlow, Killarney and Co. Sligo. His watercolours are among the finest made of this country. See text pp. 83–4.

Parsons, Lady Alicia, 1815–85
D. of the second Earl of Rosse. Amateur watercolourist, See text p. 210.

Payne, Revd John, 1700–71
B. Dublin, an amateur who painted flowers in both oil and watercolours and wrote and illustrated a book on designing glebe houses in 1757.

Payne Gallway, Louisa, d. 1872
B. Adare. Amateur landscape watercolourist, brought up in Adare. See text p. 211.

Peace, James, c. 1771–1827
B. probably Dublin, amateur, a linen draper by profession, exh. watercolour landscapes in Dublin in 1802, 1812 and 1814. He was a member of the Hibernian Soc. of Artists.

Pearsall, William, fl. 1851
A topographical watercolour of Rathmichael Church is dated 1851. May be connected with the amateur watercolourist surgeon W. Booth Pearsall, who exh. RHA 1872–1912 and became Hon. RHA 1886.

Pelham, Henry, 1749–1806 *Visitor*
American born and trained as a civil engineer, he went to England and exhibited miniatures in the RA, 1777–8. Came to Ireland about 1778/9 as agent to Lord Lansdowne's Kerry estates. Exh. Irish Society of Artists 1780. See text p. 40.

Penley, Aaron Edwin, ANWS, 1807–70 *Visitor*
Exh. two Donegal views NWS 1844 and a view of Killiney Bay in 1865. Exh. RHA 1843–56.

Perrin, Mary, fl. 1896–1902
A watercolourist principally of flowers who exhibited RI between 1896 and 1902, giving a Dublin address.

Peters, Revd Matthew William, 1741–1814
Probably b. Dublin; educ. Dublin Society Schools; spent most of career in England. See text pp. 49, 73.

Petrie, George, PRHA, 1790–1866
B. Dublin; educ. Dublin Society Schools; won silver medal 1805. Exh. RHA 1826–66. See text pp. 158–63.

Petrie, James, 1750–1819
Father of George Petrie (q.v.), a painter of miniatures who drew some pastel portraits.

Phillips, Thomas, c. 1635–93 *Visitor*
Military engineer in Ireland 1685. See text p. 18.

Phipps, Henrietta, b. 1841, d. unknown.
Daughter of Col. Pownall Phipps of Oaklands, Clonmel. M. 1885, Lt– Col William Smith. An amateur and one of the founders of the Irish Amateur Drawing Society, which became the Watercolour Society of Ireland. See text p. 221.

Piccioni, Felice, fl. 1830–42 *Visitor*
An Italian visitor who worked in Belfast during the 1830s making small chalk and wash portraits and portrait groups. Later he went to live in Cork. He exhibited in 1834, RHA, and in the Cork Art Union Exhibition 1842. See text p. 155.

Place, Francis, 1647–1728 *Visitor*
Toured through Ireland, landing in Drogheda 1698, travelling via Dublin (works dated 1698) and Kilkenny (works dated 1699) and leaving from Waterford in 1699. See text p. 21.

Plunket, The Hon Katherine, 1820–1932 and
Hon Frederica Plunket, d. 1886
Both daughters of the Bishop of Tuam, who became Baron Plunket in 1854. There is no evidence of their education. Katherine exh. in London 1881–6. She painted watercolour landscapes on the continent and in Britain and Ireland, but the sisters are best remembered for their flower paintings now in the National Botanic Gardens, Glasnevin.

Pocock, Nicholas, 1740–1821 *Visitor*
Visited Ireland on several occasions; dated works exist for 1793, Antrim coast and Giant's Causeway; 1806 and 1811, Co. Cork; 1808, Killiney Bay. Taught William Beaufort (q.v.). See text p. 82.

Pope, Alexander, 1763–1835
B. Cork; educ. Dublin Society Schools 1776 and also under Hugh Douglas Hamilton (q.v.). Exh. drawings and portraits in crayon Irish Society of Artists 1777–80, and RA 1785–1821. See text pp. 74–5, 125.

Porcher, Capt. E.A., fl. 1872 *Visitor*
Amateur; visited Ireland painting views on the Shannon and in Co. Cork 1872.

Portarlington, first Earl of, 1744–98
Amateur draughtsman and virtuoso. See text pp. 45–6.

Power, Sir William James Tyrone, 1819–1911
Amateur. An army officer whose duty took him to New Zealand. See text p. 257.

Praegar, Sophia Rosamund, 1867–1954
From Northern Ireland, she was trained at the Slade School and though she was a sculptress she drew botanical illustrations for her famous naturalist brother Robert Lloyd Praeger. She used her second name, Rosamund.

Pratt, Charles Vallancey, 1789–1869
Born in Ireland, he made his career in the army. Exh. RHA 1843. See text p. 172.

Praval, Charles, d. 1789
A Frenchman who came and settled in Ireland in 1773. See text p. 49

Preston, H., fl. 1790
Amateur, probably a member of the Gormanston family; view of Gormanston Castle dated 1790.

Pritchett, Robert Taylor, 1828–1907 *Visitor*
In Dublin for Queen Victoria's visit in 1900, when he made a number of watercolours.

Prochazka, Baroness Pauline, d. 1928
Granddaughter of the Austrian Lady Stuart de Decies by her first marriage, she was brought up in Dromana, Co. Waterford and from 1886 lived at Lyrath, Co. Kilkenny. One of the founders of the Irish Amateur Drawing Society, which became the Watercolour Society of Ireland. See text p. 221.

Prout, John Skinner, NWS, 1806–76 *Visitor*
Exhibited NWS 1839, two views of Killarney, one of Limerick, one of Glendalough and in 1840 of Killarney and Cormac's Chapel, a subject he also showed in 1852 and 1856.

Pugh, Herbert, fl. 1758–88
B. in Ireland; in England by 1758 where he appears to have lived till his death. Best known for his oil landscapes and genre paintings in the manner of Hogarth but is also known to have painted watercolours.

Purcell, Edward, fl. 1812–32
Probably Irish, working mostly as a miniaturist. Exh. in Dublin 1812 and 1815 and later worked in Waterford. Then taught in England, returning to Dublin in 1831, advertising himself as a "Professor of Drawing," Exh. watercolours, RHA 1831–2.

Purser, Sarah Henrietta, 1849–1943
B. Ireland, educ. Metropolitan School of Art and the Académie Julian in Paris. Though better known as an oil painter, she drew portraits in pencil, crayon and charcoal and used watercolours for landscapes. She is best remembered as a great patron of the arts in Ireland, both as a collector and as one of the founders of the Tower of Glass and the Friends of the National Collections of Ireland. Exh. RHA 1872–1944. See text p. 235.

Q

Quadal, Martin Ferdinand, 1736–1808 *Visitor*
From Moravia. He visited Ireland in 1779 and, meeting with success, chiefly as an animal painter, he stayed for some time. There are a number of drawings in the NGI.

Quigley, Daniel, fl. 1750–73
An Irish horse painter. See text pp. 196–7.

R

Ramage, John, fl. 1763–d. 1802
Educ. Dublin Society Schools. Worked mainly as a miniaturist and in America. See text p. 237.

Raven, Thomas, fl. 1609–35 *Visitor*
Surveyor and map-maker. See text pp. 14–16.

Rawdon, Lord, fl. c. 1780
View of Trinity Church, New York, is known.

Reed, Joseph Charles, 1822–77 *Visitor*
Exh. views of Killarney in NWS 1863, 1868–9, 1871 and 1877

Reeves, Mary, fl. 1871–1906
Amateur; lived in Cork. Exh. London 1871–87, views in Italy, France and Co. Clare; RHA 1877–1906.

Reigh, J.D., fl. 1880–after 1914
A drawing of Parnell dated 1891 is in the NGI.

Reilly, James, fl. 1745–d. 1780
Educ. Blue-coat School and Dublin Society Schools. Assisted Samuel Dixon (q.v.). Worked as a miniaturist but exhibited one crayon portrait in the Irish Society of Artists. See text p. 111.

Reilly, John, nineteenth century
Irish, four watercolours on paper in NGI of waterfall views.

Reilly, John Lushington, fl. 1810–21
From Scarvagh, Co. Down, an amateur artist who worked in pencil and watercolour. His studies made on George IV's visit to Ireland in 1821 were used by J.P. Haverty whose paintings of this event were engraved.

Reilly, Pope Stevens, fl. 1794–9
Scenes of the Church and Tower of Teghadoe, Co. Kildare, and Ballinacarrick, Co. Wicklow, are known.

Repton, Humphrey, 1752–1818 *Visitor*
Came to Ireland in 1783 as secretary to William Windham, Chief Secretary. While in Ireland he painted portraits and humorous subjects in watercolour.

Reynolds, Sir Joshua, 1723–92 *Visitor*
Some drawings in a sketch book by Reynolds, the founder of the RA, in the Ashmolean indicate that he may have visited his friend the Duke of Rutland when he was Lord Lieutenant between 1784 and 1787. The drawings include views of the Scalp, Tinnyhinch and Powerscourt waterfall.

Richardson, Frederick Stuart, RI, 1855–1934 *Visitor*
Exh. *A Limerick Peat Farm* RI 1900; RHA 1891.

Rix, Mary Anne, fl. 1834–9 *Visitor*
Wife of artist John Chase. Exh. a view of Killarney in NWS 1834.

Roberts, Thomas Sautell, RHA, 1760–1826
B. Waterford; educ. Dublin Society Schools from 1777. An artist best known as an oil painter and as the younger brother of Thomas Roberts on whose death in 1778 Sautell adopted the name Thomas as his own. Held an exhibition of watercolours in Ireland, according to advertisements in Jan. 1802, in the Parliament House, Dublin. Exh. RHA 1826, London 1789–1818. See text pp.86–8.

Robertson, Charles, 1760–1821
B. Dublin, known principally as a miniature painter but exhibited flower pieces and small portrait watercolours in Dublin in the later part of his career after 1800. Exh. London 1790–1810.

Robertson, Daniel, fl. 1812–27
An architect who painted many watercolours of houses and exhibited in RA 1812–27.

Robertson, James George, fl. 1838–51
Painted antiquities in Counties Kilkenny and Kildare 1838–41, publishing *The Antiquities and Scenery of the County of Kilkenny,* 1851.

Robertson, William, early nineteenth century
Kilkenny architect who was taught drawing by George Holmes (q.v.). See text p. 129.

Robinson, Anne Marjorie, 1858–1924
B. Belfast, better known as a miniaturist though she also painted landscape watercolours of Belfast and its surroundings.

Robinson, Thomas, c. 1785–1810 *Visitor*
Pupil of Romney, visited Dublin c. 1790, going to Ulster in 1793, living near Dromore with Bishop Percy, with whom he was friendly. 1801 went to Belfast, leaving for Dublin 1808. Though best known for his portraits, Robinson painted watercolour views notably of the gardens of Bishop Percy in 1803. See text p. 82.

Robson, George Fennel, 1788–1833 *Visitor*
Visited Ireland c. 1827. Killarney became a favourite subject. See text p. 86.

Roch(e), Sampson Towgood, 1759–1847
B. Youghal, self-taught. Known as a miniaturist but also as a draughtsman of genre subjects made of local people near his home in Co. Waterford. See text pp. 136–7.

Roe, William, fl. 1822–c. 1852
Educ. RDS Schools, 1822–9. Exh. RHA from 1826–47, mostly watercolour landscapes. He visited London after leaving the schools and moved to Cork in 1835 in which year he also visited Scotland. He exhibited in the Cork exh. of 1852. Also made many pencil sketches and painted topical genre scenes. See text p. 149.

Rogers, James Edward, ARHA, 1838–96
B. Dublin; an architect who painted architectural and marine watercolours. He travelled on the continent and published with J.P. Mahaffy *Sketches from a Tour through Holland and Germany* 1889. Exh. RHA from 1870. Moved to London 1876 where he exhibited at the RA.

Rogers, William P., fl. 1848–83
Studied RDS, gaining prizes 1850 and 1852. Exh. watercolours RHA 1848–83 and in London 1853 and 1865. He painted landscape and coastal scenes.

Rowbotham, Thomas Charles Leeson, 1823–75
B. Dublin, son of T.L.S. Rowbotham (q.v.) by whom he was taught; went to England when young, painting in Wales, Scotland and Europe. Taught drawing at Greenwich Royal Naval School. His only known Irish works are chromo-lithographs of *Views in Wicklow and Killarney.* Member of the NWS.

Rowbotham, Thomas Leeson Scarse, 1783–1853 *Visitor*
Lived in Dublin c. 1815 till mid-1820s. He exhibited from 1815 to 1819 and received a premium from the Royal Irish Union in 1816. Two of his views of Dublin and of Howth were engraved c. 1823. See text p. 91.

Russell, Charles, RHA, 1852–1910 *Visitor*
B. in Scotland, came to Ireland 1874 painting portraits from photographs. He exhibited landscapes in the RHA 1878–84 including watercolour landscapes and portraits. Exh. RHA 1869–1910; London 1889.

Russell, George William (AE), 1867–1935
Drew a number of charcoal portraits, though best known as an oil painter of landscapes and symbolist pictures. Exh. RHA 1905.

S

Sadler, William I, fl. 1765–88
Came to Dublin as a boy with his father; attended Dublin Society Schools from 1765. Exh. crayon portraits in the Irish Society of Artists 1777 and 1780. A portrait of Kemble is in the NGI.

Sadler, William II, c. 1782–1839
B. Dublin, son of the above. Better known as an oil painter but a watercolour topographical view of Slane Abbey survives.

Sandys, Edwin, d. 1708
An engraver who was employed by Thomas Molyneux because he was "a good master in designing prospects" to draw the Giant's Causeway. See Strickland. See text p. 34.

Sasse, Richard, 1774–1849 *Visitor*
Topographical watercolourist and oil painter. He published series of etchings of Irish scenery. Exh. Irish views in London 1791–1813. See text p. 96.

Scanlan, Robert Richard, fl. 1826–76
First heard of exhibiting at RHA in 1826. Later went to England, and was in Plymouth 1832 and London 1842 and 1847. Appointed Headmaster of the Cork Sch. of Design 1852, though he returned to England in 1854. He exhibited London 1832–76 and RHA 1826–64. See text pp. 154–5.

Scott, George, fl. 1833
Employed as a Civil Assistant Sketcher for the Ordnance Survey. Began work in Dec. 1833. Employed in the Survey of Co. Down.

Scully, Harry, RHA, fl. 1885–d.1935
B. in Cork, he trained as an accountant. Studied Cork School of Art 1885 and then Heatherley's in London. He travelled widely on the continent and settled in Kent in the 1920s. Exh. landscapes both Irish and English (Sussex and Newlyn) at RI 1887–96; RA, 1896–1901; and in Ireland in RHA 1893–1932. See text p. 261.

Selwin-Ibbetson, Sir John, 6th Bt, 1789–1869 *Visitor*
An amateur landscape painter. A view of *Phillipstown, Co. Offaly* survives.

Serres, John Thomas, 1759–1825 *Visitor*
Probably came to Ireland on several occasions. He was a friend of William Ashford (q.v.). He sold in 1790 a number of Irish scenes, views near Dublin and Waterford. A watercolour of the Exchange at Waterford is dated 1787. See text p. 82.

Severn, Joseph Arthur Palliser, 1842–1931 *Visitor*
Exhibited views of West of Ireland NWS 1885, 1892 and 1904.

Seymour, Robert George, 1836–85
B. Dublin, amateur. Worked in Temporalities Commission Dublin and exhibited at RHA 1876–85, mostly coastal scenes. Moved to England on his retirement. His sister, Kate Seymour, worked in oil and watercolour. Exh. RHA 1868.

Seymour, Revd, late eighteenth century
Amateur antiquarian, works in Grose's *Antiquities*.

Shackleton, Lydia, 1828–1914
Painted over 1500 flower portraits for the National Botanic Gardens from 1884 to 1907. Exh. RHA 1878. See text pp. 118–19.

Shanley, Charles Dawson, 1811–75
B. Dublin, educ. TCD and also under Brocas in the RDS. Family emigrated to Canada 1836. 1840–57 employed by the Canadian Board of Public Works, but pursued a career as a journalist, cartoonist and illustrator. In 1849 he was editor of *Punch in Canada*. Later he worked full-time as a journalist in New York. His nephews, Charles Dawson, Cuthbert William and Francis James also painted and illustrated as did their father, James. See *Early Plans and Views of Montreal*, exh. catalogue McCord Museum of Canadian History 1992, pp. 153–5 and 103–10.

Shee, Sir Martin Archer, PRA, 1769–1850
B. Dublin, educ. Dublin Society Schools and RA schools. Best known as a portrait painter in oils but he sometimes used crayons, also watercolour. Exh. London 1789–1845. See text p. 153.

Shee, Peter, d. 1767
Started as a house painter. Employed 1752–7 by Henry Delamain to paint at his Delft works. Later exhibited at the Irish Society of Artists, 1765, 1766 and 1767. These may have been oils. See text p. 62.

Sherlock, William, before 1731–1806
B. Dublin, painter and engraver. Started life as a prize-fighter. Late in life studied at St. Martin's Lane Academy and in Paris. Exh. London 1764–1806.

Skillen, Samuel, c. 1819–47
B. Cork; educ. RHA School, in London and on the continent visiting Italy and Spain. He only returned to Cork shortly before his early death. Exh. RHA 1842–3. An early watercolour of a Roman soldier dated 1837 survives.

Small, William, RI, 1843–1929 *Visitor*
Scottish visitor; exhibited genre scenes from Connemara in NWS 1872, 1874, 1878 and 1885.

Smith, Lieut–Col Charles Hamilton, 1776–1859 *Visitor*
Flemish by birth. Amateur; served in the British army. He made an extensive tour of Ireland painting topographical views of scenery and antiquities from Donegal to Dublin, Cork, Killarney and Galway. See text pp. 171–2.

Smith, Capt Robert, 1792–1882
B. Dublin, amateur watercolourist who spent from 1809 to 1832 (when he was in India) in the army. He was stationed in the 1820s in Ireland. His sketches are in the V&A. Exh. a landscape drawing RHA 1827. In 1840 became Junior Pursuivant and in 1865 Athlone Pursuivant in the office of arms, Dublin. See text p. 173.

Solomons, Estella, 1882–1968
B. Dublin, Educ. RHA School, Metropolitan School of Art, Paris under Colarossi, and London under Orpen. Though better known as an oil painter and an etcher, she exhibited a number of watercolour landscapes. Exh. RHA 1905–68.

Somerville, Edith Oenone, 1858–1949
B. Corfu but brought up in West Cork. Studied first in South Kensington School of Art, 1877, and then, Düsseldorf and Paris. Better known as an author but she was also a fine illustrator and oil painter. See text pp. 231–2.

Spilsbury, John Inigo, 1730–after 1795 *Visitor*
Employed as a drawing master by Mrs Tighe of Rosanna. See text p. 132.

Spilsbury, Maria, see under Taylor, Maria

Sproule, Robert Auchmaty, 1799–1845
Born in Athlone, probably a member of the architect family of Sproule, educated TCD but became a painter and moved to Canada in the late 1820s, working mostly as a topographical watercolourist and a miniature painter. Did lithograph for Hawkin's *Picture of Quebec*. Some of his works were engraved by W.S. Leney. He died in Ontario. *Early Plans and Views of Montreal*, exhibition catalogue, McCord Museum of Canadian History 1992, pp. 76–82 and 154–5. See text p. 243.

Staniland, Charles Joseph, 1838–1916 *Visitor*
Exhibited views of Co. Clare in NWS 1892–3

Stanley, Caleb Robert, 1795–1868 *Visitor*
Exhibited a view of the Liffey in NWS 1832.

Stanley, Catherine, née Leycester, 1792–1862 *Visitor*
B. Stoke-on-Trent, Shropshire; was taught by Paul Sandby Munn in 1809 and was also a friend of Henry Edridge – most of her husband's family were good amateur artists and her husband a clergyman, rector of Alderley, Cheshire 1805–37 and Bishop of Norwich 1837–49. Mrs Stanley was a fine landscape painter and when staying with the 11th Viscount Kilmorey at Mourne Park on Carlingford Lough in 1814 she made a magnificent panoramic view of the Mourne Mountains and Mourne park, now in the Ulster Museum.

Stannus, Anthony Carey, 1830–1919
B. Carrickfergus, educ. Belfast Sch. of Design 1850–4 and later in London. Exh. RHA 1860–81; London 1862–80. See text p. 275.

Staples, Sir Robert Ponsonby, Bt., 1853–1943
Educated on the continent and lived in England until 1905 when he returned to Belfast. Exh. RHA 1875–1928; London 1875–93. See text pp. 279–80.

Steers, Fanny, fl. 1833–d. 1861 *Visitor*
Exh. Irish views (Ballintemple, Co. Carlow) in the NWS 1846 and recollections of Killarney 1851. Exh. RHA 1852.

Stocks, Arthur, 1846–89 *Visitor*
Painted genre scenes in Ireland.

Stoker, Bartholomew, 1763–88
Educ. Dublin Society Schools. A painter of pastel portraits in the manner of Hugh Douglas Hamilton (q.v.).

Stokes, John, fl. 1830–52
Probably from Cork. Employed as a Civil Assistant Sketcher by the Ordnance Survey. Began work in Aug. 1830 "Hill Drawing" in Cos. Derry and Antrim. Mentioned under Cork artists in the National Arts Exhibition held in Cork in 1852.

Stokes, Margaret McNair, HMRIA, 1832–1900
B. Dublin, amateur archaeologist and friend of Petrie (q.v.), from whom she must have learned much, and of Lord Dunraven, with whom she collaborated. Precise drawings and watercolours influenced by the Pre-Raphaelites and Frederick William Burton (q.v.), also a friend, survive.

Stopford, Robert Lowe, 1813–98
B. Dublin, landscape and marine watercolour painter. Educ. probably private. Settled in Cork as a young man. Exh. RHA 1841–84. See text pp. 189–91.

Stopford, William Henry, 1842–90
Native of Cork, son of R.L. Stopford (q.v.). Trained in Cork School of Art and South Kensington. Later assistant master at St. Martin's. 1868 became Headmaster of Halifax School of Art where he remained until his death. Exh. London 1867–80. See text p. 191.

Stuart, Louisa Anne, see under Waterford.

Sullivan, Dennis, fl. 1824
His book *A picturesque tour through Ireland illustrated with numerous coloured views of the most interesting scenery* contains twenty-five coloured aquatints.

Swanzy, Mary, 1882–1978
B. Dublin. Studied under May Manning, went to Paris c. 1906 and studied under Delacluse and elsewhere. Better known for her oils, but her coloured chalk drawings are notable. See text p. 235.

Sykes, Isabella, fl. 1826
Probably an amateur. A pencil view of Glendalough dated 1826 survives in NGI.

Symes, Sandham, fl. 1836–7
An architect who painted somewhat naïve topographical watercolours. See text p. 144.

Synnot, Walter, 1773–1851
An amateur; army officer who painted in his postings and during his retirement. See text p. 251.

T

Tarrant, Charles, 1730–1818 *Visitor*
Spent a large part of his career in Ireland as a Surveyor and Architect in the Board of Works. See text p. 38.

Taverner, Mary, mid-eighteenth century
One of the copyists of Samuel Dixon (q.v.). See text p. 111.

Taylor, Maria, née Spilsbury, 1777–c. 1823 *Visitor*
The daughter of a London engraver, she settled in Ireland in 1813, following her marriage in 1809 to John Taylor, who lived in Dublin. She may have been in Ireland earlier. See text pp. 134–5.

Taylor, William Benjamin Sarsfield, 1781–1850
B. Dublin, educ. Dublin Society Schools 1800–1804 and became a drawing master and later

an art critic. He was involved in the foundation of the RHA but he left to live in London before its first exhibition. Exhibited watercolours 1831–3 at the NWS. He is best remembered now for his book *The Origin, Progress and Present Condition of the Fine Arts in Gt. Britain and Ireland*, 1841. Exh. London 1829–47, RHA 1826–9.

Telbin, William, NWS, 1813–73 *Visitor*
Exh. views of Co. Wicklow and Co. Dublin at NWS 1841–5 and 1848–9 and later also a view of Killarney 1865. William Telbin Jnr., his son, exhibited Irish subjects from 1860–c.1880.

Templeton, John, 1766–1825
Belfast naturalist and amateur painter, see text pp. 114–16.

Templeton, Robert, 1802–92
Son of John (q. v.). As an army doctor he travelled widely drawing flora and fauna. See text p. 114, 116.

Tenison, Louisa, mid nineteenth century
An amateur; a member of the King Tenison family of Roscommon. See text pp. 216–17.

Teynham, Henry George Roper–Curzon, seventeenth Baron, 1822–92, *Visitor*
In Ireland certainly in 1878, when he made a watercolour of Drogheda. See text p. 200.

Thackeray, William Makepeace, 1811–63 *Visitor*
The novelist, who was also an illustrator and caricaturist. He illustrated his travel book to Ireland, *The Irish Sketchbook*, 1843.

Thomas, John, fl. 1593 *Visitor*
A soldier who drew a view of Enniskillen, 1593. See text p. 16.

Thompson, Elizabeth Southerden See under Butler.

Thomson, Hugh, 1860–1920
B. Coleraine; educ. Belfast Sch. of Design. Worked in London most of his career as an illustrator. Member RI 1897–1907. See text pp. 275–6.

Thynne, Lady Mary, early nineteenth century *Visitor*
Painted Slane Castle and church and tower in Kells.

Tidey, Henry F., 1814–72 *Visitor*
Exhibited a pair of genre pictures, *The light side of Irish life*, in NWS 1862.

Tighe, Caroline, see under Hamilton, Caroline.

Timbrell, James Christopher, 1807–50
B. Dublin. Educated RDS Schools, going to London in 1830. Contributed to Hall's *Ireland*.

Tongue, R.D., fl. 1840
Portrait of *Sir Richard Courtney, Knight of Mangerton* and a lakeside castle signed "RDT" are known.

Topham, Francis William, 1808–77 *Visitor*
Exhibited Irish subjects in NWS 1845–7. He certainly visited Ireland in 1844, 1860 and 1862, and Irish subjects were among his most popular works. Exh. RHA 1856. His son, Frank William Warwick Topham, also a painter, was in Ireland with his father in 1860. See text p. 178.

Townshend, Harriet Hockley, 1877–1941
B. Ireland, daughter of Maj.–Gen. Walter Weldon. Started exhibiting RHA 1903; 1909 attended Metropolitan School of Art for a year. M. 1910, Thomas Loftus Uniacke Townshend. Worked in oils and pastels. Exh. RHA 1903–35 both under maiden name and married name. See text p. 234.

Tracey, John Joseph, 1813–78
B. Dublin, studied RDS Schools, winning prizes. Early works are frequently classical subjects but turned to Irish genre about 1842; became a picture restorer. Exh. RHA 1831–78. See text p. 177.

Trench, Henry, fl. 1705–26
Born Ireland, studied in Rome. See text pp. 23–4.

Tresham, Henry, RA, 1751–1814
B. Dublin, educ. Dublin Society Schools 1765. Went to London 1775, obtaining as his patron Lord Cawdor, with whom he travelled to Italy. He remained there for fourteen years studying art. On his return he based his life in London but visited Ireland in 1807 when he produced a number of works. Exh. Irish Society of Artists, 1768–75; London 1789–1806. See text pp. 100–2.

Trinseach, Sadbh, 1891–1918
Educ. Metropolitan School of Art. A painter of portraits in crayon and charcoal. She was associated with the Gaelic League and the independence movement.

Trobridge, George F., 1857–1909 *Visitor*
An English artist in oil and watercolour who was Headmaster of the Belfast School of Art from 1880–1901 and continued to live in Northern Ireland till 1908. Exh. London 1884–9.

Trollup, fl. 1676
Probably a surveyor. See text p. 18.

Tudor, Joseph, d. 1759
Renowned for his six engraved views of Dublin, for which four sketch drawings survive. He was awarded premiums for landscapes by the Dublin Society in 1740, 1742, 1743, and 1746. He was also a scene painter. See text p. 37.

Tuohy, Patrick, 1894–1930
A well-known pupil of Orpen; most of his work is outside the dates of this book. See text p. 283.

Turner, James, second half eighteenth century
According to Strickland, Irish born, but lived and worked in England 1745–1790, where he exhibited portraits at the Society of Artists. There are antiquarian topographical drawings by a Revd James Turner in the RIA. dating 1790–1799. They are probably two different people as the drawings in the RIA are clearly amateur but it is possible they are the same. See text p. 35.

Turner de Lond, William, fl. 1767–1826 *Visitor*
Was in Ireland in 1821; lived sometime in Scotland and painted in Edinburgh. His nationality is unknown. See text pp. 146–7.

V

Vallancey, Col. Charles, fl. 1794
Engineer, surveyor, antiquarian. Drew antiquities in Counties Clare, Limerick, Leitrim, Roscommon, Waterford, Kildare and Cork and probably elsewhere. See text pp. 44–5.

Van der Hagen, William, fl. 1721–d. 1745 *Visitor*
Visitor who settled in Ireland about 1724, probably of Dutch origin, but may well have been born in London, where several painters of the name were working. Landscape and scene painter. Strickland thought his name was Johann. See text p.37.

Vantwright, John, fl. 1856–c. 1892
A landscape painter in both oil and watercolour; studied at the RDS school. He worked as a clerk in the General Valuations Office, Dublin 1856–82 and exh. RHA 1861–71. He emigrated to British Columbia in 1882 and died some ten years later.

Varley, Cornelius, 1781–1873 *Visitor*
In Ireland in 1808; travelled from Co. Kerry to Co. Armagh. Brother of John (q.v.). See text pp. 85–6.

Varley, John, 1778–1842
In Ireland on several visits between 1812 and 1826, exhibiting mostly views of Killarney and in 1823 one of the Mourne Mountains. Brother of Cornelius (q.v.). See text pp. 85–6.

Vispré, Francis Xavier, 1730–c. 1790, and
Vispré, Victor, 1763–80 *Visitors*
Frenchmen, brothers, who came to Dublin via London in 1776, leaving in 1780. F.X. exhibited miniatures and crayon portraits, and Victor fruit pieces on glass in the Irish Society of Artists in 1777.

W

Wade, J., fl. 1801–17
Recorded by Strickland as exhibiting watercolour landscapes in Dublin exhibitions, 1801–2, 1809, 1811, and 1817.

Wakeman, William Frederick, 1822–1900
Instructed by Petrie (q.v.). Landscape painter and antiquarian draughtsman. On the closure of the topograpical section of the Ordnance Survey, he took up teaching, first at St. Columba's College and then at Portora Royal school, and gradually became more interested in archaeology than painting. Exh. RHA 1842–63. See text p. 164.

Waldron, William, fl.1766–1801
Educ. Dublin Society Schools and apprenticed by them to Delamain's Delft Manufactory in 1766. He was also a pupil of James Mannin (q.v.). Taught painting and drawing, succeeding Mannin as Master of the Dublin Society's Landscape and Ornament School in 1779. He exhibited in the Irish Society of Artists exhibitions, mostly flower paintings, though in 1777 he included three theatrical pieces and seven portraits. There is no indication of what medium he used but it is unlikely, given his links with the Schools, that he did not use crayon, pastel and watercolour as well as oil.

Wall, William Guy, 1792–after 1862
B. Dublin, educ. Dublin Society Schools. Went first to the US in 1818–32 and again 1856–62. Founder member of the National Academy of Design, New York. Noted for the aquatints after his watercolours of the Hudson River. Exh. RHA 1840–53. Died in Ireland. He had a son, also an artist, William Archibald Wall, 1828– after 1875, who, though born in New York, spent much of his later life in Ireland and in England where he died. See text pp. 238–40.

Wallis, James, 1785?–1858
An amateur from Cork, he became an army officer and spent much of his career in Australia. See text pp. 252–3.

Walmsley, Thomas, 1763–1806
B. Ireland; worked as a scene painter in the Opera House. London. In 1788 returned to Dublin where he was employed in the Crow Street theatre. From 1790 till his death he remained in England, practising as a landscape painter in both oil and watercolour. He occasionally visited Ireland; exh. *Views of Killarney* in the RA 1796 and issued a series of aquatints of Killarney, in sets of four, starting in 1795. Exh. RA, 1790–6. See text p. 89.

Walsh, Edward, 1756–1832
Native of Waterford, trained in Glasgow as M.D, returned to Ireland as Lieut-surgeon with army 1798. Posted to Canada 1803–c. 1809 where he was stationed at Montreal, Fort George and Amherstburg. See text p. 242.

Walsh, Nicholas, 1839–77
B. Dublin; studied RDS schools and RHA schools. Painted landscapes, genre scenes, sea pieces and birds. Travelled in France and Italy 1864. Returned London briefly 1872 before going to Italy, where he died. Exh. RHA 1858–77; RA 1872 (Venetian scene); other London shows including Crystal Palace 1871, where he showed fifteen watercolours done in Paris during the siege of 1870.

Walsh, Peter, fl. 1769–d. 1819
Antiquarian and patron of the arts from Belline, Co. Kilkenny. See text pp. 37–8.

Ward, John, 1832–1912
B. Belfast; studied at Belfast School of Design. Entered the artists' department of his father's business, Marcus Ward & Co, printers and publishers, in 1847. Exh. watercolours under the name Bonnington Smith. A member of the Belfast Ramblers Sketching Club. Travelled in Egypt, Greece, Sicily and elsewhere in Europe and

England. 1876–90 editor of Sir E.J. Poynter's *South Kensington Drawing Book* and published books on art later in his life. Died in Kent.

Ward, Mary, née King, 1827–69
B. Ballylin, Co. Laois, d. Revd Henry King and his wife Harriet (née Lloyd), sister-in-law of the 2nd Earl of Rosse. 1854 married the Hon. Henry Ward of Castleward, Co. Down. Her chief interest was natural history and science. See text pp. 209–10.

Warren, Edmund George, RI, NWS, 1834–1909 *Visitor*
Exh. views of Wicklow and Killarney in NWS 1871.

Warren, John, fl. 1764–79
Entered Dublin Society Schools 1764. Exh. Irish Society of Artists 1768–77 crayon and watercolour portraits, landscapes, and religious subjects, winning a Dublin Society premium in 1770.

Waterford, Louisa Ann, Marchioness of, née Stuart, 1818–91 *Visitor*
English visitor after her marriage in 1841 to the third Marquis of Waterford in 1841, in Curraghmore, Co. Waterford. Returned to Northumberland after his death 1859. A pupil of Ruskin. Her watercolours, mostly of religious subjects or genre scenes, are of high quality. Exh. RHA 1885. See text pp. 211–12.

Waters, George, 1863–1947
B. Holywood, Co. Down; studied Belfast School of Design, winning prizes. Worked as a lithographic artist. First exh. Belfast Ramblers Sketching Club 1890 and was a founder member of Belfast Art Society and the Ulster Society of Painters. Painted landscape watercolours mostly in Antrim, Donegal, Dublin and Wickow.

Watkins, Bartholomew Colles, RHA, 1833–91
B. Dublin entered RDS school 1847. Came of an artistic family. Landscape painter in oils and watercolour. Worked in England as well as all over Ireland, and visited Norway c. 1860. Exh. RHA, 1856–92, RA and other London shows 1857–75. See text pp. 266–7.

Watson, Samuel, 1818–?67
B. Cork, settled in Dublin and worked as a lithographer. Painted oils and watercolours, Irish peasant life. Exh. RHA 1845–8 and perhaps also in 1895, in which case Strickland's death is incorrect. See text p. 214.

Watson, William, d. 1765
Worked in Dublin as a portrait painter (life-size) in oils and pastels. Did occasional subject pictures. Exh. Irish Society of Artists, 1765. See text pp.73–4.

Watson, Mrs
Wife of William Watston (q.v.) exh. fruit and flower pieces in watercolour and crayon in the Irish Society of Artists 1768 and 1770–1. See text p. 74.

Webb, Josephine, 1853–1924
B. Dublin; educ. Queen's Institute where she won two silver medals for her drawing, and at the Académie Julian, Paris, 1877–8. She was a teacher in Dublin of some importance. Exh. RHA 1880–1921, in the Watercolour Society of Ireland, in the Dublin Arts Club, and in London. She held a one-man show in Dublin in 1913. See text p. 234.

Weigall, Charles Harvey, NWS, 1794–1877 *Visitor*
An English genre and history painter who exh. Irish subjects in NWS in 1837 and 1861 and exh. RHA 1847 and 1851. Contributed to Hall's *Ireland*.

Weld, Isaac, 1774–1856
A well-known secretary of the Dublin Society who painted in America in his youth. See text pp. 237–8.

Welland, William, fl. 1843–69
A member of a family of Dublin architects. A drawing of Cahir Castle dated 1843 survives.

Wellesley, Arthur, fl. 1843–4
Amateur draughtsman, son of the Marquis of Wellesley.

West, Francis Robert, c. 1749–1809
B. Dublin; son of the first Master of Dublin Society Schools, Robert West (q.v.), who taught him to draw in crayon and pastel. Exh. Irish Society of Artists 1770–80 and Dublin exhibitions 1800–1, portrait, religious subjects and genre scenes. Succeeded to the Mastership of the Schools in 1771. Exh. London 1790. See text p. 65.

West, Robert, fl. 1740–d. 1770
B. Waterford, studied Paris; the founder Master of the Dublin Society Schools. See text pp. 47–9.

West, Robert Lucius, RHA, c. 1774–1850
B. Dublin, son of Francis Robert (q.v.). Worked in oils and pastel, portraits and subject pictures. He was in London in 1808 and exh. RA 1771–1822. A founder of the RHA and exhibited there 1826–53. Master of the Figure School, Dublin Society Schools, from 1809 to 1845.

West, Samuel, c. 1810–after 1867
B. Cork. Probably studied in Cork before going to Rome. In London 1840 and exhibited RA 1840–67. Worked mostly as an oil painter of portraits and history subjects. Made watercolour copies of old masters. Exh. RHA 1847.

Wheatley, Francis, 1747–1801 *Visitor*
Worked in Ireland, 1779–83/4; apart from his major portraits and oil paintings of contemporary Irish history, he toured the country painting watercolours in Kerry, Kildare, Lismore and in and around Dublin.

Wheeler–Cuffe, Lady Charlotte Isabel, née Williams, 1867–1967
Amateur who painted landscapes and botanical illustrations; worked in Burma. She wrote and illustrated *The Burma Alphabet* in English and Burmese (Mandalay, 1913). See text p. 121.

Wheeler–Cuffe, Otway, 1836–1918
Father-in-law of above. Amateur; army officer from Co. Waterford. Two volumes of watercolours dating 1864–1870 include scenes from the British Isles, the continent and New Zealand.

White, John, b. 1540/50–?1606 *Visitor*
Englishman who was involved in the colonization of Virginia and famous for the watercolours he did during his two visits, 1585 and 1587–90. Settled on property he leased from Sir Walter Ralegh near Lismore. The author of a map of Mogeely dated 1589. See text pp. 13–14.

Wilkie, Sir David, 1785–1841 *Visitor*
Scottish visitor, who appears to have visited Ireland on several occasions. On one visit he was in Ballinahinch, Co. Down. See text p. 178.

Willes, William, d. 1851
Cork artist. Trained first in Edinburgh as a doctor, then became a pupil of Grogan (q.v.). Also studied at RA and lived in London for some time. Exh. in Cork, RHA 1843–9 and London, 1820–21. Became first Master of the School of Art, Cork 1850. See text p. 164–5.

Williams, Alexander, RHA, 1846–1930
B. Drogheda; little formal education. Painted in oils and watercolours and was probably the earliest artist to paint on Achill. Became first Secretary of the Dublin Sketching Club in October 1874 and retained the position for fifty years. Exh. RHA, 1870–1930. See text pp. 268–70.

Williams, Solomon, RHA, 1757–1824
Educ. Dublin Society Schools. Lived a great deal in London between 1789 and 1809. Exh. in London, mostly oils, frequently of historical subjects. A sketchbook (NGI) survives dated 1789, of varying subjects, animals, antique sculpture, landscape and figure subjects. One illustration is of Boswell sheltering from a shower. Exh. RHA 1826; London 1791–1826.

Williamson, James, fl. 1773–1801
Son of a Dublin print seller, publisher and picture cleaner. Exh. Society of Artists, Dublin, 1773, six landscape watercolours. Sent a still life of fruit to an exhibition in 1801. Better known as a Surveyor. See text p. 50.

Willis, Richard Henry Albert, 1853–1905
B. Dingle, Co. Kerry. Was apprenticed to an architect, and studied Cork School of Art; later in South Kensington. Became a teacher, and later, 1882–92, Headmaster at Manchester School of Art, then worked in London painting, before becoming Headmaster of the Metropolitan School of Art, Dublin, in 1904. Worked in oil, pastel and watercolour and as a sculptor. Exh. RHA 1880–1 and 1905; London 1879–91.

Wilmot, Martha, 1775–1873
B. Cork, amateur. Companion to Princess Dashkoff 1803–8. Kept a "greenbook" of watercolours of subjects and portraits connected with the princess. Travelled in south of Ireland 1808–12, when she went to England, marrying the Revd William Bradford 1812, and settling in Stomington, Sussex. Visited Paris 1817 and 1818. 1819–29 lived in Vienna, travelling in Austria, Hungary and Italy; returned to Stomington 1829 and in 1857 to Dublin. See text pp. 201–2.

Wilson, James Glen, 1827–63
An Ulster artist who settled in Australia. See text p. 255.

Woodlock, David, 1842–1929
B. Golden, Co. Tipperary and went to Liverpool aged 12, working in an outfitters. Later trained in the Liverpool Academy School and became a painter in that city. He does not appear to have returned to Ireland.

Woolley, Samuel, fl. 1791–1802 *Visitor*
Signed and dated a watercolour of the House of Lords Portico, 1797. An architect who designed house and gates at Glenenea, Co. Westmeath.

Wren, Matthew, fl. 1754–68 *Visitor*
Map-maker and surveyor. An assistant of John Rocque, he later worked on his own, producing a map of Newry (1761) and Co. Louth (1766) before returning to England. See text p. 195.

Wynne, A.B., fl. 1876–1904
Exh. watercolours RHA 1876–1904. Landscape subjects; Irish, Indian, Norwegian, North African, French, Italian, Swiss, Egyptian, German.

Wynne, Revd Samuel, fl. 1774–94
An amateur draughtsman who published eleven drawings in Grose's *Antiquities*. Worked all over Ireland, including Donegal. See text p. 43.

Y

Yard, Charles, fl. 1845–57
Dublin painter. Exh. RHA 1845–52 (mostly from London addresses) watercolours of England, Scotland and a few of Ireland: Lough Derg, Co. Clare, Waterford and Dublin Bay. Also exhibited in London 1848–57.

Yeats, Jack Butler, RHA, 1871–1957
B. London, son of John Butler Yeats (q.v.). Educ. in London Schools of Art. Worked as an illustrator in black and white 1888–98 and from 1910 for *Punch*. Watercolour was his principal medium till c. 1915, and he continued to use it throughout his life even when his main work was in oil. See text pp. 271–3.

Yeats, John Butler, 1839–1922
B. Dublin; educ. as a barrister. Took up painting late in life and studied at Heatherley's and RA schools; mostly used pencil for his superb portrait drawings. Early in his career he used gouache for illustrative work. Went to America to live in 1907. See text pp. 270–1.

BIBLIOGRAPHY

BOOKS

ADAMS, Eric, *Francis Danby, Varieties of poetic landscape* (London, 1973).

ANDREWS, J.A., *Irish Maps*, Irish Heritage Series, No. 18 (Dublin, 1978).
Plantation Acres (Belfast, 1985).

ANGELO, Henry, *Reminiscences of him with memoirs of his late father and friends*, 2 vols. (London, 1828–30).

ANGLESEA, Martyn, *Royal Ulster Academy of Art* (Lisburn, 1981).
(ed.), Richard Dunscombe Parker, *Birds of Ireland* (Belfast, 1984).

ARCHER, Mildred, *India and British Portraiture 1780–1825* (London, 1979).

ARCHIBALD, E.H.H., *Dictionary of Sea Painters* (Woodbridge, 1980).

ARNOLD, Bruce, *A Concise History of Irish Art* (London, 1969).
Orpen, Mirror to an Age (London, 1981).
Mainie Jellett and the Modern Movement in Ireland (New Haven and London, 1991).

AUSTEN, Jane, *Emma*, edition Zodiac Press (London, 1978).

Australian Dict. of National Biography, 2 vols. (Melbourne, 1966-7).

Barney Bryan's Sketchbook, published in Exeter, no date.

BARTON, Richard, *Lectures in Natural Philosophy . . . on Lough Neagh*, and *Some remarks towards a full description of Upper and Lower Lough Lene, near Killarney* (both 1751).

BARTON, Rose, *Familiar London* (London, 1904).

BASTIN, John, and ROHATGI, Pauline, *Prints of S.E. Asia in the India Office Library* (London, HMSO, 1979).

BELL, Mrs G.H., *The Hamwood Papers* (London, 1930).

BERKELEY, George, *The Querist* (2 parts, Dublin 1725, (1735)–1736).

BERRY, H.F., *A History of the Royal Dublin Society* (London, 1915).

BERRY-HILL, H. and S., *George Chinnery, 1774–1852* (Leigh-on-Sea, 1963).

BLACK, Eileen, *Paintings, Sculptures and Bronzes in the collection of the Belfast Harbour Commissioners* (Belfast, 1983).

BLACKER, Stewart, *Irish Art and Artists*, 1845.

BLISS, Alan Joseph, *A Dialogue in Hibernian Stile between A and B*, Vol. 6 of *Irish Writings from the Age of Swift* (Dublin, 1977).

BODKIN, Thomas, *Four Irish Landscape Painters* (Dublin and London, 1920), 1987 edn. introduction by Dr Julian Campbell.

BONYHADY, Tim, *Images in Opposition Australian Landscape Painting 1801–1890* (Melbourne, 1985).
et al., The Skottowe Manuscript, a commentary (Chippendale, Australia, 1988).

BOURKE, Marie, *The Aran Fisherman's Drowned Child by Frederick William Burton* (Dublin, 1987).

BOWE, Nicola Gordon, *Harry Clarke* (Dublin, 1989).

BOYNE, Patricia, *John O'Donovan (1806–1861) a biography* (Kilkenny, 1987).

BREEZE, George, *Society of Artists in Ireland, Index of Exhibits, 1765–80* (Dublin, 1985).

DE BREFFNI, Brian (ed.), *The Irish World* (London, 1977).

BREWER, James N., *The Beauties of Ireland*, 2 vols. (London, 1825).

BROOKE, Raymond, *The Brimming River* (Dublin, 1961).

Bryan's Dictionary of Painters and Engravers, 5 vols., revised edn. (London, 1903–5).

BURBRIDGE, William F., *A Dictionary of Flower, Fruit and Still Life Painters 1515–1950*, 2 vols. (London, 1974).

BURKE, Edmund, *A Philosophical Enquiry into the Origin of our Ideas of the Sublime and the Beautiful* (London, 1767), edition by J.T. Boulton (London, 1958).

BURKE'S *Landed Gentry of Great Britain and Ireland*. 1868 edition.

BUTLER, Elizabeth, *From Sketch-book and Diary* (London, 1909).

BUTLER, Patricia, *Three Hundred Years of Irish Watercolours and Drawings* (London, 1990).

CAMBLIN, Gilbert, *The Town in Ulster* (Belfast, 1951).

CAREY, Williams, *Some Memoirs of the Patronage and Progress of the Fine Arts in England and Ireland* (London, 1826).

CLARKE, Mrs Godfrey, *Gleanings from an Old Portfolio*, 2 vols. (Edinburgh, 1895).

CLARKE, Michael, *The Tempting Prospect* (London, 1981).

COLLIS, Maurice, *Somerville and Ross: a biography* (London, 1968).

COLVIN, Christina (ed.), *Maria Edgeworth, Letters from England* (Oxford, 1972).
Maria Edgeworth in France and Switzerland (Oxford, 1979).

COMYNS-CARR, Mrs J., *Reminiscences* (London, 1925).

CONNER, Patrick, *George Chinnery* (Woodbridge, 1993).

CRAMPTON WALKER, J., *Irish Life and Landscape* (Dublin and Cork, c. 1925).

CROFTON CROKER, T., *Researches in the South of Ireland* (London, 1824).
Fairy Legends and Traditions of the South of Ireland, 3 vols (1825–8).

CROMWELL, Thomas K., *Excursions through Ireland*, 3 vols. (London, 1820).

CROOKSHANK, Anne, *Mildred Anne Butler* (Dublin, 1992).
and GLIN, Knight of, *The Painters of Ireland* (London, 1978).

CURL, James Stevens, *Moneymore and Draperstown* (Ulster Architectural Heritage Society, Belfast, 1979).

CURTIS, L. Perry, *Apes and Angels; The Irishman in Victorian Caricature* (Newton Abbot, 1971).

DALSIMER, Adele M. (ed.), *Visualizing Ireland* (Boston and London, 1993).

DAY, Angelique (ed.), *Letters from Georgian Ireland* (Belfast, 1991).

DENSON, Alan, *An Irish Artist, W. J. Leech, RHA (1881–1968)*, 2 vols. (Kendal, 1968–9).

DERRICKE, John *See under* Small *and* Somers.

DOYLE, Michael, *The Doyle Diary* (London, 1978).

DUNLAP, William, *History of the Rise and Progress of the Art of Design in the United States* (New York, 1834), 3rd edition (3 vols., Boston, 1918).

EGERTON, Judy, *British Watercolours* (London, 1986).

ELLISON, Canon C.C., *The Hopeful Traveller, the Life and Times of Daniel Augustus Beaufort . . .* (Kilkenny, 1987).

FENLON, Jane, FIGGIS, Nicola, and MARSHALL, Catherine (eds.), *New Perspectives* (Dublin, 1987).

FISHER, Jonathan, *A Picturesque Tour of Killarney describing in twenty views the most pleasing scenes . . . accompanied by some observations, etc., with a map of the lake and its environs, engraved in aquatint* (Dublin, 1789).
Scenery of Ireland, illustrated in a series of prints of select views, castles and abbeys, drawn and engraved in aquatint (Dublin, 1795–6).

FISHER, Stanley William, *Dictionary of Watercolour Painters 1750–1900* (London, 1972).

FOSKETT, Daphne, *A Dictionary of British Miniature Painters*, 2 vols. (London, 1972).
John Harden of Brathay Hall 1777–1847 (Kendal, 1974).

FRIENDLY, Alfred, *Beaufort of the Admiralty, the Life of Sir Francis Beaufort 1774–1857* (London, 1977).

FROST, Stella (ed.), *A Tribute to Evie and Mainie Jellett* (Dublin, 1957).

FURNISS, Harry, *Confessions of a Caricaturist*, 2 vols. (London, 1901).

GANDON, James, Jr., and MULVANY, T.J., *The life of James Gandon Esq. . . .* (Dublin, 1846). Maurice Craig (ed.) (London, 1969).

GARLICK, Kenneth, and MACINTYRE, Angus (eds.), *The Diary of Joseph Farington*, 12 vols. (New Haven and London, 1978–1983).

GILBERT, John T., *Facsimiles of National Manuscripts of Ireland . . .*, 5 vols. (Dublin and London, 1874–84).

GILBEY, Sir Walter, *Animal Painters of England from 1650*, 2 vols. (London, 1990).

GIROUARD, Mark, *Life in the English Country House* (New Haven and London, 1978).

GLIN, Knight of, and CRAIG, Maurice, introductions to reprints of Malton's *Dublin* of 1799 (Dublin, 1978), and Malton's *Dublin Views in Colour* (Dublin, 1981).

GOODWIN, Francis, *Rural Architecture*, 2 vols. (London, 1835).

GRATTAN, William, *Patronage Analysed* (Dublin, 1818).

GRAVES, Algernon, *A Dictionary of Artists who have exhibited works in the principal London exhibitions from 1760 to 1889* (London, 1884. New and enlarged edn. 1895).
The Royal Academy of Arts: a complete dictionary of contributors and their work 1769–1904, 8 vols. (London, 1905–6).
The Society of Artists of Great Britain . . . The Free Society of of Artists (London, 1907).

GREEN, The Revd. William Spotswood, *The High Alps of New Zealand* (London, 1883).

GROCE, George C., and WALLACE, David H., *The New-York Historical Society's Dictionary of Artists in America 1564–1860* (New Haven and London, 1957).

GROSE, Daniel Charles, *The Antiquities of Ireland*, Roger Stalley (ed.) (Dublin, 1992).

GROSE, Francis, *Antiquities of Ireland*, 2 vols. (London, 1791–95).

GRUBB, Geoffrey Watkins, *The Grubbs of Tipperary* (Cork, 1972).

GWYNN, Stephen, *Highways and Byways in Donegal and Antrim* (London and New York, 1899).
Beautiful Ireland, 4 vols. (London, 1911–12).

HAIGHT, Gordon S., *The Letters of George Eliot*, 9 vols. (New Haven and London, 1954–79).

HALL, Mr. and Mrs. S.C., *Ireland: its Scenery: Character . . .* , 3 vols. (London, 1841–3).

HALSBY, Julian, *Scottish Watercolours 1740–1940* (London, 1986).

HARBISON, Peter, *Beranger's Views of Ireland* (Dublin, 1991).

HARDIE, M., *Watercolour Painting in Britain*, 3 vols. (London, 1967–69).

HARDY, Francis, *Memoirs of . . . James Caulfield, Earl of Charlemont . . .* (London, 1810).

HARE, Augustus (ed.), *Life and Letters of Maria Edgeworth*, 2 vols. (London, 1884).

HARPER, J. Russell, *Early Painters and Engravers in Canada* (Toronto, 1970).
Painting in Canada, a History, 2nd edition (Toronto, 1978).

HARRIS, Eileen, *British Architectural Books and Writers 1556–1785* (Cambridge, 1990).

HARRY, Owen, *Mary Ward* (Birr, 1991).

HAYDEN, Ruth, *Mrs Delany: her Life and Flowers* (London, 1980. 2nd edition, London, 1992).

HAYES MCCOY, G.A., *Ulster and other Irish Maps, c.1600* (Dublin, 1964).

HERBERT, Dorothea, *Retrospections of Dorothea Herbert 1770–1789*, 2 vols. (London, 1929). Reprint Louis Cullen (ed.), (Dublin, 1988).

HERITY, Michael, *Irish Passage Graves* (Dublin, 1974).

HEWITT, John, and SNODDY, Theo, *Art in Ulster*, 2 vols. (Belfast, 1977).

HOLMES, George, *Sketches of some of the Southern Counties of Ireland . . .* (London, 1801).

HOPPEN, K. Theodore, *The Common Scientist in the Seventeenth Century. A Study of the Dublin Philosophical Society 1683–1708* (London, 1970).

HOUFE, Simon, *A Dictionary of British Book Illustrators and Caricaturists 1800–1914* (Woodbridge, 1978).

HOWLEY, James, *The Follies and Garden Buildings of Ireland* (New Haven and London, 1993).

HUTTON, A.W. (ed.), *Arthur Young's Tour in Ireland 1776–1779*, 2 vols. (London, 1892).

JACOBS, Phoebe Lloyd, *John James Barralet and the Apotheosis of George Washington*, Winterthur Portfolio 12 (Charlottesville, 1977).

JACOBOWITZ, Arlene, *James Hamilton 1819–78, American Marine Painter* (Brooklyn Museum, 1966).

JOPPIEN, Rudiger, and SMITH, Bernard, *The Art of Captain Cook's Voyages*, Vol. 1, *The Voyage of the Endeavour 1768–71* (New Haven and London, 1985).

KENNEDY, S.B., *Paul Henry* (Dublin, 1991).
Irish Art and Modernism, 1880–1950 (Belfast, 1991).

KERR, Joan (ed.), *Dictionary of Australian Artists*, 2 vols. (University of Sydney, 1984, and Oxford University Press, 1993).

KONODY, P.G., and DARK, Sydney, *Sir William Orpen Artist and Man* (London, 1932).

KÜTTNER, Gottfried, *Briefe über Irland* (Leipzig, 1785).

The Ladies Amusement (London, c. 1760).

LEWIS, Gifford, *Somerville and Ross* (London, 1985).
The Selected Letters of Somerville and Ross (London, 1989).

LLANOVER, Lady (ed.), *Autobiography and Correspondence of Mary Granville, Mrs Delany*, 6 vols. (London, 1861).

LOW, William, *A Chronicle of Friendships 1873–1900* (London, 1908).

McCARTHY, Michael, *The Origins of the Gothic Revivals* (New Haven and London, 1987).

McCORMACK, Tim, *et al.*, *First Views of Australia 1788–1815* (Sydney, 1987).

MacDONALD, Patricia R., and PEARCE, Barry, *The Artist and the Patron, Aspects of Colonial Art in New South Wales* (Sydney, 1988).

McKECHNIE, Sue, *British Silhouette Artists and their Work 1760–1860* (London, 1978).

MAAS, Jeremy, *Victorian Painters* (London, 1969).

MALINS, Edward. and GLIN, Knight of, *Lost Demesnes* (London, 1976).

MALLALIEU, H.L., *A Dictionary of British Watercolour Artists up to 1920*, 2 vols. (Woodbridge, 1979).
Understanding Watercolours (Woodbridge, 1985).

MAXWELL, Constantia, *Country and Town under the Georges* (London, 1940).

MILTON, Thomas, *A Collection of Select Views from the Different Seats of the Nobility & Gentry in the Kingdom of Ireland, engraved by the best artists* (London, 1783–93).

MORRIS, Thomas, *Holy Cross Abbey* (Dublin, 1986).

MURDOCH, John, *Forty British watercolours from the Victoria and Albert Museum* (London, 1977).

MURPHY, Denis (ed.), *Triumphalia Chronologica Monasterii Sanctis Crucis in Hibernia 1640* (Dublin, 1891).

MURPHY, James Cavanah, *Plans, elevations . . . of the church of Batalha . . .* (London, 1795).

NAPIER, Robina (ed.), *Johnsoniana, Anecdotes of the Late Samuel Johnson LLD.* (London, 1884).

NEELY, W.G., *Kilkenny, an Urban History 1391–1843* (Belfast, Institute of Irish Studies, Queen's University, 1989).

NELSON, E. Charles, and McCRACKEN, Eileen M., *The Brightest Jewel* (Kilkenny, 1987).

NICHOLSON, Benedict, *Joseph Wright of Derby*, 2 vols. (London and New York, 1968).

NOLAN, William, and POWER, Thomas P. (eds.) *Waterford History and Society* (Dublin, 1992).

NOON, Brendan, *et al.*, *A Vision of Eden, the Life of Marianne North* (London, 1980).

NYGREN, Edward J., with ROBERTSON, Bruce, *et al.*, *Views and Visions: American Landscape before 1830* (Washington, Corcoran Gallery of Art, 1986).

O'DOWDA, Brendan, *The World of Percy French* (Belfast, 1981).

O'KEEFFE, John, *Recollections of the Life of John O'Keeffe. Written by Himself*, 2 vols. (London, 1826).

O'NEILL, Henry, *The Fine Arts and Ancient Civilisation of Ancient Ireland* (London, 1863).
The Round Towers of Ireland, part the first, containing descriptions of the four round towers in the county of Dublin (Dublin, 1877).

O'RAIFEARTAIGH, T. (ed.), *Royal Irish Academy: a Bicentennial History 1785–1985* (Dublin, 1985).

PASQUIN, Anthony (i.e., John Williams), *Memoirs of the Royal Academicians and an Authentic History of the Artists of Ireland* (London, 1796). Reprinted with an introduction by R.W. Lightbown (London, 1970).

DE PENCIER, Honor, *Posted to Canada* (Toronto, 1987).

PETRIE, George, *et al.*, *Picturesque Sketches of Some of the Finest Landscape and Coast Scenery of Ireland with drawings by G. Petrie RHA, A. Nicholl & H. O'Neill*, Vol. 1 (Dublin, 1835), Vol. 2 (Dublin, 1843).

PIGGOTT, Stuart, *Ruins in a Landscape. Essays in Antiquarianism* (Edinburgh, 1976).

PLATTS, Una, *Nineteenth Century New Zealand Artists* (Christchurch, 1979).

PRAEGER, R.L., *The Way that I Went* (Dublin and London, 1937).

PRESSLY, William, *The Life and Art of James Barry* (New Haven and London, 1981).

PRICE, Liam (ed.), *An Eighteenth Century Antiquary . . . Austin Cooper . . .* (Dublin, 1942).

PÜCKLER-MUSKAU, Prince, *Tour in England, Ireland and France, in the years 1828 and 1829 . . .*, published anonymously (London, 1832).

PYLE, Hilary, *Jack B. Yeats* (London, 1970).

Jack B. Yeats. His Watercolours, Drawings and Pastels (Dublin, 1993).

REID, Forrest, *Illustrations of the Sixties* (London, 1928).

ROGET, J.L., *History of the Old Watercolour Society*, 2 vols. (London, 1891).

ROWAN, Anne Martha, *et al.*, *The Architecture of Sir Richard and W.V. Morrison* (Dublin, 1989).

SHAW, W.A. (ed.), *Huguenot Society*, Vol. XVIII (Lymington, 1911).

SHEE, Martin Archer, *The Life of Sir Martin Archer Shee*, 2 vols. (London, 1860).

SHEEHY, Jeanne, *Walter Osborne* (Ballycotton, 1974).

The Discovery of Ireland's Past: The Celtic Revival, 1830–1930 (London, 1980).

SIMMS, Angret with SIMMS, Katherine, *Kells* (Royal Irish Academy, 1990).

SIMMS, J.G., *William Molyneux of Dublin*, P.H. Kelly (ed.), (Dublin, 1982).

SITWELL, Sacheverell, *Narrative pictures: English genre and its painters: with notes on the illustration by Michael Sevier* (London, 1937).

SLEATOR, William, printed by, *An Essay on Perfecting the Fine Arts in Great Britain and Ireland* (Dublin, 1767).

SMALL, John (ed.), John Derricke, *The Image of Irelande* (Edinburgh, 1883).

SMITH, Charles, *The Antient and Present State of the County of Cork*, 2 vols. (Dublin, 1750).

SNYDER, Martin P., *City of Independence. Views of Philadelphia Before 1800* (New York, 1975).

SOMERS, Lord (ed.), *A collection of scarce and valuable Tracts . . .* 2nd edition, 13 vols. (London, 1809–15), includes John Derricke, *Image of Irelande* (London, 1581).

SPENDLOVE, F. St. George, *The Faces of Early Canada* (Toronto, 1958).

STALKER, John, and PARKER, George, *Treatise of Japanning . . .* (Oxford, 1688).

STANFORD, W.B., and FINOPOULOS, E.J. (eds.), *The Travels of Lord Charlemont in Greece and Turkey, 1749* (London, 1984).

STEBBINGS, Theodore E., Jr., *American Master Drawings and Watercolours* (New Haven, 1976).

STEWART, Ann M., *Irish Art Loan Exhibitions 1765–1927*, Vol. 1, A–L (Dublin, 1990).

Royal Hibernian Academy of Arts, 3 vols. (Dublin, 1990).

STOKES, William, *George Petrie* (London, 1868).

STRICKLAND, Walter, *Dictionary of Irish Artists*, 2 vols. (Dublin, 1913).

TAYLOR, W.B. Sarsfield, *The Origin, Progress and Present Condition of the Fine Arts in Great Britain and Ireland*, 2 vols. (London, 1841).

THACKERAY, William Makepeace, *The Irish Sketchbook* (London, 1842. Edition Belfast and Oxford, 1985).

THOMAS, Earl, *Sir John Johnson, Loyalist Baronet* (Toronto and Reading, 1986).

TILLOTSON, G.H.R., *Fan Kwae Pictures . . .* (London, 1987).

TONGUE, Alan, *A Picture of Percy French* (Antrim, 1990).

TURPIN, John, *A School of Art in Dublin since the Eighteenth Century* (to be published, Dublin, 1994).

TYLER, Ron, *Visions of America* (London, 1983).

WALLACE, W.A., *John White, Thomas Harriot and Walter Ralegh in Ireland* (London, 1985).

WALSH, Edward, *A Narrative of the Expedition to Holland, in the Autumn of the Year 1799: illustrated with a Map of North Holland and Seven Views of the Principal Places Occupied by British Forces* (London, 1800).

WEDD, A.F., *The Fate of the Fenwicks, letters to Mary Hayes, 1798–1828* (London, 1927).

WILDE, Sir William Robert W., *Memoirs of Gabriel Beranger, and his Labours in the Cause of Irish Art and Antiquities, from 1760 to 1780* (Dublin, 1880).

WILLIAMS, Iolo, *Early English Water-colours* (London, 1952. Reprint, Bath, 1970).

WILMOT, Martha, *The Russian Journal of Martha and Catherine Wilmot, 1803–8* published by the Marchioness of Londonderry and H. Montgomery Hyde, 2 vols. (London, 1934).

WILTON, Andrew, *British Watercolours 1750–1850* (Oxford, 1977).

WOLF, Edwin, 2nd, and KOREY, Marie Elena, *Quarter of a Millenium. The Library Company of Philadelphia 1731–1981 . . .* (Philadelphia, 1981).

WRIGHT, Thomas, *Louthiana: or an Introduction to the Antiquities of Ireland* (London, 1748).

ARTICLES AND PERIODICALS

ADAMS, Ronald, "Andrew Nicholl," *Irish Arts Review*, Vol. 1, No. 4 (Winter 1984), pp. 29–34.

ANDREWS, J.H., "Surveyors and Surveying in James Williamson's Autobiography," *Familia, Ulster Genealogical Review*, Vol. 2, No. 7 (1991).

ANGLESEA, Martyn, "Andrew Nicholl and his Patrons in Ireland and Ceylon," *Studies*, Vol. 71 (Summer 1982), p. 134.

"Sketches of a Victorian Vicar: Narcissus Batt, 1824(?)–98," *Ulster Genealogical and Historical Guild Newsletter*, Vol. 1, No. 9 (1983), pp. 282–89.

"James Moore," *GPA Irish Arts Review Yearbook 1991–2*.

and PRESTON, John, "A Philosophical Landscape," *Art History*, Vol. 3, No. 3, (September 1980) p. 252.

ARCHER, Jean, "Geological Artistry: The Drawings and Watercolors of George Victor du Noyer in the Geological Survey of Ireland," Adele M. Dalsimer (ed.), *Visualizing Ireland* (Boston and London, 1993), pp. 133–44.

BARRETT, Cyril, "Michael Angelo Hayes RHA and the Galloping Horse," *The Arts in Ireland*, Vol. 1, No. 3 (1973), pp. 42–7.

BEAUFORT, Daniel Augustus, "Tour of Kerry," *Journal of the Kerry Archaeological and History Society*, No. 18 (1985), p. 193.

BERGER, Pamela, "The Historical, the Sacred, the Romantic: Medieval Texts into Irish Watercolours," Adele M. Dalsimer (ed.), *Visualizing Ireland* (Boston and London, 1993), pp. 71–88.

BLACK, Eileen, "James Glen Wilson (1827–1863): an Irish artist in Australia," *Familia, Ulster Genealogical Review*, Vol. 2, No. 3 (1987), pp. 37–46.

"James Glen Wilson," *Irish Arts Review* (1990–1991), pp. 99–102.

BLACKLEY, Roger, "J. Guise Mitford," *Art New Zealand 27* (1983), pp. 46–7.

BREEZE, George, "Letter to the editor: Hickey Portraits," *Apollo* (Jan. 1976) p.79.

BROOKE-TYRELL, Alma, "Mr Howis the artist of Jervis Street 1804–1882," *Dublin Historical Record*, Vol. XXXII, No. 1 (Dec. 1978), pp. 27–38.

BUTLER, Patricia, "The Ingenious Mr Francis Place," *Irish Arts Review*, Vol. 1, No. 4 (Winter 1984), pp. 38–40.

"A Designer of Distinction – William Kilburn (1745–1818)," *Friends of the Royal Society of Watercolours and Drawings* (Spring 1987), pp. 37–9.

CAFFREY, Paul, "Samuel Lover's Achievement as a Painter," *Irish Arts Review*, Vol. 3, No. 1 (Spring 1986), p. 53.

"Sampson Towgood Roch, miniaturist," *Irish Arts Review*, Vol. 3, No. 4 (1986) pp. 14–20.

CASEY, Christine, "Miscellanea Structura Curiosa," *Irish Arts Review*, Yearbook (1991), pp. 85–91.

Cn, "Gleanings on Old Cork Artists," *Journal of the Cork Historical and Archaeological Society*, Vol. VI, 2nd series (1900), pp. 106–8.

COFFEY, Petra, "George Victor Dunoyer 1817–69," *Sheet Lines, Journal of the Charles Close Society*, No. 35 (Jan. 1993), pp. 14–26.

COLVIN, Christina, "Maria Edgeworth's Bedroom," *Country Life*, Vol. 161, No. 4149 (6 Jan. 1977), p. 47.

COOPER, Richard A., "Genealogical Notes on the (Austin) Cooper family in Ireland 1660–1960," *The Irish Genealogist*, Vol. 3, No. 9 (Oct. 1964), pp. 351–5.

CROOKSHANK, Anne, "The Conversation Piece," *Decantations A Tribute to Maurice Craig* (Dublin, 1992), pp. 16–20.

DAY, Robert, "Sketches of Cork in 1838 by William Roe," *Journal of the Cork Historical and Archaeological Society*, Series 2, Vol. VIII (1902), pp. 150–4.

DEVAPRIAM, Dr Emma, "The Synott Children," *Art Bulletin of Victoria*, No. 26 (1986), pp. 15–21.

DUNOYER *see under* Coffey.

ELLWOOD, C.V., and HARVEY, J.M.V., "Lady Blake," *Bulletin of the British Museum Historical Series*, Vol. 18, No. 2 (29 Nov. 1990), pp. 145–202.

FIGGIS, Nicola, "Irish Portrait and Subject Painters in Rome 1750–1800," *Irish Arts Review, Yearbook* (1988), pp. 128–32. "Henry Trench," *Irish Arts Review Yearbook*, Vol. 10 (1994), pp. 217–22.

FFOLLIOT, Rosemary, "Provincal Town Life in Munster," *The Irish Ancestor*, Vol. V, No. 1 (1973), pp. 37–52.

GARDENER, Albert Ten Eyck, "Ingham in Manhattan," *Metropolitan Museum Bulletin*, Vol. X, No. 9 (May 1952), pp. 245–53.

GIROUARD, Mark, "Stamped, Addressed and Illustrated," *Country Life* (30 July 1970), pp. 290–1.

GILLESPIE, France, "Edith Somerville 1858–1949," *New Perspectives* (Dublin, 1987), pp. 195–206.

GILLESPIE, Raymond, "Describing Dublin: Francis Place's Visit 1698–1699," Adele M. Dalsimer (ed.), *Visualizing Ireland* (Boston and London, 1993), pp. 99–118.

HAYES, Michael Angelo, *Delineation of Animals in Rapid Motion*, a paper read before the Royal Dublin Society (Dublin, 1877).

HORNER, Arnold, "Cartouches and Vignettes on the Kildare Estate Maps of John Rocque," *Irish Georgian Society*, Vol. XIV, No. 4 (Oct.–Dec., 1971), pp. 57–76. "Carton, Co. Kildare," *Irish Georgian Society*, Vol. XVIII, Nos. 2 and 3 (April–Sept. 1975), pp. 45–104.

HOUSTON, Stuart, "Birds by Hood," *The Beaver, Magazine of the North* (Summer 1974), pp. 4–11.

IGOE, Vivien, and O'DWYER, Frederick, "Early views of the Royal Hospital Kilmainham," *Irish Arts Review, Yearbook* (1988), pp. 78–88.

"The Irish Abroad," Anon., *Ireland of the Welcomes* (July–Aug. 1992).

JENKINS, Ian, "Adam Buck and the Vogue for Greek vases," *Burlington Magazine*, Vol. CXXX, No. 1023 (June 1988), pp. 448–55.

KRIELKAMP, Vera, "Going to the Levee as Ascendancy Spectacle . . .," Adele M. Dalsimer (ed.) *Visualizing Ireland* (Boston and London, 1993), pp. 37–54.

LEASK, Ada, "Samuel Dixon," *Irish Georgian Society*, Vol. XVIII, No. 4 (Oct.–Dec. 1975), pp. 109–36, and Vol. XXIII, Nos. 1 and 2 (Jan.–June 1980), pp. 1–32. (Ada Longfield), "William Kilburn (1745–1818) and his book of Designs," *Irish Georgian Society*, Vol. XXIV, Nos. 1 and 3 (Jan.–June 1981), pp. 1–28.

LEDBETTER, Gordon T., "Alexander Williams 1846–1930: Sidelights on a Victorian Painter," *The Irish Ancestor*, No. 2 (1975), pp. 83–90.

LIGHTBOWN, Ronald, "18th and 19th century Visitors – Part II," *Old Kilkenny Review* (second series), Vol. 3, No. 2 (1985), pp. 161–73.

LOEBER, Rolf, "Biographical Dictionary of Engineers in Ireland 1600–1730," *The Irish Sword*, 1977–79, No. 79, Vol. XIII, Nos. 30–45, 50–3, 106–23, 230–55. "An Unpublished View of Dublin in 1698 by Francis Place," *Irish Georgian Society*, Vol. XXI, Nos. 1 and 2 (Jan.–June 1978), pp. 7–15.

LONGFIELD *see under* Leask

MacCURTAIN, Margaret, "The Real Molly Macree," Adele M. Dalsimer (ed.), *Visualizing Ireland* (Boston and London, 1993), pp. 9–22.

McGUIRE, Edward A., "Pastel portrait painting in Ireland in the XVIII century," *The Connoisseur*, Vol. 103 (Jan. 1939), pp. 12–13.

McPARLAND, Edward, "Emo Court, Co. Leix," *Country Life* (23 May 1974).

MAHER, John, "Francis Place in Dublin," *Journal of the Royal Society of Antiquaries of Ireland* (1932), Vol. 62 and "Francis Place in Drogheda, Kilkenny and Waterford," *Journal of the Royal Society of Antiquaries of Ireland* (1934), Vol. 74.

MALLALIEU, H.L., "Francis Nicholson," *Watercolours and Drawings*, Vol. IV, No. 3 (Summer 1989), pp. 15–18.

MASSING, J.M., "Durer's Warriors and Peasants 1521," *Irish Arts Review, Yearbook* (1994), Vol. 10, pp. 223–6.

MITCHELL, G.F., and PARKS, H.M. "The Giant Deer in Ireland," *Proceedings of the Royal Irish Academy*, Vol. LII, B (1949), p. 294.

MONTAGUE-SMITH, Patrick, "The Dexters of Dublin and Annfield, Co. Kildare," *The Irish Ancestor*, Vol. II, No. 1 (1970), p. 342.

MORRISON, Kristin, "Ancient Rubbish and Interior Spaces: M.A. Butler and M.J. Farrell, Discovered," Adele M. Dalsimer (ed.), *Visualizing Ireland* (Boston and London, 1993), pp. 23–36.

MULCAHY, Rosemarie, "Patrick Tuohy 1894–1930," *GPA Irish Arts Review Yearbook* (1989–90), pp. 107–18.

MULVANY, Thomas James, "Memoirs of Native Artists, No. 1, Mr Francis West," *The Citizen*, No. XXIV (Oct. 1841), p. 206. "Hugh Douglas Hamilton," *Dublin Monthly Magazine*, (Jan.–June 1842), p. 68.

NETZER, Nancy, "Picturing an Exhibition: James Mahony's Watercolors of the Irish Industrial Exhibition of 1853," Adele M. Dalsimer (ed.), *Visualizing Ireland* (Boston and London, 1993), pp. 89–98.

O'CONNELL, Sheila, "Lord Shaftesbury in Naples, 1711–1713," *Walpole Society*, Vol. 54, 1988 (publ. 1991), p. 162.

POTTERTON, Homan, "A Director with Discrimination – Sir Frederic Burton in the National Gallery," *Country Life*, Vol. CIV (9 May 1974), pp. 1140–1141.

QUANE, Michael, "Tour of Ireland by John Harden in 1787," *Journal of the Cork Historical and Archaeological Society*, 1953–5, Vol. LVIII, No. 187, pp. 26–32; Vol. LVIX, No. 189, pp. 34–40; No. 190, pp. 69–77; Vol. LX, No. 191, pp. 14–21.

RAFTERY, P.J., "The Brocas Family, Notable Dublin Artists," *Dublin Historical Record*, Vol. XVII, No. 1 (Dec. 1961), pp. 25–34.

RALEY, Robert, "Philadelphia's Irish Legacy," *The 1984 Antiques Show* (Philadelphia, 1984), pp. 47–54.

"Willima Roe: Views of Cork and its environs 1837–9," Anon., *Capuchin Annual* (1941), pp. 158–70.

ROSS, Ruth Isobel, "Phillips' Pleasing Prospects," *Country Life* (4 March 1976), pp. 552–3.

ROYAL DUBLIN SOCIETY, *Proceedings*, Vol. LXXXI (Dublin, 1843). Report of the first public Distribution of Premiums (Dublin 1843).

SCARISBRICK, Diana, "Companion to a Russian Princess," *Country Life*, Vol. 169, No. 4351 (Jan. 1981), pp. 76–8.

SHELLEY, Donald A., "William Guy Wall and his watercolours for the Hudson River Portfolio," *New-York Historical Society Quarterly*, Vol. XXXI (Jan.–Oct. 1947), (New York, 1948)

SINGLETON, Emer, "Charles Tarrant, Surveyor, Architect, Artist and Cartographer (1730–1818)," *Old Bray Journal*, Vol. 1, No. 5 (Dec. 1991), pp. 7–15.

SNODDY, Oliver, "An unlisted item of Carlow Printing," *Carloviana* (1969), pp. 8–11 and 22.

THORP, W.A., "The Art of the Cut Paper-cutter," *Country Life* (10 July 1943), pp. 194–96.

TRENCH, C.E.F., "William Burton Conyngham (1733–1796)," *Journal of the Royal Society of Antiquaries of Ireland*, Vol. 115 (1985), pp. 40–61.

TURPIN, John, "The Masters of The Dublin School of Landscape and Ornament 1800–1854," *Irish Arts Review*, Vol. 3, No. 2 (Summer 1986), p. 49. "The School of Ornament of the Dublin Society in the 18th century," *Journal of the Royal Society of Antiquaries of Ireland*, Vol. 116 (1986), pp. 38–50. "French Influence on Eighteenth-Century Art Education in Dublin," *Eighteenth-Century Ireland*, Vol. 5 (1990), pp. 105–16. "Irish Art and Design Education from the Eighteenth century to the Present," *Irish Arts Review, Yearbook* (1994), Vol. 10, pp. 209–216.

Vertue's Notebooks (I–VI) were published in the Walpole Society in the following volumes: XVIII (1929–30); XX (1931–2); XXII (1933–4); XXIV (1935–6); XXVI (1937–8); XXX (1951–2); an index to the first five was published in Walpole Society Vol. XXIX (1940–42).

WELD, Isaac, *Report of the first public Distribution of Premiums, Royal Dublin Society* (Dublin, 1843).

WIND, Edgar, "Shaftesbury as a Patron of Art," *Journal of the Warburg and Courtauld Institutes*, Vol. 2 (1938–9), pp. 185–8.

WYNNE, Michael, "Thomas Frye c. 1710–62," *Burlington Magazine*, Vol. CXIV, No. 827 (Feb. 1972), pp. 78–85.

"James Hore, Active 1829–1837," *Studies* (Spring 1976), pp. 46–51.

"An Influence on Robert Healy," *Burlington Magazine*, Vol. CXVIII, No. 879 (June 1976), p. 413.

"Lord Charlemont's Album," *Irish Georgian Society*, Vol. 21, Nos. 1–2 (Jan.–June 1978), pp. 1–6.

"James Hore, Gentleman View-Painter," *Irish Arts Review*, Vol. 2, No. 1 (Spring 1985), pp. 38–42.

"The Gondo Tunnel on the Simplon Pass c. 1829," *Irish Arts Review Yearbook* (1992), pp. 220–1.

CATALOGUES

ALLODI, Mary, *Canadian Watercolours and Drawings in the Royal Ontario Museum*, 2 vols. (Toronto, 1974).

The Anatomy Lesson, Art and Medicine, exhibition, NGI (Dublin, 1992).

ANGLESEA, Martyn, *Andrew Nicholl* (Belfast, 1973).

James Moore (Belfast, 1973).

Portraits and Prospects, catalogue of an exhibition of watercolours from the Ulster Museum in association with the Smithsonian Institution (Belfast, 1989).

BARRETT, Cyril, Introduction to the Rosc *Exhibition of Irish Art in the Nineteenth Century*, held in Cork, 1971.

BARRY, James *see under* Pressly, William

BATSON, Whaley, *Henrietta Johnston*, introduction to the catalogue of an exhibition held in the Museum of Early Southern Decorative Arts, Winston–Salem, North Carolina and the Gibbes Museum of Art, Charleston, South Carolina, Oct. 1991–Feb. 1992.

BODKIN, Thomas, Introduction to exhibition catalogue, *Patrick Joseph Tuohy RHA, 1894–1930*, Paintings, drawings, sketches 1901–1930, Dublin Mills Hall, 1931.

BRENNAN, Fionnuala, "Mary Swanzy," introduction to exhibition catalogue, Pyms Gallery, London (Nov.–Dec. 1989).

BROWN, David Blaney, *Catalogue of Drawings in the Ashmolean Museum Oxford by artists born before 1775* (Oxford, 1982).

BUTLER, Mildred Anne *see under* Crookshank.

CAMPBELL, Julian, *The Irish Impressionists*, exhibition catalogue, NGI (Dublin, 1984).

Mary Swanzy, introduction to exhibition catalogue, Pyms Gallery, London (Nov.–Dec. 1989).

Frank O'Meara and his Contemporaries, exhibition catalogue, Hugh Lane Municpal Gallery of Modern Art, Dublin, Crawford Art Gallery, Cork and Ulster Museum (Belfast, 1989).

Nathaniel Hone, exhibition catalogue, NGI (Dublin, 1991).

CLARK, Kenneth, introduction to exhibition catalogue, *Jack B. Yeats 1871–1957*, Toronto (1971).

COLLINS, Roger, and ENTWHISTLE, Peter, *Pavilioned in Splendour* (Dunedin Public Art Gallery, 1986).

COOKE, W. Martha E., *W.H. Coverdale Collection of Canadian Paintings, Watercolours and Drawings* (Ottawa, 1983).

CROOKSHANK, Anne, and GLIN, Knight of, *Irish Portraits 1660–1860* (London, 1969), exhibition catalogue, Dublin, London and Belfast (1969–70).

Mildred Anne Butler, exhibition catalogue, Kilkenny, Dublin and Christie's, London (1981).

CULLEN, Fintan, and MURPHY, William M., *The Drawings of John Butler Yeats*, exhibition catalogue, Albany Institute of History of Art (Albany, 1987).

DANBY, Francis *see under* Greenacre.

DAWSON, George, introduction to exhibition catalogue, *Paul Henry*, TCD and Ulster Museum (Dublin, 1973).

Richard Doyle and his family, V&A exhibition catalogue (1983).

Dublin International Exhibition, 1865, descriptive catalogue (London, 1866).

EGERTON, Judy, *George Stubbs 1724–1806*, exhibition catalogue, Tate Gallery and Yale Center for British Art (London, 1984–85).

ELMES, Rosalind M., *Catalogue of Irish Topographical Prints and Original Drawings, mainly in the Joly Collection* (Dublin, 1943). New revised and enlarged edition by Dr M. Hewson for NLI Society (Dublin, 1975).

English Drawings, exhibition catalogue, Hazlitt, Gooden and Fox (1990).

English Watercolours, Leger Galleries, London (10 Nov.–24 Dec. 1980).

FAIGAN, Julian, *Paul Sandby Drawings*, Australian Gallery Directors' Council (Sydney, 1981).

FOX, Celina (ed.), *London World-City 1800–1840* (New Haven and London, 1992).

GRAHAM, Conrad, *Mont Royal – Ville Marie: Early Plans and Views of Montreal*, McCord Museum of Canadian History (1992).

GREENACRE, Francis, *The Bristol School of Artists . . .*, exhibition catalogue, City Art Gallery, Bristol (Nov. 1973).

Francis Danby, exhibition catalogue, Tate Gallery, London, in association with the City of Bristol Museums and Art Gallery (London, 1988).

An Exhibition of Watercolours and Drawings by John Harden, Arts Council of Great Britain (Bristol, 1951).

HENRY, Paul *see under* Dawson.

HICKEY, Ted, introduction to exhibition catalogue, *Richard Dunscombe Parker's Irish Birds*, Ulster Museum (Belfast, 1980).

HONE, Nathaniel *see under* Campbell.

HUTCHISON, John, *James Arthur O'Connor*, exhibition catalogue, NGI (Dublin, 1985).

18th, 19th and 20th century Irish Paintings, exhibition catalogues, Gorry Gallery (Apr.–May 1986, Oct. 1987).

JOHNSON, Dale T., *American Portrait Miniatures in the Manney Collection*, Metropolitan Museum of Art (New York, 1990).

JOHNSTON, Henrietta *see under* Batson.

JOHNSTON, Roy, *Roderic O'Conor*, exhibition catalogue, Barbican Art Gallery, London, and Ulster Museum, Belfast (1985).

Roderic O'Conor, exhibition catalogue, Musée de Pont-Aven (1984).

M. and M. Karolik Collection of American Paintings, 1815–1865 (Cambridge, Mass., 1949).

M. and M. Karolik Collection of American Watercolours and Drawings: 1800–75, 2 vols. (Boston, 1962).

KOKE, Richard J., compiler, *A Catalogue of the Collection including Historical, Narrative and Marine Art*, New-York Historical Society (1982).

(ed.) *Artists by Themselves, Artists' Portraits*, catalogue from the National Academy of Design, New York (New York, 1983).

KOSHKIN-YOURITZIN, Victor, *American Watercolours from the Metropolitan Museum of Art* (New York, 1991).

KRAUSE, Martin F., Jnr., *Catalogue of British Drawings and Watercolours 1775–1925*, Indianapolis Museum of Art (1980).

LE HARIVEL, Adrian (ed.), *Irish Watercolours and Drawings* from the NGI (Dublin, 1991).

Compiled by, introduction by Homan Potterton, *Illustrated Summary Catalogue of Drawings, Watercolours and Miniatures in the National Gallery of Ireland* (Dublin, 1983).

Catalogue of Paintings: Exhibiting several fine Works by the Masters And a Collection of Pictures, by the Artists and Amateurs of Limerick (1821).

MACLISE *see under* Ormond.

Samuel McCloy (1831–1904), exhibition catalogue, Lisburn Museum (1981–2).

MATHEWS, Alister, *Drawings and Watercolours*, Cat. 79, No. 133, Bournemouth (Spring 1972).

MOORE, James *see under* Anglesea.

Jeremiah Hodges Mulcahy . . ., exhibition catalogue, Cynthia O'Connor Gallery (Dublin, Aug. 1980).

MULREADY see under Pointon.
MURRAY, Peter, *Illustrated Summary Catalogue of the Crawford Municipal Art Gallery* (Cork, 1992).

NASH, Robert and ROSS, Helen, *Dr Robert Templeton . . . Naturalist and Artist*, exhibition catalogue, Ulster Museum (Belfast 1980).
NICHOLL, Andrew see under Anglesea.

OBERHUBER, Konrad, and ROBINSON, William W., *Master Drawings and Watercolours: The Hofer Collection*, exhibition catalogue, Fogg Art Museum (Cambridge, Mass., 1984).
O'BRIEN see under Collins.
O'CONNELL, Daire *et al.*, *Mainie Jellett*, exhibition catalogue, Irish Museum of Modern Art (Dublin, 1991).
O'CONNOR, James Arthur see under Hutchinson.
O'CONOR, Roderic see under Johnston.
O'MEARA, Frank see under Campbell.
ORMOND, Richard, and TURPIN, John, *Daniel Maclise*, exhibition catalogue, London and Dublin (1972).
OSBORNE, Walter see under Sheehy.

PARKER, Richard Dunscombe see under Hickey.
PLACE, Francis see under Tyler.
POINTON, Marcia, *Mulready*, exhibition catalogue, V & A (London, 1986), NGI, Dublin, and Ulster Museum, Belfast (1986–7).
PRESSLY, Nancy L., *The Fuseli Circle in Rome*, exhibition catalogue, Yale Center for British Art (1979).
PRESSLY, William, *James Barry: the Artist as Hero*, exhibition catalogue, Tate Gallery (London, 1983).
PYLE, Hilary, *Jack B. Yeats in the National Gallery of Ireland* (Dublin, 1986).

RORIMER, A., *Drawings by William Mulready*, exhibition catalogue, Victoria and Albert Museum, (London, 1972).
ROWE, Rebecca, and NUGENT, Charles, *Rose Barton RWS, Exhibition of Watercolours and Drawings*, exhibition catalogue, Crawford Gallery, Cork; Fine Art Society, London; Ulster Museum, Belfast and Butler Gallery, Kilkenny (1987).
RYAN-SMOLIN, Wanda (ed.) *Irish Woman Artists from the Eighteenth Century to the Present Day*, exhibition catalogue, NGI, Hugh Lane Muncipal Gallery and Douglas Hyde Gallery (Dublin, 1987).

SANDBY, Paul see under Faigan.
SHEEHY, Jeanne, "Walter Osborne," exhibition catalogue, NGI (16 Nov.–31 Dec. 1983), Ulster Museum (20 Jan.–29 Feb. 1984).
SPARLING, Mary, *Great Expectations, The European Vision in Nova Scotia 1749–1848*, exhibition catalogue, Halifax, Toronto and Montreal (1980–81).
Canada in the Nineteenth Century: the Bert and Barbara Stitt Family Collection, catalogue, Art Gallery, Hamilton (1984).
A Spice of Life, [Staples] exhibition catalogue, David Messum Gallery, (London, Nov.–Dec. 1991).
STRONG, Roy, *A Pageant of Canada*, exhibition catalogue, Ottawa (1967).
STUBBS see under Egerton
SWANZY, Mary see under Brennan *and* Campbell

TEMPLETON, Robert and John see under Nash.
TUOHY see under Mulcahy.
TYLER, Richard, *Francis Place 1647–1728, an exhibition of his work*, York and Kenwood (London, 1971).

A Concise Catalogue of the Drawings, Paintings and Sculptures in the Ulster Museum (Belfast, 1986).

WILTON, Andrew, and LYLES, Anne, *The Great Age of British Watercolours 1750–1880*, exhibition catalogue, London, and National Gallery of Art, Washington (1993).

Jack B. Yeats 1871–1957, a centenary exhibition, 1971–2 exhibition catalogue, Dublin, Belfast and New York (Dublin, 1971).
See also under Clark *and* Pyle.
YEATS, John Butler see under Cullen.

UNPUBLISHED MANUSCRIPTS

ARMSTRONG DUFFY, Shirley, "Late Nineteenth Century Sketching Clubs," B.A. thesis (TCD, 1984).
ASTON, Dr. M., *Lord Carysfort and Sir Joshua Reynolds: The Patron as Friend* (c. 1986).

BEAUFORT, Louisa, "Scraps to amuse my dear Admiral from LCB" (1857), TCD ms. 8264.
BRENNAN HOLOHAN, Mary, "Sarah Purser," B.A. thesis (TCD, 1989).

CASEY, Christine, "Books and Builders . . .," Ph.D. thesis (TCD, 1991).

DINELEY, Thomas, *Observations made on his tour in Ireland and France, 1675–80*, NLI ms. No. 392.
DUFFERIN AND AVA, Marquess of, Typescript Diary 1839, The Dufferin Foundation, Clandeboye.

HAMILTON, Alexander, ms. diaries of A.H., 1793–1807, Hamwood Collection.
HARDING, George, *Two Tours of Ireland in the years 1792–1793*, ms. Lough Fea, Shirley Papers.
HAYWARD, Richard, ms. list of British artists in Rome, 1753–75, BM Printroom.
HUNT, Sir Vere, Typescript *Journals*, Mid-Western Archives, The Granary, Limerick.

JOHNSTON, Roy, "Roderic O'Conor," B.A. thesis (TCD, 1991).

KILRUDDERY Mss., courtesy of the Earl of Meath.

LOEBER, Rolf (ed.), "An alphabetical list of artists who worked in Dublin during the seventeenth and eighteenth centuries," unpublished typescript (Kingston, Ontario, 1973).

McCARTHY, Professor Michael, "Beyond the Grand Tour, Anglo–Irish Travellers to Greece and the Levant 1740–1750," lecture given in Toronto University (1992).
MacFARLANE, Jane, "Sir Frederick William Burton RHA, (1816–1900): His Life and Work," B.A. thesis (TCD, 1976).
MURRAY, Peter, "George Petrie," M.Litt. thesis (TCD, 1980).

O'GRADY, John, "Sarah Purser," Ph.D. thesis (UCD, 1974).

ROBERTSON, James George, album of Kilkenny material, Royal Society of Antiquaries of Ireland.

SEVERENS, Martha, *Henrietta Johnston*, unpublished lecture in connection with exhibition (1991–2); *see under* Batson.
Scottish Record Office, GD 18/4595–4648.
STOKES, Margaret, Notes for biography of Burton, NGI archives.

Unknown Diarist, Royal Irish Academy ms. 24K 14/15, 2 vols. (1801–3).

WILLIAMS, Alexander, ms. Autobiography, private collection.
WYNNSTAY mss., National Library of Wales.

INDEX

Page numbers in *italics* indicate illustrations.

MARY BATTERSBY
(National Library of Ireland)